THE ART AND POLITICS
OF WANA SHAMANSHIP

THE ART AND POLITICS OF WANA SHAMANSHIP

Jane Monnig Atkinson

University of California Press
Berkeley · Los Angeles · Oxford

University of California Press
Berkeley and Los Angeles, California

University of California Press, Ltd.
Oxford, England

© 1989 by
The Regents of the University of California

Library of Congress Cataloging-in-Publication Data

Atkinson, Jane Monnig.
    The art and politics of Wana shamanship / Jane Monnig
Atkinson.
        p.   cm.
        Bibliography: p.
        Includes index.
        ISBN 0-520-06377-5 (alk. paper)
        1. Wana (Indonesian people)—Rites and
ceremonies.   2. Shamanism—and government.   I. Title.
DS632. W34A87   1989
306'.089922—dc 19   88-27094
                                                          CIP

Printed in the United States of America

1 2 3 4 5 6 7 8 9

The passage from Ed Casteel and Jeanne Casteel, "Indonesia:
Wana Tribe," quoted on page 323 is reprinted by permission
of New Mission Inc.

For Effort

Contents

PART FIVE

Illustrations

MAPS

Preface

My aim in this book is to account for the popularity of the *mabolong*—the major shamanic ritual of the Wana of Sulawesi, Indonesia—by showing how it articulates a cosmic order and at the same time constitutes a political one. Rituals are valued by students of culture as "lenses" that bring facets of social life and meaning into focus. The Wana mabolong not only refracts multifarious dimensions of a social world, but it also conjures its own relations of power, authority, and dependence, with implications both within and beyond the ritual setting. This study examines the mabolong on its own terms, then explores how and under what conditions ritual authority can translate into political authority in other contexts of Wana life.

Early in my graduate days I considered the proposition that field researchers should not investigate religion until they had analyzed more fundamental relations of production. Rejecting that counsel, I went to Indonesia to study ritual specialization. If a Marxian gap between base and superstructure did not trouble me, a Durkheimian disjunction between society and ritual did. Although intrigued by interpretive approaches to cultural forms, I was concerned to maintain a connection between symbolism and social processes. As a consequence, my dissertation might well have been called "Wana Shamanism in Everyday Life," for in it I sought to show how shamanic ideas and practices figured not only in ritual, but in nonritual contexts as well. Only two chapters out of nine were trained specifically on ritual.

Once the dissertation was submitted, I turned to other matters. My field research had been the first extended ethnographic study of an indigenous population in Central Sulawesi since the early decades of this century. Hence there were many regional issues that required preliminary definition and analysis. I wrote on topics as varied as religion, ethnicity, and nationalism, incest and marriage, poetry and politics, and gender relations. Doing so helped me identify a political process that appeared to operate in a number of contexts of Wana social life. Briefly put, relations of authority and dependence in Wana settlements are based on differential access to special forms of knowledge that derive from sources external to the local community. Personal command of such knowledge is established through public performance of ritual and oratory.

With that model in mind, I returned to examine Wana shamanic ritual. There I found a correspondence between the ritual logic of shamanship and the practical logic of community leadership. Just as a shaman concentrates his spiritual powers and combats the entropy of his patients' souls, so a leader endeavors to attract a following and to overcome the tendency of local groups to disperse. A Durkheimian reading of this correspondence would be that the ritual is ratifying in symbolic terms the political relations in Wana society. But without ritual and oratory—shamanic and otherwise—there would be no forum for establishing political authority in Wana society (see Augé 1982; Traube 1986). Thus ritual symbolism and social relations do not parallel each other but operate as part of the same process.

Is Wana ritual then simply politics, or Wana politics simply ritual? I think not. But the overlap between the two offers a way around a problem in political analysis—namely, the question of political motivation. I would argue that Wana seek shamanic powers for a variety of reasons. Some people are "religiously musical" (cf. Otto 1950). Some want to protect people they love from illness and death. Some want to defend themselves against rivals. Some want to render themselves attractive to others. Whatever desires propel them into the mabolong arena, if they persist, sooner or later they will find themselves operating in an arena that is at once ritual and political. (This factor, I think, discourages shamanic endeavors on the part of Wana women, some of whom experiment with aspects of shamanship but seem uncomfortable asserting claims over others in a settlementwide or regional setting.)

Once I had clarified my understanding of the relation of Wana ritual and politics, I was then ready to return to my field materials on ritual. Previously I had resisted immersing myself in close analysis of ritual language and action lest I lose myself in what Geertz (1973, 125) characterized as "the kind of jejune cabalism into which symbolic analysis of exotic faiths can so easily fall." It had seemed safer to talk about Wana shamanship than to delve into shamans' talk. Yet, recognizing that Wana shamanic discourse is a political discourse (and vice versa), that it is in large measure through talk that people assert claims over others, I had reason to think that focusing on shamanic discourse would allow me to bridge the divide between ritual and everyday life. I therefore devoted a year to examining transcripts of shamans' songs. The analysis that follows is based on that endeavor.

The major portion of this book was written during a sabbatical year spent at the Center for Advanced Study in the Behavioral Sciences with the support of NSF grant #BNS 84-11738. I thank Gardner Lindzey, Robert Scott, and the Center's trustees for providing ideal conditions in which to work. Margaret Amara and Rosanne Torre of the Center's library cheerfully located countless books and articles for me. Kathleen Much, the Center's editor, offered insightful comments on a draft of the manuscript. Conversations with fellow fellows Keith Baker, Victoria Bonnell, Christine Hastorf, and Robert Netting were also particularly helpful in the development of this project. Participating in the History Discussion Group, composed of Center fellows and staff, emboldened me to attempt the historical exploration that concludes this book. Although the kind of speculative analysis I engage in there might scandalize some of the historians in that group, they should acknowledge their abetting role.

The field research on which this study is based was conducted in Indonesia from July 1974 through December 1976. I am deeply grateful to the Lembaga Ilmu Pengetahuan Indonesia for their sponsorship. I am grateful as well to the Governor of Sulawesi Tengah, the Bupati of Poso, and the Camats of Ulu Bongka and Bungku Utara for their helpful support. The warmth, hospitality, and friendship of Bapak and Ibu Kartasasmita in Jakarta, Poppy Gerungan and A. Sapri in Palu, and the Tomewu family in Ampana I shall never forget.

With its Gertrude Slaughter Award, Bryn Mawr College underwrote my field research. This, combined with a three-year NSF predoctoral fellowship and supplements from the Stanford Anthropology Department's NIGMS training grants, comfortably spared me the painful exigencies that so many of my peers have faced.

My overwhelming debt, however, is to the many Wana who overcame their grave suspicions of my presence and purpose in their region and gave generously of their hospitality, humor, knowledge, wisdom, and insight. Their faces, voices, and actions fill the chapters that follow. I hope this book will be received as a token of appreciation for the lesssons in life they have been willing to share.

Recalling the amazement and pleasure people expressed at seeing the names and photographs of their predecessors in a copy of Kruyt's 1930 article on the Wana, I have decided to use people's actual names (or teknonyms) except where confidentiality is called for. The shamans whose songs are presented here would be easily identified anyway by their words. I hope this decision is a wise one that will empower the children and grandchildren of the people described here to know and understand their own past.

This book has grown out of years of thinking, talking, and writing about the Wana. In addition to Wana themselves, many interlocuters stateside have contributed wittingly and unwittingly to my understanding of Wana ritual and politics. I can thank only a few of them here.

From the time I entered graduate school until her death in 1981, Michelle Rosaldo provided me with unstinting inspiration, encouragement, and support. She knew full well that the richness of Wana culture would lead me in directions neither she nor I could predict. I think she would be both surprised and pleased that my investigations have brought me to this present consideration of the things Wana do with words.

Working in an understudied area has drawbacks. A major one is a dearth of colleagues who are knowledgable and interested in the same ethnographic information and issues as oneself. I have had the good fortune to find two colleagues who, although they have not conducted research in Central Sulawesi, have provided invaluable insight into the problems with which I am dealing. One is Anna Tsing, whose work with the Meratus of Kalimantan prompted me to think further about ritual authority and social practice among the Wana. The other is Shelly Errington, whose comparative approach to Indonesian cultural forms has helped me to understand Wana history and culture in a regional perspective.

For their perceptive questions and valuable comments at various stages in the development of this manuscript, I thank Greg Acciaioli, Jane Collier, Elizabeth Coville, Shelly Errington, Charles Fergusson, Christine Hastorf, Deborah Heath, Ticia Horvatich, Fred Myers, Robert Netting, Renato Rosaldo, David Sapir, Anna Tsing, Terence Turner, Annette Weiner, and Sylvia Yanagisako.

An insightful review by Elizabeth Traube proved very helpful during the final revision of the manuscript. I am also grateful to Sheila

Levine and Betsey Scheiner of the University of California Press for their part in turning the manuscript into a book, and to Anne Canright for her meticulous copyediting.

It is customary for authors to acknowledge the assistance of others in typing their manuscript. Thanks to electronic technology, I typed this manuscript myself. But the same technology subsequently cost me a substantial sacrifice of autonomy and pride. Transposing files to several different operating systems and printing out on unfamiliar equipment called for a cast of what seemed like thousands. For their knowledgeable assistance, good humor, and forbearance I am particularly indebted to Effort Atkinson, Randy Collver, Mike Cullum, Dan Grey, Vicky Martin, and Susan Masotti.

The support of my parents, Eugene and Mary Jane Monnig, has ranged from emotional to editorial, from educating me to entertaining my children as I have worked.

And to Effort Atkinson, my deepest thanks—for everything.

A Note on Transcription

In transcribing the Wana language, known as Bahasa Taa, I have followed the conventions used for other languages in the region. In accordance with the new Indonesian orthography, the letter *j* is used instead of *dj* (as in *raja* instead of *radja*), and the letter *y*, not the letter *j*, is used to represent the glide /y/.

	Labial	Dental	Palatal	Velar	Glottal
			Consonants		
Stops	p	t		k	'(glottal stop)
	b	d	j	g	
Spirants		s			
Nasals	m	n		ng	
Trill		r			
Lateral		l			

/r/ when preceded by /n/ is pronounced as /d/.
/w/ when preceded by /m/ is pronounced as /b/.

Glides
y, w

	Front	Central	Back
		Vowels	
High	i		u
Middle	e		o
Low		a	

All Wana vowels may occur in lengthened form. Lengthened vowels are represented by double letters—for example, *aa*.

Vowels in initial word position are preceded by a weakly articulated glottal stop.

As in many other languages of Sulawesi, syllables generally end with an open vowel. Some words that appear in this text, however, offer partial exceptions to that rule (e.g., *Barangas, basal, Bolag, tambar,* and *tundug*). Although occasionally pronounced with a full final /i/, more typically in my experience these words were pronounced with a final consonant or a very weakly articulated final /i/. Given the infrequency of the full final vowel sound, then, I have transcribed such words here without.

Variations in the transcription of certain common words that appear in the shamans' songs throughout this book reflect the distinctive speech styles of individual performers. Bracketed question marks ([?]) indicate my uncertainty about transcription or translation.

Finally, a note about the format of the transcriptions in this book. As Alton Becker (1989) emphasizes, transcribing speech is an interpretive act in which conventions as seemingly minor as punctuation impose structure and meaning on frozen speech. I have opted to include no capitalization or punctuation in the transcriptions of Bahasa Taa (except where appropriate for clarity when used in general discussion), although these conventions are present in my English translation. Because, moreover, it was necessary to introduce line breaks in the shamans' songs owing to the technical exigencies of print, I took the liberty of using this device actively to highlight parallel constructions of syntax, sound, and sense as I construe them.

Introduction

The most popular of shamanic rituals in the Wana hills of Central Sulawesi, Indonesia, is the *mabolong*, a noisy event that punctuates the night with pulsating drum beats, sonorous gongs, and the wailing cadences of shamans' songs. The word *mabolong* literally means "drumming." The ritual takes its name from the two-skinned *bolong* drum, which, along with a pair of bronze gongs, produces the insistent rhythms that summon both humans and spirits to the ritual and accompany shamans as they dance (Fig. 9).

ETHNOGRAPHIC BEARINGS

My introduction to the mabolong was inauspicious. It occurred in the Wana village of Ue Bone, to which I had been directed for a field site by those outsiders who knew the Wana best. A teacher, Pak Darius, had spent time in the region, and he characterized Ue Bone as the center of Wana tradition. Our guide, Pak Basir, concurred. Basir, a Muslim from Southeast Sulawesi, had lived and worked as a trader in the Wana region for many years and was married to a Wana woman. When we met him he was assisting local authorities in a plan to move residents in the northern half of the Wana region to a settlement called Kilo Ono, meaning "six kilometers" from the Tojo Sea. At the request of the district head of Ulu Bongka, Pak Basir agreed to escort my husband, Effort, and me on a tour of the northern Wana region, with Ue Bone as our ultimate destination. We were joined by a military officer and several young Wana men hired to carry equipment.

Our hike began on the sandy plain that divides the sea- and trade-oriented residents of the coast from the subsistence farmers of the interior. After fifteen kilometers a mountain ridge juts abruptly upward, presaging the walk to come along steep, often slippery footpaths that wind around great mountain flanks and level out along rock-strewn riverbeds. Much of the interior is covered by dense rain forest, broken

1

in spots by hot, dry stretches of grassland. Looping in great serpentine curves from south to north is the giant and largely unnavigable Bongka River, fed by numerous mountain tributaries, which empties at last into the Gulf of Tojo, where our hike began. Although the segment of the peninsula inhabited by the Wana measures at its widest point only about 130 kilometers, the terrain and its contours translate into a coast-to-coast hike of eight or nine days minimum—in the best of weather—for all but the strongest hikers. The south coast, like the north, is set off by a mountain ridge and bordered by a flat ribbon of sand, narrower than its northern counterpart. Its seaward-looking Muslim settlements are smaller as well.

Our itinerary took us to a series of villages, or *kampung*, in the northern district of Ulu Bongka. A kampung consists ideally of two rows of well-maintained thatch-roofed houses that are elevated on stilts and set in a clearing kept neatly weeded and clear of debris. Kampung were initiated in the region by the Dutch colonial authorities early in this century after the Wana resisted administrative efforts to relocate the upland population to coastal settlements where they could be governed more conveniently. As a compromise, Wana were permitted to continue living in the interior on the condition that they build and maintain kampung. Some complied, some did not. Dutch patrols toured the region regularly to check on the condition of the kampung and to arrest "runaways" (*tau miyai*) who refused to "make villages" (*mangingka kampung*). In lieu of on-site surveillance of upland communities, Indonesian national authorities in the 1970s resurrected the plan abandoned by their Dutch predecessors to resettle Wana at the coast. During my fieldwork official visits to the interior were rare, and consequently village maintenance was lax.

Where kampung are maintained, they are not necessarily occupied but may serve chiefly as sites for official visits and sometimes for large festivals. Indeed, Wana typically reside in their rice fields, not in their kampung. Wana practice swidden farming (a horticultural technique also known as slash-and-burn), producing rice, maize, tubers, bananas, sugar cane, and numerous fruits and vegetables. Hunting, fishing, and gathering supplement this production. Wana locate their thatch-roofed houses directly in their swidden fields (Figs. 1, 2). Over the course of a farming year these houses grow from hastily built field huts into commodious dwellings elevated on stilts. After the rice harvest, houses are converted into granaries as people move on to make the next year's fields and homes.

Wana favor large settlements, with as many as ten or twelve households (typically composed of a conjugal couple and their dependents, both old and young) farming contiguous plots in a single large clearing. Leadership is provided by mature people (usually men) with knowledge of rice ritual, customary law (*ada*), and shamanship—forms of knowledge quite different from the Indonesian language skills that the government expects of village headmen (*kepala kampung*) and scribes (*juru tulis*).

Our initial trip was a tour of kampung, not of the farmsteads we came to know on subsequent hikes in and out of the region. As we entered each kampung word would be sent to local farming settlements that visitors had arrived. Eventually food would be sent (rice and vegetable condiments, without the chickens and rice beer that we later learned to recognize as Wana hospitality), and a village headman, sometimes accompanied by a few other brave souls, would arrive to discuss plans for resettlement with our escorts and to size us up. We used the time we spent waiting in deserted villages to engage in language lessons with our Wana guides.

On the eleventh day of our hike we arrived at Ue Bone. With great relief, weariness, and anticipation, we entered the empty kampung. Eventually we were greeted by a handful of people and provided with some rice and unripe bananas to be cooked as a side dish. I gathered from our guides that this fare was only marginally acceptable. Word arrived that a mabolong would be held that night in one of the swiddens. Our companions expressed hope that we might attend what was described as a quintessential Wana event. That hope was subsequently dashed by the report that our presence at the mabolong was undesired and that some people had fled in anticipation of our attendance. To compensate for his neighbors' lack of hospitality, a local man, the official liaison—who I gathered made no shamanic claims—gamely staged a "mabolong" for our enjoyment. Rounding up some courageous adolescents to play a drum and a pair of gongs, he sheepishly bobbed about in a clowish imitation of a shaman's dance. Amid the din, Effort and I struggled to sleep away the aches of our long walk.

The situation did not improve at daybreak. Distressed by our presence, residents of the area were reputedly poised for flight. To our immense relief, the soldier in our party received radio instructions to return at once to Marowo. Although nothing could relieve our strangeness, we figured the departure of our military escort could only help. Pak Basir decided we should leave our heavy packs in Ue Bone and hike eastward to visit some other settlements, where harvest festivals were under way. As it later turned out, he had a motive in mind.

After overnight stays in the villages of Kalinsu and Ue mAtopa, we crossed the Bongka River and paid a visit to the village of Ue nTangko. Like the residents of Ue Bone, the people of Ue nTangko were for the most part not affiliated with a world religion. In official parlance, such people carry the label *suku terasing*, "isolated ethnic group," which connotes their distance—spatial, material, and spiritual—from Indonesian nationalist culture.[1] Unlike the inhabitants of Ue Bone, however, the people of Ue nTangko were newcomers to the region where they now resided. Most had come from settlements in the southern district of Bungku Utara the decade before. Like the people of Ue Bone, they distinguished themselves from other residents of Ulu Bongka who belong to the To Linte branch of the upland population. (Most people in the Ue nTangko area were identified with the Barangas branch; Ue Bone residents identified themselves with the Kasiala branch.)

Basir had close ties with members of this community from the days when he lived in the interior and traded cloth for rice to sell at coastal markets. For his sake, if not for ours, we were hosted well. After the experience of being shunned, I now felt awash in human kindness and sympathy (a premature sensation, as it turned out). I recall being particularly struck early on by the warmth of a beautiful, outgoing young woman called Indo Lina, by the proud bearing of Apa Iki, an influential old man of the community, and by the curiosity of Apa Nedi, pitifully crippled with rheumatoid arthritis, who wore a tattered old T-shirt emblazoned with the word *LOVE*.[2]

From Ue nTangko, our plan was to return to Ue Bone by way of a harvest festival in the village of Rompi. After crossing the Bongka River and discussing the matter with Basir and a Mori teacher living in Ue mAtopa,[3] we began to have second thoughts—some of them carefully planted by Basir and the teacher, each of whom, for different reasons, thought it preferable that we live in Ue nTangko rather than Ue Bone. Exhausted by more than two weeks of hiking, attracted by the hospitality of the people of Ue nTangko, and more than ready to settle down, we agreed.

Our return to Ue nTangko, however, was a cause for some consternation on the part of our hosts, who had tolerated having us as visitors but were reluctant to have us as residents. At the time I was not aware of the extent of their apprehension, but in the wake of its ambiguity, had I not been too weary to walk, I would gladly have hiked back out to Marowo. Local trust developed slowly as we proved our good intentions by negotiating and paying rent (2,500 rupiah—slightly more than six dollars—per month), by dispensing medicine, and by not perpetrating atrocities on local residents (as many fully expected we would). It was only much later, with the help of Indo Lina, Apa Iki, Apa Nedi, and their neighbors, that I began to piece together the millenarian schema through which Wana were attempting to make sense of our presence in their land.

Some five thousand people were officially identified as Wana during the time of my fieldwork. I cannot presume to represent all of them equally in this study. When I speak of "the Wana," I resort to ethnographic shorthand for "the people whom I know best" among the Wana population. Associated as I was with so-called *suku terasing* settlements, I did not come to know Muslim and Christian Wana communities very well (although I did know many Wana who were or who had been Muslims or Christians). My work reflects that fact.

From September 1974 through December 1976 I based my research in a community affiliated with Ue nTangko, located on the east side of the flood-prone Bongka River (Map 3). Near the border of the districts of Ulu Bongka and Bungku Utara, this settlement was a four-day hike (local conditions permitting) from either the northern or the southern coast of the Wana region. Four other settlements—one large, three small—were located within an hour's hiking distance of the settlement where I lived. Across the river was the kampung of Ue mAtopa. Because most of my neighbors came from the areas of Manyo'e and Bino in Bungku Utara, there was a steady flow of visitors from that direction and I had occasion to visit a number of settlements in that area.[4]

In the early months of fieldwork, my husband and I lived in the house of Apa Iki and his wife, Indo Ngonga. Apa Iki was the farming leader and legal expert of the community (Fig. 8). Indo Ngonga was an experienced performer of a variety of nonshamanic healing rituals (Fig. 7). Also living in the house were their younger son, his wife, and the senior couple's orphaned adolescent granddaughter. As the months went on, I grew quite close to Indo Lina, the daughter-in-law of my hosts and the wife of Apa Mene, the most prominent shaman in the community (Fig. 3). Eventually Effort and I joined their household, which included as well Indo Lina's daughter, Apa Mene's son, Apa Iki's widowed first cousin, and *her* two children. I remained in this household after Effort returned to the United States in December 1975. Readers will become quite familiar with Indo Lina, Apa Mene, and their neighbors over the course of this book.

Once we had settled in Ue nTangko, our neighbors became aware of our willingness to treat them with aspirin, sulfa, tetracycline, and other rarely available potions. With our medicines at hand, they declared, it would no longer be necessary to stage mabolong. Considering it unthinkable to withhold whatever medical assistance I could lend, I despaired of being able to study Wana shamanic practices with any thoroughness.

Such pessimism was naive, however, because their assertion and my resignation revealed both an overestimation of our medical know-how and an underestimation of what mabolong are all about. Regarding undue faith in our medical skills, Effort and I found ourselves lacking both the supplies and the knowledge to treat many of the serious diseases we encountered. My first patient, a child with a raging fever, wracking cough, and diarrhea, died within a week of my attempts to treat him. Only after I experienced the nonfebrile stages of malaria myself did I realize my error in administering aspirin to people complaining of acute headaches. Effort and I learned on the job, but our successes lay, for the most part, in treating sores and minor skin ailments.

The prediction that our medicines would render shamanic performances obsolete proved unfounded as well, and not merely on account of our ineptitude. Illness is only one excuse for a mabolong. Anticipation of misfortune, successful recoveries from previous illnesses, marriages, farming festivals, visits by prominent shamans, as well as a general desire to party, are all reasons to hold a mabolong. Considerably more mabolong were held during my second year of fieldwork than during my first, not because people were any sicker, but instead because there were more residents (including more shamans) in the community and they had had a better harvest—with, consequently, more plentiful supplies of rice and beer.[5]

RITUALS AND POLITICAL ORDERS

Mabolong are events that bring neighbors together. Apart from mabolong, weddings, funerals, and four annual farming festivals, it is rare for co-residents of a swidden settlement to congregate as a group. These collective rituals convene a community under the auspices, and through the exercise, of distinctive forms of authoritative knowledge—shamanic, legal, or agricultural, depending on the event.

The challenge of the present analysis is to treat both the expressive and the political dimensions of this ritual without collapsing the two together. The expressive potentialities of the mabolong and other Wana rituals are not limited to producing or reproducing political relations. Likewise, Wana politics—broadly defined as the way people make claims over one another—is confined neither to shamanship nor to ritual. And yet ritual processes and political processes intersect in distinctive ways in the Wana hills. Close attention to one ritual will highlight the nature of that intersection.

Any form of expressive culture worth its salt necessarily entails a politics of meaning. No matter whether access to and control over valued symbolic forms are actively contested or accepted as given, political relations among ritual participants are affected. The political salience of Wana ritual, however, is particularly significant for several related reasons.

First, the Wana are located in a region of the world where the spiritual and political are intricately intertwined, both in the local societies themselves and in terms of their analysis by Western scholars. Relations of authority and dependence have been etched indelibly in conceptions of the spiritual throughout this Southeast Asian archipelago. Ritual and ceremonial displays of power and hierarchy appear integral to the workings of a wide array of political orders. This assertion appears equally apt whether applied to royal cremations in Bali (Geertz 1980), funeral feasts in Tana Toraja (Volkman 1985), house raisings in Timor (Renard-Clamagirand 1982), headhunting celebrations in Luzon (M. Rosaldo 1980), or healing ceremonies in Kelantan (Kessler 1977). All are occasions when political relationships are brought into being. By hosting or being hosted, by staging, staffing, supplying, or staying away, people array themselves in a manner that—for a moment—articulates patterns of authority and dependence, of cohesion and competition. Far from merely reflecting "a real political order" that exists in other spheres, these rituals create an order and freeze it for a moment in a cosmic frame. How and to what degree such orders coincide with nonritual practice or can be sustained by it is an open and difficult question.

A second reason has to do with the particular nature of Wana social order and its relation to other populations in the region. For this small, dispersed, and relatively egalitarian population, ritual operates as a primary means of political organization and integration. But Wana do not exist in a vacuum. In the last century and a half, Wana have experienced regional warfare, the hegemonic outreach of neighboring coastal kingdoms, and the imposition of state rule by the Dutch, the Japanese, and, most recently, the Indonesian nationalists. As Hocart (1970) would have predicted, rituals for the procurement of life have assumed complex political functions in response to changing political conditions in the region.

A third reason follows from the second. Wana have long existed on the geographical and ideological peripheries of more centralized and powerful polities. Recent work by Geertz, Errington, and others has illuminated the cultural dimensions of power at the centers of the former Indonesian kingdoms, or *negara*. Less understood are the relations of peripheral populations to those historical centers (see Bentley 1986). This book analyzes an instance of hegemonic relations between center and periphery from the vantage of a marginal people. In doing so, it brings out congruences between symbolic forms and social processes and continuities between ritual performance and political practice, issues underplayed in prominent cultural analyses of Indonesia's powerful centers.

FROM CENTER TO PERIPHERY

The political dimensions of ritual in Southeast Asia are nowhere more dramatic than in the courtly ceremonies of the former kingdoms of mainland and island Southeast Asia. As Benedict Anderson (1972) insightfully wrote of the Javanese, power in the traditions of these kingdoms is culturally conceived to be a cosmic, generative energy that individuals can attract to themselves through ascetic practice. Political success is attributed not to one's outward deeds in the world, but to personal possession of mystical power. The fortunes of a realm likewise can be read as reflecting the concentration or dissolution of power at the center, as personified by the ruler. Likened to a lamp whose intensity is greatest at the center and diminishes as it radiates outward, a ruler's power dictates the range of his influence. The role of ritual and ceremony as a means of manifesting a ruler's power becomes clear when understood in the context of indigenous political philosophy. So too does the mandalic shape of traditional kingdoms, the potent centers of which matter whereas the vague borders do not. Anderson's work has ably demonstrated the significance of this cultural notion of power in modern politics of the region.

In Java, concentrating power is not an activity restricted to rulers; puppeteers, peasants, and even pedicab drivers seek to accrue power through ascetic and mystical practice (see Keeler 1987). Nor is the "politics of the center" restricted to royal capitals (or, in the local idiom, royal "navels"). Errington (1989) and Wolters (1982) have both argued eloquently that although the political philosophy of Southeast Asian kingdoms was glossed in Sanskrit, their political ideas and dynamics have deep roots in the cultures and history of the region. Tambiah (1985a, 253–54) makes a similar point when he identifies mandalic schemata among Indonesian swidden populations characterized by segmentary lineage systems. Indeed, striking continuities can be seen in the symbologies of power from political centers to the hinterlands. But just how symbolic expressions of power are established and sustained in practice both within and beyond the ritual context and across political formations has not been clarified.

Geertz (1980), for instance, has made a strong case that the power conjured in Balinese courtly ritual was not a reflection of "real power" located elsewhere in the state; instead, it was simply what power there was. But as his account demonstrates, staging grand rituals and ceremonies on the scale of these Balinese performances calls for complex networks of patron-client relations through which resources can be marshaled. Moving down and out to the peripheries of such systems, we find that ritual serves there too as the stage for demonstrating power. But the leverage of leaders to marshal large followings is considerably diminished, and as a consequence, so too is the scale and grandeur of collective celebration. More obvious in a setting like the Wana hills, where the trappings of armies, riches, and courtly refinements do not apply, are the strenuous efforts by leaders to create for themselves the grounds of their authority. Lacking the props and supporting casts available to actors at center stage of the theater state, leaders must rely on their own persuasive talents as performers to conjure the power that attracts and maintains constituencies.

Wolters has sketched a possible political lineage connecting early swidden populations in Southeast Asia to the later historical kingdoms. Common to all, he suggests, is a cultural matrix in which unequal spiritual powers, demonstrated through ritual and ceremony, generate political hierarchy and relations of dependency. As we shall see, this model captures well some critical features of Wana shamanship. Local "men of prowess" transformed themselves into royalty, Wolters (1982, 10–11) proposes, by adopting Hindu concepts that glossed heroic prowess as a spiritual achievement and cast it in divine terms.

Wolters's argument rests on the notion of a prehistoric kernel of political inequality that subsequently germinated as a result of cultural contact, growing into the hierarchical kingdoms of Southeast Asia. His is a purely cultural model that omits factors like subsistence technologies, population pressure, and warfare—the standard "prime movers" in comparative theories of political evolution. He succeeds in delineating an enduring pattern that transcends a range of societal types in Southeast Asia, but not in explaining its dynamic transformations, something I shall attempt for a region of eastern Central Sulawesi.

Wolters applies his model to literate populations whose religious and political notions have become fixed in the form of written texts. Although he begins his argument by focusing on swidden farmers in the Southeast Asian forests, precursors of contemporary populations like the Wana, he does not return to them for the following reason:

> Many people lived in distant highlands and were beyond the reach of the centres where records survive. The *mandala* were a phenomenon of the lowlands and even there geographical conditions encouraged under-government. Paul Wheatley puts it well when he notes that "the Sanskrit tongue was chilled to silence at 500 meters." One cannot assume that powerful overlords in the plains always ignored the natural resources and manpower in the hills and mountains, but the historian, relying on written records, has to remove vast territories from the historical map of earlier Southeast Asia.
>
> (Wolters 1982, 32)

Whereas Wolters considered the political forms of Southeast Asian swidden populations to be the precursors of the later kingdoms, the twentieth-century Wana must also be viewed as successors and former vassals of these kingdoms. The Wana come into historical view only as the sultanates that ringed coastal Sulawesi were snuffed out in the twentieth century. These royal centers were themselves Islamicized transformations of the negara, the Indonesian version of Southeast Asian mandalic polities.[6] Indeed, as Wolters suspected, the "overlords" on the coastal plains that border the Wana area did *not* ignore "the natural resources and manpower" of the upland region. A history of engagement with coastal polities has shaped political processes in the Wana hills in important ways, and with intriguing parallels to other areas of Southeast Asia, such as the Kachin hills of Burma (see Leach 1954).

CULTURE AND PERFORMANCE

My aim is to show how the mabolong is at once both meaningful and operative in Wana social life. Doing so will involve analyzing the mabolong not simply as an expressive text but also as a dramatic performance, with links to wider social practice that go beyond cultural commentary. By tracing these connections I hope to reveal the historical construction and practical dynamics of power in this peripheral region of Southeast Asia.

In doing so, I shall move analytically as well as geographically from the interpretive tradition that has dominated recent study of Indonesian culture and politics. Interpretive approaches broke the hold of structural functionalism in American anthropology in the 1960s by challenging the practice of reducing symbolic forms—through which human thought, feeling, communication, and meaningful action are organized—to the social order, to patterned relations among people and institutions. Cultural analysts have succeeded exceptionally well in convincing at least one wing of the discipline that cultural meaning deserves study in its own right. Their success has been so great, in fact, that in some quarters a counterargument has been necessary—an explication of meaning alone does not constitute a full analysis of social action.

The initial import of symbolic anthropology was to pry culture away from its means-to-an-end role as sustainer of social structure. Once that was accomplished, it became both undesirable and impossible to "put Humpty Dumpty together again"—in other words, to return to treating cultural forms as mere epiphenomenal offshoots and mechanistic reinforcers of social structure. Indeed, interpretive anthropologists have often gone to great lengths to keep expressive dimensions of culture free from imputations of instrumental or pragmatic action. The strength of this approach is the nonreductive portrayal of other systems of thought. Its weakness is the disengagement of expressive dimensions of culture from other social and historical processes.

Coincident with these American developments, the work of Pierre Bourdieu, Anthony Giddens, and others has in the meantime offered less static, more temporal ways of conceptualizing social processes, human agency, and consciousness· than did the postwar Parsonian models that cultural analysts were challenging. The issue, as many see it, is no longer the maintenance of absolute distinctions between the "logico-meaningful" and "causal-functional" orders (see Geertz 1973, 144–46), but rather the successful integration of cultural forms and social practice.

Indeed, Geertz regards social action as the focus of his work. Yet because his best-known essays place such emphasis on interpretation, he is criticized for failing to show what social action can accomplish beyond communicating meaning.[7] Such criticism is in line with Bourdieu's (1977) argument that anthropologists overprivilege rules, maps, and meanings in their accounts of other people's experience precisely because, as observers, they lack both native competence and vested interest in the social practices they study. The point is that people use words and other symbolic forms for purposes other than rendering themselves intelligible. While intelligibility may be the first order of business in practical terms for the fieldworker new on the scene, it can be presumed by more experienced social actors whose interests go beyond making themselves understood. The critique also brings out the point that cultural meanings are not always shared but often are contested.

In the field of ritual studies, concern with social practice has taken the form of new and renewed interest in ritual performance. This interest draws inspiration from such forebears as J. L. Austin, whose notion of language as conventional activity has been applied to ritual by Tambiah (1985c), and Victor Turner, whose emphasis on the theatrical dimensions and transformative properties of ritual is reflected in the work of anthropologists like Kapferer, Myerhoff, and Schieffelin. Instead of presuming that cultural meanings unfold uniformly and automatically, performative approaches call for an investigation of the ways ritual symbols present themselves to ritual participants. Emphasis on ritual performance is a useful corrective for overemphasis on symbolic meaning, but only, I submit, if what Victor Turner (1968) called "storehouses" of symbolic information and Tambiah (1985b, 2) speaks of as "performative blueprints" are not reducible solely to the effects they have on the consciousness of cultural subjects (see Atkinson 1987).

In presenting the mabolong, I want to highlight what Tambiah (1985c, 124) deems "the dual aspect of rituals as performance." Kapferer (1983, 239) declares that "one, perhaps, never steps in the same ritual twice," calling attention to the fact that rituals are not timeless: they develop and change. Rituals have histories. Performances build on one another and are affected by, and in turn affect, what happens more generally in the world. Moreover, their outcomes are not predetermined; performers and performances can succeed or fail, their aims and uses can change, they may have unintended consequences. Yet by definition, rituals are more structured—more objectified—than nonritual life. Indeed, their structures model aspects of their wider social context (see T. Turner 1977, 59). It is therefore vital to explore ritual logic as well as ritual improvisation in order to grasp the dynamic relation between ritual and ongoing social processes.

To return to Heraclitus, one may not step in the same river twice, but one can be reasonably certain that one is still stepping in a river. Likewise, no two mabolong performances are ever identical, but ethnographer and locals alike generally know when they are experiencing one. For this reason (without putting too Platonic a twist on it), I take the liberty of generalizing about "the mabolong" from my experiences in the mid-seventies in Wana settlements along the border of the districts of Ulu Bongka and Bungku Utara. Participant observation and close analysis of transcriptions from events of this genre, however, combined with my reading of the single prior ethnographic account of the Wana, published by the Dutch missionary A. C. Kruyt (1930), suggest to me that the mabolong performances I attended in the 1970s may be quite different in form and efficacy from the mabolong of the 1890s. Not only does it seem that the contemporary mabolong may have appropriated elements of another ritual popular in the last century, but it may also be the case that shamanship, as practiced in the mabolong arena, has shifted and heightened its profile over the last half century. Once again, transcriptions of ritual performances contain clues to these changes.

PRESENTATION

The organization of this book follows my argument that the mabolong, rather than being a neat reflection of preexisting social relations, in a real sense constitutes them. Given this premise, one option would be to treat the ritual and its broader social context simultaneously in a "totalizing" effort (see Tambiah 1985a, b). In order to sustain a sense of the ritual's integrity, however, I have chosen instead to focus the first four-fifths of the book closely on the mabolong. Only then, after the expressive and performative dimensions of the ritual itself have been explored, will I move out to the wider dimensions of Wana society and history. Were I to begin with a thoroughgoing examination of Wana society and history before analyzing the mabolong ritual, both author and readers could too easily lapse into a familiar way of viewing the expressive dimensions of the ritual as a cultural gloss on the "real" nature of Wana social structure.

Many rituals can be characterized as "liturgy-centered." By this I mean they are dominated by orderly sets of ritual procedures which coordinate the actions of practitioners and congregants. By contrast, a ritual like the mabolong is more "performer-centered": governed less by liturgy and more by the actions and inclinations of individual practitioners. This quality of the mabolong becomes intelligible when one understands that the mabolong is the principal arena for achieving a shamanic reputation. As they go about their shamanic tasks of convening spirit familiars and treating patients, Wana performers must at the same time create and confirm the grounds for their personal shamanic authority.

Mauss ([1902–3] 1972, 9) observed that in comparison to "religious rites," "magical rites" (a category that for Mauss included the shamanic) "seem to require much more ingenuity and *savoir-faire* from their practitioners," perhaps, he speculated, because "they are practised by individuals who are outside the social group, who act in their own interests or in the interest of other individuals, or in their name." For Mauss, magic lay in the shadows of organized social life. Like magicians elsewhere, Wana shamans derive their power from extrasocietal sources, but to succeed as shamans, they must bring personal powers back from the peripheries to the heart of a community. In the mabolong, individual performers endeavor to identify their own interests and those of their patients with the greater interests of the community, and in this way to serve as benefactors for the collectivity. Ingenuity and savoir faire are essential for their pursuit of legitimacy.

One might well find that the contrast I draw here between performer-centered and liturgy-centered ritual parallels a distinction between shamanistic and priestly ritual, or between charismatic and routinized religious practice. Later I will compare the mabolong to a more liturgically centered ritual called the *salia*, which enjoyed great popularity in the nineteenth century during a time of greater political centralization in the Wana area. This ritual was performed by liturgical experts under the auspices of Wana chiefs known as *basal*. Its purpose was to promote the well-being of the entire congregation. Thus, it resembles rites in other chiefdoms where collective welfare is "achieved not piece-meal, but by one all-inclusive rite" (Hocart 1970, 60). The decline of the salia has accompanied the erosion of regional leadership in the area. I shall argue that with the disappearance of Wana chiefs, local reliance on the charismatic leadership of Wana shamans both within and beyond the ritual setting has apparently grown.

As a performer-centered ritual, a mabolong cannot be described or analyzed as a preordained progression of delineated steps to which ritual practitioners and congregants collectively conform. It is rather a repertoire of ritual actions available to performers acting independently in the ritual arena. This repertoire divides into four general categories, recognized by cultural actors and characterized by distinctive segments of song and dramatic action: summoning spirit familiars, treating patients, traveling up to the sky to negotiate with the Owner on behalf of a patient, and requesting foods for spirit familiars. My analysis of the mabolong (Parts One through Four) is therefore organized around transcriptions of shamanic songs representing each of these four performance categories. Disembodied as they are from actual events, these transcripts cannot fully convey the sights, sounds, smells, and experiential immediacy of the ritual moment from which they are drawn. Nor can analysis of the texts alone account for the impact of their performance on a Wana audience. But given their richness, the texts will provide an entry into my analysis of how the ritual works. In presenting these materials, I intend to show that careful attention to ritual texts will not contract into obscurantism but instead will, in Paul Ricoeur's (1971, 544) words, "open up a world."

Throughout a mabolong performance, shamans sing. Their songs are couched in a speech style quite distinct from the one used in everyday conversation. Shamanic vocabulary borrows eclectically from other languages as well as from archaic and arcane ritual forms. Familiar Wana words are transformed by substitutions, contractions, and reduplications of sounds. Parallel constructions abound (see Fox 1988). Wana shamanic song is on the "freer" end of what Charles Ferguson (1987) has called "formatted discourse," speech that is formulaic but not fixed. Tambiah (1985c, 142) has noted the usefulness of parallelism for performers' construction of such discourse: by stringing together parallel phrases, a performer can draw out a thought, embellish it, and play on multiple meanings. Such constructions permit performers to attract attention, add emphasis, and stall for time.

Performers keep their audiences apprised of ritual action—namely, shamanic dealings with hidden spirit agents—through their songs. Although use of this speech style distinguishes performers as "people with spirit familiars" (which is what Wana terms for "shaman" mean), shamans' songs are fully comprehensible to Wana audiences.[8] A mixture of stock formulae and improvisation, the songs reveal the challenge their performers face: to create distinctive reputations for themselves, but to do so in ways that conform with audience expectations of what powerful shamans are.

RITUAL ACTIONS
AND SHAMANIC CAREERS

At the start of a mabolong and on throughout the evening, performers repeatedly summon their spirit familiars—the "owners" of powerful knowledge on which shamanic prowess depends. In Part One I will explore both the cultural and performative implications of these invitations. Examination of shamanic invocations reveals that Wana shamanship is predicated on a division between ordinary existence and hidden realms of experience. Shamanic power derives from hidden realms to which human access is restricted. As he congregates his spirit allies around him, a performer asserts his ability to mediate between his human community and more powerful spirit realms.[9]

Part Two addresses Wana techniques of shamanic therapy. Just as

Wana notions of shamanic power presume a divided reality, so shamanic therapy presumes that human beings possess hidden dimensions to which only shamans have access. A person's life depends on the condition of these vital components of being, but shamans alone can monitor and manage them. In this way shamans assert control over people's very lives.

The most powerful Wana shamans exercise this control by making dramatic trips to the sky to negotiate with the Owner of the world. In Part Three I draw on theories of exchange and sacrifice to show how shamans can create and sustain authority over ritual communities through mediation with a high god. Although the religious historian Mircea Eliade (1964) regarded such visionary travel as the Ur-form of shamanism, there is reason to think these journeys to the sky and their focus on a high god may be a new emphasis, if not an altogether new development, in the mabolong. I shall make the case that these ritual changes are linked to political changes in the Wana region over the last century.

The texts I present in the first three sections of the book will create an impression of the ritual centrality and power of their performers. But the model of shamanic authority put forward in performers' songs is not consonant with the practice of Wana "shamanship," by which I mean the art or skill of performing as a shaman. The politics of Wana shamanship is "egalitarian," in Morton Fried's (1967, 33) sense of the term, in that there are no "means for fixing or limiting the number of people capable of exerting power." What seems presumed in shamanic songs is in fact what performers must strive to achieve in the course of performance—namely, recognition of their shamanic claims. Part Four explores shamans' dependence on one another and on their audiences as revealed in the requests they make on behalf of their spirit familiars.

Once the mabolong is recognized as an arena for the creation of shamanic reputations, these four segments of ritual song and action can in fact be seen to recapitulate the shamanic career. By summoning spirit familiars—the first act—performers publicly assert their claims to hidden powers. Until such claims have been made, a performer cannot convincingly undertake the other three segments. Treating patients—the second act—logically follows the summoning of spirits, both as a sequence of ritual action and as a more advanced stage of shamanic endeavor. The third act, "going to the Owner," is an optional measure undertaken after a performer has summoned spirits and examined patients. To initiate such a journey, one should be an experienced and respected shaman with the confidence and authority to commit others to future outlays of food and demonstrations of support for the endeavor. The fourth act, "requesting food for spirit familiars," is a rite of rebellion in which performers of any degree of expertise may engage. Like other rites of rebellion, it reveals the "underbelly" of the institution of which it is a part. Requests for food, I shall argue, expose the fact that a shaman, on whom others ideally depend, is in practice dependent on the support of his audience.

The four ritual segments around which my analysis is organized thus form both the building blocks of this performer-centered ritual *and* the stages in the career of a successful shaman.

RITUAL AND EVERYDAY LIFE

Ritual, here as elsewhere, poses a set of possibilities apart from the everyday social world. As Victor Turner (1981, 159) put it, ritual operates in the "subjunctive mood," in contrast to the "indicative mood" of daily life. Turner's own work on rites of passage empha-sizes what he came to call *sparagmos*: the "dismemberment" of order in the context of ritual liminality, the "time out" from social life that ritual affords in the process of transforming participants' identities and consciousness (p. 160). By overturning the structures that govern ordinary social experience, liminal phases of ritual allow the free play of *communitas*, a sense of oneness unfettered by the social divisions and demands of daily life.[10]

As we shall see, the Wana mabolong offers experiments in the dis-memberment of order. But assertions of form in the mabolong are also squarely in the subjunctive mood; they pose a possibility of social authority, cohesion, and order that far exceeds the indicative reality of Wana social life, a point I shall develop in Part Five. Wana settlements display a greater degree of what Moore terms "social indeterminacy" than do many more highly structured societies (Moore 1975; Moore and Myerhoff 1977). Repeated dislocations over this century, to be described later, have no doubt exacerbated this quality.

Instead of presuming the contours of quotidian existence and then overturning them, as the Ndembu rituals analyzed by Turner appear to do, Wana ritual poses an order that exceeds the order achievable in nonritual reality and then—as we shall see—threatens its audience with disruptions of that ideal order. For a society in which authority is informal and relies on consensus, in which not due process but the threat of spiritual sanctions upholds community norms and values, shamans can represent order in their own right instead of posing a challenge to secular authority. This fact may go far toward explaining why successful shamans are the pillars of Wana communities, and not marginals or outcasts. It also hints at why Wana have historically made use of ritual practice to cope with political turmoil.

As this book unfolds, the reader may well wonder why the political emphasis in expressive dimensions of Wana society should be so great, when the political stakes for the Wana seem so low. After all, at the time of my study they were a population of only some five thousand swidden cultivators living in small scattered settlements with little regional integration, apart from often frustrated efforts by Indonesian district officials to administer the interior region. I will attempt to account for that disparity first by exploring how shamanic authority can operate as an organizing factor in and between local settlements; then, drawing on Kruyt's 1930 account of the Wana, I shall reconstruct (as far as possible) a picture of political processes at work in the region since the middle of the nineteenth century. In this way I hope to show how the political implications of Wana shamanship may have been heightened by historical developments over the last century as close readings of ritual texts reveal the links between contemporary shamanship and the politics of an earlier time.

THE TEXTUAL CORPUS

A mabolong is a bewildering event for the uninitiated. Drum and gongs pound. People chatter. Performers sing and dance independently of one another. No overall structure appears to govern the occasion. Without prior knowledge of conventional scripts of ritual action, one is at an utter loss to comprehend the scene. The conditions of a performance, moreover, make it very difficult to elicit on-site explanations from one's companions. Hence, long before I understood what was going on during a mabolong performance, I made it my habit to record as much of the audible portions of shamans' singing as possible and to jot down notes about what people in the room were doing.[11]

More than fifty mabolong performances were held in the neighborhood where I lived during my twenty-two months of residence in the Wana hills. Performers included both local novices and experts, as well as visitors from other settlements both near and far. I also had occasion to attend mabolong in other settlements. My tape recorder captured expansive monologues, emotional dialogues, and brief snippets of song broken off by the din of drum, gongs, and other voices, or by a performer's own distraction. Fixed once on magnetic recording tape, these discourses would be fixed once again as written texts. Enlisting the help of patient companions, I would replay the tapes one phrase at a time until I had transcribed the performers' words (and relevant audience comments when possible) and the gist of my conversations with my fellow transcribers about what we had heard (Fig. 5).

My associates in this task were generally not shamans. Most were women, including the wives and daughters of shamans, who would help out during breaks in their farm work. One was the precocious young son of a shaman. Two were crippled, housebound men who found these sessions an entertaining diversion. We would lounge about in the vicinity of the tape recorder, with ample supplies of betel and tobacco. As we worked, other tasks, such as mending clothes, weaving mats, delousing friends, shooing chickens, and tending children, would be accomplished. We would occasionally direct questions to experienced shamans who were sometimes in the room as we conversed. But as a young woman with a nonconfrontational disposition, I was hesitant to request the assistance of the noted shamans in my neighborhood to transcribe these texts. Whereas these same men proved quite willing to teach me secret knowledge, I sensed their impatience with the tedium of playing and replaying tapes of public performance. One shaman gruffly referred to my lengthy and gossip-filled chats with his wife and other women as "talking lies." After all, it was the secret magic of the performers, not their songs, that was culturally regarded as efficacious. Owing to the circumstances of my research, then, my understanding of shamans' songs derived largely from discussions with nonexperts (cf. Lewis 1980). Not being in search of a Don Juan or an Ogotemmeli, I did not regard this fact as a failing. More recently, I have come to realize the value of those countless sessions of "talking lies" with nonexperts—especially women—for offering me an understanding of Wana shamanship from the perspective of shamans' constituencies, a point I shall elaborate in Part Five.

I have based my choice of transcripts for presentation here on several factors. One is relative completeness. The audibility of performers' voices is often cut off on my tapes by drums, gongs, and other noises, and shamans also start and stop their songs without warning. Instead of stitching together snippets of songs, I looked for uninterrupted examples of ritual actions. Another issue is translatability. I have greater understanding of some of the episodes I recorded than others because of when they occurred during my field stay, my familiarity with the actors, my awareness at the time of what was transpiring, and the quality of my subsequent discussions with others about the performance. Readers may note that I rely heavily on the performances of two men in particular. One, Apa Mene, is the shaman in whose house I lived. The other, Apa Linus, was a close neighbor and a frequent performer. The people who assisted me in transcribing tapes knew these men and their shamanic exploits well. Hence, discussions about their performances were particularly rich. At the same time, I did transcribe significant portions of performances by a dozen other performers. Performers differed in their singing style, vocabulary, and phrasing, as well as in the personal spirit familiars they employed, but they shared much in common. The transcripts that I present here are unique in that not even the same performer would ever duplicate them exactly (although he might use certain phrases over and over again). Clearly, we are not dealing with invariant texts; nevertheless, I feel quite confident that these transcripts are not aberrant, but instead are representative of shamanic performances in the general time and place of my research. Comparisons with Kruyt's 1930 account of the Wana and Adriani's texts from the neighboring region of Poso (Adriani 1932; Adriani and Kruyt 1950), moreover, reveal a high measure of stability in ritual language and procedures in this century.

Recognizing the challenge of developing an analysis based on lengthy transcriptions of ritual performances, I have sought to make my presentation of both text and analysis as lucid as possible. Signposts are provided throughout to give readers a sense of where we have been and where we are going. At the risk of annoying some readers with excessive "scaffolding," I hope in this way to render a detailed account of a complex ritual more intelligible.

PART ONE

1

Summoning Powerful Allies

The decision to hold a mabolong is typically made by a household that wishes to host a ceremony, in conjunction with a shaman who is willing to perform. The performance may be held in the hosts' house or, if that dwelling is too small to accommodate a throng, in a larger house in the settlement. Preparations include securing a drum and gongs, locating appropriate "foods" for the spirit familiars of the shamans who are likely to perform, and notifying others in the settlement that the event is about to take place.

The drum and gongs, essential for a mabolong performance, are generally shared within settlements. Questions of ownership arise only if communities divide. The wooden drum, covered on each end with the skin of a python, large lizard, or monkey, can be made locally. Gongs, made elsewhere, are in short supply. If it is necessary to borrow an instrument from another settlement, an invitation is extended to members of that community to come "party" (malae).[1]

As for the "rice of the spirits" (baku mwalia), this typically consists of plants from the forest—tender shoots, glossy leaves, pretty berries, and the hallmark of all Wana spirit familiars, a fragrant basil called wunga. Individual shamans and their familiars have particular tastes, which are known to their hosts through experience (if the shaman is a member of the community) or inquiry (if he is a visitor from elsewhere). A shaman's children are often a useful source for this information and, if young, may be prevailed on to search for special items.

The decision to stage a mabolong, especially in the event of an illness, is often sudden. Sometimes neighbors learn of the performance only when the drum and gongs mark its start. Generally word spreads informally as people visit one another's houses, meet on the trail, or congregate at the water at day's end. Should there be visitors to the settlement, or should people have errands at other farmsites, invitations may be extended to other communities. If the mabolong is being held in fulfillment of a vow (see Part Three) and food supplies are ample, then plans are generally made at least one day and often several days in advance and care is taken to circulate news of the event in other settlements.

Whether one receives a direct or formal invitation to a mabolong is unimportant. It does not matter how or from whom one receives notice. The hosts want the event to be well attended. A well-attended performance will last longer, entice more shamans to perform, and generate enough rice beer to keep the shamans entertained and entertaining.

People go to mabolong to enjoy themselves, to receive treatment, and to demonstrate *kasintuwu*, "mutual support," an important social value. *Tuwu* means "to live." With the prefix *sin-* it means "to live together." People who are *masintuwu* should demonstrate neighborly care, concern, and assistance when it is needed, with the expectation that others will do the same for them. Within a farmsite, neighbors are expected to share large catches of meat and fish and to respond to requests for items like betel fixings, tobacco, and salt. It goes without saying that they should attend one another's mabolong, weddings, and funerals, as well as the community's farming festivals, and should supply food and beer when the occasion warrants. People of different settlements may make a point of expressing kasintuwu by attending these festive events.

Staging an ordinary mabolong is not an expensive proposition for a household. Some homemade rice beer should be on hand, although members of other households with patients to treat will typically supply some as well. In addition there should be tobacco and betel fixings, also locally produced. Although technically only shamans must be provided with beer, betel, and tobacco, more abundant supplies make the event more festive and entertaining. The outlay is greater if the mabolong is being staged to fulfill a vow (see Part Three). A vow is a set of conditions offered by a shaman to Pue, the deity above the sky, to spare the life of a patient. These conditions generally involve slaughtering a specified number of chickens, preparing a specified number of rice offerings, and serving a specified number of bottles of beer to one and all—in short, holding a feast. Once again, neighbors can be counted on to furnish part of the spread. And it is not uncommon for a community to hold a single feast and mabolong to repay all the vows made for constituent households at once.

A mabolong is held in the evening after dark. (Beating drum and gongs during daylight calls down dangerous spirits and is to be avoided on all but one special occasion: ritual dueling performed in fulfillment of a vow [Figs. 29, 30].) When the evening meal has been completed, the enameled tin dishes washed and put away, a member of the hosting household (typically a woman), prepares the *lango*, or offering tray (Fig. 11). In a woven winnowing tray or shallow basket, she places refreshments for the shamans and their spirit familiars. These consist of betel fixings (areca nut, piper leaf, and lime), locally grown tobacco and corn husks for wrapping cigarettes, the assorted "foods of the spirits" mentioned earlier, a bottle of rice beer, a metal betel box, a cup of uncooked rice, some cloth (spirit familiars like to see that prestation, even though its human owner will retrieve it after the performance), and any other items that particular shamans may require to make their spirits strong and eager to perform.

The mabolong is "officially" under way when a man places the two-skinned drum sideways on his lap and beats out an opening refrain with the palms of his hands to alert both spirits and humans that the ritual is about to begin. After this *topo*, or "slapping" (so termed in reference to the way the drum is played), the drum is suspended from a rafter. From then until the end of the performance, the drum will be played by two people using drumsticks. Once the topo has sounded, young people begin to throng around the drum and gongs to take turns playing. Typically, young men and boys play the drums, and young women and girls the gongs, which are hung on either side of the drum. The drum provides the main rhythm, called a "song" (*linga*), the words to which the audience knows. The themes of these drum songs range from courtship to spirit encounters, from head-hunting days of old to contemporary poverty. Not uncommonly, drummers flatter and embarrass young women by playing songs that include their names. Although drum songs tend to be intricate, the accompanying gong beat is simple to master. Gong players answer each other with a single beat, either slow or fast depending on the rhythm set by the drum player or the shamans, who later on in the evening will stand to dance.

Once the music has started and the audience congregated, the host will urge the prominent shamans present to take their place beside the lango, drink beer, chew betel, smoke, and converse. Sometimes a shaman will begin his performance directly. Or he may wait half the night to begin his work. At some point he will take up his *papolonsu*, a cloth he will use to handle his patients' soul parts, and some wunga, the fragrant basil that attracts spirit familiars. Sniffing the wunga and rubbing it over his body and shaman's cloth, he whispers secret names and magical spells to make his person and his paraphernalia effective and attractive to his spirit allies. Then, after emitting some loud whistles to alert his familiars, he starts to sing in a resonant tone, drawing out his syllables and casting his voice in long, lingering cadences.

kupeboo pokio	I call, I summon
powira layo layoda	the leader, Layo Layoda,
powira we'a ntiara	the leader, Woman of the Pearl,
powira peda mlilo	the leader, Peda mLilo.
mai pampemai	Come, come,
pei soara luya	and face the betel offering,
panta ja komi wegangku	each of you, my spirits.
o peboo joa joamo joa sondo	Oh, call your followers, your followers, handsome followers.
panta naka sondili ri luya	Have each one arrive at the betel offering.
o imba to yoyo nsimata	Oh, where is the One of the Succulent Shoot,
guruku baratapa	the teacher I met while keeping vigil?
penanya komi wegangku	Experienced you are, my spirit.
kasidomu poroia	Assemble everyone.
o imba to ri mata ntasi	Oh, where is the One from the Source of the Sea,
wega ngkaramat	Spirit of Karamat?
kasidomu panta panta	Assemble each and every one.
kita masondada luya	Together we shall face the betel offering.
o imba to ri buyu sinjuyu	Oh, where is the One of Adjoining Mountain Slopes?
mai mpapaemai ri sori guyano	Come, do come, to the edge of the betel offering.
o kasidomu panta panta	Oh, assemble each and every one,
ri sori ngguyano	at the edge of the betel offering.
o sidomu panta	Oh, assemble each,
o sidomu samporoia wegangku	Oh, assemble all, my spirits.
maka melengke sangkio wega	Take a little look, spirits,

pei ngande lai guyanoku	and eat down here at my betel offering.
pei sibuka ntinombo	And drink of the beer,
pai sibuka	and drink,
. . .	[unintelligible]
nake dole masanang	so you'll be happy, content.

With these words, Apa Weri, a skilled hunter and subtle speaker, assembled his spirit familiars one evening (Fig. 12). On another occasion his brother-in-law and chum, Apa Mene, sang the passage that follows (Fig. 13).[2] Apa Mene's voice is as harsh and loud as Apa Weri's is reedlike and refined. But shamans are not judged by the beauty of their song, but by the hidden powers they are thought to wield.

i lilo mpopoyu	Oh, you of the Lilting Whistle,
paka mosu mosu	come close, close.
komi kusonaru	You I rely on.
i lilo mpopoyu	Oh, you of the Lilting Whistle,
to pongkami tongku	the One Who Guards the Mountain,
mai mai papemai wo'u	come, come, make haste again.
saito sabengi mantidang sili	Night by night set a limit to this illness.
mai mai papemai ruyu	Come, come, hurry come soon.
guru taa ginuru nabi ponuntu	Teacher never studied [i.e., the shaman acquired this teacher on his own without studying with other mortals], *nabi* to heed, traveling together over every mountain crest,
majue majuyu ponto rapa buyu	using the path of the source.
paka jaya mpu'u	You I depend on.
komi kusonaru	Come lend your aid.
ma'i matulung	The One Who Sits with Legs Bent to the Side
mungku to lamungku	
jaya katuntu	[whose] path is the epic
ri pada kamumu	through the Purple Grassland.
e jaya ntundug	Hey, the path of shaman's allies,
komi tayu to sansala	you, people on a separate path,
powira ntana sanai	[your] leader from Tana Sanai,
naka rangku mai	conversing as you come.
buyu to saito to samba'a	On the next mountain over,
naka gai mai	making an approach, comes
rede malangang	Short Tall One.

e ne'e kojo mbojombojo wega	Hey, don't you dare take offense, spirit.
mbenumo tundug	Where's the shaman's ally,
rata mitulung	come to help?
naka nggai rede malangang	Making an approach, Short Tall One,
tutu'a bolag	the Elder of the Bolag spirits,
to ri tondo nggele	those from the Direction of Laughter,
to tu'a mapewe	the Old One in the Loincloth,
joa nsareareme	followers of Sareareme.
o mai mai papemai mai	Oh, come, come, hurry up and come.

SHAMANIC SOBRIQUETS

With such a song—known as a "summons," or *patoe*—a shaman calls his spirit familiars from distant haunts to join him at the lango. He addresses them not by their true names—potent words that he alone knows—but rather by nicknames (*pangki*). These epithets often link a spirit to a particular place, typically a wild and distant one. The place may well be the spot where the shaman first encountered the familiar, as in the case of Tondo Nggele mentioned by Apa Mene. A shaman who addresses a spirit as *to ri rapa bente*, "the One from the Fortified Crest," hints that he met this ally atop a mountain, a spot made doubly frightening and powerful through its association with the violence of a former era. A shaman who summons *to ri watu buya*, "the One at the White Rock," similarly alludes to a meeting he had with a spirit in a distant and lonely place.

At other times, place names associate the spirit with a mythical topography. *Pada kamumu*, the "Purple Grassland" that Apa Mene's spirit traverses, is such a place. It is a familiar site in epic tales called *katuntu* and in shamans' journeys above the earth. So too is *mata ntasi*, the "Source of the Sea" from which Apa Weri's ally hails. Performers may call on *kuasa ri tunda ntana*, "the power at the seat of the earth," where the land, still joined to the sky, was first set down, or the power from the *siyonso*, the boundary of land and sea far off where the sun sets.

Sometimes epithets draw on the language and imagery of the sultanates that formerly dotted the coast of Sulawesi. The epithet *wega ngkaramat* in Apa Weri's song makes use of a term for sacred power (*karamat*) associated with rajas of days gone by. It is not uncommon for shamans to invoke powers of the kingdoms side by side with the powers of the wild, as Apa Mene does here:

raja pologoti	Raja of the Pologot [a term for shamans' familiars],
ma'i mitolongi	come lend your help.
ma'i raponsarumaka komi	Come, you, be depended upon.
to ri buyu kandoli	The One at the Leaning Mountain,
mampolemba wonti	disguised as a monkey,
ne'e kojo kaumboli	don't you dare have a change of heart.

For the Wana, who have been historically peripheral to coastal centers, the powers of the wild and the powers of the civilized centers are equally remote and equally impressive. Both are beyond the ordinary Wana world and so serve as resources for shamans.

Some epithets are old ones associated with shamans of the past. I recorded invocations to *to ri lemba nsinara*, "the One on the Flank of Mount Sinara," which A. C. Kruyt (1930, 449) transcribed a half century ago. Mount Sinara is reputed to have been rich in resin trees. Men probably tapped both resin and spirits on their soujourns there. Likewise the spirit from *mata ntasi*, "the Source of the Sea," shows up in both Kruyt's (ibid.) transcripts and my own. Using epithets associated with a well-known shaman identifies one as a protégé or, perhaps, as one brave enough to have waited by the shaman's freshly dug grave in order to win the spirit familiars who gathered there. Two shamans may also use the same epithet for different spirits, and shamans who are close friends or related as teacher and student may, in a gesture of solidarity, call on each other's spirit familiars in the course of a performance.

Spirit epithets may allude in poignant ways to shared experiences of a community. When Apa Mene concluded a string of epithets with the phrase "Followers of Sareareme," he implied that the spirit or spirits named earlier were led by one whose name plays attractively on the word *reme*, meaning "light" or "clear." Apa Mene and Indo Lina had had a baby boy whom they called Sareareme and who died a month after birth. Apa Mene has since communed with the child's spirit. Apa Linus, Apa Mene's younger cousin, alludes to some of his own familiars as "followers of Sareareme," an appellation that Indo Lina finds deeply moving.

The adoption of a new epithet by a shaman in his chant, be it original with him or not, suggests the acquisition of a new familiar. For example, during my field stay Apa Mene began summoning *to tu'a matoko, to tu'a masowo*, and *to tu'a pungku*—the Old One with the Staff, the Old One with a Goiter, and the Old One with Stumped Limbs. People familiar with his spirit epithets pointed out to me that he had entered into a new alliance.

Epithets like these are puzzling to the sociologically minded ethnographer. Because of the parallel construction of Wana shamans' songs, it is unclear whether we are dealing with one spirit or several. Moreover, Wana pronouns are not marked for gender. Time and again, when companions referred to a kind of spirit, I would ask if the spirit were male or female. People would ponder the matter, then reply that there must be males and females, and children too, or how would they propagate? As we shall see in the next chapter, Wana conceive of spirits as living in communities just as they themselves do. And like Wana communities, spirit communities have distinguished leaders. In their invocations, shamans typically address the "leaders" (*powira*) of their spirit familiars and instruct them to organize their "followers" (*joa*) to assist in a joint undertaking.

CONCENTRATING POWER

As the opening passages of this chapter reveal, a patoe is an insistent call to distant spirits to "come close," to congregate around the shaman at the lango. Patoe convey a dramatic sense of the distance these spirits are expected to traverse at the beck and call of their human friend. The following is a portion of a Wana "summoning" transcribed by Kruyt (1930, 448–49; I have transposed the passage to conform to current conventions of transcription and supplied my own translation):

imba to re'e tamungku	Where are the ones of the mountain?
solu ma'i ruyu	Come, arrive here first.
to la'u togongi	The ones down on the Togi Islands [in the sea to the north of the Wana],
ira soe ndopi	Leaf Swinging on a Wooden Plank,

solu paka joli	hurry up and arrive!
to la'u winanga	Those down at the mouth of the river [probably where the Bongka River pours into the sea, days away from most Wana settlements],
ma'i paka sara	come, make haste.
to ri mata ntasi	Those at the source of the sea,
kasolumo ma'i	come, make your arrival.

To draw them close, a shaman flatters his spirits, referring to them with such phrases as "my esoteric teacher" (*guruku masusi*), and "[the One who] refuses to be surpassed" (*bo'onya ri ara*; literally, "who refuses to be on the bottom"). The performers quoted above admire their spirits' retinues (*joamo joa sondo*) and stress their own reliance on the aid of these hidden friends. In lavishing praise on his spirit familiars, a shaman does not neglect himself. Note how Apa Mene in his patoe refers to one of his spirits as "teacher never studied," meaning that the shaman won this spirit alliance through personal quest, not from study with another mortal. Similarly, Apa Weri sings of meeting his "teacher" To Yoyo nSimata while keeping vigil, a testimony to his shamanic efforts.

In addition to flattery, a shaman nags: "Don't have a change of heart," "don't take offense," "come, be depended upon." Spirit familiars need constant encouragement and persuasion. They also apparently respond to invitations to approach the lango:

kasidomu mai	Assemble, come,
kasidomu panta panta	assemble each and every one

and to indulge in the the refreshments that await them there:

to maransa poransamo	Those who dance, proceed to dance.
to mongande pengandemo	Those who eat, proceed to eat.
to moluya peluyamo	Those who chew betel, proceed to chew.

The shaman thus appeals to his familiars as a host appeals to guests. He urges them to make themselves "happy, content," before assisting him in the evening's tasks.

KEEPING SECRETS

As he sits at the lango, the shaman surveys a landscape vivid to him but invisible to his human audience. He addresses familiarly and with reference to past experience powerful beings whose very names are kept secret from the shaman's human audience: "Ah, here comes the One of the Lilting Whistle! And there is the One Who Guards the Mountain, Short Tall One, and the Old One in the Loincloth!" Along with these leaders come throngs of supporters, chatting with one another as they cross the mountains. The shaman, as I have noted, deals with the "leaders" of the spirit hosts, and thereby displays parity with them. An invocation creates the sense of dense masses of invisible beings crowding around the shaman at the lango. When shamans perform together for the first time, they make a point of introducing their spirit familiars to one another to insure harmonious relations among their respective retinues. Colleagues like Apa Weri and Apa Mene, by contrast, need not resort to such measures, because their spirit familiars have a long history of collaboration.

The patoe is a communication between shaman and spirits. It is distinguished from ordinary conversation by the fact that it is sung and by the fact that it is cast in language very different from that of everyday conversation, in both vocabulary and linguistic embellishment. To communicate with these beings from beyond the human community, shamans use words associated with distant times and places. For example, some vocabulary comes from the *molawo*, an esoteric chant regarded as the "mother" of shamanic performances. Others derive from epic songs about a bygone era of magic (*katuntu*). Apa Weri's song is rich with such vocabulary. Expressions like *soara luya* and *joamo joa sondo* are stock phrases from these forms. Foreign terms are also incorporated; words like *guru* and *nabi* have been in the tradition so long that their alien origins are forgotten, but others, like *karamat*, probably still carry a foreign cachet. Borrowings need not come all the way from India or the Middle East; indeed, languages of neighboring peoples are a fertile source of differentiated vocabulary. Other words are conventional shamanic substitutes for ordinary vocabulary: *sangkio* instead of *sangkodi*, "a little"; *melengke* instead of *malo'a*, "to look," are but two examples.

It is vital to emphasize, however, that shamanic speech, although different from ordinary conversation, must be intelligible to Wana audiences. Unlike Kuna songs of ritual healing, which are neither addressed to nonspecialists nor widely understood by them (Sherzer 1983, 134), a Wana shaman's song admits a human audience as witness to his engagement with spirits. The significance of this fact will become apparent as my analysis unfolds.

The explicit purpose of the summons is for a shaman to assemble his spirit familiars and to enlist their aid for the evening's activities. Each shaman has his own style of patoe, which he varies during a single performance and from evening to evening. Moreover, whereas every shaman's mabolong performance starts with a patoe, the patoe is by no means limited to the beginning of the mabolong. After his initial summons, a shaman repeatedly calls on and encourages the same spirits throughout the evening and summons new ones as well. With each new patient he examines, too, a shaman sings a patoe. And after a pause in his labors to converse with people in the room, he may begin anew by calling once again on his hidden companions. Thus, a shaman's performance at a mabolong does not take the form of a single narrated journey in which spirit familiars are assembled, travel off together in pursuit of patients' souls, then return to their starting point. Although this format, characteristic of the esoteric molawo ritual (see Part Three), is applied when the mabolong performer makes a special trip up to the Owner, such a journey constitutes but an optional episode in the mabolong, not the structure of the ritual in its entirety.

The continual repetition of the patoe throughout a shaman's mabolong performance is evidence I shall invoke later to substantiate my argument that the mabolong is to a great degree "about" the power a shaman derives through his relationship with his spirit familiars. But that point cannot be made without a full appreciation of what spirits and power are in Wana culture.

2

A Divided Reality

> Here we have the basic idea behind magical actions, an idea involving immediate and limitless effects, the idea of direct creation. It is the absolute illusion, the maya as the Hindus so aptly named it. Between a wish and its fulfillment there is, in magic, no gap.
>
> Mauss, *A General Theory of Magic*

> All magical operations rest on the restoring of a unity; not a lost unity (for nothing is ever lost) but an unconscious one, or one which is less completely conscious than those operations themselves.
>
> Lévi-Strauss, *Introduction to the Work of Marcel Mauss*

When he summons his spirit familiars to the lango, a shaman addresses a cohort invisible to his human companions.[1] Through his song, he simultaneously grants his audience access—albeit indirect—to a hidden dimension of their world and maintains its exclusivity. This chapter will explore the cultural construction of this divided reality. Chapter 3 then examines how differentiated realms of experience provide the conditions for social distinction and inequality.

DIFFERENTIATED BEINGS

My first intimations of the divided nature of the Wana world came one hot day during my first month of fieldwork as Indo Lina and I were lounging indoors, avoiding the noonday heat and working to remedy our language gap. In striking contrast to nearly all her neighbors, Indo Lina, the young wife of the settlement's most prominent shaman, had openly and immediately welcomed my presence and curiosity about Wana life. What is more, she did not hesitate to express her curiosity about my life as well.

Looking out over the densely forested mountain flanks that faced us, Indo Lina explained that those forests were full of "people" (*tau*) who for some reason were not seen, people who lived and farmed like the people here but who kept themselves hidden from sight. My first thought was of what Indonesians call *orang berliar*, "wild people," who hide in the forests to avoid being governed. I had been told by Indonesian authorities that the Wana area was full of such people, presumably those who refused to register as kampung members. The vividness and certainty with which my companion spoke made these unseen forest dwellers seem very real indeed. I had not yet begun to appreciate how my companions treated aspects of "nonordinary reality"—not "as if" they were real, but rather "as real" (Castaneda 1971, 14).[2]

I noted then my perplexity about these elusive people who Indo Lina said live and farm like others but stay out of view. Later I was to learn that these neighbors are called the *tau bolag* or *tau wuni* ("invisible people") and constitute another *bangsa*, another "category" of people like the Wana themselves.[3] Unlike the Wana, however, the Bolag are said to possess *jampu*, the power to become invisible. Using jampu, they conceal themselves from their Wana neighbors and allow themselves to be seen only when and if they choose. The terms Indo Lina used to characterize the Bolag were, as I recognized even then, terms that applied to ordinary Wana settlements. It was only later, as my knowledge of Wana language and culture advanced, that I could be sure that these hidden people was not humans such as you or I might ordinarily meet, but a spirit population whose characteristics were drawn from Wana social experience. Tau bolag were, as people succintly put it, *tau ewa kita si'i, pei si'a*, "people like us here, but not."

DIFFERENTIATED REALMS

At the same time that she was revealing to me the existence of the tau bolag, Indo Lina was also pressing me to reveal my knowledge of another kind of division in her world. She outlined for me the existence of two realms, *tana salebe*, where the Wana live, and *tana saruga*, a wonderful place where people are white and beautiful and there is food without work. She was curious how much I knew about the latter place. In time I came to understand the profound significance of her question, which applied culturally available constructions of reality to the perplexing presence of two Americans in the Wana area. The derivation of the place names she used came to me only later. *Salebe* is the Wana rendering of Celebes, the former Dutch name for Sulawesi, the island the Wana inhabit. In fact, neither *salebe* nor *sulawesi* is a common term in Wana parlance. Instead, Wana speak of *tana wana*, "the Wana land" (as opposed, for example, to *tana bugis*, the place where Bugis people come from). The outsider's term, *tana salebe*, enters Wana discourse only in consideration of the place of the Wana in the wider cosmos. (I use the word *cosmos* here rather than, say, the designation Republic of Indonesia, because my sense is that *salebe*, no longer the name of the Indonesian island now called Sulawesi, is associated more with ultimate reality than with more proximate political, economic, and ethnic issues.) As for *saruga*, the term derives from the Sanskrit word *svarga* ("heaven") and, as a borrowing from Bahasa Indonesia, is used by Muslims, Christians, and pagan Wana for the afterworld (see Atkinson 1983).

That morning's conversation stands out in retrospect as my first introduction to Wana ideas about a multifarious reality. Indo Lina's account, corroborated and enhanced over and over by others is founded on divisions of experience expressed in terms of spatial and visual separation. The tau bolag live alongside the Wana but maintain their invisibility. Saruga, as I later learned, is conceived to exist alongside the earth, although no longer continuous with it, and to be cloaked by invisibility. Contained in both conceptions is the premise that there are realms of reality ordinarily inaccessible to people in everyday life. Moreover, these divisions are conceived to be functions of a temporal process.

The vision of the world as divided into ordinary and hidden realms is not an idle cosmology, but a powerfully generative theodicy. History and experience are conjoined in this framework, of which shamanship and its millenarian offshoot are critical linchpins. By positing dimensions of reality beyond everyday experience, it establishes the cultural preconditions for Wana shamanship—namely, the possibility of marshaling valued resources exogenous to Wana society by extending social relations beyond the bounds of the human community. By identifying both the unknown and the seemingly uninhabited regions of the world as the homes of hidden beings, Wana map out a geography of power.

In a treatment of Southeast Asian cosmologies, Robert McKinley (1979, 317) identified "a felt tension between culture and nature" at work in traditional shamanic complexes: in contrast to Hindu conceptions of divine kingship, which place power, embodied by raja, at civilized centers, the shamanic systems of upland swidden populations locate power in the wild. In its broad outlines, McKinley's account applies to the Wana case, although Wana do not rely on shamans to appease the natural realm on which their farming communities encroach, as McKinley's argument suggests they might. By deeming the forest to be the locale of other-than-human beings, Wana emphasize the difference between their own social world and the uncultivated tracts of forest beyond Wana farming communities. Power, in Wana terms, originates not within human settlements, but in the wilderness. The Wana shaman at his lango is in some respects like a raja at the "navel" of his kingdom. Both embody concentrations of magical power, but the raja derives his power by "staying put" as the center of his kingdom, whereas the Wana shaman has ideally sought his power through lonely and frightening quests in the forest.

DIFFERENTIATED EXPERIENCE

The distinction of realms I am treating here is more than spatial. It expresses not only a physical separation between human communities and what lies beyond them, but an experiential one as well. Wana characterizations of reality are, I submit, not about "reality" per se, but rather about the relation of a cultural subject to his or her world. Familiar Euroamerican dichotomies like natural/supernatural, physical/metaphysical, and empirical/nonempirical concern the nature of phenomena that stand apart from the self and hence provide only a rough approximation of the distinction at work here.

Instead of carving up reality without reference to a knowing subject (see Hallowell 1967, 92), Wana express the nature of the world in terms of differential access to varieties of experience. To this end, they recognize a world in which it is possible to see and interact with that which is not ordinarily seen or engaged. To take an example, on our arrival Effort and I were accepted as part of the world, albeit a puzzling and disturbing part. We were people not ordinarily encountered in the Wana land who were now visible and accessible to all. If indeed we were from Saruga, such a situation would be an ominous portent of the end of the present order, for it would mean that the dead were mingling with the living without restriction. The problem was phrased not in terms of our essence, but rather in terms of our presence and general visibility in Wana communities.

Charles Frake's (1980) contrast of the "ordinary" and the "extraordinary" is more useful here than conventional oppositions such as "natural" and "supernatural," which presume differences "in the world out there." When applied not to ontology but to epistemology, the terms *ordinary* and *extraordinary* can be used to highlight what cultural actors take to be likely and possible in human experience, as opposed to objective properties of the world. In this fashion, "ordinary" would apply to what people are thought capable of experiencing in daily life, whereas "extraordinary" would apply to what is both beyond most people's firsthand experience and impossible for everyone to experience in the world as it is presently constituted. To tailor this contrast more precisely to suit Wana talk about hidden facets of experience, we should distinguish the "ordinary" not from the "extraordinary," but from the "hidden." More about that in a moment.

The contrast I am drawing turns on a capacity for experience. Just because something is unlikely to be experienced does not put it in the realm of the extraordinary. For example, all Wana can speak of the town of Poso, even though the overwhelming majority have never been there. Were they to go to Poso, however, they would presumably be able potentially to experience what anyone else might experience in that town. All share that experiential capacity equally. But people *do* differ in their capacity to experience some other dimensions of reality.

A typical Wana story illustrates the distinction. Two men were camping together by the bank of a river to fish at night. One evening the two heard the sounds of drum and gongs signaling the start of a mabolong. Here they were, off in the forest far from any human settlement. Eager to investigate, they looked about for a route to the source of the sounds. One man saw a path that led him directly to the festivities. Yet in the same place, his friend saw only a steep cliff covered with impenetrable forest. Thus one man went off to live with the tau wuni, the "invisible people," while his friend, lacking such good fortune, was left behind. Both men were able to *hear* the spirits' music, but only one could *see* to reach its source. Access to extraordinary experience is phrased in terms of sight, not hearing, a point that I will examine more closely later on.

Extraordinary realms of experience, then, are those to which some people, but not all, have access. The extraordinary, as I use it here, need not be a surprise. Indeed, extraordinary experiences are expected to happen to some Wana some of the time. The potential for extraordinary experience is an "ordinary" assumption, if you will, in Wana life.

Events such as falling sick, being bitten by a snake, or losing one's house to flood or fire are, for Wana, ordinary in that it takes no special capacity to be able to experience them. Yet mundane events may be interpreted either as ordinary events in the course of things *or* as events that have behind them a special reason—what the Wana would term a "source," "origin," "foundation," or "base" (*pu'u*). Thus, a person may experience an event that is provoked or motivated by an "extraordinary" source and lack the capacity to apprehend the source directly. This is not to say that a person could not suspect what the source might be, but without a special capacity, that person could not verify the source, let alone take effective action in regard to it.

To summarize my discussion so far, Wana distinguish ordinary dimensions of reality—namely, those to which everyone, in theory, has access—and extraordinary dimensions of reality—those to which access is limited. Events in the world may be quite ordinary; for example, a stomachache may be caused by eating too much fresh meat or young corn. Like the Azande, Wana freely grant the efficacy of "ordinary" aspects of the world, including human carelessness, inattention, and stupidity. But events in the world may be motivated as well by sources beyond the direct ken of ordinary people. Direct access to and influence over these sources is restricted to a fortunate few. These points provide both an epistemology and a charter for Wana shamanship.

Although not everyone can experience hidden possibilities in the Wana world directly, all can be conversant with them. Through the use of conventionalized narratives (what Ortner [1973] has termed cultural "scenarios")[4] that outline typical sequences of action involving extraordinary dimensions of reality, people can discuss and interpret events with reference to hidden sources. For instance, people may ponder whether an accident was the result of clumsiness or a ghost's provocation, whether heavy rains are simply "seasonal" (*temponya*) or constitute retribution for an act of incest, whether a child's incessant crying is due to possession by a changeling spirit (*tau tolo*) or merely the product of a whiny disposition. Interpretation, then, is not limited to the few who claim firsthand experience with hidden realms and spirits. Through allusions to mutually shared scenarios, people are free to interpret experience in terms of what they themselves cannot directly apprehend.

To this point I have sketched how a contrast between ordinary and hidden dimensions of reality operates experientially and exegetically for cultural subjects. As Lévi–Strauss ([1950] 1987, 19) observed for normal and abnormal behavior, the relation between ordinary and extraordinary reality is both complementary and dynamic. Subsequent analysis will highlight the involvement of this relation in practices fundamental to Wana life and society.

DIFFERENTIATION AND NARRATIVE

Elizabeth Traube's (1989) characterization of the epistemology of another Island Southeast Asian people, the Mambai of East Timor, applies verbatim to the Wana: "[Both] conceive of their society in narrative terms, as a transformation of an earlier state of unity and wholeness." In contrast to Mambai thought, however, the Wana cosmology carries both a cosmogony and a distinctive telegnosis. Not only do Wana posit a prior state of unity followed by a series of separations, partings, and dispersals, all of which have led to the present state of impoverishment, but they also anticipate a reunion of that which was divided at the original source.

In their historical moment, after dispersal and before reunification, Wana portray themselves as existing in a cosmic state of entropy, which, mimetically, their discourse about the past represents. Wana assert that the cosmogonic "stories," the *serita*, are no longer known in their entirety. Unlike in Mambai society, where cosmogonic narratives support ritualized exchange and where restricted access to cosmogonic knowledge constitutes social hierarchy, Wana cosmogony serves neither as a charter for human social exchange nor as the dominant form of ritual knowledge for which cultural actors compete.[5] Nevertheless, as subsequent examination will reveal, these cosmological narratives are homologous to a variety of forms of social action, including historical processes of settlement formation and dissolution, millenarian endeavors, ritual healing, and the mabolong performance.

Like the Mambai, Wana regard their cosmogonic tales as powerful. Were they to be recited in their complete form, their telling would take seven days and seven nights. A recitation of this sort would have to be accompanied by an offering tray, or lango, such as the one prepared for a shamanic performance, because these stories possess *baraka*. Whereas for coastal Muslim culture baraka is an attribute of royalty and the powerful paraphernalia with which sovereigns surround themselves, Wana consider baraka to have its source in the Wana homeland. In this way, Wana assert their own primordial centrality over and above the power claimed by coastal political centers. The use of the lango for a recitation of cosmogony is revealing. Just as a shaman's lango serves as a central point to which exogenous powers from distant places are drawn, so the storyteller's lango serves as a point of concentration for powers that have dispersed to the ends of the earth.

My own recitation of these stories requires no lango, for the snippets culled from my associates contain no secret and potent names of powerful beings, nor do they represent the corpus in its entirety, an ideal that my sources believe once existed but does no longer. Kruyt's collection of Wana cosmogonic stories gathered in 1928 is likewise scattershot. Wana make no pretense—unlike Mambai ritual specialists—of full knowledge of cosmogonic stories, nor do they go to lengths to judge "narrative competence." (Such judgments are, however, applied to performance in other arenas, such as shamanship and legal debate.) Yet people did specify how a ritual performance of powerful cosmogonic tales would be conducted: it would begin at the beginning, with the *potudu*—the "descent" of earth, mountains, animals, plants, and people from the heaven (see Kruyt 1930)—and then proceed with a series of separations—the parting of the earth and sky, the distancing of the earth and the sun, and the parting of the morning and evening stars.[6]

The Departure of Knowledge, Power, and Wealth

My own recitation will begin with the former golden age. "In the past," it is told, the Wana land was populated by *tau baraka*, "people of power." Those were the days of *wali mpanto'o*—literally, "the becoming of the word." In that time one needed only speak a wish, and it would be realized. The formula for such a wish is called *adi adi*; by closing one's eyes and reciting, "adi adi indo dua apa, to si aku to momonso, kulepa matak. . ." ("*adi adi* of mother and father, mine is the truer;[7] I have only to open my eyes. . ."), there appeared whatever it was one wished for. Tales of the days when wishes so easily came true are called katuntu. Their characters use adi adi to obtain food, houses, wealth, and trips to far-off places.

Alas, the golden age was not to last. The tau baraka departed from the Wana land to go to the "end of the earth" (*joe ntana*). Some went in bodily form, using vehicles of transport characteristic of katuntu such as flying rainhats (*toru*), shields (*kantar*), and chairs (*gadera*). Others became *tompuso* first, meaning that their bodies turned into features of the landscape (typically rocks) as their spirits went off to join the others. (Wana millenarian leaders have promised both kinds of departures to their adherents.) With these people went power (*baraka*), knowledge (*pangansani*), and wealth (*kasugi*) (including, some say, *pabriik*, or "factories"—the source of valued material goods).[8] What was left to the Wana seemed poor indeed, such as implements to make barkcloth (*ronto kojo*), considered grievously inferior to cotton cloth.

Significantly, the names given to two of the three departing entities, baraka and kasugi, are borrowed from the dominant Islamic coastal peoples who in Wana history have held a regional monopoly on power and material wealth. The story of the departure serves as an explanation for the political and economic disparity Wana see as existing between themselves and their coastal neighbors. As for the third item, pangansani, its name is important for Wana shamanship. *Ansani*, "to know," is a familiar Wana word that applies to the possession of ordinary commonsensical sorts of information and know-how. The nominal form, *pangansani*, however, does not apply to commonplace knowledge. Instead, it pertains both to the knowledge that charac-terizes that earlier golden age and to the knowledge of a person who controls powerful magic (*do'a*) deriving from hidden sources in the Wana world today. In other words, there is still pangansani to be found—although people are quick to say it is nothing compared to the powerful knowledge of the past. In contrast to that former age, however, powerful knowledge is no longer commonplace but is limited to a very few. The departure of the tau baraka, then, has left today's Wana powerless, poor, and limited in their access to knowl-edge.

The Disenchantment of the World

A second cluster of stories accounts in a somewhat lighter vein for another set of miseries. The figure to blame here goes by the name of

Langesong, a spoilsport who went about ruining people's comfort by "remarking" (*magagang*) on the way things worked, thereby causing those things to lose their efficacy. Before Langesong spoiled things, tools and implements performed on their own without engaging human toil. For instance, carrying baskets known as *kalando* once walked by themselves. Then along came Langesong, who urged the owner of a basket to hurry up because it was about to rain. From that time on, baskets have had to be carried. It is likewise because of Langesong that the wild tuber *ondo* can no longer be eaten raw but must be leached first, and that bees sting, thanks to the sharp thorn he placed on the apian posterior.

Far more serious was the suffering Langesong inflicted when he interfered with a *measa*, a demon who in those times ate only the insides of rocks and trees. One day a measa was hammering at a rock to get at its core, or "liver" (*ate*). Langesong passed by and remarked, "Don't eat the insides of rocks. They are hard. Eat the livers of people. They are tender." The demon pondered the matter, then went to the Owner (*pue*), who granted the demon permission to eat the livers of people, but only when they are ripe (*matasa*). Consequently, when a person's life is destined to end, it is said that a demon "eats out one's liver" (*mangkoni yau atenya*). Similarly, having developed a taste for human livers, demons now steal them or harm their owners before the appointed time. Shamans are the Wana defense for such unauthorized poaching.

Langesong, it seems, would stop at nothing. I once heard a woman declare that Langesong, "curse his eyes," was responsible for the fact that women rather than men bear children!

Langesong did not refrain from badgering the powerful. At the time of the exodus of tau baraka from the land, Langesong's tongue was not silent. Seeing someone depart in a boat flying above the treetops—a normal event in that age of power—Langesong exclaimed, "What's that fellow doing committing *asa*?" (*asa* being an act that is unnatural, and hence ill-omened). As Langesong uttered those words, the boat promptly fell from the sky.

The efficacy of Langesong's words represents the reversal of the efficacy of adi adi. Instead of producing desirable consequences by uttering a formula, Langesong subverts them with his speech and also marks a switch from public magic to private magic. To report on an extraordinary feat (in Wana terms, to *magagang*) is to cause it to fail; for example, should one witness a shaman walking in the air and proceed to announce the fact, the shaman will fall. Miracles can still happen, but only in secret.

The Separation of the Living and the Dead

I mentioned the separation of earth and heaven (*saruga*) at the start of this chapter. Once, it is said, people traveled freely between the two places. But heaven was becoming too full, so free access was barred to insure that the earth would be inhabited. Saruga was set off from the earth by a barrier (*yondo, tida*) of darkness (*wengi, wuri*). Now to enter heaven one must "store one's body" (*sombo lemba*), leave the "light" of this world, and pass through the "barrier of darkness." The word *lemba* refers both to one's earthly body (which remains as a corpse after death) and to garments. At death, in order to enter heaven a person discards his or her body as one would shed one's clothes. (When examining patients, shamans sometimes inspect the "buttons" that hold a patient's body and soul together.) As it now stands, the living of this world and the dead of Saruga are forbidden to meet as long as the living still wear their lemba.

Stories also say that in the past death was a temporary state from which people returned in three days. Then Ngkasi, the Wana trickster, cried and stamped the ground in rage (*mangaru*) when a person died; thereafter death was permanent and people's rotting bodies had to be buried.

The separation of heaven and earth, of living and dead, is a central theme in both shamanic and millenarian practice. Millenarian predictions forecast a reunion of heaven and earth when the living and the dead will once again mingle together freely (*sagala wo'o*—literally, "to mix heads," as people in a crowd). In the meantime, shamans mediate a divided world as they treat the sick and the dying.

The Parting of Religions

The clusters of stories summarized thus far present the economic, political, and theodical conditions of present-day Wana life as the unfortunate result of a variety of separations. Another set of stories explains the religious divisions of the current world as being the consequence of siblings parting. In his 1930 article on the Wana, Kruyt (p. 418) recounts a tale of two siblings, one pagan and one Muslim;

since that time, a third sibling has been added to account for Christianity, the newest religion in the area.

In these tales, the eldest sibling remains in the Wana homeland to maintain the traditional religion, while the younger siblings go off and establish Islam and Christianity. For example, one man renowned for his stories told me of *nabi noho* (probably "the Prophet Noah" in local Muslim parlance), who had three children. One went to *maka* (Mecca) and became a Muslim; another went to *belanda* (the Netherlands) and became a Christian; and one stayed with the father and "held on to the Wana religion" (*mangkongo agama alae*). The scenario of siblings' parting surely corresponds to the historical experience of the Wana, as converts to world religions and hence to coastal culture moved from the homeland and down to the sea. During the first year of my fieldwork, the Christian and Muslim communities of the district of Ulu Bongka were resettled on the coast under the directive of the Indonesian Social Ministry, an exodus that repeats earlier ones in Wana memory.

Like the stories of the departure of knowledge, power, and wealth from the Wana homeland, stories of the origin of the religions derive what is significant in intercultural relations—in this case religion—from a Wana source, thereby underscoring the primacy of Wana culture (see Atkinson 1983). Also as in those stories, in millenarian forecasts a return to the source—in this case, to the Wana religion—is anticipated. It is widely held among Wana that when everyone has chosen to convert to either Islam or Christianity, religious war will erupt. Many suspect that national elections are a poll to determine which side, Islam or Christianity, has more adherents. Given the religious agenda of Indonesian political parties and the fact that election results do measure the strength of certain religious factions, these suspicions have some basis in political reality. There was a strong conviction among my pagan neighbors that it was their task to maintain the traditional Wana religion to the end in order to gain salvation when those powerful beings who departed their homeland come back to their place of origin in Wana.[9]

Abandonment by Spirits

A final set of stories built around the theme of separation addresses the divisions that Indo Lina outlined, namely the divisions among inhabitants of the Wana land. Whereas once upon a time the Wana and their neighbors mingled freely, today all but the Wana conceal themselves with jampu, "invisibility." I heard several reasons for this separation. One popular account describes how in the past the Wana and their close neighbors, the tau bolag, were *masintuwu*, "living together." Thus, the Bolag and the Wana exhibited neighborliness, cooperation, and mutual support, as closely related communities are ideally expected to do, with acts that demonstrate this cherished value including participation in each other's festivities.

A death occurred among the Wana, so the story goes, and the tau bolag asked when the funeral feast would be held. The day after tomorrow, came the reply. In fact, though, the feast was scheduled for the next day. Why the lie? Out of stinginess, I'm told, and a fear that there would not be enough food to go around. On the appointed day the tau bolag arrived carrying food and drink, as good neighbors should, only to discover that they were a day late. Insulted by the deception, they left their contributions to the feast and departed, vowing to have nothing more to do with the Wana. Other stories cite parallel breaches of etiquette on the part of the Wana and "small feelings" (*kodi nraya*) on the part of the tau bolag as reasons for the latter's withdrawal. Today it is only a rare and fortunate Wana who realizes the hope of encountering a tau bolag.

Wana regret the invisibility of the tau bolag because these good beings are desirable company. There are other populations in the Wana land whose invisibility is despaired, however, not because of their goodness, but because of their malevolence. Invisibility gives these harmful beings an advantage in their efforts to injure Wana. The invisible enemies include among their ranks the liver-eating demons (*measa*) mentioned above, as well as changeling spirits called *tau tolo* who trade souls with infants, place spirits called *salibiwi* who punish people for improper words and behavior in particular locales, and headhunting spirits—the *sangia, tau sampu'u,* and *tambar*—who use the rainbow as their path and inflict excruciating headaches, muscle aches, and fevers on innocent victims. Like the benign tau bolag, these beings too are thought to live in communities that resemble Wana settlements, but unlike the tau bolag they behave hostilely toward Wana. Particularly extreme are the measa, who regard humans as game. Yet in characteristically relativistic fashion, Wana assert that in their own communities *measa* are good folk of pleasant appearance who don hideous exteriors only when roving in search of human prey.

These harmful beings are often referred to as *soba*, a term that applies as well to pestilence and to harmful agents that damage rice crops, such as rats, birds, insects, drought, and blight. Like rice, humans have their own pests who beset them out of capriciousness or in response to provocation. Over time, Wana claim, the soba that afflict them have multiplied. Correspondingly, Wana have grown smaller and weaker. Time, by the Wana equation, spells degeneration.

Cut off as they are from their spirit neighbors, both malign and benign, the Wana are doubly disadvantaged. First, they can no longer see the enemies who would attack them. Second, the spirits to whom they might turn for help are equally hidden from sight. The spirits' assumption of invisibility does not mark a change in their nature or way of life, only in their access to humans. A human may walk directly past their dwellings and see only impenetrable forest. Should they grant a person the privilege of meeting them, their homesteads will be unmistakable: where ordinary mortals see only trees and dense brush, the lucky one sees houses and farms. Whether one sees or not depends on a lucky conjunction of personal fortune, spirit approval, and, in some cases, special knowledge of ways to entreat potential, yet hidden, benefactors.

Hope lies on two fronts. On the one hand, shamans can tap the assistance of spirits to combat human misfortune. On the other, millenarian movements occasionally promise to resolve human estrangement from hidden beings, mobilizing adherents, for example, with the pledge that as a group they will don invisibility and go off to join the tau bolag. These millenarian movements, commonly inspired by fear of impending danger, propose simply fading away as a solution to existential problems. Hence, the confusion I felt in trying to distinguish between spirits and government runaways in Indo Lina's account was not without foundation, though I did not know it at the time.

DIFFERENTIATION AND POWER

I have reviewed five clusters of stories. The narrative structure of each involves the division of a prior state of unity. Whereas unity spelled strength and vitality, division spells weakness and unviability. In each cluster, a separation or dispersal in the past has left the Wana poor and vulnerable.

Wana adopt a distinctive ethnic stance regarding their sense of what Traube (1989) terms "lost plenitude." During my initial survey of the Wana area, I was repeatedly struck by the way in which Wana, especially senior men, would approach me with what I can only characterize as "sob stories"—pathetic portrayals of themselves as poor and orphaned. At first I read these performances as blatant requests for handouts. But in time I came to see that these self-characterizations went beyond bids for charity, representing instead a theodical strategy, fine-tuned to a distinct cultural logic. To be poor and parentless is to be bereft of security and guidance in the face of danger; it is a stance designed to invoke the pity of more powerful agents. Whereas a mature and respected Wana man would not promote a self-image involving abject poverty and abandonment to those he considered equal to or weaker than himself, to potential benefactors from afar he might very well represent himself, and thereby his people, in negative relief against a wider and threatening universe (see Atkinson 1984b).

The rhetorical power of such self-presentation shares the terms of the cosmogonic narratives that derive present-day conditions from a series of separations: the division of the land from heaven; the departure of power, knowledge, and wealth from the Wana land to the end of the earth; the parting of Wana from their place of origin; the division of religions; and the isolation of Wana from their spirit neighbors. The hope that lies behind these supplications turns on the anticipation that ultimately there will be a reunification of the world as what has parted will return "to seek its source."

Separations—of heaven from earth, life from death, knowledge, power, and wealth from their homeland, magic from work, spirits from humans, other peoples and religions from the Wana—have left the Wana powerless in their own eyes. These separations also set the preconditions for societal differentiation. For the Mambai, cosmogonic knowledge itself is "conceived of as a hidden treasure of unspoken words, and converted into hierarchical status" (Traube 1989). For the Wana, what is to be treasured and coveted is not the narratives about the division of the cosmos, but instead the words that pass across the partition.

Wana access to hidden realms of experience is limited, but there is a lively commerce across the divide. The next chapter will explore what Mauss (1967, 13) termed "the connection of exchange contracts among men with those between men and gods." Specifically, it examines the nature of spirits' "gifts" to humans and the place of these gifts in human transactions in Wana life.

3

Hidden Knowledge

> The secret offers, so to speak, the possibility of a second world
> alongside the manifest world; and the latter is decisively
> influenced by the former.
>
> Simmel, *The Sociology of*
> *Georg Simmel*

In trying to define my reasons for coming to live in the Wana land,
my companions and I hit on the word *moguru* "to study," as a characterization of my aim. The word derives from the Sanskrit term *guru*,
or "teacher." In adopting *moguru* as a label for my intentions, I hoped I
was conveying—as best one could to people unfamiliar with Western
educational institutions—my desire to "study" what shamans do. I
was soon to learn that *moguru* was not a contrived gloss for a foreign
practice:[1] "studying spells" is an established form of exchange with
clearly defined procedures.

It wasn't long before I frequently was finding myself seated in private with a teacher who would whisper to me in hushed tones the
knowledge he or she assumed I sought. This would consist of a series
of magical names and spells that would be repeated as many times as I
needed to inscribe them in my notebook. (Invariably my teachers
would comment on how my ability to write accelerated what would
otherwise be a lengthy and tedious process of memorization.) If my
teacher happened to be a shaman and the magic involved shamanic
performance, our sessions would conclude with applications of
chicken blood to our hands and feet to insure the continued "freshness" and efficacy of the magic for both my teacher and myself.

I found "secret" knowledge not only baffling, but also initially dis-
appointing. As a cultural anthropology student of the seventies, I took
it as axiomatic that cultural knowledge must have interpretable
meaning.[2] For me, learning secret knowledge implied achieving a full
and explicit reckoning. For my teachers, to know the secrets was
to memorize precisely the content of spirits' communication with

humans—however cryptic those communications might be. Enigma, not explanation, was its essence. But then, their relation to Wana ritual healing was different from mine. What I wanted to know was what they already took for granted—namely, the language, imagery, and principles of shamanic ritual. As it happened, I learned Wana shamanship backward, by moving from secret knowledge to common knowledge. In doing so, I began to see how much of the secret knowledge consisted of condensed allusions to the public dimensions of healing ritual. Interpretation, as it turned out, had a place in the enterprise after all. But the power of Wana magic lies not in the "meaning" of particular spells, but rather in the social relationships it constructs.

Elsewhere in Parts One and Two of this book, I begin with text, then move to context. Given the nature of Wana secret knowledge, however, in this chapter I follow the insight of other students of ritual secrecy (Barth 1975; Myers 1983) and reverse that order. To appreciate what one has learned, one must have a sense of its value. Hence, before exploring the content of magic, I shall examine its social value and management.

As we have seen, Wana characterize the present-day world as a diminution of the past. Among the most dramatic shifts from the prior age to the present was the changeover from a time when wishes came true (or, as Wana put it, "words happened" [*wali mpanto'o*]) to the current state of affairs where people must toil to achieve what little they have. Today, verbal magic provides a semblance of the former power of words. Magic very simply consists of words told by spirits to humans. Although barriers now exist between Wana and "those people who are like us but not," limited communication still takes place. But the "knowledge" (*pangansani*) that can be acquired in the Wana world today is meager compared to the pangansani of the "people of power" (*tau baraka*) who have long since deserted the Wana land.

The word *pangansani* is limited to the knowledge of an earlier age and to the magical knowledge of outstanding shamans and other who can perform incredible feats, such as defying bullets and knife blows, through the use of spells. But knowledge of magic is by no means so restricted in Wana society. Some individuals possess vast numbers of magical spells, but my companions asserted that no one utterly lacked spells. I came to recognize the truth of this statement when I discovered that even a partially deaf and consequently retarded child in my household had her own scant repertoire of magic to help her with her daily chores.

THE POWER OF THE WORD

The word *do'a* epitomizes magical knowledge derived from spirits. In fact, the magic imparted by spirits to humans may take one of three forms: "names" (*sanga*), "spells," (*do'a*), or "medicines" (*pokuli*). The first two forms are verbal; the third consists of material substances that are magically efficacious. What I say in reference to spells holds true for names as well, unless a specific contrast between the two is drawn. Names and spells occupy a more prominent place in Wana shamanic practice than do medicines, for reasons I shall explore at the end of this chapter.

True magical knowledge, be it a name, a spell, or a medicine, originates with spirits who communicate it to humans. The transaction may occur during a vigil undertaken for the express purpose of meeting spirits, during a chance meeting in the woods, or in a dream. And some magic, passed along from generation to generation, derives from the powerful beings who once inhabited the Wana land.

To obtain magic directly from a spirit is a matter of good fortune and perseverance. One must have a "palm line" (*ua mpale*) that disposes one to such luck (judgments of whether or not one possesses a lucky palm line are generally retrospective pronouncements based on past successes or failures). A person in search of spirits may seek the assistance of a shaman to learn special names, spells, medicines, and procedures to help with the quest.

SEEKING MAGIC "ON ONE'S OWN"

The forest is the place to go in search of spirits. One may either "walk" about (*malinja*) or "keep vigil" (*baratapa*) at a place or object. The former strategy can be combined with an otherwise ordinary trip to the forest in search of meat, plant foods, or materials with household uses; the latter is usually done in the dark of night solely for the purpose of meeting spirits. With either method, it is best to dress as poorly as possible to evoke the pity of the spirits. It is not uncommon for one who is skilled at playing a musical instrument such as flute, tuning fork, or stringed chest resonator to play haunting and plaintive songs to attract hidden beings.

One may choose a strategy for one's search according to the kind of knowledge or spirit one desires. For example, a person in search of spells to use in childbirth may tie a string around the just-budding fruit of a banana tree, then threaten not to remove the string until the spells are given. After a while, the plant should start to whimper. Finally, the plant's tutelary spirit (*nabi*) will emerge and offer the desired spells for speeding the delivery of a child in exchange for releasing the banana fruit. Alternatively, one could use the same technique to ask the nabi for spells to stop one from choking. The homeopathic principle at work in both cases is obvious.

Someone in search of magic to make wounds vanish might choose to guard a caged bat, which is said to lick its torn wings to render them whole again. One man I knew kept vigil at a river for a related sort of spell to make him impervious to cuts. He sat in the dark, striking the water repeatedly with a knife. The logic of this act was to gain knowledge that would make him as resistant to knife blows as water is.

The examples cited so far contain an association between the object over which one keeps vigil and the type of knowledge one wishes to obtain. One may also guard an object in order to meet a particular kind of spirit. For instance, one shaman of my acquaintance kept watch over a rice mortar and was visited by *wata podo*, a demon whose name translates to "short trunk" (Wana mortars are carved from tree trunks). A person in search of *pontiana*, the spirit that plagues women in childbed, might keep vigil over a chicken or its eggs, which have important associations with motherhood and childbirth. A grave is an unparalleled site for meeting "demons" (*measa*) and "ghosts" (*wonggo*). Not everyone in search of magic and spirits is so specific in the quest. One may simply go looking for spirit revelation in general and take whatever knowledge is offered.

A person in search of spirits sets out with certain expectations based on a rich and very public lore about what happens in encounters between humans and spirits. A supplicant should dress in rags and carry no food or blanket, and betel offerings are essential to entice spirit visitors. One fully expects to be visited first by menacing beings who test one's courage and resolve; by keeping in mind that one will be tested, one can interpret frightening shapes, sounds, and irritants—be they demons, snakes, centipedes, or mosquitoes—as challenges from spirits. If one can withstand these threats, then a benevolent spirit will emerge at last and ask "for what are you suffering?" (*saa raposukar*).

The spirit should then reveal what the seeker asks. The experience at this point may not be entirely clear. Even if the knowledge imparted by the spirit is garbled, however, one should not tarry but return home to sleep. One will then dream back the words correctly and remember them.

Conventionalized narratives or "scenarios" about what happens during spirit quests "both formulate appropriate goals and suggest effective action for achieving them" (Ortner 1973, 1341). They offer procedures to follow and a cultural framework in which personal experience can be cast. Visionary techniques such as isolation, fasting, and repetition of monotonous acts are built into the scenarios, which serve as directives for would-be shamans. Vigilants' retrospective remarks that they did not understand at the time what was happening to them suggest that these narratives may be of use in ordering an initially ambiguous experience into an intelligible sequence.[3]

STUDYING MAGIC

"To acquire [knowledge] on one's own" (*rata ngkalionya*) is an enviable accomplishment that not everyone can achieve. Most Wana do not obtain magic directly from spirits, but through transactions with other human beings. To "study" (*moguru*) magic, one needs to find a willing teacher. There are good reasons for wariness on the part of both teacher and student. Magical efficacy is premised on exclusivity; if magic is bandied about freely, it loses its effectiveness.

Studying spells implies a level of trust not all people share. People sometimes suspect that their teachers have deceived them by changing a word here and there to render the magic ineffective. In the case of sorcery magic, some say, a reason to deny requests for spells is that a teacher is highly vulnerable to magical attacks by a student. Others say people refuse to share their magic because they want to retain all its benefits for themselves. As we shall see, magic can be what distinguishes people from their peers in this relatively egalitarian society. Withholding magic, like withholding food or other desired items, can breed resentment.

In spite of such cultural justifications for *not* sharing magic, there decidedly are incentives for doing so. One is payment. People are often reluctant to share their knowledge with casual acquaintances. They justify their reluctance with the claim that to retain their efficacy, spells must be paid for. In the case of important magic, even a child should make token payment to a parent, who otherwise would be willing to give the magic freely, in order to assure the continued efficacy of the knowledge.

Payment for magic may take the form of cloth or clothing, chickens, dishes, old Dutch coins, modern currency, or other valued items. Payment is not calculated by the number of spells or names taught, but rather by the importance of the knowledge for the owner and by the nature of the relationship between teacher and student. Under-payment may mean that the spells will not prove effective for their new owner. Overpayment, however, could mean a loss of efficacy for the teacher.

A second reason to share spells is the opportunity it offers to create and affirm relationships. In cases I witnessed, the greater the desire and commitment for friendship or patronage between two people, the less the concern over payment. Thus two shamans cementing a part-nership might eagerly and conspiratorially huddle to exchange secret knowledge. A man with a close attachment to a relative and neighbor would share hunting spells with him. By contrast, one old couple withheld spells from a young kinsman who had left their following and moved elsewhere. A woman known to have spells to avoid child-bearing complained to me about importunate visitors from other set-tlements who would appeal to her friendship and ask for her secrets, but offer nothing in return.

Withholding magic draws a line between "us" and "them." Such distinctions are seldom made between close relations. In most instances my teachers would reveal their magic to me in the presence of spouses, children, and grandchildren, and they often cited their spouses and parents as sources of their knowledge.

I can only speculate about people's willingness to share spells with me. My willingness to pay was clearly a motivating factor, although I did not pay by the spell, and I sometimes was told magic with no expectation of payment. Nearly all the magic I was taught came from the kindred of the couple with whom I lived, people who wanted to please me and help me in some way with my work. By no means was all the magic I received considered powerful or highly consequential, although Apa Mene dictated an enormous number of names and spells, including major magic for sorcery and shamanship.

At the time, I did not question the accuracy of the magic I was given. After all, my aim was to interpret the magic, not to use it (although I do confess—as I suspect other fieldworkers might—to testing a spell every now and then.) In retrospect, I wonder whether in the case of extremely potent or dangerous magic my teachers did not on occasion scramble a word or two in self-defense. Whether they did or not makes no difference for my understanding of the nature of Wana magic, but it is a significant question in relation to the politics of ethnography—and on this point I can say no more.

Spells are termed *mata*, or "fresh," when they are new and highly potent. Over time, a spell may become "worn out" (*mariwam*) or "scarred" (*royom*). It is my sense that loss of freshness is a concern particularly for spells with shamanic application, as opposed, say, to rice magic, which has come down "from the creation of the world" (*ungka kare'e nu lino*).

When shamanic magic is exchanged, it is essential to set out an offering of betel for the spirit owner of the spell (who functions as a spirit familiar) lest the latter be attracted by recitation of the magic, then provoked by a lack of hospitality to harm the parties to the transaction. To retain the "freshness" of a spell for both teacher and student, a succulent plant called *samata* (literally, "something fresh")—known for retaining life and moisture even when picked—may be placed in the betel box. After the magic has been revealed to the student, both parties to the exchange hold the samata between their flattened palms. The samata is then replanted. The hope is that, like the samata, the magic will be resilient through its transfer.

Blood taken from the comb of a live chicken may be smeared in a line up the palms and feet of the learner. "Living blood" (*raa tuwu*) also has a place in farming rituals to insure continued success from one phase of the farming cycle to another. As the blood is applied, words are spoken to the effect that as the spells remain potent for their old owner, so they will also be potent for their new owner.

THE SOCIAL USES OF MAGIC

Magic is an accompaniment to every pursuit in Wana life, There are formulae for farming, hunting, fishing, and gathering honey in the forest and for promoting beauty, courtship, and contraception. Health and life depend on the power of magic, as do strength, courage, oratory, and economic success. Magic assists one with life's trials, both small and great. There are spells to soothe a crying child, to insure that one's bamboo water tubes fill quickly, to make one's guests feel full after only one plate of rice. There are spells to dispel the wrath of others, to make an enemy smile and be conciliatory, to make two people love or hate each other (a popular one for parents who wish to manage their children's affairs).

Success for Wana is predicated on the effective use of magic. Just as people assume that other-than-human beings shape outward events in the ordinary world, so too do they assume that their human companions are using magic, whether or not there is direct evidence to that effect. Given that assumption, people seek and use magic themselves, both as a defense against the hidden influences acting on them and as a way of obtaining their own aims and desires. It is assumed that people who excel in enterprises like farming, hunting, trading, oratory, shamanship, or love owe their success to powerful magic as much as to diligence and hard work. It is not that one could succeed in practical pursuits with only magic and no effort: success of that kind was possible only in the former age when wishes came true. Rather, it is through magic that the extra measure of success in an endeavor is presumed to come. Evans-Pritchard (1937, 477) noted a similar tendency among the Azande to attribute success to magic: "Success is often expressed in terms of magic—e.g., a successful hunter gets a reputation for magic. People therefore attribute his success to his magic whether he possesses medicines or not."

In fact I discovered that, quite often, successful people did indeed possess the magic to match the accomplishments for which they were renowned. Expert farmers knew farming spells; women with few or no children owned contraceptive magic. Indeed, the fact that they possessed the requisite magic is an indication of their commitment to their goal.

And what of those who have the magic but fail to achieve their desires? A variety of explanations covers this contingency. Perhaps their teacher played them false. Perhaps their magic has lost its efficacy through time and teaching. Or perhaps they have failed to maintain the prohibitions their magic carried. Then again, perhaps they simply lack the "fortune" (*dale*) or "palm line" (*ua mpale*) to succeed in the particular pursuit on which they embarked.

Wana magic is bound to the structure of desires. It offers a course of action to the motivated individual as well as a plausible way of interpreting events in terms of human feelings and motivations. People use magic to achieve their desires and presume that others do as well. The association of spells and desires is nicely revealed in an expression that was current during my fieldwork. A standard Wana phrase for expressing distaste or disinclination is *taare rayaku*, "I have no feelings [or inclinations] for that." Young women of my acquaintance, when teased about an alleged attraction to certain men, emphatically declared, "Taare do'aku": "I have no spell for that."

KNOWLEDGE AND SOCIAL
DIFFERENTIATION

Although Wana assert that no one is without magic of some sort, they are likely to attribute more magic to certain people than to others. Attributions of significant knowledge roughly relate to adulthood, masculinity, and social prominence. This is not to say, of course, that special knowledge is never attributed to the young, to women, or to those with little social influence, but in the absence of personal familiarity with an individual, people do simply presume that a mature and respected adult man possesses important magic.

This presumption is revealed in the kinds of interpretations placed on instances of illness and death. Children and women are typically regarded as the victims of spirits, but mature men who take sick and die may be regarded by their next of kin as suicides. Although accounts of their deaths suggest bouts of serious and sudden illness, survivors would explain that the dead men had enlisted the help of their spirit familiars to commit suicide. By making a special offering to the spirit owners of his magic, a man requests to die within a specified interval of time; he will then become ill, and death will soon follow. By this interpretive framework, adult men more than others, and influential adult men in particular, are regarded as authors of their own deaths rather than hapless victims.

The differential attribution of knowledge according to social standing is nowhere clearer than in Wana sorcery. Wana sorcery is not set apart from other kinds of magic; instead, it is simply one category of magical knowledge. Men in particular, because they more often travel beyond their settlement, are expected to possess magic for self-defense. The expression *pake pake langkai*, "men's accoutrements," refers to the defensive magic a man needs to guard his person, especially in the company of potentially hostile strangers in distant settlements and coastal markets. One crippled man denied knowing sorcery by saying that he did not travel far and hence had no need for it.

From a young age Wana children are taught that angering strangers brings reprisals, especially in the form of sorcery. Sensitivity to that fact provides a reason to behave. Wana toddlers are continually told not to walk in front of strangers or to offend them in any way lest a spell be cast on them. Children learn the idiom early and well. When a little girl carried off my towel on her way to bathe, her young companion expressed disapproval by warning that I may have used sorcery on it. Children also learn how to gauge the power of an adversary. When I joined several women in criticizing the cocky pre-adolescent son of a prominent shaman for making fun of a crippled woman's gait, he defended his insulting behavior by saying he possessed sorcery magic, whereas the woman and her companions—poor and dependent women from a distant settlement—did not.

The significance of sorcery as an index of social relations, revealed tellingly in children's understandings, takes its fullest form in adult interactions and commentary on their social world. Unlike the pattern of "voodoo death" described by Cannon (1942) for northern Australian aborigines, in which the community isolates a doomed victim, Wana rarely make their acts of sorcery public to either victim or community. Nor does a community cut off a victim as being beyond help or hope. Although no consensus is ever arrived at concerning a diagnosis of sorcery or justification for it, parties to a bad relationship or third-party observers may impute sorcery to occasions of illness by matching them to states of ill will. Sorcery is viewed as a predictable way to vent anger or hurt feelings. To provoke such feelings in others is to invite sorcery in retaliation. A diagnosis of sorcery is not a pronouncement of death; it is, however, reason to enlist a trusted shaman to fight back.

Magic is woven into the pattern of community life and sentiments, as the following two cases illustrate. Apa Leru had a history of quarrels and bitter feelings with Apa Mina (pseudonyms), a rivalrous nephew of his own age. After a series of crop failures, Apa Mina and his followers claimed that Apa Leru had used magic to destroy their crops. Apa Leru, stung by the accusation, moved his family to a settlement several days' walk away. Later, when commenting on Apa Leru's move, Apa Mina and his neighbors attributed the success of their subsequent harvest to Apa Leru's absence (although in other contexts they attributed their bountiful harvest to their move up from a river plain to a forested hillside with fewer pests).

After a year or so, Apa Leru returned to visit his aged father in a neighboring settlement. He made a point of not passing through Apa Mina's farmsite lest he be accused of harming the rice crop. Not long after his visit, though, several of Apa Mina's relatives fell victim to leg ailments: his father developed crippling numbness in one leg, and an aunt experienced a flare-up of an old sore on her calf. During a mabolong Apa Mina's brother-in-law, a prominent shaman, claimed to discover, with the aid of his spirit familiars, that Apa Leru had placed sorcery magic at a site where both victims had walked. The diagnosis was consistent with the history of bad feelings between Apa Leru and Apa Mina, and thus made sense as an explanation. Two additional points may be noted. First, the accusation was made in the "sorcerer's" absence: Wana rarely accuse sorcerers directly, and they rarely attribute acts of sorcery to members of their own community. (When Apa Leru was rumored to have cast sorcery on Apa Mina's rice, he was living in a separate farmsite.) Second, accusations of sorcery heighten existing tensions. Much of the ill will between Apa Leru and Apa Mina derived from intimations of sorcery, which fueled their distrust and resentment.

Sorcery is not the only form of disruptive magic afoot in Wana life. One woman described to me how she had once been affected by a young man's love magic. When not in his presence, she would cry and refuse to eat. An observant grandparent diagnosed the young woman's behavior and treated her accordingly with an antidote to love magic. After that, the woman claimed, she was free of the effects. Apart from whether or not the youth had indeed used love magic on the woman (if he desired her, most likely he had), the woman and her relative regarded her emotional state as the young man's doing and not as a condition deriving from her own feelings or subject to her own control. By declaring her emotional state to be produced by someone else, her grandparent took responsibility for ending the external influence and, by my companion's account, freed her from its disturbing effect.

MAGIC CONCEALED AND REVEALED

To this point I have dealt with the social management and implications of magic. Now I shall turn to the nature of magic itself. As I
noted earlier, verbal magic comes in two varieties: "names" (*sanga*)
and "spells" (*do'a*). Sanga are the secret names of spirits, objects, and
afflictions. The significance of sanga is rooted in the premise that reality extends beyond our everyday perception of it. Everything is
thought to possess a "real name" (*sanga kojo*) unknown to people at
large, as well as an everyday name by which it is generally known.
Everyday names, likened to people's teknonyms and nicknames, carry
no power or importance in and of themselves. "Real names," however, give one influence or control over their referents. For example,
knowing the name of the first demon to descend to earth (*sanga nu
measa uyu ngkatudu*) may halt an attack by a liver-eating demon. The
secret name of rice may be used to destroy another person's rice crop.
Knowing the names of pythons and crocodiles can insure that one
does not meet these animals on a journey. The name of rice beer can
prevent drunkenness. A shaman uses the secret names of his shamanic
paraphernalia to make the articles useful during a performance. My
associates did not seem perturbed by the idea that two people might
know different secret names for the same being or object, such as the
Owner (*pue*). As long as the names come from spirit sources, they are
monso, a word that—quite tellingly—can be glossed as both "effective" and "true."

Do'a often contain sanga, but they include other words as well,
such as directives to the referents of those names, phrasings of the
goals of the spell, and a variety of words, many of them borrowed
from Islamic prayers (such as *sumila, ala ta ala,* and *salama*), that contribute to the spell's efficacy. Spells may also contain apparently
irrelevant or uninterpretable words and phrases, called *pangego nu do'a*,
"expressions" or "embellishments of the spell," which "carry" (*mangkeni*) the verse.

Spells often, but by no means invariably, consist of verses of equal
meter and final rhyme. They also often make use of parallel constructions, as do shamans' songs, formal storytelling, legal oratory, and
spirit invocations. Sometimes these constructions are direct borrowings from other forms of stylized speech. The following spell, used to

stop heavy bleeding, illustrates the use of parallel construction and syntactic repetition:

> siko raa moili
> kupowolili muni
> kukunsi kupaka inti
> sumiaa sumisi
>
> You, floating blood,
> I send you back again.
> I lock, I make tight.
> *Sumiaa sumisi.*

The verse *kukunsi kupaka inti* expresses one action in two ways using the same grammatical form. In doing so it repeats the syntax of the preceding verse. All three phrases consist of verb forms prefixed with the first person singular pronoun *ku-*. The repetitions lend emphasis, highlight agency, and serve practically as a mnemonic device for learning and recalling the formula.

Wana spells are typically laced with Islamic vocabulary. These elements are regarded not as cultural borrowings, but as an integral and potent part of Wana magic. The next two spells are used at the clearing stage of the swidden cycle. The first one makes a plot smaller and hence lightens the task of the farmer. It may also be used on a journey to make the distance seem shorter. The second is used after the farm work is done to return the land to its former size.

> siko do'aku samila
> kurukaku wawo nia
> kainti ndo'a sumila
>
> You, my good spell,
> wrinkle up the surface for me.
> Firmness of the spell, *sumila.*
>
> siko do'aku salama
> yambarakakaku tana
> kusamila kusalama
>
> You, my good spell
> spread out the land for me.
> I *sumila,* I *salama.*

The term for spell, *do'a,* itself derives from the Arabic word *doa'a* (*doa* in Bahasa Indonesian). The words *sumila* and *salama* are plays on renderings of *bismillah* ("In the name of God"), *salaam* ("peace"), and *selamat* (Bahasa Indonesian for "safe," "happy"). *Sumila* is, in Wana usage, a proper ending for a spell as well as a term that contributes to a spell's efficacy. *Salama* similarly reinforces the effect. Not just magic, but Wana culture generally, makes free use of Islamic vocabulary; such words as *nabi, jimi (jin* in Bahasa Indonesian), *seta (setan* in Bahasa Indonesian), *karamat,* and *baraka* abound in Wana usage, although the meanings they carry do not always match those of Muslim Indonesian society. *Nabi* in Wana usage, for example, does not carry the sense of "prophet," but rather designates a kind of guardian spirit.

The eclecticism we find in Wana magic and shamanship derives from an emphasis on innovation and entrepreneurship in dealings with hidden dimensions of reality. A premium is placed on seeking new and powerful forms of knowledge. New embellishments arise as seekers of magic and spirit alliances display their personal associations with hidden beings. Shamanic speech absorbs new concepts, imagery, and vocabulary that distinguish it from ordinary talk. In contrast to shamanic speech, words delivered by spirits to humans are fixed but their form and language are not restricted by traditional canon. Magic will not be denied efficacy on account of peculiarities in its wording or structure; consequently, there is ample room for creativity, including linguistic borrowing, in both private magic and public shamanship. The difference is that creative phrasing in shamans' songs is credited to the singer, whereas distinctiveness in magic is attributed to its spirit owner, not its human recipient.

Despite the latitude allowed them in the composition of magic, it must be said that spirit owners often adhere to certain conventions of style and content. Although I was often baffled by the magic I studied, I eventually discovered that much of it related quite directly to conventionalized narratives about the etiology and ritual management of conditions it addressed.

This discovery came slowly. In my seventh month of fieldwork a young woman taught me a spell to counter the effects of *dosa,* or "sin," brought on by abuse of the bond between parent and child. Acts of dosa may include cursing a parent or child or mishandling procreative substances, menstrual blood and childbirth blood in particular. Dosa usually reveals itself in conditions such as jaundice, swelling of the abdomen, coughing, and weakness. These were the words she gave me:

> e raa e raa
> raa ntau masina
> kaliu la'u limbo
> mii kunsani siko
> i logu mwuya
> i nabi jampang
> bole ri yangi
> sumila

> eh blood, eh blood,
> blood of a malicious person,
> passing down at the lake.
> Mii, I know you.
> Oh, *logu* [?] of the moon,
> vigilant *nabi*,
> open the sky.
> *Sumila.*

The words made little sense to me. (One—*logu*—still doesn't.) When I pressed her to explain the verse (something Wana teachers of spells are not normally asked to do), my teacher, an articulate woman, began to tell me what shamans do when they treat someone who is suffering from dosa. The lake mentioned in the spell, she explained, is located near the Owner's place directly up above us. Shamans often visit it on their travels in search of their patients' souls. A shaman may discover his patient's *tanuana*, or "dream agent," standing in water up to its armpits, or even up to its chin! He then rescues the tanuana from the lake and returns it to its rightful place in the top of its owner's head.

This explanation was the first I had heard (or at least understood) about the *rano mwe'a* ("lake of women") or, as it is sometimes called, *rano ndosa* ("lake of sin"). Later I learned that this lake is a customary stop on the itinerary of shamans and their spirits in the esoteric molawo performance, as well as in the mabolong, which offers an abbreviated version of the same kind of journey (see Chapter 8).

Through further investigation of shamanic management of dosa, I could begin to piece together a better sense of what the spell was "about." It begins with a reference to the blood of a sinful person at the "lake of women." The allusions to blood, to Mii (a secret name for the *nabi*, or spirit of a child in the womb), and to the moon all refer to women's reproductive cycles, which are regulated at the lake. The reference to the ill-intentioned person at the lake may also call up an image of a woman aborting a fetus: women bathe with spells to end a pregnancy, and abortion is one act that brings on the condition of dosa. The use of the potent name Mii is emphasized by the phrase "I know you," a common one in Wana spells that underscores their possessor's special knowledge and hence control over powers in the world. The spell invokes another powerful agent, *nabi jampang*, a spirit who protects human lives. *Logu mwuya* similarly is most likely the name of another spirit whose powers are being invoked. The phrase *bole ri yangi* appears to be a request or command to these powerful beings to release the patient's suffering by intervening at the "lake of women." The spell concludes with the word *sumila*, a Wana rendering of the Arabic "In the name of God."

The spell contains, then, a highly condensed reference to a major scenario that shamans act out in formal ritual. The private user of the spell would apply it to someone she suspected was suffering the effects of dosa. If her diagnosis was correct and the spell is itself a "true" or "effective" one, the patient's symptoms might be alleviated. If the spell did not work, it could be that the diagnosis was incorrect, that the spell was not effective, or that the problem was so severe that shamanic intervention was indicated. In the last case, words derived from spirits are not enough. The spirits themselves must be called on to help.

As I became more familiar with both Wana spells and Wana ritual, I came to see that often a spell is a condensed allusion to standard narratives concerning the etiology of an illness and its ritual management. Consider the following spell.

> tuma pai ura
> rapasiwaka mangunda
> siko ala dunia
> torungi manusia
> nawoe mpeka
> sumila
>
> Body louse and shrimp,
> put together to boil.
> You, Allah of the world,
> protecting humankind,
> unbend the hook.
> *Sumila*

This very typical Wana spell is used to avert the dreadful consequences of mixing meats from land and from water in a single meal, an act that brings angry reprisals from Lamoa, the punitive spirit of thunder and lightning. Within the general prohibition on mixing foods, the field mouse represents the most dangerous food from land to eat with a food from the water. Indeed, field mice should not even be cooked with water. The owner of this spell explained that the word *tuma*, which means "body louse," is the "name" of the field mouse. Thus, the spell joins field mouse and shrimp—a combination that some will not even pronounce together, let alone eat together. The first two measures of the spell, then, portray the fearful act of mixing shrimp and land meat together in a pot.

After pronouncing the dreadful deed, the spell addresses the Owner with the aim of negating the threat of pain and illness that is certain to follow in retaliation. The being addressed here is not Pue Lamoa, but the Pue whom shamans visit on their trips to the sky (see Part Three). This deity, represented as a protective parent shielding a child by means of a broad-brimmed rainhat called a *toru* (Fig. 6), is addressed here not as Pue, which is standard in Wana conversation and ritual, but as Ala, a borrowing from Islam. The use of an Islamic term is quite typical of both Wana spells (which regularly borrow "potent"-sounding words from Muslim prayers) and Wana secret names (which, being arcane, often contrast to ordinary usage). Other foreign borrowings in this spell are *dunia*, an Indonesian term for "world" that substitutes for the Wana term *lino*, and *manusia*, "humankind," a term from Bahasa Indonesia that has no exact equivalent in the Wana language.

The "action clause" of this spell is a directive to Pue to pry open a hook. It is the habit of Lamoa, when angered by some human infraction, to cast down metal objects from above—hooks, axes, knife blades, and the like. Lodged in a person's body, these weapons cause acute pain and fever. Treating a patient who is diagnosed as a victim of Lamoa therefore involves removing these objects, and this is done in a ritual called the *pantende*, which is directed specifically at treating conditions attributed to Lamoa. The words of the pantende chant speak of making his implements soft and flexible, then prying them open and removing them from the flesh. As with dosa, such a spell could be used in place of a ritual—in this case, the pantende. If the spell did not prove efficacious, the ritual itself would then be performed.

MEANING AND EFFICACY

From the sample of Wana magic presented here, it would appear that
Wana spells are rich in interpretable meaning. Let me assure the reader
that for every spell that can be neatly unraveled, I could provide many
more that are far less accessible. I would venture the hunch that spells
that have been passed along frequently from one person to another are
more likely to assume an intelligible form than are at least some of the
spells received directly from spirits. But interesting as pursuit of this
point might be for anthropologists, it would be of no interest to
Wana, for whom magic is magic if it was given by a spirit to a human,
regardless of any peculiarities of form or meaning. This principle was
illustrated for me when a playful shaman of my acquaintance taught
his teenage brother the following spell:

> wuti palaku
> wuti palaku
> anto nika aku
> sumila
>
> A lie, a falsehood,
> a lie, a falsehood,
> a deception I am making.
> *Sumila.*

This verse resembles a spell in its use of meter, parallel construction,
and an Islamic term (*sumila*). Yet its meaning suggests that the spell is
a lie. The boy, well acquainted with his brother's humor, was unsure
whether he was being put on or not. (He was.) When I asked one
connoisseur of spells about the verse, he declared that if a spirit had
indeed given those words to a vigilant, they would constitute a potent
spell. In the course of studying spells myself, my teachers and I would
be both amused and perplexed by words ranging from the obscene to
the extraneous. But the principle held—if the words were exactly
those of the spirit source, the spell was both "true" and "efficacious"
(*monso*), which for Wana means the same thing.

The effectiveness of magic does not lie in the sense or beauty of the
words any more than it lies in the creativity of the magician. Instead it
lies in the correct recitation of the original words as spoken by a spirit
to a human and in proper management by its human owner. Thus,
highly potent magic may consist of puzzling, unintelligible, or

extraneous language, whereas false or worn-out magic may be attractively worded.

In a suggestive comparison of Azande and Trobriand magic, Evans-Pritchard (1929) sought to explain the contrast between Trobrianders' emphasis on fixed magical formulae and Azandes' indifference regarding exact repetitions of magical performances, postulating that fixed formulae are a consequence of restricted ownership of magic by a social group, such as a family, clan, or other corporate unit. For the Wana, ownership of spells is an individual, not a corporate, matter, and spells may be passed along from one person to another without regard to kinship. Yet Wana spells are attributes of their possessors every bit as much as Trobriand magic is distinctive of particular kin groups. Personal ownership of spells is, in the Wana context, closely tied to and protected by an insistence on precise memorization. But social function alone does not account for form here: a cultural focus on original sources (*pu'u*) is equally at play. Verbatim recitation of a spirit's words across the division between human and hidden realms is not simply an assertion of ownership. On the contrary, it is a reenactment of a transaction with a powerful source of knowledge in the Wana world.

APPLYING VERBAL MAGIC

The form of Wana verbal magic recalls other special speech styles, including shamans' songs, legal oratory, and public invocations of spirits. But these other forms are spoken openly, whereas magic, even when performed publicly, should not be pronounced intelligibly lest others might learn and know the words. Verbal magic is performed by reciting a name or spell over some medium, which is then brought into contact with the person or object one wishes to affect. The nature of the contact depends on whether the magic is being used overtly or covertly, and on the specific aim of the magic.

Healing magic is generally performed with the knowledge and compliance of a patient through an act called *mangerus* (literally, "to spit on"). A person who wishes to be treated typically offers betel fixings to a healer. The healer first chews a betel quid consisting of areca nut, piper leaf, and lime. The lime turns the mixture red, and once this has happened, the healer mutters a spell and spits a fine spray of betel juice onto the affected area of the patient's body. (If no betel is available, one may use "white spit" [*ngeru buya*] or ordinary saliva to apply the spell.) One may treat oneself in the same way. Should it be impossible to reach the affected part of one's own body with the mouth, one may spit on one's thumb, then touch it to the appropriate area.

Another technique for using magic is to murmur it over a cup of water, which is then drunk or poured over the patient's body (one's own or another's). Typically this method is used when the aim of the magic is to remove an undesired condition from the body. Spells to abort a fetus or hasten the delivery of a child use this principle; so too do spells to rid the body of the weapons of Lamoa, described earlier. Alternatively, water treated with beauty magic may be applied to the body "to make attractiveness mount" (*paka pone yawa*). Water is also the medium for certain forms of rice magic, in which magically treated water is cast widely over the rice in a field.

When a patient is not present or if the need for treatment or protection is anticipated but has not yet arrived, a magical formula may be spoken over a betel nut, an onion, or an aromatic plant, which is then saved for later use. This method permits a person's magical knowledge to be used in its owner's absence without a revelation of its contents. Travelers, especially those journeying with small children, often request a treated object from a shaman to carry as protection on the trip; when in need of the magic, the traveler may chew the treated areca nut and then proceed to mangerus the person requiring protection. Onion is not chewed, but is rubbed on the body. Substances used defensively in this way are often plants with strong odors, such as onion and wild cinnamon, that are thought to repel dangerous spirits and to mask the "unfamiliar" odors of newcomers to a place. For the same reason, strong-smelling plants are used at childbirth to conceal the smell of a neonate, which attracts demons and disturbs other spirits of the locale.

Betel is the most common vehicle for magic that is openly used. A substance bound up with cultural notions of sociability and hospitality, its use in healing is likewise a sociable gesture, precipitated by the hospitable act of offering betel to the healer. Following treatment, the patient temporarily bears the red stain of betel spit on the skin, public testimony to the healing act. Other substances leave evidence of treatment on the patient's body in the form of a strong odor. By contrast, magic to cleanse a person of an unwanted condition signifies the removal of the condition by leaving no trace of its use.

Magic may also be used covertly to affect the dispositions, health, and lives of others. It may be whispered over food, beer, betel, clothing, gifts—in short, over any object the target is expected to use. It may be spoken upstream into the water in which the victim will bathe (to achieve effects as various as leprosy, ringworm, and love). Sorcery may be murmured over sharpened pieces of bamboo, bits of glass, or pieces of wood, then fired into the body of a victim. The following spell can accomplish that end:

> siko i nabi mbalo
> paka nga'a kuwaro
> nja'u sule nu pago
> ate ranta maka
>
> You, oh Spirit of Bamboo,
> make light as I throw.
> Over there is the heart to head for.
> Make the liver fall out.

In addition to such offensive acts, magic can be used defensively to guard rice granaries, coffee plants, coconut trees, chests of cloth, and other possessions. One may speak magic over a thread and string it across a path leading into one's coffee patch; should someone come in contact with the thread, the trespasser's genitals may enlarge grossly and painfully. A protective spell on a chest of cloth might cause the hand that opens it to break out in horrible sores. The magic would harm any transgressor, even the owner of the possessions should he or she fail to "deactivate" the magic before approaching the site of the sorcery.

People may be affected by magic, then, without their knowledge. Even apparently hospitable offers of betel, food, and drink may disguise attempts to influence another's thoughts, feelings, and well-being. And whether deserving or innocent, one may find oneself the victim of a hidden attack of sorcery.

MEDICINES AND THEIR PLACE
IN WANA SHAMANSHIP

So far I have dwelt exclusively on verbal magic. In contrast to "names" and "spells," pokuli consist of physical substances, not words. (One person highlighted the difference nicely by saying that

spells are "recited" [*raguyu*], whereas pokuli are "wood" [*kaju*].)
Typically, pokuli are plants, but they may consist of other substances
as well. Wana do use the term *pokuli* to refer to the various phar-
maceutical potions (aspirin, malaria pills, sulfa, and vitamins) that are
sold at the coast; medicines of this sort may be called "store medicine"
(*pokuli ntoko*) to distinguish them from *pokuli wana* or "plant medicines" (*pokuli ngkaju*). The term includes more than cures for bodily
ills, however, applying as well to substances used to induce effects
other than healing in humans, spirits, and objects. There are pokuli to
enhance farming, oratory, beauty, bravery, courtship, and countless
other endeavors in Wana life. Like verbal magic, medicines augment
activities of every sort.

Pokuli typically consist of substances that resemble—by their
name, form, or some other property—the desired end their user
seeks. For example, tenacious roots and vines are used to invoke taut
firmness in both hunting dogs (to keep them on the trail and prevent
them from scattering) and new mothers (to restore tone to abdominal
muscles and organs). Scrapings from a dog's nail or a cat's dried
placenta will speed delivery in childbirth because their owners deliver
their young quickly. Plants with names like "bountiful"(*maniu*),
"numerous" (*sipalagi*), and "stationary" (*rodo*) are important rice
medicines because their use invokes those properties for the harvest.

Wana medicines may be eaten, drunk, chewed as part of a betel
quid, mixed with food, drink, or tobacco, rubbed on the body, or
worn as amulets. As with other forms of magic, medicines may be
used overtly or covertly. Generally, efforts at healing are overt,
whereas hostile attacks or efforts to alter a person's attitude are covert.

Like names and spells, medicines derive in theory from spirits. But
although power is thought to reside in both verbal formulae and material substances, verbal magic takes precedence over magical materials,
particularly in Wana shamanship. Quite likely the emphasis on verbal
knowledge has been underscored by contact with Islamic peoples,
who also stress the primacy of verbal formulations. But the centrality
of spells in Wana life cannot, I think, be written off to culture contact.
It speaks instead to something more fundamental in Wana conceptions
of the world. Verbal knowledge is social knowledge. A spell is a token
of a conversation between a hidden spirit and a human being: it testifies to a special bond that transcends the barriers of the present world.
Even though medicines, too, can represent a communication between

a spirit benefactor and a human recipient, because these substances are common objects evident in the everyday world, they are a step removed from the special transaction implied by the spell. This difference is reflected in the fact that whereas sometimes people speak of medicines as secret knowledge obtained from spirits and revealed only in return for a gift, at other times they speak of medicines as popularly known substances that circulate without restriction in the public domain. Thus the category pokuli spans a continuum—from casual and freely known information to esoteric secrets—considerably wider than that of spells and names.

Medicines, in contrast to names and spells, are not a requisite for shamanhood, nor is their use a part of shamanic performance, whereas without verbal magic a shaman is not a shaman. Although possessing medicines is certainly not a liability for shamans, neither is it essential. Two men I knew—one a prominent shaman, the other a novice— explicitly avoided gathering medicines to treat illnesses because, they said, they lacked "a light hand" (that is, one that would insure the success of the treatment). If use of a medicine was indicated for one of his patients, the senior shaman would recommend that his wife locate the substance. To be unable to handle therapeutic substances is not a handicap for a shaman who, to effect a cure, relies on his verbal knowledge and his personal influence over the spirits from whom his knowledge derives.

By contrast, one domain in which medicines figure prominently is rice ritual. Here tradition rather than spirit quest is the source of ritual expertise; hence, the importance of spells as indicators of personal spirit ties does not apply. Pokuli also had a place in the headhunting celebrations of an earlier time. At the end of the three-day festival that followed a successful raid, warriors would share a meal of *baku ragi*, consisting of "white and dark glutinous rice and *uwi kojo*, a tuber with a red peel," topped with pieces of an enemy scalp, then mixed together with a sword (Kruyt 1930, 525). This act was called "eating medicine" (*mampokoni pokuli*) and was intended to strengthen those who partook of the meal. We could liken the scalp brought back from war to the magic brought back from spirit quest. Both are exogenous to the community (unlike medicinal plants gathered in the swidden), and their acquisition is limited to the brave.

Another reason for the primacy of spells has to do with the premises of shamanic performance. Shamans investigate hidden sources of events in the world—as in the area of healing, where they treat not overt symptoms, but unseen causes. Like Ilongot healing in Northern Luzon, which moves from an emphasis on physical ailments to a concern with spiritual ones depending on the gravity of patient's disorder (M. Rosaldo 1973), Wana healing shifts from simple applications of medicines and basic spells to shamanic journeys into spirit realms. Whereas spells play a role all across this continuum, medicines, being substances of the everyday world that are typically matched to symptoms, not to sources of illness, are useful primarily at its simpler end. The sense that verbal magic might be a weightier matter than use of medicines is conveyed by the claim of one woman that the recitation of spells to prevent childbirth invites the dangerous, debilitating condition of dosa, or "sin," but using medicines to accomplish the same end does not, because medicines are "simply a technique" (*ojo salaak*).

Finally, words, as opposed to substances, possess an exclusivity that underscores the special power of their owner. Cultural conditions of efficacy demand secrecy. As one person put it, a spell loses its power if young children know the words and go about singing them. Whereas the public performance of Wana verbal magic simultaneously reveals the fact that magic is being used and conceals the content of the magic, there are no established procedures for the public use of medicine that both broadcast its use and protect its secrecy. Verbal magic, unlike material magic, symbolizes and reinforces the exclusive and private relation between its wielder and its hidden source.

KNOWLEDGEABLE MEDIATION ACROSS DOMAINS OF REALITY

To return now to the mabolong, where our shamans sit summoning their spirit familiars, we can take stock of the ritual action to this point in light of Wana cosmology and epistemology. In congregating his personal familiars, a shaman mediates the division between hidden and everyday realms. Although his own origins are in the powerless human realm, nevertheless through his summons he asserts influence over hidden beings: the sources of magical power and spiritual assistance.

The words he sings simultaneously reveal and conceal. They imply familiarity with hidden beings based on past encounters and the ability to see what other human beings in the room cannot. They conjure the sort of commensal relation between Wana and spirit communities that is thought to have once existed but does no longer. The shaman's song also appropriates the reputations of past shamans as it promotes his own. At the same time, his language conceals the true and potent names of the shamans' friends, maintaining the secrecy of the magical knowledge bestowed on the shaman by his hidden comrades. In the very act of singing, of adopting a distinctive style of speech, the shaman sets himself apart from his human companions and underscores the exclusiveness of his relations with spirits.

The shaman's summons has the potential to be at once nostalgic and powerful: nostalgic because of its multiple allusions to past shamans and to an era of magic, powerful because the shaman conjures a potent concentration of hidden beings around him. His is not the still and inward contemplation of the mystic—of, for example, the Javanese "man of Power," who is characterized by "his ability to concentrate: to focus his own personal Power, to absorb Power from the outside, and to concentrate within himself apparently antagonistic opposites" (Anderson 1972, 13). Instead, the shaman conquers oppositions in the world by actively transcending the barriers between settlement and wilderness, between humans and spirits, between visible and hidden reality. Through his magical knowledge he *absorbs* power, not only from beyond his person, but from beyond his community as well, concentrating it not so much within himself as around himself. And he focuses power, not in tranquil meditation, but (as we shall see in Parts Two and Three) in protagonistic action on behalf of his patients and community. Like a Javanese "man of Power," the Wana shaman exemplifies a concentration of spiritual potency (see Errington 1989; Wolters 1982); their contrasting practices, however, reveal the differences in power and its operation at the center and at the periphery of Southeast Asian polities.

PART TWO

4

Therapeutic Endeavors

In Part One I explored Wana constructions of a divided reality and the power inherent in words derived from spirits. In Part Two I will consider how secret knowledge and spirit alliances are put to work in the context of a mabolong performance.

Once the shamans of the evening have begun to summon their familiars, people wishing to be examined may indicate their desire by placing a betel quid on the lango for the shaman of their choice. When a shaman indicates that he is ready, the patient offers forth his or her hands with palms together. The shaman blows on the patient's hands, places one end of his shaman's cloth on the patient's head and one end at his own mouth, and murmurs spells to promote the life of the patient. To investigate further, he may hold his cloth like a screen between the patient and himself as he summons his spirit familiars with his song to come examine the patient's condition. In this action, the patient's body is transparent to his gaze. He then may touch the patient's body with his hands to detect further what may be wrong. Depending on what he detects, he may proceed to draw out harmful intrusive objects from the patient's body and to recover lost elements of the person's being and return them to their rightful owner.

The following texts trace the verbal dimensions of these acts. None, however, come from mabolong performances. Instead, all were sung as part of healing rituals called potudu. A potudu (literally, "to bring down" the spirit familiars) can be roughly characterized as a mabolong minus the theatrics, politics, and audience; it follows the script of a mabolong, but without the accompaniment of drum and gongs. Unlike a mabolong, it typically involves a single shaman, a single patient, and the members of a single household. The shaman summons his familiars to the lango and examines his patient just as he would at a mabolong, but should he determine it necessary to cast off intrusive objects from his patient's body or recover missing elements of his patient's being, instead of dramatically enacting those proce-

79

dures himself to the accompaniment of drum and gongs, he simply recounts them in song.

I have substituted potudu texts for mabolong texts in this section for three reasons. First, very simply, it was difficult to make audible recordings of shamans singing as they treated patients during mabolong performances, for the sound of drum and gongs effectively drowned out this portion of the songs. Second, it is my impression that shamans are not as verbally explicit in treating patients at mabolong as they are at potudu performances; at the mabolong, they can *act out* their treatments in ways that convey what they are doing in channels other than the verbal. Finally, mabolong are in general less patient-centered than potudu: the portions of shamans' songs that are audible to their audiences typically concern matters other than routine treatment.

In the absence of good transcripts of mabolong, one might ask why I offer a substitute. Recent anthropological work has criticized cultural analysts' preoccupation with text, noting that the significance of cultural experience is not indexed by its verbosity (e.g., R. Rosaldo 1984). In the case I am considering here, however, the dramatic action of Wana healing *is* richly depicted and accessible in the potudu form. These texts make explicit the premises and procedures fundamental to all Wana healing. Although the mabolong often condenses these into shorthand form or conveys them nonverbally, they are nevertheless known and understood by Wana audiences. Hence, one who is familiar with these scripts is equipped to read the dramatic action of a mabolong performance.

In the following song, Apa Linus is recovering the lost soul parts of his own sick child (see Fig. 20). Known for his beautiful singing voice, Apa Linus had recently begun to perform again after a long illness during which he repeatedly coughed blood. In this passage, the reader will note, Apa Linus continues to summon and encourage his spirit familiars throughout:

e nau yugo rapobente lio	Eh, even if weakened, changed in appearance,
deja malanya ja muni	they make it possible again.
e ane panta nggomi suolangku	If each of you, my spirit familiars.
o to ri lengku nsalu	Oh, the One by the Stretch of River
mamposisi watu	who implants the stone,
mai metulungi ruyu	come help first,

nggomi suolangku	you, my spirit familiar.
o to ri ue wengi oti	oh, the One at the Dark and Dried-up Stream,
mampolemba wonti	disguised as a monkey,
matundug tonsi	allied with a bird,
mai mai mpapomai ruyu	come, come, come hither first,
nggomi suolangku	you, my spirit familiar.
ne'e mesonaru yau wo'u	Don't turn over the task to others at this stage,
nggomi suolangku	you, my spirit familiar.
panta ja joangku	Each of my following,
ne'e mesonaru	don't delegate the task to others.
nau ri luo saluo	Even if it's in another place,
deja malangku ja muni	I can retrieve it again.
mai mai mpapemai ruyu	Come, come, come hither first.
e nggomi suolangku	Eh, you my spirit familiars,
mai nggita mansoe solimbu	come, let's swing the cloth.
lima nggomi mo ri ara	Your five are on the bottom.
limangku yako ri dawo	My five are on the top.

Here he is referring to the cloth he uses to capture his patient's lost soul parts. By "your five" and "my five," he is referring to his own hand and the hands of his spirit familiars.

nggomi suolangku boros	You, my numerous spirit familiars,
mai mpapemai ruyu	come, come hither first.
ne'e sonda rajumo mangande	Don't arrive wanting to eat.
rianya undo ngkunti	There is no shadow of a drum.

Here he cautions his familiars, lest they be disappointed, that there is no mabolong going on and refreshments are wanting.

nggita ojo sonda	We'll only arrive
da luya buke singgayano	to find betel filling the offering tray.
e mai ganta mbalo lue	Eh, come, Ganta mBalo Lue.
e to ri lengku nue	Eh, the One from the Stretch of River,
mai tamponganti muni	come, fetch back
bayo ngkoro uli	the shadow of the soul,
nja'u ri luo saluo	off in another place.
e ne'e mesonaru yau	Hey, don't leave the task to others,
suola menanyamo	experienced spirit familiars.
manayamo seja mantompale yugo	Experienced also at treating feebleness,
nau yugo rapoyugo	even feebleness compounded.

e manayamo seja	Eh, experienced too,
ojo manaya kalidonya	only experienced on their own.
e deja malanya ja muni	Eh, they can get it back.
e nggomi suolangku	Eh, you, my spirit familiars.
si'a ojo naoamo	It's not just a pretext,
nggomi suolangku	you, my spirit familiars.
e o mesonaru	Eh, oh, delegating.
si'a ojo naoa	It's not just a pretext,
panta seja solu	each one also appears,
panta seja dongka	each one also arrives.
e nau ri luo saluo luo saluo	Eh, even if off in a further place, a further place,
deja malanya ja muni	they can get it back,
deja malanya ja muni	they can get it back.
e mbenu to pu'u mpowadi	Eh, where is the Source of the Epic Song?
guru pangansani	Teacher of Knowledge,
kasolumo ma'i	come appear.
kita da monganti muni	We are going to recover [the soul part of]
pomuli kionya	the small child.
nja'u ri luo saluo	Even if they're off in another place.
ane panta ja nadongka	If everyone arrives,
ane panta ja nasolu	if everyone appears,
e mai tongkeni solimbu	and comes to carry the shaman's cloth.
lima nggomi mo ri ara	Your five are on the bottom,
limangku yako ri dawo	my five are on the top,
taponganti muni ruyu	as we first retrieve
bayo ngkoro uli	the shadow of the soul.
nau ri luo saluo	Even if it's in another place,
deja malangku ja muni	I can retrieve it.
e ne'e kaumboli yau	Eh, don't go off hurt,
ne'e kaumbojo yau	don't go off offended.
seja suola munanya	Here's an experienced familiar
nanganganti ruyu muni	retrieving it first.
mai mpapemai ruyu	Come, come hither first.
o bisa nggomi suolaku	Oh, effective you are, my spirit familiar.
e nggomi suola	Eh, you, spirit familar.

Now Apa Linus is restoring his daughter's missing soul parts:

e ne'e ojo liu	Eh, don't just pass by,
ne'e ojo ndeu	don't just go by.
mai posaligi ruyu muni	Come, re-enter again first.

nja'u ri lemba to mbawo	Go down into the body on top,
nja'u ri lemba mokumba	go down into the thick body.
ne'e ojo liu	Don't just pass by,
ne'e ojo ndeu	don't just go by.
mai wuuigika lo'u muni	Come, blow it down again.
ria yosaku mawuui	It is not my breath that blows.
yosa ntundugi mawuui	It's the breath of the spirit ally that blows
bayo ngkoro uli	the shadow of the soul.
e nau ri luo saluo	Eh, even if it's in another place,
deja malanya mo ja muni	they could bring it back again,
nanganganti muni bayo koro uli	taking back the shadow of the soul
nja'u ri luo saluo	even if it's in another place.
to ri tondo nggele	The One from the Direction of Laughter,
juyu insareareme	companion of Sareareme,
o ronda nto ri rapa bente	oh, partner of the One at the Fortified Hilltop,
to tu'a bupewe	the Old One in the Loincloth,
biasa monggengge	accustomed to chortling.

Here Apa Linus refers to his spirit familiar from "the Direction of Laughter" as the companion of Sareareme, Apa Mene's familiar discussed in Chapter 1, and to "the Old One in the Loincloth," also an associate of Apa Mene. (Apa Linus himself is Apa Mene's younger cousin and sometime "student." In Part Four we will have further occasion to consider the relationship between this junior shaman and his more prominent relative.)

mai wuuigika lo'u ruyu muni	Come blow it back in again.
to buyu mandao tu'a nauwamo	The One of the Open Mountain Flank, the Old White-haired One.
to ponsoe lango	The One Who Swings the *Lango*,
yako seja ia rango	that one also arrives.
mai posaligi ruyu muni	Come, enter [the soul] back in again first.
togo wuri togo bengi	Three nights, three evenings.
ewa ulu mpemononya	Like it was in the beginning.
e mo nggomi suolaku	Eh, you, my spirit familiars.
ne'e ojo liu	Don't just pass by,
ne'e ojo ndeu	don't just go by.
o pantamo kuanti muni	Oh, I bring each one back,
koro uli koro tongo segi	the first soul, the middle soul now.
posaliki muni ri lemba badunya	Re-enter within the cover of the body.

o to ri lengku nue	Oh, the One at the Stretch of River,
to saru mbarue	the surrogate of Barue.
e ne'e ne'e doya ne'e doya	Eh, don't, don't be lazy, don't be lazy.
wuuigika lo'u muni	Blow it down again.
yosa to mayui	Breath that is long,
yosa to umuri	breath that is long-lived.
o mo nggomi suolangku	Oh, you, my spirit familiars.
si'a ojo naoamo	It is not just a deception.
nggomi djo panta	You, each one,
o ne'e tuna	oh, don't hesitate,
ne'e yole	don't stay away.
lele limakaku ruyu	Pass your hands over for me first.
lele limakaku muni	Pass your hands over for me again,
naka ewa uyu mpemononya	so it will be as it originally was.
e nja'u ri luo saluo	Eh, even if off in another place,
o deja malangku mo muni	oh, I can bring it back again.
panta suola nasonda	Each spirit familiar has arrived.
panta suola nasolu	Each spirit familiar has appeared
tantompale pomuli pomuli kionya	to treat the child with its hands, the little child.
e taa kuwai tuna yau	Eh, I don't permit you to waste away.
e to rapa buyu	Eh, the One at the Mountain Crest,
majaya lambuwu	who travels on a whirlwind,
tundugi kadudu	spirit ally Kadudu,
yako mo to ruyu	you who goes first,
nansanimo pu'u	who knows the source,
mai posaligi muni	come put [the vital elements] back again.
to ri lengke mwuri	The One at the Shadow of Night,
i nabi masusi	oh, esoteric *nabi*,
e wuuigika ruyu muni	eh, blow back again first,
yosa maumur	long-living breath.
e mo suolangku	Eh, my spirit familiars,
mai mpapemai ruyu metulungi	come, come hither first and help.
mantompale panta panta	Touch with your hands each one, each one.
nutampale mpuraia	Pass your hands over all.
e wetu mo nggita suola	Eh, like that are we spirit familiars,
wetumo nggita pelogoti	like that are we spirit friends.
to ri tondo ngkule	The One at Tondo ngKule,
mampolemba kuse	disguised as a monkey,
mai tundugi tute	come ally, demon cat.
si'a naoamo	It's not a deception.
mai mpapemai ruyu suolangku	Come, come hither first, my spirit familiar.

o yako seja rata	Oh, there also arrives
i ndei ngkaraka	Ndei ngKaraka, the one with the bumps,
i molemba bawa	the one wearing the guise of a toad.
mai nutompale ruyu	Come to touch first
pemuli kionya	the little child.
mayugo ntuo lembanya	Feeble in the extreme, her body.
yugo sala ngkayugo	Feeble, fault of feebleness.
e ne'e tuna ne'e yole	Eh, don't wither, don't spoil.
nggita monayamo seja	We are experienced also,
e mantompale yugo rapoyugo	eh, at treating with out hands enfeebled feebleness.
deja malanta ja muni	We can get it back,
e suola sala suola	spirit familiar not the familiar.
si'a ojo naoa	It's not just a deception.
e mai mpapemai ruyu	Eh, come, come hither first,
mai taponganti muni	come retrieve
bayo ntanuana	the shadow of the dream agent,
e nja'u ri luo saluo	eh, off in another place.
deja malanta ja muni	We can bring it back again.
e o to lemba nsinara	Eh, the One from the Flank of Sinara,
i du'a [tu'a] makaba	Old One *makaba*[?],
yako seja ia rata	that one also has arrived,
matukangi ganta	an expert in managing fates.
e mai tongkeni solimbu	Eh, come, carry the shaman's cloth.
lima nggomimo ri ara	Your five are on the bottom,
limangku yako ri dawo	my five are on the top,
paiwa raanti muni	so it can still be retrieved again.
pomuli sala pomuli	The child, not a child,
pomuli kionya	the little child.
miyugo ntuo lembanya	Feeble in the extreme, her body.
ne'e mosonaru ne'e layo yau	Don't delegate, don't go off on your own,
nggomi suolaku	you spirit familiars of mine.

On another occasion Apa Mene performed a potudu for a young boy whose penis was bleeding excessively following the incision of his foreskin, a procedure performed on preadolescent boys. Apa Mene had done the procedure and was clearly worried about its aftermath.

mata tomali	Mata Tomali,
to pongkoli janji	who transfers fates,
mai mpapemai mai ratulungi	come, come, come assist.
kulimba muni ri kaju	I move it again to a tree.
kulimba muni ri watu	I move it again to a rock.

o wega mai muni ratulungi	Oh, familiar, come back, assist.
o wega kulimba yau ri kaju	Oh, spirit, I move it off to a tree
kulimba yau ri watu wega	I move it off to a rock, spirit.
mai ratulung	Come, let it be helped,
mai rapemono muni	come, let it be begun again.
mai ratulutulungi	Come, let it be helped, helped.
mai pai kukunsi	Come, and I lock it,
kupowolilika muni	I make it go back again.
o wega kuanti ja muni	Oh, spirit, I take it back,
o wega mai kita mantompale muni	oh, spirit, come, we'll heal it over again with out hands.

Now Apa Mene removes an intrusive object from the boy.

nempo molulapi mwuku	Even if layered over with bone.
nempo molalapi mpela	Even if layered over with skin.
dja totende mai ja	It will come shaking forth
ri doe lima ntundug	on the hand of the ally,
ri doe lima nsuola	on the hand of the familiar.
ratimbeka soba	The enemy is combatted.
bara nja'uwa yabinya	Maybe there's still a remainder in there.
deja malaja ntundugi	The ally can manage it,
napomono ja muni	make it happen again.

Now he attends to recovering the boy's soul parts, including the soul in his back (*koro uli*), his dream agent (*tanuana*), and gemlike pulse points in his hands and feet (*tolowu*), concepts that will be explored in Chapter 6.

kuanti malaja muni	I can take it back again,
bayo ngkoro uli	shadow of the *koro uli*.

The shaman interrupts his song to say, in ordinary speech, "It fled, the soul of the fellow with the bleeding penis" (*niyaimo ngkoro uli ngkai maraa toyunya*). He resumes:

wuuigika muni bayo ngkoro uli	Blow the shadow of the *koro uli* back in place.
masaliki muni	Enter it back again.
taa ja i maria wei	There's no problem.
nawuui muni	It's blown back in
ntundug lele naugi	by spirit ally Lele Naugi.
o wegaku	Oh, my spirit familiar,
kusonaru lo'u wo'u	I depend on you again.

kuwuui saito bayo ntanuana	I blow the shadow of the dream agent.
napolele muni lo'u saito wo'u	Make it cross back down there again.
samba'a tolowu mwitinya	One *tolowu* of his feet,
kuanti malaja muni	I can take it back again.
wuuigi muni yosawa ntundugi	Blow back the breath of the spirit familiar,
wuuigi muni tolowu mwitinya	blow back the *tolowu* of his feet.

In my final example of a healing text, Apa Mene treats me for an attack by headhunting spirits who, among other things, have stolen my scalp—a theft whose metaphysical base will be explained in Chapter 6.

mbenu to la'u siyonso	Where is the one down at the meeting of earth and sea?
mai kuanti mala ja	Come, so I can take what's there.
da kuanti yau	I shall take it out.
kupekibolosi bayo nu balengka	I shall exchange it for the shadow of the scalp.
mai kabolosi wega	Come, make the trade, spirit.
ane ja'u natumana	If there's something stuck down there,
deja totende mai ja	make it come shaking forth.
pei ransa pei nantundugi	And cast it off and perform as an ally.
pei ransa pei nansuola	And cast it off and act like a spirit familiar.
to la'u siyonso	The one down at the meeting of land and sea,
biasa mangoko	accustomed to taking
bayo pela mwo'o	shadows of the skin of the head.
ne'e kojo mosanaru komi	Don't you dare delegate to me.
mantulungi aku	Help me.
maya kupansaruka komi	I can delegate to you.
nempo longko naka wao	Even if it has gone far,
kuanti mala muni	I can retrieve it again.
bayo nu balengka	The shadow of the scalp,
njo'u ira ngkanau	gone forth on a palm leaf,
njo'u mata npanai	gone forth on the point of a sword.
wali mpeboon	Her ability to call,
wali mpekion	her ability to summon,
ininya rakinya	her sweat, her grease,
kuanti mala ja	I can retrieve them.

komi ja tundug	You, spirit ally,
mai nu tulung	come to help,
ma'i nu pemole muni	come to make well again.
njo'u waka mpelagam	Over there is the site of the wound,
njo'u nu pemole muni	over there, make it well again.
mbenu to ri tondo nggele	Where is the One from the Direction of Laughter,
we'a matungkeke	the Woman with her Skirt Hitched Up?
rata mampolengke	Come, have a look.
paka mala mala muni	Make it possible, possible to retrieve.
ne'e kojo malawudi	Don't you dare prevaricate.
ane bisa ja tundug	If you're effective, ally,
mai mantolele muni	come pass over again,
penade taa ja marugi	and insure that there's no ruin.
yako mala mala muni	Possible, possible to bring it back.
paka mala mala mantompale maya	Make it possible, possible, able to heal.
bayo nu bayonya bayo nu balengka	Shadow of its shadow, shadow of the scalp.
o nuwuui ntundugi	Oh, blown by the spirit ally,
bayo nu balengka	shadow of the scalp,
tudu nasintaka muni	descend, attach again,
nawuui ntundug	blown by the ally.
mai lele mpale muni	Come, cross with the hand again.
njo'u nawuui tundugi	Over there, blown by the ally.
komi lima moliara	Your hand tends.
limaku ri dawo	My five are on top.
lima mansoe salangki	Five swinging the shaman's cloth.
kuantika muni bayo ngkoro uli	I retrieve again the shadow of the soul,
naka naanti ntundug	so the spirit ally can take it,
paka mala muni anti	make it possible again to retrieve,
paka mala mala	make it possible, possible,
bayo ngkoro uli	the shadow of the soul,
paka naanti ntundug	make it so the ally retrieves it,
naanti maya ja muni	can retrieve it again.
wega kusonaru	Spirit I rely on.
e komi pei nansuolaku	Eh, you, whom I use as a familiar,
penaja ntundugi	as an ally.
mai ratulungi	Come, let it be helped.
ne'e nu boboli aku	Don't trick me.
ne'e kojo malawudi	Don't you dare prevaricate.
malaku ja muni bayo ngkoro uli	I can retrieve again the shadow of the soul,

kawe naka koko muni
pai naanti ntundug
mai ratulungi ruyu
njo tanakabe nu lima
tundugi antika kita
e nawuui ntundugi
mai mantolele muni
mangantika koro uli
posalika muni sei taa napomarugi

sei taa napomayugo karo

taa naporangguni
taa napobente lio
ewa ulu pemononya
ewa uyu penajadi
guruku mawali

saito to samba'a
kuanti mala ja
bayo ntanuana
komi tundugi mananya
mantompale gana
anti paka mala mala

pai rawuuigi muni
komi penaja ntundug
mai pei pidari muni
waka mpolegaleganya

mai tapomele muni
waka mpewongowongo
mai kuwuuigi muni
bayo ntanuana wega

lo muni masaligi
nawuuigi muni ntundugi
lindo lindok
rapia muni waka puwongonya
pidari matao tao
pidari maruna runa
balo pomuya to pongkami luya

palenya maruna rapidari muni

wave it back close again,
and the ally retrieves it.
Come, let it be helped first.
Reach forth with the five.
Ally, retrieve it for us.
Eh, the ally blows it.
Come cross over again.
Retrieve for us the soul.
Enter it back again so that there will
     be no loss.
So that the body won't be
     enfeebled,
not jaundiced,
not changed in appearance.
Like it was in the beginning,
like it was at the creation.
My teacher who makes things
     happen.
That one.
I can retrieve
the shadow of the dream agent.
You, experienced ally,
lay on your hand enough.
Make it possible, possible to
     retrieve
and be blown back in place.
You, who perform as an ally,
and pinch together again
the site of the little game [i.e., the
     damage done by the warrior
     spirits to my scalp].
And heal again
the site of the mischief.
Come, I blow back
the shadow of the dream agent,
     spirit.
Down again it enters,
blown back by the spirit ally.
Happy, happy I am
to heal over the site of the mischief,
to mend it nicely, nicely,
to mend it neatly, neatly.
Planted Bamboo, the One who
     Guards the Betel,
by their hands, it is mended neatly
     again.

lemo lambayo	Lemo Lambayo,
suola lola lolamo	spirit familiar, *lola lolamo* [old, elderly?],
da saito to samba'a	that one will be the one
nantika mala	who can retreive
bayo ntilowu mwitinya	the shadow of the *tolowu* of her feet,
da simalaja muni rawuuigi muni	who will make it possible to blow back
tolowu mwitinya ewa uyu pemonya	the *tolowu* of her feet, as they were before.
taamo maranindi loto marasisi	No longer shivering cold.
pura kuwuuigi muni	I have finished blowing back
pasi tolowu mwitinya	even the *tolowu* of her feet.

Several initial observations can be noted about these texts. First, simply because he is now treating particular patients, a performer does not abandon his patoe; he continues to summon and encourage his spirits throughout his performance. Second, the shaman and his spirits are working together in a special partnership: "your hand is on the bottom, my hand is on the top" is a characteristic way of expressing the cooperation between shaman and spirit agency. Third, the texts portray a side of the patient's being that is known directly only by shamans and their spirit familiars. The items being returned to and removed from the patients' bodies in these texts belong to a dimension of reality that lies beyond most people's perception but at the same time concerns their very survival.

5

Shamans as Seers

If I did not feel some responsibility to identify the Wana *tau kawalia*, or "persons with spirit familiars," with the wider literature on shamanism, I would be tempted to follow E. M. Loeb's example and refer to the Wana shaman as a "seer,"[1] for "seeing" is what defines a Wana shaman. Wana express distinctions among various forms of "seeing." In an ordinary state, one is said to see with one's "hard eyes" (*mata mako'o*) or one's "real" or "bodily eyes" (*mata koro*). Quite different is to see something with the "eyes of one's dream agent" (*mata ntanuana*). Dreams—perceived through the agency of one's tanuana—are most people's only direct access to spirits and the hidden realms of existence. Dreams may contain truths, deceptions, foreshadowings of events (*sabalera*), or disguises of what is to come (*sule, salekong*), as well as expressions of the dreamer's personal thoughts or desires (*wali nraya*).

Important knowledge of spells, names, and medicines may be imparted in dreams. One old woman of my acquaintance claimed that the ghost of her aunt or some other spirit being would often appear to her in a dream and reveal a medicine to her when someone in the community was ill. For example, when a neighbor was suffering from a prolapsed and bleeding rectum, a cure for the man's problem came to her in a dream. Her remedy was tried and proved successful; grateful for her help, the man asked for the medicine and offered payment for it. The woman told me that her uncle declared that her dreams were not visitations by spirits, but instead simply the product of her desire to obtain remedies—literally, "the coming into being of her wishes" (*wali nraya*). The woman rejects her relative's skepticism and cites the efficacy of her medicines as evidence that they do indeed come from spirits.

SHAMANIC VISION

Shamans see in waking states what others can see only in dreams. When a shaman encounters a spirit in the course of ordinary life, he does so with his mata mako'o—that is, the way one ordinarily observes a mundane event. The experienced shaman, however, has another form of vision available to him. When a shaman assembles his spirit familiars, he augments his ordinary perception with the "eyes of the spirit familiars" (*mata mwalia*). With his faculties so enhanced, he can perceive dimensions of existence that are hidden to people around him: he can scrutinize the state of his patients' inner beings, facets even their owners cannot know; and, while remaining physically in the room, he can witness events transpiring in spirit realms. With vision comes control. Just as his spirit familiars enable him to see what is ordinarily hidden, so too can they extend his power to feel and manipulate what lies beyond the touch and grasp of most people.

People liken the experience of a performing shaman to "the state of a person dreaming" (*ewa kare'e tau mangipi*). The comparison is telling, not only because it characterizes a performing shaman's condition as what we might gloss "an altered state of consciousness," but also because both dreamers and shamans are thought to rely on special agents to perceive hidden realities. My companions compared a shaman's vision to a particularly "clear" or "vivid dream" (*pangipi manopa, pangipi manasa*). In contrast to a dreamer, however, the shaman is conscious, and instead of relying on a "dream agent," or tanuana—a faculty possessed by everyone—he employs the agency of his spirit familiars. The difference is illustrated by a crippled man's report of seeing a throng of little children approaching as he dozed during a mabolong performance. He figured that they must have been spirit familiars (*walia*) coming to help the shaman, and his own dream agent intercepted the shaman's vision. Whereas the shaman could see his spirit familiars in a waking state, though, this man could see them only in a dream.

What is it like for a shaman to "see" as he performs? One man explained that when he closes his eyes, he sees as one would see a vivid dream; when he opens them again, his "thought snaps back" and the vision is gone. There is no elaborated transition between "states." As they sing, shamans close their eyes and see the spirit world. It is not unusual for them to interrupt their singing to open their eyes and speak in an ordinary manner. Conversations and joking alternate with singing and "seeing." According to this man, his thoughts and feelings are "different" when he is performing than they are in ordinary life, but he adds that they are not "extinguished" (*pika raya*) as they are for a person who has lost control over his sensibilities. In the latter state, one no longer has any good thoughts or feelings (*taamore raya to matao*). One could kill in such a state without feeling pity. The shaman's state is different. He continues to be aware of his thoughts and feelings—though, as we shall see, they might be unlike those he usually experiences in ordinary life.

ENGAGING SPIRIT FAMILIARS

The agents who enable a shaman to "see" are precisely the same agents from whom magic derives. Although everyone is thought to possess magic, not everyone performs as a shaman; most people use verbal formulae without directly engaging their spirit owners. A performing shaman, however, summons the "owners" of his spells (*pue ndo'a*) to serve as his spirit familiars. Their presence will transform a shaman's consciousness and his perception of the world.

Achieving a working relationship with spirit familiars is neither automatic nor easy. A person who possesses both the requisite magic *and* the potential to become a shaman must first learn to recognize and act on the arrival of his spirit familiars. Such a person should come to experience a sense of excitement and an urge to dance when the drum and gongs are played.[2] The sensation of arousal is described as a shaking or quivering of the body, brought on by one's walia. I was told of one shaman who, because he could not wait until he was in the house to begin dancing, could be found jumping up and down through the rice fields on his way to a performance.

The process of learning to recognize and to act on the arrival of spirit familiars is often supervised by an expert shaman. This teacher is commonly a close senior relative—a father or an uncle, an older brother or a cousin. In private, a teacher may provide the novice with secret knowledge for meeting spirits in the woods; in public, he may guide the novice's performance at a mabolong (Fig. 19). There are various ways a senior shaman can promote the arrival of spirits. For example, he may "implant" (*mamposisi*) a walia-attracting object—such as betel nut, the succulent *samata* plant, or a pretty stone that appeared from nowhere, called a *tolowu*—in the top of the novice's head; the object lodges there and serves as a "bridge for the spirits" (*tete mwalia*). Later, in private, the teacher reveals to the novice secret names of spirits and shamanic accoutrements such as basil and the special cloth (*papolonsu*) shamans use to treat patients.

The novice embarks on the public side of shamanship by dancing at mabolong performances. Shamanic dancing is called *motaro*, which means "to jump up and down" (Fig. 14). It is done with the knees bent and flexed, the torso rigid, and the eyes closed. The posture resembles that of Wana infants who are held under the arms and bounced up and down to the gleeful amusement of both the child and its older audience. This act of childish play is also called motaro and is done in explicit imitation of a shaman's dance during actual performances. Dancing for an adult may recall the early pleasure of being bounced, admired, and amused as a tiny infant. Bouncing a baby may also afford an adult, shaman or not, the pleasure of physically responding to the compelling beat of drum and gongs.

There is a variety of motaro known as *salonde*, (literally, "something beautiful"), which is a woman's style of dancing (Fig. 15). It involves the same vertical up-and-down movement as the male style, but instead of bending her arms at the elbow and holding her hands at the height of the rib cage, the dancer casts her arms gracefully from side to side. The salonde has aesthetic appeal and can be done without implying that the dancer is embarked on a shamanic career. For a man to motaro suggests that he is attempting to engage spirit familiars; for a woman to salonde may suggest either that she has shamanic aspirations or that she is simply showing off her skills as a graceful dancer. The equivocality of the interpretation placed on a woman's dancing reveals a tacit but powerful assumption that Wana shamanship is largely a male game (see Chapter 14).

Senior shamans encourage their protégés to dance. They may also perform public acts to encourage the walia to come to the novice: they may wave their shamans' cloths over their students' heads or blow spells through the cloth onto the crown of their heads. Should a senior shaman be making a special journey upward to request "breath" for a patient, he may urge a novice to dance along with him. Sometimes, too, a novice may be given a routine task to carry out, such as recovering a lost soul or some other part of a patient's being. The novice may not be able to "see" the elements he is handling, but his teacher will guide his hand. Following directives, the novice snatches at what seems to him to be "empty air" (*rao soa*), then presents the cloth to his instructor, who inspects the catch and informs him of what he has accomplished. During lessons of this sort, a novice is urged to go through the motions of performing as a shaman, even if he cannot see what shamans see; his teacher then confirms the success of his actions, which the novice himself cannot yet verify. Shamanic vision, it is said, will come later.

Those who have tried to perform but have failed in their attempts to "see" joke about clutching at "empty air" and perceiving only vast darkness. They typically credit their lack of vision to the fact that they were not meant to be shamans. One young father, however, who performs occasionally, told me that in fact shamans see nothing, that all their talk and gestures are simply "decoration" (*bubunga*). According to him, the only true part of the performance is the magic shamans use. Interestingly, he asserts the genuineness of spells and the visitations by spirits who deliver the spells to solitary mortals, but he denies the claims of shamans who say they see hidden realities as they perform.

I asked a senior shaman about the young man's remarks. He answered:

> [The skeptic] is inexperienced. If one only dances a few times as a joke, one does not see. There must be "people," "spirits." If one has thirty spells, one has thirty spirit allies. If one is experienced, one will see them. Yes, if one has effective spells, one can recover souls and the like if they are close, for a sickness that is not very serious—even if one can't see. But if you can see, you look for it. Even if it [the patient's soul part] is far, you can find it. [The skeptic] who doesn't see, cannot.

This shaman told me he performed for two years before he came to see. Other experienced shamans also speak of performing for months or years before attaining shamanic vision.

A middle-aged widow who was on her way to becoming a shaman criticized young boys who would dance for a little while, then sit down and declare they saw nothing. As she put it, "The path of the spirit familiars is not like a road that is stepped on. They want it to stretch out like a walking path." She herself has seen spirits outside the ceremonial context, but she had yet to see much as she danced at a mabolong.

The relationship of a shaman and his spirit familiars is complex, and it shifts over the course of a mabolong performance. At the outset, the shaman is an ordinary person distinguished from his human companions only by his ability to summon spirit allies from distant haunts. In the course of performing, the shaman augments his person by surrounding himself with hidden and powerful beings. His song emphasizes the fusion of his spirits' capabilities and his own. In distinguishing shamans from spirit mediums and other ritual specialists, Eliade (1964), Reinhard (1976), and others emphasize that shamans control their spirit agents instead of being controlled by them. The repeated invitations, instructions, and rebukes that Wana shamans deliver to their spirit familiars—"come, come," "oh, don't hesitate, don't stay away," "don't take offense"—underscore the Wana shaman's directing role.

VAMPIRES, WARRIORS, AND SHAMANS

Wana culture offers a contrast to the shaman in the person of a human vampire. Shamans are "people with spirit familiars" (*tau kawalia*). Vampires are *tau kameasa*, "people with demons." In fact, many shamans count "liver-eating demons" among their spirit familiars. A measa who is "domesticated" or "cared for" (*rapiyara*) by a shaman will help to heal a sick person when serving as a shaman's aide, whereas the same demon acting on its own would viciously prey on human victims. Even its appearance changes, depending on whose agent it is: as a free agent, the demon is a huge ugly beast with distorted features; as a shaman's walia, it is a small and benign-looking spirit. In partnership with a tau kawalia, a demon can be a blessing for a shaman's followers. In possession of a tau kameasa, however, a demon can be a death-dealing curse. The demon causes its human counterpart to lust after human livers, and together they prey on human victims. The victim of a vampire who sees his or her predator in the woods is, from that moment on, doomed. Soon after a vampire's attack, the victim will suddenly take sick and die.

A person may become a kameasa either by predisposition or by engaging in improper acts. Just as some people have the "palm line" to become shamans, others have the palm line to become vampires. The trait sometimes recurs in families or people of "one vine" (*sambiaa*): parents may induct their children into the practice, as in the case of a vampire mother who reportedly fed her daughter human insides. Eating raw bird meat is also said to make people "turn into demons" (*kature yau*), because demons supposedly fly through the air. (Some shamans, by contrast, *walk* in the air.) Certain forms of magic—such as *doti lamu*, which gives people x-ray vision, the ability to see the insides of objects—are thought to provoke the phenomenon. With such an ability, one can see not only the insides of things (such as a standing column of water instead of the bamboo tube that contains it), but the insides of people as well. The risk is that one may become desirous of those insides and want to eat them—which is the act of a kameasa. Shamans with such magic insist that they possess such vision only in the context of a shamanic ritual, whereas vampires use such vision at all times. Kameasa become lustful at the sight of blood and particularly at the sight of a human placenta—stories tell of kameasa parents and grandparents devouring the placenta of newborn babies and then proceeding to eat out the infants' insides as well.

A vampire—a person with a demon "on his or her back"—is characterized as someone who has lost the qualities of a human being. Typically, it is said, such a person stops bathing, starts sleeping alone, and begins to speak incoherently. Often a vampire flees human company, talks to him- or herself, and otherwise acts strangely. Clearly, people suffering certain forms of mental illness would fit the label *kameasa*. Yet, not all vampires exhibit the telltale signs. In such a case, people remark on the discrepancy between the individual's outward manner and the horrible practices of which he or she is suspected.

A vampire is regarded without question as a killer. Should a number of people in an area take sick and die, someone suspected of being a vampire may be thought responsible. In earlier times, such a person might have been subjected to a *polobiang*, or test. For example, burning resin would be poured on the suspect's hand: if the skin developed wounds as a result of the test, the person would be judged a kameasa and would be promptly killed. (Today, fear of government reprisals discourages this practice.) In the past and now, objections of the suspects' kin function as a check as well. Sometimes, though, even close relatives may lose their patience with a person perceived to be a danger to the well-being of all. Such was the experience of the uncle of an old woman I knew, who assisted in the murder of his aunt and cousin, two women who lived apart from others and behaved peculiarly. When a vampire is executed, it is essential that a mabolong be performed to prevent the dead person's demons from possessing the killers and turning them into vampires as well. After the killing of his aunt and cousin, my acquaintance's uncle told his niece that shamans removed a variety of insects, bats, and other creatures from the bodies of the killers, a sign that the dead women's demons had already invaded them.

The sense in which a tau kameasa is regarded as totally bereft of any redeeming human qualities is found in people's pitiless accounts of these individuals, in the attitude that suspects should be executed the moment their guilt is established, and in the absence of any of the funeral observances that ordinarily mark the passing of a human life.

The kameasa is in some sense the reverse of a kawalia. Whereas kawalia control spirits, kameasa are controlled by spirits. The kameasa may represent a twist on another prized role of former times as well, that of a headhunter. After a victorious headhunt, warriors are said to have consumed a feast of *baku ragi*, rice mixed with pieces of their victim's scalp. It is my impression that such consumption in nonritual circumstances would turn a person into a kameasa, and that those who partook of such a feast under formal circumstances were protected by ritual measures.[3] Like a shaman and a vampire, a warrior has a spirit attached to him—namely, the ghost of his victim. When under the influence of this spirit, the warrior experiences murderous rage. His ears swell, his face turns red, and he knows no pity. But unlike a kameasa, the warrior destroys enemies beyond his community rather than preying on his neighbors, and the act of killing is so highly ritualized that untoward consequences for himself and those around him are effectively prevented.

Like the warrior, the shaman also may come dangerously close to crossing the divide between social and antisocial commerce with dangerous powers. Shamans, through their associations with spirits, possess the powers to harm as well as to heal, and some even press the boundary between kawalia and kameasa. I have heard of powerful shamans whose demonic familiars would kill patients instead of curing them. One shaman of my acquaintance who led a millenarian movement in the 1960s was shunned as a healer for a time by some of his relatives because his spirit familiars had turned murderous. (Interestingly, instead of being viewed as incompetent because his patients were dying, this shaman was judged, by his associates at least, as especially powerful.) Another shaman I knew well would occasionally flirt with the image of a kameasa, claiming to crave patients' insides and placentas. In this way he underscored his reputation for consorting with dangerous demons.

FUSION OF SHAMAN
AND SPIRIT FAMILIAR

I have described the difference between a shaman or a warrior and a vampire as being one of control: the former two control their spirits, whereas the latter is possessed by them. Yet in the ritual context, just as a shaman employs the perception and power of his spirit familiars, so too may he assume the personalities and desires of his spirit allies. For instance, some shamans cry freely and often in the course of a performance, something they are unlikely to do in everyday life. Such emotional alterations are attributed to the presence of a shaman's walia, who bring their own characters to bear on his own. In the case of experienced shamans, audience members can sometimes tell which of a shaman's spirit familiars has "arrived" by the way the shaman dances. For example, Apa Mene leans on a staff to dance when he is visited by *tau tu'a matoko*, an old spirit who walks with a staff; when *tau tu'a masowo*, "the Old Goitered One," arrives, he is unable to lower his chin enough to see the floor. Another shaman, when visited by a spirit he met while keeping vigil over an eel (*masapi*), becomes slippery with sweat and cannot be held. Others suddenly lose the power of speech when the mute "Owner of the Pigs" (*tau pue mwawu*) arrives.

The fusion of human and spirit personalities is most clearly displayed when a shaman requests a baku mwalia, "rice" or "food of a spirit familiar" (see Part Four). The reader will recall that the lango is stocked with items that the performing shamans' spirits are known to crave. In addition, spirit familiars may make special requests to the audience through their shaman hosts. By eating, drinking, or doing what the spirit has asked for, the shaman can satisfy his hidden ally's craving. Although these requests are called baku mwalia, they are not necessarily limited to edible items. Some familiars wish to hear the sound of a louse being crushed with a fingernail on a tin box. There are shamans who call for prickly substances to wipe on their bodies. Some shamans are known for wiping lime in their eyes, for sucking blood, for eating fire. A few spirits even have a predilection for quaffing bowls full of urine and chicken excrement. Other requests are more aesthetically pleasing, such as for pretty berries, glossy shoots, and honey. Be the substance or the action pleasurable or revolting in ordinary life, a shaman who indulges in it on behalf of his spirit familiar typically savors it.

Not only do the shaman and his spirit familiar act as one in the enjoyment of a baku mwalia, but if the baku mwalia is not forthcoming, the shaman and spirit familiar may together take offense. If the audience fails to assuage their merged feelings, the shaman's soul may depart his body and go off in the company of his walia (Fig. 28). In the event that an unconscious shaman cannot be brought around by his human companions, the shaman, it is held, will die. Good reason to humor the desires of a shaman and his spirit familiars! (This dramatic episode will be the focus of Part Four. I introduce it here to demonstrate the nature of the alliance between shaman and spirits in the course of a mabolong performance.)

A Wana shaman, then, is someone who can augment his perception, power, and personality by summoning spirit familiars. In their absence, the shaman is like other mortals in his perceptions and experience. Unlike others, though, he has both special knowledge and associates of which he can avail himself should he care to do so. A shaman thus is distinct from, yet allied with, his spirit familiars. Although they do not reside within him as an integral part of his being, when summoned, they will come great distances to join him. They are external to him, yet when present they fuse with his personality and transform his thought, perception, and behavior. When he performs, a shaman represents a concentration of powerful forces; at the end of a performance, however, his spirits depart and only their potential for being summoned again stays with the shaman. They remain part of his reputation, not an integral part of his being.

In their partnership, a shaman and spirits retain their independence, yet the magical knowledge they hold in common forges a link between them. That link is evident in the food prohibitions shamans and others with powerful knowledge observe. A person with special relations to tau bolag avoids eating certain kinds of beans; someone who counts demons among his friends may avoid particular varieties of hearts of palm. Violating the dietary preferences of one's spirit familiars can result in illness. Indo Lina attributed her shaman husband's bout of laryngitis to his having eaten rice dished up with a ladle that had been used to serve tree fungus: his spirit familiar Wata Podo, "Short Trunk," had taken offense. Once when I fell sick, those around me declared that the spirit owners of some magic I had studied objected to my having eaten the fermented mash of dark glutinous rice.

Spirit familiars may exert other forms of unpetitioned influence over their human companions outside of ritual contexts. For example, lascivious spirits called *jimi* may induce lasciviousness in their shaman friends; other spirits may bring on sickness or madness in their human companions. The process by which this happens is called *mangou* and applies to any spirit's willful possession of a human being. One junior shaman of my acquaintance claimed the ghost of a headhunting victim as one of his familiars. Like a headhunter of old, he would occasionally be possessed by this spirit. If the spirit arrived during a mabolong performance, the shaman would order the drummer to play a head-hunting song and he would demand blood as a baku mwalia. If the spirit arrived outside the ritual setting, its human friend would experience bouts of violent fury.

With a sense now of the nature of the working partnership between a shaman and his spirit familiars, we can proceed to examine just what it is these partners work *on* in the course of a mabolong performance.

6

An Anatomy of Dependence

Just as the possibility of magic is predicated on the existence of hidden realms of reality, so the possibility for shamanic healing is predicated on facets of the person over which only shamans and spirits have control. Dependence on shamans is encoded in the depiction of the person presented in Wana talk about illness. Shamanic healing operates on the premise that a person's life requires the presence of a cluster of vital elements a step removed from the self-awareness of their owner. These special elements are separable from their owner and are ordinarily invisible. They participate in hidden dimensions of reality and are subject to influence by agents and factors beyond their owner's knowledge and control. In health they are subsumed as part of the person; they come into their own in sleep, sickness, and death. Thus mortals, lacking direct access to hidden dimensions of the world beyond themselves as well as to the inner elements on which their very beings depend, must rely on shamans to mediate relations between these two realms.

PERSONHOOD VERSUS PATIENTHOOD

The sketch of personhood that I am about to present derives from shamanic discourse. It stands apart in significant ways from talk about ordinary sensations, emotions, and thought. In ordinary life, people phrase states of conscious thought and feeling in terms of a person's "inside," or *raya* (for example, *moru rayaku*, "I am worried," or *poraya*, "to feel or care for"). The elements of being with which shamans concern themselves are not identified with this phrasing. Nor are they associated with expressions concerning "thought" (*pompobuuka*) or "sensation" (*epe*).

To say that vital elements of being are distinct from experience of bodily, emotional, and intellectual states is not to say that no relations are drawn between these elements and a person's thoughts, feelings,

102

and physical well-being. An unpleasant experience may cause one's vital elements to flee, just as the departure of these elements can bring their owner illness or death. Despite such interconnections, the cluster of vital elements enjoys considerable autonomy from the rest of a person's being and experience.

Distanced as they are from direct and conscious knowledge of the vital elements on which their being depends, people do hold shared and public understandings of what typically goes on with these hidden facets of self. As in the case of hidden dimensions of the world beyond the self, stock scenarios provide public accounts relating states of being to interaction between a person's hidden facets and the world beyond. Then, too, although in most cases only shamans traffick with spirits, ordinary people may have experiential glimmers of hidden sides of their own beings. Dreams and hallucinations during illness are cited as direct evidence of one's metaphysical complexity. My neighbors mused about such matters in a startlingly Tylorian fashion, pondering how it is possible to dream about people long dead and places far away, and drawing conclusions about the nature of the soul and hopes for a hereafter.

In the following pages I will profile the elements of the person with which shamanic ritual is concerned, examining them with reference to their use in conversation, their ties to experience, and the part they play in diagnosis and healing (as illustrated by the textual materials in Chapter 4).

BODY AND SOUL,
TOGETHER AND APART

As a prelude to this inventory, consideration of two key concepts, *koro* and *lemba*, is in order, to provide a sense not only of the "mechanics" of shamanic healing, but also of an ethos that disparages outward appearance in favor of hidden reality. The word *koro* pertains specifically to a vital element of being to which shamans devote considerable attention; but its wider set of meanings provides a framework for understanding a cultural conception of the person as a physical and metaphysical being.

In contrast to the word *lemba*, *koro* defines a living state. *Koro* is the term applied to a living body as both a physical entity and an animate being: one's koro is one's physical being, that which gets dirty, itchy, bathed, and groomed, that which feels strong, weak, healthy, or sick. Used with the second-person possessive suffix, *koro* is a term of address for a companion. Peppered through conversation, it serves as an exclamation that adds emphasis to assertions. In talk about illness and healing, it applies to a soullike component of the self, hidden from ordinary perception, but essential for life. The koro, in this last sense, resides in a person's upper back, except for temporary absences during illness. After death, it continues its existence in heaven (*saruga*). The body of a dead person can no longer be called a koro: it is now a lemba.

Unlike the term *koro*, *lemba* can apply to both a corpse and a living body. When used for a living person, it distinguishes the physical exterior from the person who inhabits it. The term *lemba* is characteristically used to disparage outward appearance and contrast it to inner self. A lemba is in no sense animated—it is conventionally likened to clothing, which may be discarded. At death, it is "shed" (*wonsu lemba*), and the koro is freed to proceed to heaven. People often characterize themselves as trapped in their poor and ugly lemba for the present life. Once released at death from their pitiful exteriors, their beautified koro may live on forever. *Koro*, then, refers to an animated being: in this life, one's body and vitality; in the next life, one's immortal soul. *Lemba* refers to mortal exteriors: one's much deprecated appearance in life and one's physical remains at death.

As is probably clear by now, for Wana things are not always as they appear to be—the contrast of koro and lemba demonstrates that point well. Beneath the surfaces lie deeper realities. Humans are not the only beings in the world to be clothed in deceptive attire. Spirits, too, have lemba, external guises not in consonance with their inner beings or koro. Liver-eating demons, for example, are said to possess attractive koro, but when confronting humans they assume hideous exteriors. Animals seen in the forest—especially monkeys and forest oxen—are not uncommonly spirits in disguise. (When a shaman sings of his spirit familiar who is "disguised as a monkey" [*mampolemba wonti*], he is indicating that his hidden companion adopts such a disguise.) In stories about the former age of magic, heroes typically start out wearing deceptive guises: some are ugly and grimy, others appear as animals. My own favorite among Wana heroes is Totokumu, a young man still enveloped in his placenta. Like the Frog Prince, all these peculiar-looking fellows eventually shed their unattractive exteriors and reveal their handsome koro.

Whereas the heroes of these stories can achieve such transformations in life, people today must die in order to free their beautiful koro from their despised lemba. Legend has it that human beings were supposed to receive the breath of something regenerative, such as the moon, a snake, a shrimp, or a cricket—all of which are said to shed their old exteriors and assume new ones. But while the Owner's assistant was gone in search of regenerative breath, along came someone (some say it was Langesong, the spoiler) who gave the breath of a tree to humankind. And so people, like trees, "fall over" and die when their time has come, leaving their physical remains to rot and disintegrate. Accounts of people's passage to heaven often include an episode in which the newcomers bathe, their old exteriors fall away, and they emerge in a form fit for heaven.

The song of Apa Linus presented in Chapter 4 illustrates how a shaman endeavors to keep his patient's koro and lemba together. With the assistance of his spirit familiars, he blows the shadow of his daughter's soul (*koro*) back into her "body on top," her "thick body" (*lemba to mbawo, lemba mokumba*). As we shall see, the refined spiritual elements of a person often resist being rejoined with the unpleasant corporeality of a human lemba.

HIDDEN ELEMENTS OF BEING

The "Soul"

Koro in the sense of "soul" is featured strongly in shamanic discourse. A variety of names distinguishes this koro from the "living body" accessible to all; these include *une ngkoro* (literally, "the inside of the body"), *koro uli* or *koro samba'a* ("the first soul"), *koro tongo* ("the middle soul"), and *koro nonong* ("the genuine soul"). Although some people assert that these terms are all the same, others differentiate among them. For example, I have been told that the *koro uli* is small and shiny like a firefly, whereas the *koro tongo* is larger. The *koro nonong* (identified by some as the *tonii*) pertains specifically to the transformed soul that dwells in heaven.

According to Wana forebears, I was told, a human being has seven koro (seven being an auspicious number associated with long life), but no one I asked could name them all. I am tempted to think that the differentiation of koro derives at least in part from stylistic and performative considerations of shamanic songs. These songs, like other forms of Wana oratory, depend heavily on parallel constructions in which the same idea is conveyed in several balanced phrases (such as the line "koro uli koro tongo segi" in Apa Linus's song). People joke about the effects of such repetitions in legal oratory—unless one knows that the same fine is being expressed by several different metaphors (*ligi*), one could end up making a payment for each metaphor!

The koro resides in a person's upper back and resembles its owner in appearance. It does not engage in mundane aspects of life, nor does it experience human emotions. But under certain circumstances it may leave its owner's body, either of its own volition—when its owner suffers illness or injury (including shock or surprise in the case of a child)—or at the instigation of a spirit. Its absence from the body may precipitate illness or result from it. As the body of its owner languishes, weak and sick, the koro thrives elsewhere.

The Dream Agent

A more playful and engaging element of being is the tanuana, the "dream agent" we met in Chapter 5. The tanuana is a tiny image of its owner, residing in the crown of the head at the fontanel. Of all the hidden vital elements, the tanuana most resembles its owner in feelings and behavior. In contrast to the koro, which is something of a homebody, the tanuana is a wanderer (*taa rodo*—literally, "not settled"), the only vital element that can safely leave its owner without bringing on illness. While its owner is sleeping the tanuana travels about encountering spirits of all sorts, including the tanuana of other dreamers. The owner witnesses the adventures of the tanuana in the form of dreams. When recounting a dream, a Wana speaks of the dreamed self as "my *tanuana*" and of other people in the dream as "a person like so-and-so." Dreams are valuable sources of insight into what may be happening in the spirit world and what is to come in people's own experience.

In addition to traveling as its owner sleeps, a tanuana may flee from its owner's body during waking life, as when its owner experiences shock or surprise. (The phrase "my *tanuana* flees" is an expression of alarm on the order of the English phrase "scared out of my wits.") The departure of one's tanuana under such circumstances can result in illness. Small children are particularly susceptible to such flights.

For example, a dogfight was cited as the reason why one small baby suffered a relapse of illness after being treated by shamans. In another instance, a mischievous little boy who had been disturbing a family dinner was suddenly grabbed by his father and tied up—to the merriment of other members of the household. Some time later when the child took sick, a shaman discovered that the child's tanuana, frightened by the father's act, had fled. Like a small child, rice is thought to have a tanuana too that is sensitive to disturbances, shock, and alarm; measures are taken to insure that its tanuana is not startled, for if it flees, rice plants—like humans without their tanuana—are weak and unproductive.

Fright is not the only reason the tanuana will flee one's body. Like the koro, the tanuana distances itself from an owner who becomes sick or injured, seeking enjoyment elsewhere. Thus Apa Linus sings that his little daughter's tanuana is "off in another place." Shamans report the problems they sometimes encounter in luring a reluctant tanuana back to its enfeebled owner. Vivid dreams during illness are sometimes attributed to the fact that one's tanuana is "living it up" somewhere else.

The mere absence of the tanuana from its owner's body implies a weakened state of health, and sometimes the nature of the suffering is specifically related to what the tanuana is experiencing. For example, in the case of a child beset by seizures, it may be said that the patient's tanuana has been captured by seizure-causing spirits (*tumpu ntomua*) who have caged it in an iron chicken carrier and are tormenting it. In such an event, a shaman must win the release of the tanuana and return it gently to its owner. A conventional diagnosis for a person who has grown thin and sickly is that the patient's tanuana is being smoked over a fire by a demon who lives in the direction of the setting sun (a direction associated with death). Again, a shamanic rescue is in order. Shamans are forever rescuing people's tanuana that have been trapped beneath smoldering logs in the smoky fires of *sauju*, a condition brought on by improper marriages that cut across affinal relations of other kin and disrupt lines of generational authority.

One of the most popular diagnoses involving the dream agent is called *kakayuka* (from the term *ayu ayu*, meaning to portray or act something out so it will come true).[1] The name refers to the notion that ghosts of the dead (*wonggo, langgiwo*) may perform funeral rites for the tanuana (and often the koro) of a living person; when the rites are complete, the owner will die. Hence, shamans treating such a case may have to dig up the soul parts of the patient from the spot where the ghosts have buried them.

A friend told me that her father had once been brought back from the dead through shamanic intervention. She says he remembered traveling far along the path to Saruga, as far as a place near heaven called pada kamumu ("Purple Grassland," a site traversed by one of Apa Mene's familiars discussed in Chapter 1). There, two people approached him and told him he could not proceed. His daughter and a companion agreed that the two were the spirit familiars (*walia*) of the shaman who was treating him. The sick man reported that he picked flowers from a tree at the spot, but when he was told he could not go on, the flowers went back of their own accord to the places from which he had picked them. He told the two people that he did not know the way back. They advised him that the path was wide and instructed him to lift up the tree that had fallen across the path and to pass under it (they did not pass under it with him). As he did so, he re-entered his earthly body (*lemba*) and came back to life. The imagery of the dream is highly salient in cultural terms: Wana associate a dead person with a fallen tree; moving under the fallen tree is easily read as the soul's return to its stricken body.

Besides the koro and the tanuana, which stand in metaphoric relation to their owner, a person possesses a variety of other elements of being that are metonymically related to their owner and that also may be lost and subsequently retrieved by shamans. Intriguingly, these components seem to span a division Westerners might draw between corporeal and incorporeal, material and spiritual, essences.

Gems of the Hands and Feet

The term *tolowu* (which I left untranslated in the transcripts in Chapter 4) refers to small gemlike elements that reside one in each hand and foot. Equated with the pulse (*sule*), they are linked in some sense to body temperature. Thus they represent critical vital signs. Like the koro and tanuana, they are particular to an individual; if lost, they must be recovered and restored to that owner. In addition to the tolowu that each person possesses, there are also tolowu which are gifts from spirits. These may be used as amulets, and some shamans as well have them implanted in their bodies to attract their spirit familiars.

Breath

Another critical element that shamans must seek for their patients is "breath," or *nosa* (also called *yosa, yowe,* and *nyawa* in shamans' songs). In contrast to the other aspects of the person I have detailed to this point, "breath" is not a personalized entity that must be found and restored to its proper owner. Instead it is a life-sustaining quality procured directly from Pue, the Owner, in an act of supplication known as *manyomba* in which the shaman "requests breath" (*parapi nosa*) for his patient (this act will be detailed in Part Three). *Nosa* here, then, is equivalent to life, and giving "breath" to a patient is equivalent to granting the patient an extension of life. A person whose life has been saved in this way is sometimes said to be alive on account of *nosa mwalia,* the breath furnished by a shaman's spirit familiars. One dying woman was described to me as having no vital elements left at all— only the "breath" supplied her by a shaman.

The Wana idea of breath is elaborated further in the notion that every human being possesses two *balo nosa,* "bamboo tubes of breath," one located in the chest below the throat, the other up at the place of the Owner. The balo in a patient's body may crack, in which case a shaman will seek to repair or replace it. Alternatively, the balo in the Owner's realm may be damaged or tampered with by a hostile spirit. If the patient is destined to die, the shaman may find the balo turned upside down (just like the bamboo tube placed in the house over a grave). If it is possible to postpone the patient's death, a shaman may set this balo aright. If not, I was told, the person's soul (*une ngkoro*) goes to the Owner's place to receive its balo nosa, then passes on to heaven (which incidently is not above the earth, but next to it, hidden by a great darkness). In the same vein, a shaman who wishes to commit suicide may have his spirit familiars destroy his own balo nosa in the course of a journey to the Owner.

Other Vital Properties

The reader will recall from Chapter 4 that Apa Mene restored my "ability to call," my "ability to summon," along with my "sweat" and "grease." Other vital characteristics that may be restored to a sick person include "strength" (*roso*) and "blood" (*raa*). These elements do not figure prominently in conventional narratives about the etiology or treatment of illness, but references to them in shamans' songs underscore the life-restoring actions of the shaman. They appear to be secondary to a patient's condition. For example, I heard one man who was suffering a malarial attack remark that his body was not sweating any more. Someone in the room responded that he was not sweating because his "soul" (*une ngkoro*) had fled. The significance of these properties is their association with life: a corpse does not sweat, bleed, produce body oils, or exhibit strength. These properties distinguish a healthy person from a sick or dying one. Like "breath"—but unlike tanuana, koro, and tolowu—these qualities are not personalized in the course of shamanic treatment.

The Liver

Three other significant aspects of the person figure in Wana shamanic healing. They are the "liver" (*ate*), the "skin of the head" (*pela mwo'o*), and the "brains" (*uta*). In contrast to the other properties discussed above, these three are not sought on spirit journeys to hidden realms above and beyond the earth; instead they are sought among ferocious spirits who inhabit the Wana land. What is more, in contrast to the other elements, the absence of which may be associated with a wide variety of causes and conditions, the loss of these three items signals one of two very specific kinds of spirit attacks.

The loss of the liver (also called the *bui*, which in ordinary conversation designates the xiphoid process) can only mean the attack of a demon (*measa*) whose right it is to devour the liver of a person fated to die. Demons, however, do not always wait for divine orders before seizing livers. What is more, they often do not act on their own, but rather at the behest of a human sorcerer.

Shamans, through the agency of their spirit familiars, can detect the absence of a liver and determine whether it can still be recovered. If the shaman determines that it cannot, he may do what one shaman of my acquaintance supposedly did when called on to treat a young man who was feeling unwell. Recognizing that the young man had been "eaten out" by a measa and could not live, the shaman, rather than causing alarm by revealing his discovery, simply administered a spell and went home. Not long after, the young man died. (It is evident here how a claim of shamanic omniscience may be cited to gloss an apparent oversight.) The posthumous explanation was that a demon had attacked the youth in the forest, cut open his chest, and eaten his liver, then closed up the wound. The victim, not remembering what had transpired, lived on for a while. On the day of his death he went out birdhunting, returned to the house, and cooked his catch, but he did not live to eat it. His sister's family asserted that the demon had been sent by the victim's uncle, who was angered because the youth had impregnated his daughter and wanted to marry her over her father's opposition.

A shamanic ritual is not necessary for recovering a liver. A person with powerful magic can recover a liver from the demon who took it, typically by murmuring a spell, leaving the house momentarily, and returning with something clutched in his hand to be worked back into place in the patient's midriff—perhaps producing blood on his hands in the process. I was taught some spells for recovering a liver by an old man who was not a shaman. He explained that if one were not a shaman and hence unable to "see" demons, it was necessary to prick one's gums to obtain blood when recovering a liver. For the shaman who could actually "see" the demon and the liver, the blood would occur perforce. Months later I mentioned the old man's counsel to a friend who was startled to learn of the gum-pricking. But, she declared, it is the efficacy of the spell that matters: if the spell is "true," so too is the cure.

Corresponding to the narrow application of diagnoses pertaining to the liver, far fewer conditions of illness involve the loss of a liver than involve the loss of other properties described thus far. Moreover, and in contrast to those other elements, attacks on the liver may be associated with localized pain. Yet such association is not necessary for concern to arise about the state of a person's liver; for example, if a person experiences a fright in the forest (the habitat of measa), there is cause for worry.

Like the koro and the tanuana, the ate is a personalized aspect of its owner that only shamans can see. But unlike the former, it stands in metonymic rather than metaphoric relation to its owner. The ate also has a somewhat more tangible quality than other elements of the person in which shamans traffic. Not only does it correspond to an organ by the same name found in animal and human bodies, but its material nature is emphasized by the use of blood in its recovery, a literal gesture missing from shamans' management of other elements, including such seemingly physical properties as blood, sweat, and grease. In a sense, the liver is midway between what we might term body and soul. Its consumption by a demon accompanies every death, no matter what other afflictions the dead person suffered. The act of a demon preying on a person's liver signifies the separation of the animated koro from its earthly guise, the lemba, soon to be a corpse. As the connection between koro and lemba, the ate assumes the properties of both.

The Scalp and Brains

Like the liver, the scalp and brains have their own distinctive predator, a cooperative trio of spirits known as the *sangia, tau sampu'u,* and *tambar,* modeled on the avenging headhunters of the Wana past. According to a classic scenario, a little yellow-haired tambar spirit spots a human being coming along the path. This spirit, quite invisible to its victim, promptly sits down and sticks out its arms and legs, whereupon the hapless human obliviously jostles it. At that provocation, the tambar shrieks that it has been assaulted by a human and cries for its kin, the tau sampu'u and the sangia, to come to its defense. These large spirits are dressed and armed like warriors. Their bodies, some say, are red on one side, green on the other—like the rainbow, which they use as their path. With their headhunting knives drawn, they descend on their victim. They hack the person's torso from the shoulder down through the chest; they rip off the scalp and crack open the skull to remove the brains; they carry off the scalp on sharp fronds of the *kanau* palm in the fashion of headhunters long ago. The tambar does its share as well: too small to inflict downward blows on the victim, it strikes upward with its knife into the victim's forehead.

A typical workover by these spirits resembles in its details a headhunter's raid, including an association with rain that falls when the sun shines. The characteristic symptoms correspond to symptoms produced by a variety of mosquito-borne viruses endemic to Central Sulawesi, including encephalitis and malaria. Just as pain in the xiphoid process is associated with the loss of the liver, so the distinctive headaches and backaches caused by these viruses are attributed to the slashing knife blows of spirit headhunters.

Indicative of the discrete nature of this condition is the fact that it has its own special healing ritual, called the *posuyu* after the resin torches (*suyu*) used to threaten the enemy spirits. A posuyu specialist I knew well claimed that she could call back a patient's tanuana only if it had been frightened by the headhunting spirits' attack; if the case were more severe and her treatment failed to work, then a shaman would have to perform either a potudu or a mabolong to recover the "scalp" and the rest of the patient's vital elements, as Apa Mene did for me in the text presented in Chapter 4.

It is my sense that the "scalp" and "brains" are treated less literally than the "liver" in Wana ritual, perhaps because, in contrast to the latter, they do not define life versus death. As illustrated by Apa Mene's words in Chapter 4, shamans chant about "the shadow of the head, taken off on a *kanau* leaf, taken off on the blade of a sword." *Bayo* is a shamanic term for "shadow" and is used to qualify lost elements of the person, such as the tanuana and koro—signifying perhaps the intangibility or special nature of the properties in which shamans deal. Although I have attempted to clarify the subtle differences between what we might term physical and metaphysical or tangible and intangible properties of the person, it is important to note that shamanic discourse groups all these qualities as essential to life and health and subject to shamans' manipulation.

CONDITIONS OF PLAUSIBILITY

In his 1937 book, *Witchcraft, Oracles, and Magic Among the Azande*, Evans-Pritchard explored the subtle interweaving of empirical and nonempirical explanations of misfortune in Azande talk. Challenging the sense conveyed by Levy-Bruhl's writings on "primitive mentality," namely that much of the world walked around in a mystical fog, oblivious to constraints of reality, Evans-Pritchard sought to demonstrate how the Azande invoked alternative logics in attributing causes to events in the world. Similarly, although here I have abstracted a series of "vital elements" from Wana talk about the etiology and treatment of illness, it is well to bear in mind that the interplay of hidden and ordinary dimensions of reality in this discourse is complex—as the following case will illustrate.

A young boy whom I will call Ede went off with a friend to play by the river. In a demonstration of agility, Ede scrambled head first down an inclined log in a clownish imitation of a monkey. He lost his balance and plummeted into the rock-strewn river below. His companion managed to pull the stunned boy out of the water, and moments later Ede, his lip split and his handsome face swollen and bloody, was brought by his father to a shaman, who treated the boy with spells. The boy was treated subsequently both by shamans at a mabolong and by his father, who performed the posuyu. This last treatment inspired great mirth. Several relatives who were present at the posuyu declared the performance inept. But what struck them as particularly ludicrous was the implication that tambar spirits and their associates might be responsible for the boy's injuries: the boy's own "foolishness," not a tambar, was at the heart of the matter, they declared. Their amusement suggests the inappropriateness of attributing visible lacerations to spirits known for invisible assaults. To treat the boy's bruised face with a posuyu performance was to treat a spirit attack with misplaced literalness.

Although it may have been inappropriate to treat actual cuts and bruises with a ritual meant for hidden wounds, attributing overt physical symptoms to hidden agents is what shamanic healing is all about. No one laughed when a shaman pronounced that Ede's mother's ghost had provoked his fall. No doubt the shaman's diagnosis was better received in part because its author was held in higher esteem than the boy's father, but its logic was deemed more reasonable as well. The diagnosis identified a hidden motivation behind an observable event. The shaman claimed that the boy took a risk and fell because his mother's ghost, lonesome for her son, encouraged him to do so in the hope he would join her as a ghost. The bruises, blood, and pain were the result of falling on the rocks, but the accident was motivated by a hidden agent. This explanation was acceptable to my companions, whereas the suggestion that spirits had beaten the boy's face to smithereens was taken as a joke. Thus attributions of events to hidden factors are subject to cultural judgments of appropriateness—sharp-tongued Wana find as much to ridicule in far-fetched diagnoses that confuse dimensions of reality as Azande found in a thief's claim that witchcraft made him steal.

From the account given so far, it should be evident that the person, in the terms of shamanic healing, is a fragile concatenation of hidden elements that are prone to disperse of their own accord or at the will of external agents. Not only is a person's integrity threatened by the centrifugal qualities of its hidden elements, but it is also subject to invasion by external hidden objects and agents—a condition that leads in turn to the dispersal of vital elements.

INVASIONS OF THE PERSON

Intrusive Objects

A *ransong* is an object placed in the body by a hostile source that results in intense localized pain. It may be any sort of material object—a piece of glass, the tooth of a comb, or a sharpened stick of bamboo, for instance, in which case a human sorcerer is likely at work, or perhaps stones, leaves, and other natural items, for which demons are typically responsible. Lumps of earth, reminiscent of graves, are characteristic missiles of ghosts. Lamoa, the punitive spirit of thunder and lightning, casts dreaded metal objects, including fishhooks, axes, and knife blades. Forest spirits called salibiwi punish boisterous or blasphemous people in their vicinity with bits of branch and sand that cause pain in the mouth, ears, eyes, and joints. And those who act disruptive in the fields at harvest time may have grains of rice fired into them by the rice spirits (*toloniu*).

A final sort of intrusive object reflects not on the malice of a hostile agent or the improper behavior of a victim, but rather on the power of two categories of people: prominent hunters and shamans. The pieces of "hoof" from a great hunter's catch and "fingernails" from a great shaman's spirit familiars sometimes lodge in the bellies of tiny children and must be removed.

A person with appropriate spells can "suck out" (*pangepe*) a ransong with no more ceremony than is required for the administering of a spell. In the context of a healing ceremony, a shaman can detect the ransong in the patient's body, then use a spell to draw it close to the surface. He may then suck it out with his mouth or draw it out into his special shaman's cloth. This is one of the actions depicted in the text of Apa Mene's treatment of the boy with the bleeding penis in Chapter 4 ("Even if layered over with bone, even if layered over with skin, it will come shaking forth on the hand of the ally").

When removing a ransong from a patient's body, a shaman may or may not produce an object visible for all to see. To do so is by no means essential for verification of therapeutic success. People are aware that sometimes shamans hide objects ahead of time, which they then pretend to extract from their patients. The issue for my associates was not the tricks or "embellishments" (*bunga bunga*), but the power of the shaman's magic.

Fates

Another serious invasion of the body involves a *tuka* or *janji*, which fates one to die at a certain time. The word *janji*, or "promise," is a borrowing from Bahasa Indonesia. The word *tuka* also refers to the rung of a ladder, for in other contexts ladders and steps paced on the ground are associated with the lifespan. Some people asserted a difference between *tuka* and *janji*, others claimed they were identical; as with names for the soul, the two terms may well represent a proliferation of names for a single notion, resulting from the performative challenges of healing rituals.

A shaman at a mabolong may use his shaman's cloth (*papolonsu*) to remove a "fate" from the throat of a patient where it lodges (it was this procedure, modified for a potudu performance, that Apa Mene used on the young boy in Chapter 4). He then dramatically disposes of it: admonishing everyone in the room to stay seated (lest they be struck by the flying fate), he begins to dance; gripping one end of the papolonsu, he snaps the cloth and fires off its contents. A typical destination—the one to which Apa Mene sent the boy's fate—is "a rock split in two equal halves" or "a tree split and dried." In fact, I was told, this "expression is deceptive." Because a fate means that someone must die, what the shaman actually attempts to do is insure that the victim will not be his patient. The fate he casts off will thus lodge in someone else. It follows that illness is sometimes attributed to a fate cast by a shaman somewhere else. One night in a house where I was staying, a young child awoke with night terrors. A shaman immediately set about to perform a potudu and discovered that the child had been struck by a fate thrown by someone performing audibly at a mabolong in a settlement nearby. In sending the fate on its way, the shaman I witnessed sang, "Oh, go back, turn back, and head for the place of the drum"—that is, return to the mabolong from which it had been sent.

The negotiation of people's fate takes place at a higher level as well, as we shall see in Part Three when shamans go to supplicate the Owner on behalf of their patients. What is interesting about the notion of tuka or janji is the way in which an abstract concept is concretized for shamanic manipulation. An impending death is represented as something that attaches itself to the body and may, with proper knowledge, be removed. In a similar way, shamans may attempt to remove other sorts of unfortunate predispositions. For example, shortly after one acquaintance of mine—a young man twice widowed—took a third wife, a shaman altered the "palm lines" of the couple to insure that the pattern would not continue.

Flying Fetuses

Intrusions into the body are not restricted to inanimate objects. Knowledgeable shamans are thought capable of removing a fetus from one woman's womb and placing it in another's—a procedure that can be carried out without the women involved knowing. Shamans' claims to have moved children around in utero are frequently made post facto. For example, a shaman may let it be known that he alone realized that a woman was pregnant when she should not have been, perhaps because she was unmarried or had conceived the child incestuously. Discreetly he moves the fetus to the womb of a properly married woman who then undergoes a normal pregnancy and delivers the child. The child, however, is still regarded as the progeny of the couple who conceived it. I know of one marriage that some people regarded as highly incestuous because a shaman asserted that one partner was in fact the child of the other partner's close relations. Sometimes women who become pregnant again almost immediately after giving birth claim that the new fetus must be a "hurled child" (*ana waro*).

Changeling Spirits

People may also be entered by spirits, as the case of the human vampire discussed in Chapter 5 chillingly demonstrates. The other major form of spirit possession involves changeling spirits (*tau tolo*). Motivated, some say, by a desire to enter the heaven where humans go, tau tolo seek to trade places with human souls. A baby who cries constantly, eats ravenously, and fails to grow is often regarded as the victim of a tau tolo. A shaman then endeavors to rid the child of the intruding spirit and return the child's own soul to its body.

SUMMARY

This chapter has catalogued the assemblage of hidden components that make up the person, as well as a series of intrusive elements that may threaten the integrity of that being. For readers familiar with anthropological interests in personhood, this itemization may seem a trifle odd. The inventory I have presented here falls short as a reckoning of the "symbolic means by which to sort people out from one another and form an idea of what it is to be a person" (Geertz 1983, 65). Instead, it is part of the specialized discourse of shamanic healing, which ignores the frameworks through which people locate and conduct themselves in social intercourse. The shamanic construction of personhood is largely irrelevant in ordinary life; it comes into play only when health and life are threatened. Precisely because of its restricted applicability, however, it offers telling insights into the Wana social order and worldview.

The person, like the cosmos, possesses hidden as well as accessible dimensions. What is more, the hidden aspects of the person interact with the hidden aspects of the world beyond the person. Shamans alone can mediate that interaction. Because the well-being of a person is dependent on the behavior of others, both spirits and humans through their actions can intentionally or unintentionally disrupt one's state of health. A person's well-being rests on a fragile assemblage of hidden elements: when these elements are concentrated in their proper places, the person thrives; when they are dispersed, the person grows weak and sick. In this sense the person and the polity are homologous. Like a person, the Wana homeland prospered when "knowledge," "power," and "wealth" were concentrated at their source, but when these elements departed for the "end of the earth," this prosperity declined. Only when these elements are reassembled at their origin will the homeland recover, like a patient whose soul parts have been restored. This homology of person and polity underwrites shamans' claims to be sustainers of order for both individuals and communities—a point that I will develop further later on.

Although health and life depend on the concentration of vital elements of being, there appears to be nothing that holds a person together from within. Rather, cohesion is dependent on powers external to the person (a point that holds for Wana communities as well). A person cannot monitor, let alone control, his or her own hidden elements of being. Indeed, the notion that people lack control over their own well-being is underscored by the very location of the two most important vital elements, the soul and the dream agent, one residing in the upper back, the other in the crown of the head. In contrast to parts of the body that are active and expressive, such as the face and the hands, these regions are passive and uncommunicative (see Helman 1978, 115); and in contrast to regions of the body that can be directly seen and protected, such as the chest or the navel (see Errington 1983, 547–48), they cannot be observed or easily guarded by their owner. Rather than managing these elements on one's own, a person must submit to the care of a specialist who can know more about one's ultimate state of being than one can know oneself. (Even a shaman must call on another shaman to monitor his own state of health and well-being.) In this way, dependence on shamanic mediation is built into the very constitution of the person.

7

Power and Therapy

> In general, it is clear that medical rites are eminently sugges-
> tive, not only as far as the patient is concerned. . . but also for
> the other participants who feel the strain and for whom the
> magician's gestures, sometimes his trances, provide a fascina-
> tion which moves them to the core of their beings.
>
> Mauss, *A General Theory of Magic*

Returning now to the three transcripts of shamanic healing presented
in Chapter 4, we can begin to follow their cultural logic. In the first,
the shaman recovers the lost soul parts of his patient. In the second, a
fate is removed from the patient and an intrusive object cast out. And
in the third, the shaman recovers the scalp as well as the soul parts that
fled when the patient was attacked by headhunting spirits.

As noted in Chapter 4, the "summoning" that opens a shaman's
performance does not end when the shaman turns to treating patients.
The shaman continues to call his spirits, offering them both blandish-
ments ("Oh, effective you are, my spirit familiar") and chastisements
("Hey, don't leave the task to others"). New spirits keep arriving to
be enlisted in the effort to treat the patient.

The shaman underscores the power he holds ("even if it's in yet
another place, I can retrieve it again") but at the same time attributes it
wholly to his spirits ("It is not my breath that blows, it is the breath of
the spirit ally that blows"). In the partnership between spirits and shaman, the spirits lead the way—*their* hands are under the shaman's,
guiding them along. One shaman stated that performers were "fool-
ing" when they touched their patients; after all, he indicated, it is the
spirit familiars who do the work.

PROCEDURES OF SHAMANIC
TREATMENT

As I explained earlier, the texts presented here come from potudu
performances. At a potudu, there is no drum or gongs. The shaman

sits by his patient's side with his eyes closed and sings. As he sings he uses "the eyes of his spirit familiars" to see hidden aspects of the world. With his shaman's cloth, he removes hidden objects from the patient's body and flings them away. He then reaches out and snatches with his cloth hidden elements of being that he and his spirit allies have found. Once he has grasped an element, he places the cloth at the appropriate part of the patient's body (the crown of the head for the tanuana, the upper back for the various koro, the feet and hands for the respective tolowu, the top of head for the "scalp") and blows through the cloth to return the item to its proper place in the patient's constitution (hence the references to "blowing" in the texts). Throughout, he continues to sing the names of his spirit assistants, praising their skill and diligence and urging them not to lag in their efforts. He may also address the elements he is replacing ("don't just pass by, don't just go by") and urge them to stay put instead of flying away again. The shaman's song and gestures keep the audience apprised of what is transpiring in his efforts to reconstitute the patient's being.

At a mabolong, the shaman's gestures are more dramatic. Instead of remaining seated next to his patient while his spirits move about performing the requisite tasks, the shaman, empowered by his spirits, works with them. If recovering hidden elements of being is in order (as it usually is), the shaman will rise to face the drum and gongs. At this point, members of the audience insure that the players of the drum and gongs are capable adolescents or adults, not the small children who swarm to play the instruments when their elders' interest lags. Should a drum or gong player make an error during a shaman's dance, the shaman may trip or fall on his journey, causing his own soul parts to flee. For this reason a dancing shaman is given a wide berth by others in the room, and he is watched for any signs of loss of control or balance. If there is a suspicion of trouble, several strong men will stand by him ready to catch, hold, or restrain him.

Gripping his shaman's cloth in front of him, the shaman, eyes shut, bounces up and down on his journey in search of his patient's soul parts. As he travels, he "sees" spirits and places through the agency of his spirit familiars. Some of the places he visits can be identified as a familiar part of the everyday landscape; others are spirit realms that people ordinarily cannot see. The shaman whispers into his cloth the secret name for the missing element he is seeking along with the name of his patient. When the "eyes of his spirit familiars" spot this missing part, the shaman lunges forward to catch it in his cloth (Fig. 22). Sometimes requiring the support of other men in the room, he lowers himself to his knees, opens his eyes, and approaches his patient with whatever it was he retrieved on his journey. He then restores the hidden element to its proper place in the patient's body, just as in a potudu performance (Figs. 23, 24). Occasionally a shaman may "see" as he dances an escaped or stolen element of someone other than the immediate patient, in which case he may recover it also and return it to its unsuspecting owner.

When casting out an intrusive object from a patient's body, the shaman may either suck out the offending entity or have his spirit familiars draw it forth into his shaman's cloth. Thanks to the power of his spirit familiars, he can draw forth even an object that is lodged deep within the patient ("even if it is layered over with bone, even if it is layered over with skin"). He then instructs his familiars to tend to any "leftover" (*yabinya*) that remains. Once he has caught the object in his cloth, the shaman stands to "cast it off" (*waro*). With his eyes closed, he faces the drum and gongs and begins to dance. When ready, he winds up and whips his cloth forward to fire the unwanted item between the gongs and over the heads of the drummers, watching its flight with the "eyes of his spirit familiars." Occasionally he will see that the object has returned, in which case he must retrieve it and cast it off again. If the intrusive object was sent by a human sorcerer, the shaman may send it back to strike its owner. If the object is a fate, he may instruct everyone in the room to stay seated lest it enter any of them by accident.

One of my neighbors told of a time her brother-in-law and a fellow shaman arrived at her house to announce that they must perform a mabolong for her that evening. She learned they had performed together the previous evening and had cast out a fate from a patient, which they saw cross the river and strike her. Even though she felt in the best of health, they knew better. Shamans can also create quite an uproar among women at a mabolong by threatening to throw a fetus, which could land in one of their wombs and result in an unwanted pregnancy.

THE LOGIC OF SHAMANIC TREATMENT

The shaman's onstage efforts on behalf of patients must be considered in relation to his offstage adventures with spirits. Off stage, an experienced shaman is expected to maintain private relations with his spirit familiars; on stage, he engages those spirits publicly in the ritual context. Spirits—denizens of distant haunts—are exogenous to the human community. In ritual, the shaman is able to concentrate their powers within the community and around himself: as he outwardly enacts his private relationship with spirit familiars, inwardly he possesses the ability to see and to manipulate hidden dimensions of existence. In determining the state of his patients' constitutions, he demonstrates access to and control over aspects of their persons that the patients themselves cannot perceive or control. Although these aspects are by definition inherently centrifugal, nevertheless health and well-being require that they be integrated in the person. Given their tendency to roam and their owner's lack of control over them, shamanic intervention offers the necessary counterforce to insure continuation of life.

To accomplish this intervention, the shaman and his spirit familiars travel to distant realms in pursuit of lost aspects of a patient's being. In doing so they recapitulate not only the flight of the patient's missing elements but also the shaman's own quests beyond the community in search of spirit powers. The centrifugality of the patient's vital elements is matched and conquered by the centrifugal path of the shaman and his familiars. Because of the powers he has concentrated about himself—powers derived from the wild—the shaman is able to overcome both his own and his patient's flight and to return himself, his spirit familiars, and the patient's vital parts to the human domain.

THERAPEUTIC EFFICACY

Once the domain of anthropologists and historians of religion, shamanism has in recent years entered the purview of medical anthropology, with considerable attention having been devoted to the therapeutic potential of non-Western healing techniques in general and symbolic healing in particular.[1] Hence, my decision to write a book about a major shamanic ritual that centers on cultural and political rather than medical aspects of meaning and performance requires comment. A general study of how Wana manage illness could not zero in on the mabolong alone but would have to cover a range of other ritual and nonritual contexts in which healing techniques are employed. Although the mabolong is the most popular of healing events, its popularity comes from the fact that it involves much more than healing. Indeed, all but one of the therapeutic measures and conditions that appear in the mabolong appear in other healing contexts as well. The one exception is the use of drum, gongs, and dance, which, while certainly aiding shamans in achieving altered states of awareness, may have therapeutic consequences as well.

Whatever therapeutic potential resides in the conditions of performance, in cultural terms therapeutic efficacy is strictly a function of the potency of a shaman's spells and spirits. A shaman's words and actions are not in themselves considered efficacious—Wana dismiss these as *bunga bunga*, "embellishments." Paradoxically, of course, only this ornamentation, and not a shaman's hidden dealings with spirits, is accessible to patients and audience.

The role of a patient at a mabolong is passive and usually minor. In fact, the patient need not even be conscious or present for treatment to occur; a shaman may retrieve hidden elements for someone not actually in attendance at the ritual and store them in a surrogate vessel, such as a bottle or another person. For cases in which a person would be hostile to treatment (a suspected human vampire, for instance), a shaman may treat a housepost in the patient's stead. Attacks of sorcery may be waged in the mabolong, but their intended victims are far away and unaware.

Even when the patient is present, no involvement in the proceedings is required. The patient is expected neither to engage in dialogue with the shaman (in contrast to the Kelantanese *main peteri* [Kessler 1977]), nor to show signs of physical or psychic transformation in the course of the evening (as in the case of Sinhalese exorcisms and Ethiopian *zar* cults). Any potential for dynamic engagement of shaman and patient is suppressed in the mabolong in favor of the shaman's heroic initiatives.

Much of the research on symbolic healing has stressed the power of words on the patient's consciousness and unconsciousness. Although the shamans' songs presented in Chapter 4 would certainly seem to be reassuring to a patient, it should be remembered that those songs come from potudu, not mabolong. In the mabolong, the patient often will not hear much if any of such words, either because the drum and gongs drown them out or because the shaman relies in his performance more on physical enactments than on verbal accounts of his efforts on the patient's behalf. In contrast to the Kuna patients who often cannot understand the shamans' songs to which Lévi-Strauss attributed abreactive potential (Sherzer 1983), when Wana patients fail to catch their shamans' verbal account of what is being done it is not because shamanic speech is unintelligible, but because it is inaudible. But like Kuna patients, Wana patients (beyond early childhood) already know and understand shamanic procedures and their underlying assumptions. Therefore, what a shaman is actually doing may be less important for them than the mere fact that he is doing it.

Prince (1982), Scheff (1977, 1979), and Schieffelin (1985), among others, have argued that too much emphasis has been placed on cognitive, especially verbal, aspects of healing (such as the efficacy of symbolic texts on patients' conscious or unconscious state), and not enough on noncognitive dimensions of performance. If it is granted that the music and dance of the mabolong may heighten its overall effect, it should be recognized that this would occur not only for patients but for everyone in the room (see Chapter 5, note 2). In calculating the performative effect of the mabolong, one is dealing not simply with a healer-patient dyad, but with several shamans, a number of patients, and an audience as well. This point illuminates the significance of the homology of person and polity discussed in the last chapter. Because persons and polity are culturally constituted in the same way, because both possess hidden dimensions that require mediation by people with access to exogenous powers, and because both can suffer the loss of their vital elements, shamans' performances frequently apply to much more than a particular patient's condition. Thus the audience—be they patients, patients' close kin, or members of the community at large—can be drawn into the drama of a shaman's performance because it opens up to a wide range of existential concerns.[2] Parts Three and Four will examine how the mabolong engages audiences, transforms them into communities, and establishes shamans as their preservers and defenders.

PHOTOGRAPHS

Photography by
Effort Atkinson and Jane Atkinson

1. Members of a farming community build their houses in conjoining swidden fields.

2. Neighboring houses.

3. Indo Lina

4.   Two friends relax during the heat of the day. The bottle in the foreground is tied to the base of a basketry funnel containing fermenting rice mash.

5. A transcribing session

6. A *toru* is a broad-brimmed hat that protects the wearer from both sun and rain. An essential accoutrement for parents of young children, it is a symbol of nurturance and parental protection.

7. Indo Ngonga wears a *toru* and holds a betel box as she carries an infant for its first descent to the ground.

8. Apa Iki, the husband of Indo Ngonga and leader of a farming settlement, performs a ritual of thanksgiving at harvesttime for the benefit of his community.

9. The mabolong ritual is named after the two-skinned drum (*bolong*) that along with two bronze gongs accompanies shamans as they dance.

10. The drum and gongs are a favorite spot for children to congregate at a mabolong.

11. The *lango* holds refreshments—including betel fixings, tobacco, rice beer, and basil—for shamans and their spirit familiars.

12.   Apa Weri seats himself by the *lango*, takes up a sprig of basil, and begins
to summon his spirit familiars.

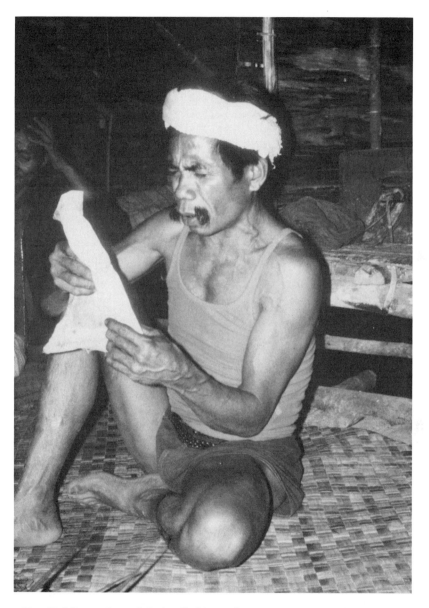

13.   Holding a piece of cloth called a *papolonsu*, Apa Mene invokes his spirit familiars.

14. A shaman faces the drum and gongs as he dances (*motaro*).

15. Women's style of dancing, known as "something beautiful" (*salonde*), is aesthetically prized.

16. One evening as she danced, a young girl saw the apparition of her dead mother.

17.   Her aunt steadied her.

18. She sat, head covered, before coming around.

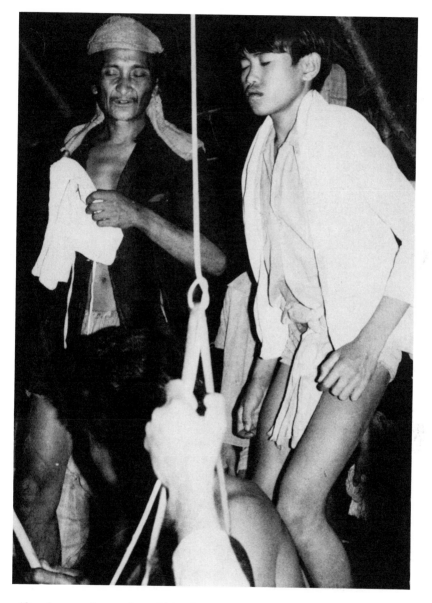

19. A young boy and would-be shaman accompanies his uncle, Apa Eri, an eminent shaman, as he dances.

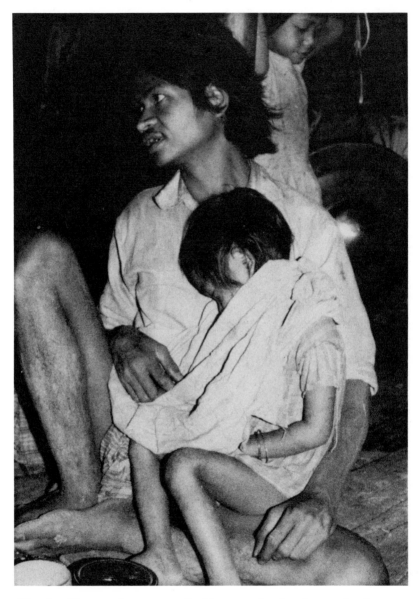

20. Apa Linus awaits treatment for his young daughter by a senior shaman.

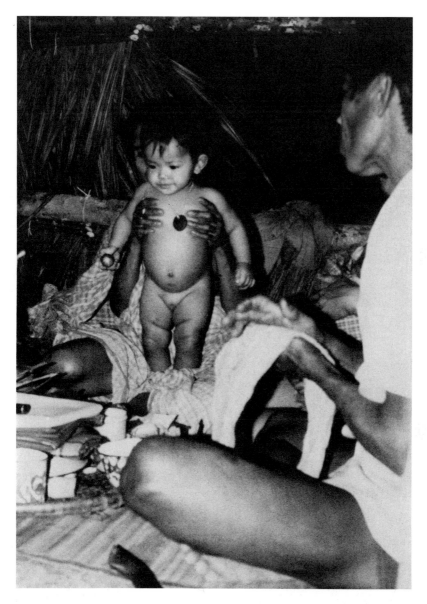

21. Young children are a principal focus of shamanic treatment.

22.   Apa Weri lunges to capture a patient's missing soul part.

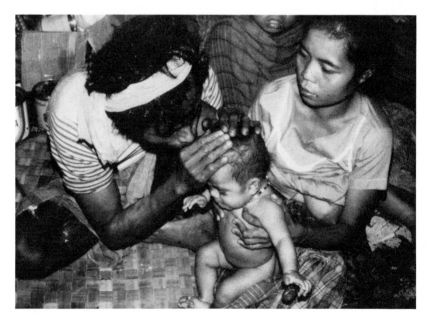

23.   The dream agent (*tanuana*) is restored to the top of a patient's head.

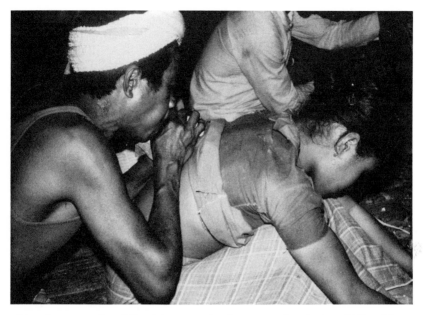

24.   A recovered soul (*koro*) is returned to its proper place in the middle of the back.

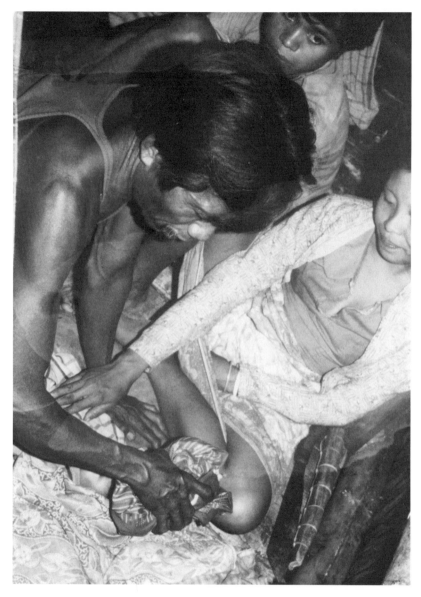

25. Apa Mene wraps a betel offering to carry to the Owner on behalf of a patient.

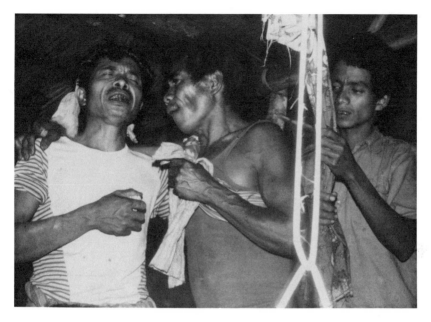

26. Two shamans engage in dialogue, as Apa ngGoru stands by to overhear their desires and to steady them in case they fall. One reason for special caution is the betel offering, representing the life of a patient, which Apa Mene (center) carries in a sarong tied to his torso.

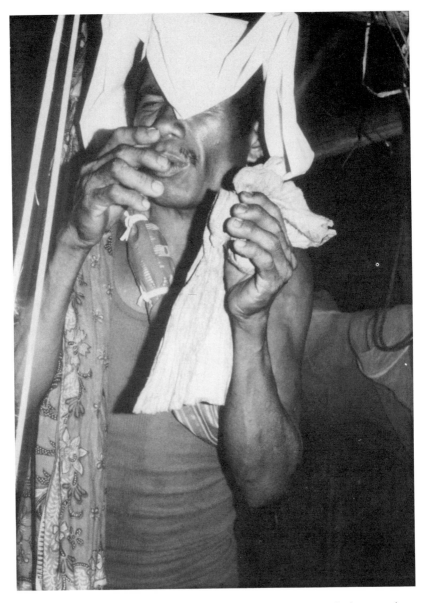

27.   With a betel offering tied to his torso and a gift of white cloth protecting his head, Apa Mene addresses the Owner.

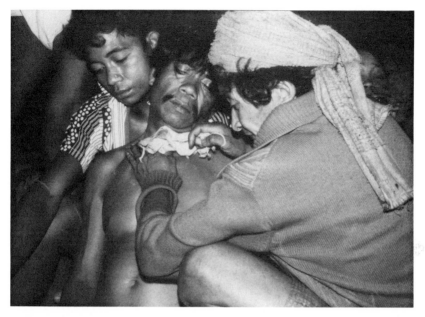

28. A shaman who experiences "small feelings" may fall unconscious and require treatment by another shaman.

29.   Repayment of a vow to the Owner may include a performance of ritual dueling—a legacy from a war-torn past—as well as a feast. As a gesture of gratitude and celebration, relatives of recovered patients pour rice beer down the throats of prominent shamans such as Apa Eri and Apa nTode, pictured here.

30. In contrast to stylized dueling in some other parts of Island Southeast Asia, Wana combatants carry a shield but no weapon. They feint but do not fight.

PART THREE

8

Ascents to the Sky

For Mircea Eliade, the eminent religious historian, shamanism is defined by an ecstatic experience of a distinctive kind: a spirit journey whereby the soul takes leave of its owner's body and travels up to the sky or down to the underworld. Such travel has a theological raison d'être. A shaman's journey either upward or downward is predicated, in Eliade's view, on a belief in "Supreme Beings." In reconstructing the history of shamanism in North and Central Asia, Eliade ([1951] 1964, 505) claimed that a celestial Supreme Being, once important throughout the area, was eclipsed in time by a host of lesser beings, "the gods of storm and fertility, demiurges, the souls of the dead, the Great Goddesses." Even when a high god is relegated to the status of a *deus otiosus*, however, the deity's former centrality can still be detected in the shaman's journey.

In Part Three I shall examine Wana shamans' ascent to the top of the sky. According to Eliade, this journey should be the very essence of Wana shamanism. Yet it is not an essential element of a mabolong performance. Indeed, a case could be made that its use in the mabolong is a recent development or emphasis. The purpose of the shaman's travel is to appeal to Pue, the "Lord" or "Owner," to spare the life of a patient.[1] Although Pue closely resembles the Supreme Being Eliade postulates for early Siberian shamanism, there is reason to think that Pue has emerged only in the last few decades as a focus of both Wana shamanic practice and general cultural concern.

My analysis of this segment of the mabolong will address issues of ritual and religious change in the Wana region. Given the paucity of historical documentation, more questions will be raised than answered; but in light of what documentation there is, it would be folly to attempt an analysis of the ritual without recognizing historical dynamics at work. This section will also lay the groundwork for my claim that the mabolong not only expresses a cosmology but constitutes a polity as well. Drawing on theories of exchange and sacrifice, I

159

shall consider how a shaman's negotiations with the Owner bear on his relations with his own community.

TRAVELS UPWARD

First, the journey itself. The episode I am going to examine can be phrased in a number of ways. The shaman is said "to go to the Owner" (*yau ri pue*), "to climb upward" (*mandake*), "to carry a betel offering" (*keni kapongo*), "to supplicate" (*manyomba*), to make or to fulfill a "vow" (*nia, pantoo*). The aptness of these phrases will be brought out in what follows.

In contrast to the staples of a mabolong performance—summoning spirit familiars and treating patients as described in Parts One and Two—a journey to the Owner is an option undertaken only when a shaman deems all other treatments insufficient unless a higher power is consulted. A shaman's determination in this matter is based not on the patient's outward appearance but rather on the patient's hidden condition as ascertained by a shaman and his familiars. A person who appears to be in the best of health and one who is obviously near death may each possess a "fate" (*tuka, janji*) to die in the near future; both may be equally in need of a reprieve from Pue, who dwells above at the "peak of the sky."

To make an appeal to Pue, a shaman carries a betel offering on the patient's behalf. Called a "complete betel offering" (*kapongo gana*), this prestation consists of either three, six, or seven slices of areca nut, a matching number of piper leaves, a tiny packet of lime, and some tobacco. The number of slices of areca nut that are carried depends on the age of the patient. Because the number seven is associated with a full life span, to use seven slices for a tiny child may imply that the child is closer to completing a full life than is in fact the case. Hence some people indicated that a smaller number of slices is advisable for a little child.

A shaman and the patient's family prepare the betel offering, wrap it in a corn husk, and place it in a sarong (Fig. 25). The offering is then tied to the shaman's back in the manner of a baby carried on its parent's back. The association of the shaman with a nurturing parent and of the patient with a tiny child is explicit.

The shaman now summons his spirit familiars to accompany him on his journey upward to the Owner's place. As he does so, others check to see that experienced players are stationed at the drum and gongs. Because he is carrying what is in essence the patient's life on a long and perilous journey, the quality of his accompaniment is of special concern. For the same reason, strong men may be called on to stand near and prevent him from falling as he dances by treacherous points on the journey, such as the "whirlwind" (*lambuwu*) that may spin him about (Fig. 26).

The shaman now switches his song from the standard style used in the mabolong to the style used for journeys of supplication to Pue in an esoteric ritual called the molawo. He may also at this point summon along with his personal retinue of spirit familiars other companions such as Woti ngKila, Balo Ransa, and Sori Wunga—traditional walia or pelogot who are said to have been helping Wana shamans for generations—whose epithets are similarly associated with the molawo ritual (about which more in a moment).

The destination of the shaman and his companions is the Opo Bira Lima. An *opo* is a locality associated with an authority; before the Dutch attempted to organize them into villages in the early decades of this century, at least some Wana were associated with the locality of one or another *makole*, a representative of a coastal raja (see Part Five). As for *bira*, although my companions could not gloss it, among the Pamona speakers to the east the term means "side." Opo Bira Lima may thus mean "the Place of the Five Sides," but as far as those I asked were concerned, the phrase is simply a standard designation for the Owner's place.[2]

The Owner's place is located at the "peak of the sky."[3] This site may be reached in a variety of ways. A trip to the Owner requires a *jaya*, a word that carries the double sense of a path and a means of conveyance. Were one performing a molawo ritual instead of a mabolong, the journey would be long and slow. Likewise, the molawo chant is lengthy and explicit. To give the reader a sense of shamanic travel as experienced on a "slow boat to heaven," I shall present a synopsis of a molawo journey before presenting the text of a mabolong journey, which is condensed and cryptic in the extreme. I shall also explain how the mabolong episode derived from the molawo ritual. Prior acquaintance with the molawo plot will, I hope, make the mabolong text easier to follow.

THE MOLAWO:
A SLOW TRIP TO THE SKY

The molawo performance I summarize here was performed by an old, blind shaman, Apa nSempa, on behalf of two women and their children who were suffering fatigue—and on my behalf as well, for he knew I wanted to hear this rarely performed chant. Ideally I would present the text and verbatim translation of a molawo text, but given that Apa nSempa's performance (the shorter of the two I transcribed) is some sixty-five hundred words, a synopsis plus a snippet of text must suffice.[4]

As the chant begins, several spirit familiars assemble their retinues at the house of Indo Tina, the spirit owner (*pue*) of wild pigs. (Apa nSempa happened to have been a great hunter in his younger days. His choice of venue alludes to his secret knowledge associated with the hunt.) The spirit familiars fetch betel to chew and strong vines with which to construct a vehicle for their voyage. This task provides an occasion for divination. If the areca nuts fall "badly," the soul parts of the patients will not be recovered successfully; if they fall well, the patients will be restored to health. As it happens, the areca nuts fall well—not onto the ground, but into the hair knots and sarong folds of the female spirits and onto the knife and spear points of the male spirits. Then the areca palm and vines are healed over as though they had never been cut—a sign that the soul parts of the patients, too, will be returned as new.

Taking auspices at the start of a journey was standard practice for Wana war parties in the last century. Much as warriors went forth, according to cultural logic, to insure the prosperity of their communities, the contingent of spirit familiars goes upward to insure the well-being of the patients. The people of Poso, the western neighbors of the Wana, explicitly compared the travels of male headhunters in this world to the skyward journeys of female shamans who performed a ritual called *polawo*, which closely resembles the molawo chant (Adriani 1932). Another molawo performer of my acquaintance has his spirit familiars use a method of divination that was employed by headhunters of old.

Returning to the house of Indo Tina, the spirits perform a counting ritual to insure long life and health for all. They then set about constructing the vessel in which to travel. They use the vines they have collected to fasten boards together and then test the vehicle to make sure it does not creak. (The word *po'us*, "to bind together," applies to the construction of material objects ranging from ladles to houses. It figures as well both in shamans' talk about "fastening together vehicles" [*po'us jaya*] and in legal talk about marriage payments that "bind" a couple's union.) They pause to chew betel before embarking. An excerpt from this episode will give a sense of the elegant imagery and exacting detail of a molawo chant:

natotele wo'u mpongulu	Again the leader speaks,
sidomu nggita joa	let us assemble our followers.
ane pantamo sidomu	If everyone has assembled,
raantimo luya segi	take the betel here,
rasayo ri rodo lima	slice it in the palm of the hand.
mpela patolepe yau luya	Peel the areca fruit from its skin.
kusali sonda randa	I bring it within [?],
kusalo luya ri pongana	I place the betel in the mouth.
ane nja'u ri pongana	If it's there in the mouth,
ralodu silele yau luya	bend and follow out the betel.
kusalo wo'u longkindi woto ngkidoya	Now I place piper leaf from the side of a tree
nja'u dawo luya ri pongana	there on top of the areca nut in the mouth.
ralodu nsindarandara	Bend together.
natampe wo'u tiyula	Added now is the lime,
ewa gawu limu lanto	like a low-lying, foggy mist.
gawu tiyula ratade ri pongana	A fog of lime is tossed in the mouth.

These lines depict in elaborate detail the common and habitual act of chewing a betel quid, which comprises a slice of areca nut, a shred of piper leaf, and a pinch of lime. It likens the chewing of betel to the up-and-down dance of the familiars as they "bend their knees" (*lodu*) to propel their vessel—hence the admonition to "bend together." The leader's words synchronize the crew's efforts as they chew and as they dance. Many of the words in this passage are either distinctive to shamanic chants (such as *nggita* for *kita* ["we"], *segi* for *si'i* ["here"], *dawo* for *wawo* ["on top of"]) or are used in special metaphor—for example, *rodo lima*, in which the word for "sedentary," "at rest," is combined with the word for "five" to mean the palm of the hand, juxtaposed to five mobile fingers. (The usual term for the palm of the hand is *dada mpale*.)

To return to the general outlines of the plot, the spirits, now refreshed, mount their vehicle and bounce up and down to propel themselves upward through the air. People liken their bouncing to that of a shaman as he dances, as well as to babies who are bounced up and down in suspended cloth cradles.

The initial progress is duly calculated as the vessel mounts to the house porch, then the tobacco racks, then the chicken's roost, then the tops of a series of increasingly taller trees. It finally passes through several layers of clouds. The shaman depicts the vessel as it sails through the air with flags flying, musical instruments ringing out, birds perched on its railings, and peopled by spirits with straight bangs and arched backs. The spirit leaders urge their crew on, telling them not to be lax or to lag as they rock their vessel ever upward. The inexperienced are counseled not to look down lest they become dizzy and fall out. One garrulous spirit on this trip is repeatedly admonished to stop talking and to devote his strength to bouncing the vessel upward.

The song recounts sights along the way, such as the boundary between light and dark, the rays of the sun, and the "fork of eight roads" (*panga njaya wayu*), which is on the path to heaven (*saruga*). At last the spirits dock at a lookout point known as *pangonda nsala* and survey the realms. Their leader identifies the locales and their inhabitants for them:

> Listen, listen as I talk. Listen as I talk, you followers, every follower.
> Listen as I tell you.
> Look, look over there at the distant lands.
> There are the Ones of the Striped Reed.
> There are the Ones of the Headscarf's Hurling.
> There are the Ones of the Areca Shoots.
> There are the Ones of the Red Clouds.
> There are the Ones of the Land of the Dead.
> There are the Ones of the Summoning Drum.
> There are the Ones of the Drum of One Song.
> There are the Ones of the Land of the Dead, the place of the
>   stillborn children.

The residents of the last-named land, startled by the spirit's vessel, part the thatch of their houses to look up at the arrivals. At first they think that "perhaps the sky is falling, perhaps the land is collapsing." But then they see the expedition. Says one tiny soul to another, "Take a look for me. Perhaps my mother has come. Perhaps my father has

come." Such poignant yearning can bring a performing shaman, as
well as his audience, to tears.

These realms hold bittersweet associations for Wana audiences. The
imagined beauty of these haunts and their distance from earthly
misery have great appeal, but these are also places to which people's
souls flee. Should a person's soul parts grow too happy in these
hidden realms, their owner may be lost to the caring friends and family
of this world.

Shamans play on themes of separation and loss. For example, in
one episode, reminiscent of the myth of Demeter and Persephone, a
performer wept as he sang of watching a mother and child picking the
sour fruit of a *katimba* tree on the path to Saruga. A soul that eats the
fruit of this tree can no longer be restored to its owner's body. In the
shaman's vision, the mother was peeling fruit for the child; if the child
were to taste the fruit, some living child would die. The performer
declined to identify the people in his vision but assured the audience
that the child was not of their own community.

From the lookout point, the spirits resume their journey upward to
the place of Pue to inquire about the fate of several patients. They
converse about propelling their vessel, the sights they see, and their
efforts to locate lost soul parts and to drive off dangerous elements
from their patients' bodies. At last they arrive at the Owner's house
and convene on the "wrestling ground" (*tompo mpogula*, a feature of
dwellings mentioned in molawo and katuntu, epics of the prior
magical age). The point of their visit is to ask who is responsible for
the patients' illnesses. Pue may deny responsibility and direct them to
another spirit realm—for example, the place where the spirits who
punish bad marriages live. Alternatively, Pue may claim responsibility, in which case the shaman's contingent must negotiate for the
patients' lives (as in the mabolong text that follows).

In Apa nSempa's molawo performance, the spirit familiars inquire
about their patients, two women and their children. Their poor health
was thought to be due to the fact that the women's menstrual cloths,
hung out to dry, had been blown away by the wind. As the substance
from which human life is created, menstrual blood must not be
burned. Had the lost rags been consumed by fire—say, in the burning
of a new swidden—they might be the "source" of their owner's sickness. Pue informs the familiars that the women's skirts were not
improperly destroyed, hence the women and their children are not

in peril. The shaman advises the use of a special spell to ward off any dangerous effects from the loss. Once they have received clarification from Pue, the familiars begin their return trip. This stop at the Owner's was quite brief. Had it been necessary to plead for the patient's life, it would have been considerably longer.

From the Owner's place, the familiars now stop at the "summoning drum" (*ganda mokio*). They beat the drum to attract the spirit inhabitants of the various realms. Along with the spirits come the souls of sick people to join what promises to be a festive occasion. The spirit familiars seek out the wandering souls of their patients amid the throng and thereby retrieve them for their owners.

One old woman described to me how her own soul was retrieved at this stop in another performance. The spirit familiars detected the footprints of her "first soul" (*koro samba'a*) traveling back and forth between the place of the rise spirit and the place of desires. They beat the summoning drum to lure her soul. When all the spirits had gathered to dance to the rhythm of the drum, the familiars spotted her dream agent (*tanuana*). "Wild" at first, it eluded them. But they encouraged it to dance and to show off its skill. (The woman herself is an admired dancer.) Lavished with praise by the spirit familiars, the dream agent grew tame and allowed the spirit familiars to carry it back to its owner. The shaman diagnosed that the woman was pining and sick because, despite her diligence, her rice crop had failed again, whereas her neighbors' had thrived.

In Apa nSempa's chant, the spirit familiars now set off from the summoning drum on their descent. They pass the earlier sites they saw, making a final stop at the land of the ghosts (*luo langgiwo*) to determine if the dead are causing any trouble for their patients. The ghosts admit that they have done so, but only because they take orders from those more powerful than themselves.

At last the spirit familiars arrive back at Indo Tina's house, where they hang up the clothes they have worn on the journey. Then they blow the soul parts they have rescued back into their patients and thus restore their patients to their former state of health.

Several contrasts to the mabolong episode I describe next are worth mentioning here. One striking difference is that a molawo performer recounts his journey in song, whereas the mabolong performer enacts his in dance. Moreover, the molawo performer does not figure as a protagonist in his own recitation; instead, the protagonists are the familiars who lead their followers on the expedition, and at the end it is they, not the shaman, who return the lost soul parts to the patients. By contrast, the mabolong performer is more central to the adventure. As for comparing the "ecstatic experience" of the two kinds of performance, opinion varied. Some individuals told me that the molawo was simply a litany and required no shamanic prowess. Others assured me that performance of the molawo yielded a clearer view of hidden worlds than did the mabolong.[5] Finally, the molawo journey is not part of a larger ritual, but constitutes the ritual in its entirety; the trip, from start to finish, is expected to last all night. By contrast, because a mabolong performer takes time out from his other ritual activities to make the trip, it is generally completed in an hour or so.

A JOURNEY TO THE OWNER, MABOLONG-STYLE

With a sense of the molawo journey, let us now turn to the mabolong performer as he undertakes his ascent. In the following text, the shaman Apa Mene carries a betel offering to the Owner on behalf of a pregnant woman:

kajaa yau towolu	The bells jangle forth.
karengge yau,	Jingling they go,
karengge kajaa yau	jingling jangling they go,
karengge kajaa ma'i	jingling jangling they come.
i sala layo layoda	Here's the path of Layo Layoda,
i sala insada sanggona	here's the path of Sada Sanggona,
sala i mantopi wunga	here's the path of Mantopi Wunga [traditional epithets of spirit familiars associated with the molawo].
nto'u naka ende ende	Going upward, dancing, dancing.
nto'u naka juyu juyu	Going upward, together, together.
nto'u opo bira lima	Going up to the Opo Bira Lima,
nto'u opo wai yowe	going up to the Place that Gives Breath.
to liu luo langgiwo	Past the place of the ghosts—
koro doe madondong	how happy, joyful indeed,
koro masanang	how content are
komi langgiwo to ele	you ghosts of that place.
taaware nu pangansani	There is not yet knowledge,

taaware nu papoiwa	there is not yet speech.
suola taawa mananya	Familiar not yet experienced,
taawa kuiwaka yambe	not yet do I speak the steps,
taawa kuisaka sala	not yet do I count the path,
liu ri langgiwo	as we pass by the ghosts.

In explaining that it is not yet time to "speak" or "count the steps," the speaker seems to be instructing a novice on the trip. As we shall see, the traditional molawo spirits are accompanied by the shaman's new personal familiars who are making their "maiden voyage" to Pue.

o to komi tayu pomouluku	Oh you people whom I lead [?],
natolele lima mpale	cross over the five fingers of the hand,
natolele lima mpale	cross over the five fingers of the hand,
natolele ombo ombo wega	cross over cloud, familiars,
mojaya kila majoli	traveling on swift lightning,
mojaya kila mureme wega	traveling on shining lightning, familiars.
to liumo balibali	We've left the enemies behind.
i yadu woti ngkila, balo ransa,	Oh Woti ngKila, Balo Ransa,
luegia balo tanda	Luegia Balo Tanda,
mosumo makoko wega	you are near now, close, familiars.
peaja komi suola	Wait up, you spirit familiar.
peaja komi tomundo wega	Wait up, you ally, familiar.
tomundo ia manau	The ally, he is experienced.

This is our first indication of what we are soon to learn—that the shaman's new familiars, novices in this enterprise, are proving to be fast travelers and are outstripping the old guard in speed.

woti ngkila, balo ransa,	Woti ngKila, Balo Ransa,
luegia balo tanda	Luegia Balo Tanda
rata njaria	have arrived there.
katoto yau tamburu	The tuning fork beats out.
kajaa yau towolu	The bells ring out,
karengge kajaa ma'i	jingling jangling they come.
karengge kajaa yau	Jingling jangling they go.
o wegaku lioku sondilo ruyu	Oh familiars, I'll look, examine first
muli kiondodi nja'u	the tiny child there
ri luo langgiwo wega	in the place of the ghosts, familiars.
ane mewalili muni	If [we] turn back again,
pai kuanti mala ja ruyu	then I can take it first.

The traveling party pauses so that the shaman can go back to rescue the soul of the pregnant woman's child from the place of the ghosts.

ewa noti rauso	Like a hurled shaft,
sala i sada sanggona	the path of Sada Sanggona,
sala i layo layoda wega	the path of Layo Layoda, familiar.

Now one of the novices wants to stop for a snack—a desire to which spirit familiars are prone (see Part Four).

o raju ntuo kupongande	Oh, I'd dearly love to eat,
porosoku yau	to strengthen me,
ayu wense ngguma to winayo	the hair of a copper-clad sheath.[6]
koro raju kupongande yande nto tu'a masowo	Truly, I want to eat the food of the Old Goitered One.
koro liu ngkabelonya	Truly outstanding, its deliciousness,
wense ntongguma winayo	the hair on a copper-clad sheath.

The shaman's aunt ventures the guess that he is asking for the human hair or horsehair that decorates a wooden shield called a *kantar* (Figs. 29, 30). The riddle thus likens a shield that protects a warrior to a sheath that protects a knife.

bara i elemo wega	Maybe it's that, familiar.
manopa ntuo kusulu	Clearly indeed I see
wense tongguma winayo	the hair on the copper-clad sheath.
rata ja bela belaku	There arrives a friend, my friend,
balaku to taawa mananya	my friend who is not yet experienced.

The new arrival is the spirit who wants the hair from a shield. As it turns out, there is none to be had in the house.

ane taaria to ele	If there is none of that,
bandaka donganya	grant me his wish,
bandaka donganya wegaku	grant me his wish, my spirit.
baluwa ntau mawuni	Hair of the invisible people.

A member of the audience guesses *woale*, moss that hangs from trees in the forest.

bara i elemo wegaku	Perhaps it's that, my familiar,
boluwa ntau mawuni	hair of invisible people.
rarombaka kunti	Let the drum be beaten.
taamo kuiwa taamo kudange	No more do I speak, no more do I hear.

simbau simba'a mba'a	One, one thing.
ne'emo raromba[ka?] yadu	Don't let it be beaten anymore for me.
maledo ntuo tangamo	Your hand is exceedingly active,
taane maledo ntuo limamo	your hand is exceedingly active.
ne'emo manini nini	Don't [?] anymore.
koro liu kabelonya	Indeed, it has surpassed goodness.
koro liu kagondonya	Indeed, it has surpassed happiness,
natae i woti ngkila	says Woti ngKila,
natae balo ransa	says Balo Ransa,
luegia balo tanda	Luegia Balo Tanda.
imbamo tu'a matoko	Where's the Old One with the Staff?
imbamo tu'a masowo	Where's the Old Goitered One?
natae i suri wunga	asks Suri Wunga.
nto'umo kaende ende	Up there already, dancing, dancing.
ia layo lamba	There is Layo Lamba,
ndate opo bira lima	up there at the Opo Bira Lima,
natae insala sanggona	says Sala Sanggona.
koti wimbamo naika	Gee, how did they do it?
simba'a masowo sowo	One of them is goitered, goitered.
simba'a matoko toko	One of them hobbles, hobbles with a stick.
mbenu majoli kojo	How swiftly indeed
mawali pangulu nto'u	they became the leaders up there,
mawali pongulu bae	became the great leaders,
natae insori wunga	says Sori Wunga,
natae insori wunga	says Sori Wunga.
taa kuiwa taa kunsani, wega	I don't know, I don't know, familiar.
samba'a matoko toko	One hobbling, hobbling with a stick,
samba'a masowo sowo	one goitered, goitered.
karangonya liu	Their desire to surpass,
re'i liu ntuo ngkajolinya	here surpassing indeed their speed,
liu ntuo kagasinya	truly surpassing their swiftness,
ndate ia mampopea aku	up there they wait for us [literally, he waits for me],
nadate opo bira lima	up at the Opa Bira Lima.

We now know that the new spirit familiars on the journey are called "The Old Goitered One" and "The Old One with the Staff."

Next the travelers are going to "count the path" to protect themselves from the dangers of approaching the Owner.

isa isa meisamo	One, one, one has been counted;
dua meduamo	two, two has been counted;
togo mentogomo	three, three has been counted;
opo meopomo	four, four has been counted;
lima molimamo	five, five has been counted;
ono meonomo	six, six has been counted;
pitu pitu ntinuwu	seven, sevenfold life.
taa kupobente lio	I do not grow pale of face,
taa kupoundo ntuwu	I do not grow short of life,
taa kupomurangguni	I do not grow weak and jaundiced
maronggeni luya	as I carry a betel offering
nto'u opo bira lima	up to Opo Bira Lima.
luya gana gana, o wega	A betel offering, complete, complete, oh familiars.
isa lodu oda	One bend of the knee,
dua lodu oda	two bends of the knee,
togo lodu oda	three bends of the knee;
togo metogomo	three, three have been done;
opo meopomo	four, four have been done;
lima melimamo	five, five have been done;
ono meonomo wega	six, six have been done, familiar;
pitu mepitumo lodu oda wega	seven, seven bends of the knee have been done, my familiar.
o pesua petunda la'u ruyu	Oh enter, sit down there first.
kubisaramo majoli	I shall speak quickly.

Now the shaman reports that one of the members of the audience, "in the shadow of the drum," is gravely ill, so ill that the shaman's spirit familiar is brought to tears by the sight.

o wegaku	Oh, my familiar,
pomuli sala	one child,
pomuli pomuli saito wegaku	child, one child, my familiar,
koro manopa kusulu	how clearly indeed I see.
koro liu ngkaledonya	How truly excessive its crying.
masiyoe ntuo weganya	Wretched indeed, his familiars.
belaku ronta salu i jongi	My companion sheds tears
mansulu sondilo ruyu	to look and inspect first.
pei matungko mapari wegangku	The condition is grave and serious, my familiars,
tane ri undo ngkunti wegaku	in the shadow of the drum, my familiars.
wegaku koro masiyoe yasi wega	My familiars, truly poor pathetic, familiars.
o banda sangkio tinumbo	Oh, give me a little beer,
nempo ojo kio kio	even if it's only a little.

Now the shaman seems to address the Owner.

nutaeka nggomi	Speaking to you,
kutaeka nggomi segi	I speak to you now.
luya kuronggeni luya	I carry a betel offering, betel,
ono nsoi ono nsaja	six slices, six slivers,
luya bana nja nunjawe	betel . . . [?],
luya mamporapi yowe	betel to ask for spirit,
luya mamporapi yosa	betel to ask for breath
ndate opo bira lima	up at the Opo Bira Lima,
ndate opo wai yowe wega	up at the Place that Gives Breath, spirit.
ane yakowa nu banda	If extra [breath] is given,
mangaku sala suola	the spirit familiar assumes the debt,
mangaku sala tomundo	the spirit ally assumes the debt.
natae ruyu ntomundo	The spirit ally speaks first.
ewa ele poromunya	If the total is like that—
togo mpulu pitu yama	thirty-seven plates
togo mpulu pitu yamanya	thirty-seven its plates,
pitu tomou molano	seven chickens,
pitu tonumbo mabelo	seven bottles of good beer,
pitu pesolonya	seven offering tubes,
dua ito dua nsala	two there, two of them—
ane nu baika iwa [ia?]	if it's given to that one,
ane nu waika aku	if it's given to me,
dua ito dua mba'a wega	two there, two of them, spirit,
imba ane ewa ele	what if it's that way?
natae ntu'a matoko	says the Old One with the Staff,
natae ntu'a masowo	says the Old Goitered One.
mangaku sala suola	The spirit familiars assume the debt.
mangaku sala tomundo	The spirit allies assume the debt.
togo mpulu pitu	Thirty seven,
togo pitu tinumbo mabelo	three, seven bottles of good beer,
pitu pesolonya	seven offering tubes,
pitu tomou malano	seven chickens,
pitu tinumbo mabelo	seven bottles of good beer.
imba ane ewa ele	How about if it's that way,
ewa ele pangaku sala suola	like that, the burden undertaken, spirits,
pongaku sala tomundo	the burden undertaken, spirit allies?
ane doe madondong ewa ele	If it's happily pleasing like that,
natae nsuola	says the spirit familiar,
natae ntu'a matoko	says the Old One with the Staff.
koro dondong seja aku	I too am contented indeed,
koro doe masangang	happy and contented indeed.

o ane ewa ele koro doe madondong	Oh, if it's like that, happy and contented indeed,
koro doe masangang wegaku	happy and pleased indeed, my spirit.
o wegaku duo ito dua nsala	Oh, my spirit familiars, those two, that pair.

We have just heard one side of the shaman's negotiation with Pue. Now the shaman and his familiars break off again to ask for food.

ane manaya ja nggomi	If you are experienced,
to randa mbombaru	you who are in the house,
bandaka yadu nande	give me food,
nande to mabelo wegaku	a food that is delicious, my familiar,
salu madanda ri lobo	water at the temple,[7]
salu madanda ri lobo	water hanging in a row at the temple.
o raja ntuo kupongande wegaku	Oh, I dearly want to eat, my familiar.
salu madanda ri lobo	Water in a row at the temple.

Someone guesses that he is asking for water in a bamboo pipe. (Wana fetch water in lengths of bamboo that are kept in a line near the hearth.)

o rianya to ele wegaku	Oh, it's not that, my familiar,
bela pai kutaeka nggomi nggomi	friend, but I ask you, you,
salu madanda ri lobo wega	water in a row at the temple, spirit.
bia boakamo	Never mind, forget it.
taa siwee nundanda	It's not deeply desired.
wetumo kami suola	We're that way, familiar,
wetumo kami tomundo wegaku	we're that way, ally, my familiar.

Someone guesses dew on the ends of the roof thatch.

rianya to ele pai donganyamo	It's not that which he wanted.
o wegaku taa siwee nundanda	Oh, my familiar, it's not greatly desired.
wetumo to tu'a matoko	The Old One with the Staff is that way,
wetumo tu'a masowo	the Old Goitered One is that way,
to tu'a masowo	the Old Goitered One.
koro doe madondong	Happy and joyful indeed,
koro doe masangang	happy and joyful indeed,

wegangku bela
omo saito sangkodi nuwolili muni
koro doe madondong
woti ngkila, balo ransa
luegia balo tanda
mbenu i tu'a motoko

imba to tu'a mosowo
paka joli tima toko
paka joli tima toko
kita da waleko muni
kita da lo'u lo'umo
taamo rabandaka toko
bia bia boakamo
omo tongkeni mongkeni wega

my familiars, friends.
Only one little while 'til we return.
Happy and joyful indeed.
Woti ngKila, Balo Ransa,
Luegia Balo Tanda.
Where is the Old One with the
    Staff?
Where is the Old Goitered One?
Hurry up and get your staff.
Hurry up and get your staff.
We're about to turn back.
We're going to go down, down.
The staff no longer is given.
Never mind, don't bother.
He'll just hold on to the sling, spirit.

Here the shaman had been calling for a staff that he had used earlier when his familiar who hobbles with a stick arrived. Someone finally gave him the staff, but he dismissed it and held on instead to a cloth cradle suspended from a rafter.

omo rombakaku kuntinya

bara kudange muninya
natolulu lele nto'u
natolulu layo layoda
mbenu layo layoda
mbenu to sada sanggona
mbenu lele manga'a
woti ngkila, balo ransa
luegia balo tanda
woti ngkila, lele lima
natolulu maka nto'u
pei kita natanaka
mbenu to tu'a matoko

mbenu to tu'a masowo
natae nto sori wunga
natae nto sori wuya
koro liu ngkajolinya
koro liu nggasinya
kaliu ri opo reme
kaliunya opo bira
natae i sori wunga
natae i . . .

Just have them play their drum for
    me.
Perhaps I'll hear it again.
Following on the journey up,
following Layo Layoda.
Where is Layo Layoda?
Where is Sada Sanggona?
Where is Lele Manga'a?
Woti ngKila, Balo Ransa,
Luegia Balo Tanda,
Woti ngKila, Lele Lima
followed going up.
But we ask,
Where is the Old One with the
    Staff?
Where is the Old Goitered One?
say the ones of Sori Wunga,
say the ones of Sori Wuya.
They are truly surpassing in speed,
truly surpassing in swiftness,
passing up to the shining *opo*,
Their passage to the Opo Bira,
says Sori Wunga
says [unintelligible]

yosa kuwuuigi wo'u	Breath I blow back again.
yosa naporapika nsuola	Breath requested by the familiars,
suola tu'a matoko	familiar, the Old One with the Staff,
suola tu'a masowo	familiar, the Old Goitered One.
nempo ojo santutu mwua	Even if only one pounding of betel.
nempo ojo santutu ntaku	Even if only one pounding of lime.
da kuwuuigi ruyunya	I'm going to blow first.
e matao kukita	Oh good, I see.
matao kojo kudonge	Very good, I hear.
masilulak suola	The familiars are chasing each other,
masilulak tomundo	the allies are chasing each other.
tomundo tu'a matoko	The ally, Old One with the Staff,
tomundo tu'a mosowo	the ally, Old Goitered One.
koro liu kajolinya	They are truly surpassing in speed,
koro liu kagasinya	they are truly surpassing in swiftness.
ia mampake kuasa	They use power.
ia mampaka bisanya	They use their potency.
ombo nsese mampotonda kasuola	They leave in their wake a cloud of flowers, the familiars.
siwaju kuwuuigika yosa	The same, I blow the breath.
yosa mawuuigi	The breath blowing,
silele taa maowe taa maonda	continuing, not stopping, not ceasing,
mawuui silele lele mawuui	breathing continuously, continuously breathing,
saeo eo	day after day,
mawuui simburu mburi	breathing night after night.
napongaku nsuola mangaku sala suola	Undertaken by the spirits, the familiars assume the responsibility.
kuporapika ri opo wegangku	I requested at the *opo*, my familiars,
asali loto ja ue nalombu	that cool would be the water that is waded.

This text hardly matches the preceding synopsis of the shaman's molawo journey. Of course, a summary cannot take the place of actual text. But even so, whereas the molawo text is an explicit and largely self-contained narrative, complete from beginning to end, the mabolong text presented here seems fragmentary and requires considerable contextual information to be understood. The performer's words, which are central to the molawo, may in fact be incidental in a mabolong performance. Often a shaman's song goes unheard because of the din of drum and gongs: I was able to record shamans' journeys to the Owner only on occasions when shamans asked that the drum and gongs be silenced, presumably to allow the audience (and the anthropologist) to hear their words.

Instead of tediously constructing and propelling a vessel for the journey upward, the mabolong performer and his entourage take a swift route—"the path of a lightning flash" (*jaya bata bila*), "the path of the blink of an eye" (*jaya sampida mata*), or "the path of the wind" (*jaya ngoyu*). The contingent of the text cited here uses lightning for its path.

Unlike a molawo performer, the mabolong performer does not bother to recount everything he passes. The only site along the shaman's route that Apa Mene mentions is the "place of the ghosts," and he mentions it for a particular purpose, namely, to rescue the soul of the patient's baby.

As in the molawo text, conversation among the shaman's spirit familiars is prominent. Apa Mene's associates fall within two camps: the traditional walia who make journeys to the Owner and his own personal walia, whom he had only recently engaged. There is a comical contrast between the traditional walia with their graceful epithets (Woti ngKila, "Flash of Lightning," Mantopi Wunga, "The One Who Wears Basil for a Hat,") and the shaman's personal walia, "Old Goitered One" and "Old One with the Staff." Apparently it is the latter the shaman speaks of early in the text as being inexperienced, not yet familiar with the protocol of making a trip to the Owner. Yet in the end this spirit or these spirits (in some contexts the epithets appear to apply to the same spirit, in others to two different spirits) surpass the experienced ones in speed and conduct the negotiations with the Owner. By outperforming the classical walia, the new walia cast glory on themselves and their shaman associate.

Another important feature of the text involves the shaman's frequent interruption of his activities to request a "food of the spirit familiars" (*baku mwalia*). To do so, he poses a riddle to the audience (whom he has been ignoring up to now), and his audience must attempt to guess what it is he has asked for. The significance of such requests will be explored in Part Four; here it suffices to note that these requests serve to keep audience members engaged and attentive to the performance.

Shamanic antics aside, what has transpired in this text? The shaman's contingent has approached the Owner's place, negotiated a
deal, obtained "breath" for the patient in return for a promise, and
returned to its starting place. This sequence needs to be spelled out and
explained in some detail.

In contrast to encounters with spirits on earth and in the realms
along the path to the Owner, a direct encounter with the Owner
requires pronouncing a special ritual formula to prevent a condition
called *buto*, which may include such symptoms as bloating of the
abdomen, jaundice, and unremitting fatigue. Buto is brought on by
violations of hierarchy, improper claims to rank, and acts of disrespect to authority: one who misuses the legal system may be *buto
ada*; one who unrightfully claims a rank or office may be *buto pangka*;
one who unworthily assumes the name of an important person may
be *buto sanga*; one who is disrespectful to a parent-in-law may be *buto
to manua*; and one who adopts or mishandles the insignia of a warrior
may be *buto koje*. Likewise, approaching the Owner of the world
carries the danger of buto. Consequently it is essential to "count"
to seven, the auspicious number of longevity, lest one's life be
shortened. Reciting the formula underscores the risks the shaman
undertakes on behalf of his patient.

Once they have reached the place of the Owner, the walia begin to
negotiate. We hear only the shaman's half of the dialogue. The shaman
informs the Owner (or the Owner's go-between, the *leangi mpue*) that
he bears a betel offering to ask for breath on his patient's behalf. Note
that he requests *breath*—not the other elements of being that flee from
a person's body in time of illness. Breath here stands for life and its
continuation (as indicated in the final lines of the song). The shaman,
then, is asking for an extension of the patient's life.

To win breath from the Owner, the shaman must make a vow
called a *nia* or *pantoo* (the word *nia* in Bahasa Indonesia refers to
an intention or plan). In essence, he and the spirit familiars are
contracting a "debt" (*inda*) or agreeing to pay a "fine" (*sala*) in return
for the patient's life. A typical fine in the context of a mabolong
involves four categories of items: rice beer, chicken, leaf plates full of
cooked rice, and tiny bamboo tubes filled with rice and chicken
feathers. (In some cases the shaman may also promise a performance
of ritual dueling in which celebrants carrying shields charge each other
a specified number of times [Figs. 29, 30].) The size of the fine is

auspiciously phrased in threes and sevens. Thus the shaman in the text above promises thirty-seven little plates of rice, seven chickens, seven bottles of beer, and seven small tubes.

Once a bargain has been struck, the shaman and his spirits retrace their path down to earth, the betel offering still bound to the shaman's back bearing the "breath" they have won for the patient. In the final lines of the text above, the shaman concludes his journey by placing the betel offering on the patient's head and blowing the breath from the Owner into his patient. The packet of betel now has a special relationship to the patient, representing both an extension of life and a debt to be paid. It must be kept in the roof of the house where the patient lives until the vow to the Owner has been fulfilled; should the patient move to another house before the debt has been paid, the betel offering must be moved as well.

The shaman's "vow" to the Owner must now be "repaid" (*rabayar*) with a feast. To celebrate a patient's recovery, the patient's household slaughters the promised number of chickens, fills with rice the promised number of leaf plates, and provides the promised bottles of rice beer for friends and neighbors. Commonly, households with vows to fulfill coordinate their efforts, and other households in the settlement are expected to demonstrate neighborliness (*kasintuwu*) by contributing food and drink to the feast. If food abounds, other settlements may be notified of the event; those guests, too, would be expected to bring at least some rice beer. Thus the burden of feeding the community is shared by all.

After the meal is eaten, a mabolong is held. Once again, the shaman makes a journey upward to the Owner's place, this time to inform Pue that the vow has been fulfilled. Now he carries not only the betel offering that before served as the vehicle for breath, but also *pesolo*, the small bamboo tubes filled with rice and feathers from the chickens slaughtered in fulfillment of the vow. As he addresses Pue, close relatives of the recovered patient place a white cloth on the shaman's head to demonstrate the "whiteness" of their feelings (*kabuya nraya*)—in other words, the gratitude they feel, a gratitude that extends both to the Owner and to the shaman (Fig. 27). It is wise and proper for them later to insist that the shaman take the cloth.

Once the vow has been fulfilled, the betel packet and the pesolo are hung from the roof beam of the patient's house, where they remain as long as the house stands.

9

Exchanges with the Owner

> Exchange is not a complex edifice built on the obligations
> of giving, receiving and returning, with the help of some
> emotional-mystical cement. It is a synthesis immediately
> given to, and given by, symbolic thought, which, in exchange
> as in any other form of communication, surmounts the con-
> tradiction inherent in it; that is the contradiction of perceiving
> things as elements of dialogue, in respect of self and others
> simultaneously, and destined by nature to pass from one to the
> other.
>
> Lévi-Strauss, *Introduction to the Work of*
> *Marcel Mauss*

> Even if reversibility is the objective truth of the discrete acts
> which ordinary experience knows in discrete form and calls
> gift exchanges, it is not the whole truth of a practice which
> could not exist if it were consciously perceived in accordance
> with the model.
>
> Bourdieu, *Outline of a Theory of Practice*

The purpose of "going to Pue" is to rejuvenate human life. Elsewhere
in the Pacific, human life (along with other key social values) is often
regenerated through exchange. Such exchange may involve gifts
ranging from betel, food, shell valuables, and ax blades to fine mats,
cloth, brides, babies, and human bones (see Weiner 1985, 1989). The
Wana shaman's negotiation with Pue also involves exchange—not
ceremonial gift exchange on a human plane, but rather what Mauss
([1925] 1967, 13) labeled "gifts to gods."

In their 1898 study of sacrifice, Hubert and Mauss focused on the
richly documented priestly traditions of Hebrew and Vedic ritual. In
keeping with the nature of their source materials, their essay focuses
primarily on the liturgical dimensions of sacrificial ritual (see Valeri
1985, 64). They did not at that time systematically investigate connections between sacrifice and the wider social context in which it occurs,
nor did they analyze ethnographic accounts among nonliterate peo-

179

ples. Dismissing efforts along those lines by such British theorists as Tylor, Robertson Smith, and Frazer, they stated:

> It is likewise impossible to hope to glean from ethnography alone the pattern of primitive institutions. Generally distorted though over-hasty observation or falsified by the exactness of our languages, the facts recorded by ethnographers have value only if they are compared with more precise and more complete documents.
>
> (Hubert and Mauss [1898] 1964, 8)

By the 1920s, however, Mauss judged ethnographic documentation of Polynesia, Melanesia, and the Northwest Coast of North America adequate to serve as the focus of his *Essai sur le don*, published in 1925. (In the interim, of course, ethnographic fieldwork had gained in both rigor and respect as a result of such pioneers as Franz Boas, Bronislaw Malinowski, and A. R. Radcliffe-Brown, on whose work Mauss drew.) And in contrast to the earlier study of sacrifice, the *Essai sur le don* addresses the wider connections between a ceremonial act and the social world of which the act is an integral part.

In his treatment of the gift, Mauss ([1925] 1967, 13) observed that "the connection of exchange contracts among men with those between men and gods explains a whole aspect of the theory of sacrifice." He did not there attempt, however, to trace the links between "total prestation" and the phenomenon of sacrifice which he and Henri Hubert had explored a quarter of a century earlier. Because his concern was exchange on the human social plane, Mauss explored the relation between exchange and sacrifice only in the context of gift giving between humans in which gods and nature figure as a wider and impressionable audience. He proposed, for example, that destruction of property in the potlatch of the Northwest Coast and of Northeast Asia was in fact a form of contractual sacrifice to spirits and gods embodied by human potlatch players (Mauss [1925] 1967, 14). Thus in potlatch systems "gifts to gods" and "gifts to men" overlap (see Gregory 1980).[1]

Whereas Mauss in *The Gift* focused on exchanges between humans which presumed a nonhuman audience, I am going to analyze the shaman's negotiations with Pue as an exchange between a shaman and a spiritual being which presumes a human audience. Here the offering is one "in which a direct relationship between the giver and god predominates," as opposed to cases of "gifts to gods" in Papua New

Guinea and the Northwest Coast "in which the relation of giver to god is manifestly a vehicle for the expression of relations between men" (Gregory 1980, 644). I shall begin with an examination of the ritual itself, then explore the implications for understanding ritual and political relations in Wana communities.

Valerio Valeri's recent analysis of sacrifice and hierarchy in ancient Hawaii will aid me in this task. Valeri (1985, 70–71) treats Hawaiian sacrifice as a performative act that "effects transformations of the relationship of sacrifier, god, and group by representing them in public"; in what follows, I shall pursue Valeri's insight for a shamanic ritual and show how the relationship of the *sacrificer* to patient, god, and group receives particular emphasis in this ritual process.

OFFERINGS AND INDIGENOUS PHRASING

A tradition among twentieth-century writers on sacrifice cautions against reducing sacrifice and other forms of ritual exchange to the utilitarian market relation so familiar to Euroamerican society. Mauss offered such a warning with reference to A. C. Kruyt's Sulawesi ethnography: "This uncertainty about the words which we translate badly as buying and selling is not confined to the Pacific." He cited Kruyt "as one of the better ethnographers [who,] while using the word 'sale,'" portrays Toraja exchanges with spirits as a system not of "sale and purchase" but "of gifts and return gifts" (Mauss [1925] 1967, 98, 30–31).

Like their neighbors to the west, Wana have borrowed the Malay word *bayar* to speak of "repaying a vow" (*baya nia*). They use the same word to refer to "paying" a legal fine. Indeed, the promise to fulfill a vow is sometimes referred to by the terms for a legal fine (*saki*) or debt (*inda*). Be it a legal fine or a vow to Pue, the point of repayment is not commerical transaction, but the re-establishment or renewal of a relationship through deference to authority (that of ada or Pue). The act of assuming responsibility for restitution is called *mangaku*, a verb form of the first-person pronoun *aku*. Thus to mangaku is to take upon oneself a special burden or responsibility for restoring social relations disrupted by social conflict or threatened by illness. In ada negotiations, a measure of authority may accrue to one who assumes responsibility for another's debt. (As we shall see in Chapter

15, the nineteenth-century practice of debt slavery operated on that principle, as does the ongoing practice of creating political constituencies by articulating lines of authority and dependency.) Likewise, in negotiations with the Owner, shamans assert their authority and others' dependency by assuming responsibility for fulfilling vows on behalf of their patients. Local notions of debt and repayment in these legal and sacrificial contexts bear the mark not of commerical exchange, but of political hierarchy and patronage in the region.

GIFTS TO (AND FROM) GOD

Bourdieu (1977, 5), in his critique of Lévi-Strauss's critique of Mauss's *Essai sur le don*, argues that time is fundamental to the structure of exchange. Indeed, temporal intervals are intrinsic to both the logic and practice of Wana offerings to Pue. The shaman's vow (*pantoo*) involves two stages: an initial approach to the Owner to request an extension of life for a patient, and a subsequent celebration for the continuation of life. Sacrifice proper occurs only after the Owner has granted the boon; rather than being a gesture of abnegation or renunciation, then, it is a celebratory communion of continuing life.

Like the ritual sequence itself, my analysis unfolds in two stages: first, an examination of the objects that constitute the gifts between mortals and the Owner, and second, a consideration of the fact that a shaman is involved in their transfer.

Betel

By carrying an offering of betel to Pue, the shaman (in Maussian fashion) initiates a state of mutual obligation between humans and the Owner. Both are ideally committed to receive and to give: the sociable offering of betel obligates the Owner to entertain the shaman's request, while the shaman's vow commits the shaman, his patient's family, and, by extension, the community to celebrate the granting of breath. The shaman initiates a cycle of exchange that brings the community and the Owner into communication.

As Valeri (1985, 65) would anticipate, betel represents the sacrifier—the patient on whose behalf the supplication is made. Betel is a token of sociability for Wana, as for other Island Southeast Asian populations. Betel is offered to humans and spirits alike as a prelude to

conversation and an overture to negotiation across all contexts of
Wana life. In various ways areca nuts, betel quids, and betel paraphernalia all represent persons in Wana rituals. For example, in the molawo
performance each patient is represented by a whole areca nut that,
incised in a distinctive way, serves as the vehicle for its owner's vital
elements—in contrast to the mabolong, where a patient's soul parts
are retrieved and transported in the shaman's cloth (*papolonsu*). In the
salia ritual (no longer performed in most Wana regions), each participating household was represented by a *wua ntuwu*, an "areca nut of
life," along with a small bowl of rice and a cordyline leaf. Whereas a
whole areca nut stands for a person or a household, a sliced areca nut
represents a request for treatment of a person or household. At the
salia, each household placed a sliced areca nut on a tray. Likewise, at a
mabolong a person requesting treatment from a shaman will present
him with betel fixings at the offering tray.

Betel figures in nonshamanic ritual as well. As in other Island
Southeast Asian societies, Wana marriage negotiations involve a complicated etiquette of betel prestation, and divorce is effected by tearing
a piper leaf (an essential element of a betel quid) in two. So closely is
betel associated with social persons that stepping over the betel bag of
one's parent-in-law is tantamount to stepping over that person's
body. The consequences of either act—*buto to manua*—are dire. At
death, the betel bag of the deceased represents its owner's continued
social presence through the funeral observance until finally it is carried
to the gravesite, thus signaling the departure of the dead from the
community.

During the course of the vow's formulation and fulfillment, the
packet containing betel fixings is sequentially transformed: first from
an assemblage of substances involved in everyday social intercourse
into a medium of communication between the human and the deity;
subsequently into a vehicle for the Owner's gift of breath and a surrogate for its human recipient; then into a token of a life extended and a
debt outstanding; and finally into a symbol of a petition granted and a
vow fulfilled. In this process the betel offering is not alienated, as in
the destruction of a sacrificial victim, but rather is augmented: it is a
gift to which significance accrues as it changes hands. Yet transferral is
not explicit. Gregory (1980, 640) has likened a gift (in the Maussian
sense) to "a tennis ball with an elastic band attached to it. The owner
of the ball may lose possession of it for a time, but the ball will spring

back to the owner if the elastic band is given a jerk." Indeed, the betel, although it is carried to Pue, resides there only long enough for the shaman to make his appeal; it then returns to the patient enriched with the Owner's gift. Thus it symbolizes the open flow of continuing life, instead of serving, say, as a sacrificial substitute for the patient.

Festive Food

In Hubert and Mauss's terms, the betel used in the pantoo would constitute an offering, not a sacrifice (but cf. Valeri 1985, 37, 64–65). Like a sacrifice, an offering is "consecrated," meaning that it moves from a secular into a "religious domain," and it serves as an "intermediary" between a deity and the person or object that is to benefit from its presentation (Hubert and Mauss [1898] 1964, 9, 11). But unlike a sacrifice, an offering in Hubert and Mauss's terms is not destroyed in the ritual process—quite the contrary in the case of the Wana betel offering and the pesolo (to be discussed momentarily), which survive the rite as tokens of the Owner's gift and the people's gratitude, respectively. These items remain integral, whereas the chickens, beer, and rice are consumed. In Wana terms, one of these gifts—the chicken or chickens slaughtered in payment of the vow—is singled out explicitly as a sacrificial victim whose life is substituted for the patient's. The following passage is taken from a sacrificial invocation outside the context of a mabolong (and as such is addressed to two Owners, not one, for reasons I shall discuss in the next chapter).[2]

maka etu ja i neli etu	Look, there is Neli there,
taa ja e nakaus yau etu	she didn't die there
e kare'e yantu etu	at the birth of Yantu there.
si'i joni etu	Here's Joni there,
maka taa ja e kabus yau	look, she didn't die.
nse naka aku sei wetu e kuika	That's why I'm here doing this,
maka maya rato'o rasi semo aku sei	because, it could be said, these are my very feelings,
maka maya rato'o aku ndende semo	because, it could be said, I'm genuinely joyful.
maya rato'o kabuya nrayaku semo	It could be said, this is in fact the whiteness of my feelings.
sei e naka kitamo	That's why you are seeing
buya nrayaku etu sei	the whiteness of my feelings there.
togo manu da kusambale	Three chickens I'm going to slaughter

ri wawo mwiti tau dua sana etu	over the feet of that parent and child.
maya rato'o e tau dua sana	It could be said that parent and child,
maya rato'o opo e sana etu	it could be said, those four family members.
sira wetu da kuika mangingka	They are the reason I'm going to do what I do.
taa kuwutis taa kuwai e bobos	I don't lie, I don't offer a deception.
pasi e paiweri e maya rato'o	Even PaiWeri, it could be said,
nangansanga e samba'a etu	as that one there is named,
ia e ma'i e seja e etu	he has come also.
e taamo e mampeasi wengi etu	He no longer waits for nightfall.
taa e napeasi soyo eo etu	He doesn't wait for sunset.
ia e mangkeni tule etu	He is bringing rice beer.
ia e mangkeni gombo etu	He is bringing words.
ia e makuasa etu	He is empowered.
ia e kusarumaka	On him I depend.
boo siko boo siko boo siko	Hey you, hey you, hey you.
ne'e potanaka salam siko etu	You there, don't ask your fault
sambalemo ri wawo mwiti	as you are cut over the feet
joni sira dua i neli etu	of Joni and Neli there.
salama komi salama aku	You are safe, I am safe.
e maya rato'o aku mamporayang komi	Eh, it could be said I feel for you.
aku e porayang seja aku	I, eh, feel also for me.
se taa e mosa seja aku	I am not wearied either.
masusa kojo naepe	It feels very difficult.
e maya rato'o ewa walia etu	It could be said, like that spirit familiar.
nse ngingka aku sambale manu	That's what I am doing, cutting the neck of a chicken
e ri wawo mwiti	over their feet.
ne'e potanaka salamo	Don't ask your fault.
siko e marugimo	You are ruined.
saro ngkoro joni sira dua i neli	Surrogate for Joni's body, along with Neli's.
semo manu se	That's what the chicken is,
ri wawo mwiti i neli sira dua joni	over the feet of Neli and of Joni.
taa bara e kuwutis	It's not that I would lie.
taa bara e kubobos	It's not that I would deceive.
se'e naika ntau	That's what people do.
se'e naika mwalia etu	That's what spirit familiars do.
kandende e nwalia	Joy of the spirit,
kandende e nsuola	joy of the familiar.
togo manu kusambale	Three chickens I cut

ri wawo nwiti joni sira dua neli	over Joni's and Neli's feet,
naka aku ndende aku buya rayaku	because I'm joyful, my feelings are white.
ne'e potanaka salamo	Don't ask your fault.
ratamo botunya	The limit has been reached.
taamo kuwutis komi	No more do I lie to you.
taamo kubobos komi	No more do I deceive you.
ne'e potanaka salamo	Don't ask your fault.
wetu komi pangaku ngkomi	That's the duty you've assumed
ungka re mula jadi	since the beginning of creation.
wubu baru ri nganga mpala [Kepala]	Pour beer in Kepala's mouth.
taa ja namate yau neli etu muana	Neli didn't die giving birth!

Here the sacrificer addresses the sacrificial victims directly. He juxtaposes his pity for them and his joy for the patients' recovery. (The joy expressed in this text is no doubt amplified because the sacrificer—Apa Mene—is also husband to one patient and father to the other.) He directly labels the chickens as surrogates for the patients' lives and declares that role to be the animals' "duty." The flow of the chicken's blood onto the women's feet places the victim in direct contact with the persons who benefit from the sacrifice (see Hubert and Mauss [1898] 1964, 43). The outpouring of this vital substance contrasts the continuous flow of breath assured by the sacrifice, spelling ruin for the victim and life for the patient. The other substance mentioned in this text is rice beer, which is joyously poured into the mouth of a celebrant.

The sacrificial chickens not only serve as surrogates for a patient's life but also are consumed along with rice and beer in a feast of "communion"—not of the totemic variety postulated by Robertson Smith, but a celebration that nonetheless "nourishes social forces" (Hubert and Mauss [1898] 1964, 102). A personal crisis of illness, once past, thus furnishes an occasion for creating a sense of community. The patient's household gives up chickens, rice, and rice beer, a sacrifice that elicits demonstrations of mutual support—the value of "living together" (*kasintuwu*)—as neighbors are expected to gather with contributions to the meal. In practice, households with vows to pay commonly team up and celebrate together, thus distributing responsibility for the provision of food and making the occasion more festive. The theme of such "sacrifices" is by no means deprivation but instead celebration. In this way a personal crisis is transformed—through shamanic action—into an occasion to create and renew a community. It should be noted in this treatment of ritual logic that in practice, as Bourdieu (1977) would anticipate, repayment of vows does not occur automatically. People may put off the event until goaded into it by the threat of subsequent illness (interpreted as a divine reminder) or by some party (often a shaman) who wants to precipitate a festive event.

Pesolo

On his second journey to Pue in fulfillment of the vow, the shaman adds the small bamboo tubes known as pesolo to the bundle containing the patient's betel offering as testimony that the conditions of the promise have been met. The pesolo, which contain rice and feathers from the slaughtered chickens, represent the collective feast held in fulfillment of the vow. Indeed, they may well represent all three components of the feast—rice, chicken, and beer—since *large* bamboo tubes are used to collect the rice beer as it drains from the basketry funnel in which it ferments (Fig. 4). (Later, too, bamboo tubes may serve as containers for rice beer, although glass bottles are more common.)

It is also tempting to draw a connection between the bamboo pesolo and the "bamboo tube of breath" (*balo nosa*) that each person is supposed to have simultaneously in his or her chest and up at the Opo Bira Lima (the Owner's place) alongside one's *kaju nabi* a "tree of the *nabi* or spirit." Damage done to either the kaju nabi or the balo nosa results in sickness or even death for its human owner (when one dies, one's tree is felled and one's tube of breath destroyed). Shamans and their spirit familiars therefore check their patients' trees and bamboo tubes during their trips to the Owner's place, sprucing them up or clearing away obstructions if necessary. Alternatively, a malicious shaman may damage a person's tree or bamboo, and a suicidal shaman may destroy his own and die soon after.

A connection between the pesolo and the patient's balo nosa likely exists, although no one ever made the association for me, nor did it occur to me to ask anyone whether such a link was plausible. But it is tempting to see how the pesolo, as a symbol of the person and god-given breath, may represent the connection between the patient and the deity as mediated by the shaman.

Pesolo invoke another set of associations with historical implications for ritual and hierarchy in the region. They appear in Kruyt's 1930 report on the Wana in connection with offerings to keep epidemic-bearing spirits at bay, in which context they served as tokens of collective feasts—of rice eaten and chickens slaughtered. Although Kruyt does not mention the following practice, my companions gave pesolo a central place in Wana relations with coastal raja as well. Before the coming of the Dutch in the early 1900s, the Wana paid tribute first, they said, to the raja of Ternate, and later to the raja of Bungku and Tojo, located on the southwest and northwest coasts of the Wana region, respectively.[3] These raja did not exercise direct control over the Wana but ruled indirectly through Wana representatives called *makole* and *basal* (see Chapter 15). To the raja of Bungku Wana in the southerly regions offered in tribute beeswax (*taru*), along with rice and white hens. (Kruyt 1930, 465–70, provides an account of these relations with Bungku. I shall consider them further in Part Five.) To the raja of Tojo Wana to the north offered tiny bamboo tubes filled with uncooked rice, together with pairs of white chickens. Given the ambivalence expressed in Wana trickster tales and millenarian legends toward raja as both oppressors and embodiments of spiritual power, one wonders whether there was any conscious and perhaps subversive meaning to the fact that Wana gave the same items—pesolo and live chickens—to the raja of Tojo as to epidemic-bearing spirits in downstream regions. (Tojo is in fact downstream from the Wana region.)

More easily argued is the relation between offerings to the raja and modern harvest practice. Like a shaman, a farming leader makes an annual vow (*pantoo*) on behalf of his community (Fig. 8). Like a vow made by a shaman for a patient, this pantoo also entails chickens, rice, beer, and pesolo. At harvest's end, to celebrate the vitality of persons and rice, a feast is held and pesolo affixed to granaries testifying to the fulfillment of the vow. In earlier times, the raja had a part in assuring the health and well-being of people and crops. The success and prosperity of Wana farming communities was ideologically contingent on the payment of tribute to the raja, the "owners of the land" (*pue ntana*). Pesolo, then, have been both separately and simultaneously celebrations of life and gestures of homage. Their use in the mabolong draws on both conventions: we shall return again to the implications of a shaman negotiating a tributary relation between a community and a divine lord.

After the mabolong, the pesolo are suspended along with the betel offering in the rafters of the patient's house. Their placement is thus spatially between the patient and Pue, whose relationship they have mediated.

Breath

Exploring the concept of sacrifice in light of both a Maussian conception of the gift and a phenomenological notion of religion, van der Leeuw (1938, 354) observed that the point of sacrifice "is not that someone or other should receive something, but that the stream of life should continue to flow."[4] This sense is captured in the Owner's gift of "breath" for the patient—as characterized in Apa Mene's song, "breath blowing continuously, neither stopping nor ceasing, breathing continuously, continuously, breathing day after day, breathing night after night,"

Breath is distinguished in this ritual from elements of a person's being such as the dream agent, multiple souls, and the pulse points of the hands and feet. Soul parts are conceived as entities; breath is portrayed as a process. Soul parts are sought in a variety of spirit haunts; breath comes only from Pue. Soul parts are personalized components of an individual's being; breath is impersonal life, personalized only as a gift negotiated by a shaman.

The next chapter explores how seeking breath from the Owner has its parallel in Wana mythology. In journeying to Pue the shaman replicates the act of Pololoiso, the culture hero, who sought but failed to obtain eternal breath for humankind. To grasp the significance of that replication, we must consider the shaman's role as a mediator between the Owner and the human community.

SHAMANS AND SACRIFICE

Hubert and Mauss ([1898], 1964, 11) define a sacrificial object as "an intermediary" between the person or object to benefit from the sacrifice (in the present case, the patient) and "the divinity to whom the sacrifice is usually addressed." They underscore that "man and the god are not in direct contact." Up to now I have focused on what Hubert and Mauss would call the consecrated objects that are "interposed between the god and the offerer" for the latter's benefit (p. 11). As we have seen, these offerings represent the patients and the community on whose behalf the ritual actions are taken; in Valeri's (1985, 65) terms, they are "the subject in an objective form." What has been left out so far is the human intermediary: the shaman. In contrast to a priest who makes oblations to a god on behalf of other persons, a Wana shaman directly and dramatically contacts the Owner. In doing so, he takes on aspects of a consecrated offering or sacrifice that links his community and the godhead.

At the start of the ritual, the patient's fate, represented by the betel offering, is literally bound to the shaman who will bring the patient into direct contact with Pue (see Valeri 1985, 130). By undertaking the journey upward on his patient's behalf, the shaman places his own life in jeopardy: as the shaman's song indicates, the performer risks the debilitating and ultimately fatal condition of buto for presuming to approach the Owner and must recite the formulaic count to seven to ward off that danger. Absent from the text, but articulated clearly in talk about the ritual, is the danger the journey poses for a shaman and his children. The shaman approaches Pue to learn if the patient is fated to die. The Owner may say, No, I am not responsible for the patient's illness. Go check at some other spirit realm for the problem—perhaps the place of incest and bad marriages. Alternatively Pue may say, Yes, I am responsible, I have willed a death. In that case, someone must die, and the shaman endeavors to insure that the one to die is not the patient but instead some stranger in another place. The Owner may, however, agree to spare the patient only on the condition that the shaman, or perhaps one of his children, must die. To acknowledge and to ward off this possibility, a patient's family should present a shaman with a *toru*—literally, a rain or sun hat—to protect him and his family from harm. Generally the toru given to a shaman for "going to Pue" is a length of white cloth, the color signifying the "whiteness" or gratitude (*kabuya nraya*) the patient's family feels for the shaman's efforts.

It is easy to read the potential for exploitation in this practice, a potential occasionally recognized by Wana themselves. Shamans may decline to perform for a patient until the patient's family indicates that a gift is forthcoming. But a shaman's bid for a gesture of support from his patient's kin cannot be read simply or solely as a crass demand for payment. Hubert and Mauss ([1898] 1964, 28) argue that sacrifice demands a "credo. . . a like constancy in the mental state of sacrifier and sacrificer"—that is, between the person or persons who are to benefit from the sacrifice and the person who is to perform it. This constancy is sought as shamans press their patients' families for evidence of commitment to both patient and shaman. In a serious case, a shaman may ask his clients, "Which one will you sacrifice, the child or the spirit familiar?" In other words, "Whom will you allow to die, the patient or the shaman?" A wise answer would be, "I don't sacrifice the spirit familiar, neither do I give over the child to ruin. Better we pay. Whatever must be assumed, however much is fined, we accept the debt." In this way, a patient's family assures the shaman that they are fully behind his efforts.

The likelihood that the shaman will extract such assurance increases as the social distance between a shaman and his patient increases. The matter would not be broached (as far as I have seen) when a shaman is performing for someone near and dear to him. I have seen the issue pressed by a shaman who resented the continual requests for treatment by distant kin who had declined to join the shaman's settlement. On one such occasion, the married daughter of a household asked the shaman to perform for her mother, who suffered from a chronic lung problem. Her request came at an especially busy time for the shaman; his wife had just given birth and their rice required harvesting. The shaman's wife suggested to the woman that she and her husband might help them with the harvest—an unusually direct statement that shamanic treatment might be contingent on reciprocal labor.

A mabolong was held for the old woman. The shaman performed an augury to see if the patient would live and concluded that she would not. To forecast someone's imminent death would be a grave insult outside a shamanic context; within one, it means that a shaman must perform heroics to save the life. Having determined the old woman's fate, the shaman threatened to withdraw from the case. The daughter responded by declaring fervently, "White indeed were our feelings in asking you to perform. It wasn't a joke." The shaman talked of how much happier the dead are than the living and instructed the woman's two daughters simply to let her die. After all, she was old. The elder daughter then asserted how "strong" she and her family felt about enlisting his aid.

Declaring that with "just a little pinch, this old one will flee" (that is, leave this world), the shaman said he had never been so blunt with anyone before. He claimed it was no longer possible to save the woman, and given how much work they had to do (it *was* the harvest season) it would be better if they stopped their efforts and got some sleep. He added that he was not asking for wages (*ragajis*) or trying to "extort from little children" (*balelus ngana miyunu*). At that, the elder daughter placed a sarong on the offering tray. A struggle ensued between the shaman and the daughter in which each one denied that they were speaking in metaphor. He *meant* it, he declared, when he said that he wasn't bidding for payment, that there was no use trying; she, she declared, *meant* it when she said she wanted him to try. Eventually the shaman consented to "go to Pue" on the old woman's behalf.

Demonstrations of "white feelings" toward a shaman and his spirit familiars are often pro forma. For example, it is customary to place some fine cloth on the offering tray to "strengthen" the resolve of the shaman's spirit familiars to work on the patient's behalf. This cloth generally is not given to the shaman but returns to its owners. Then, too, when people insist on giving a shaman a gift, the shaman may refuse to accept it until the patient has indeed recovered, lest the patient die and embarrass him. In the case of the old woman, several days after the mabolong she herself presented the shaman with her daughter's sarong. When he resisted, the woman said that if it hadn't been for him, she would have died—and for that reason she didn't want to "fool the spirit familiars." Her household likewise then assisted in harvesting the shaman's field.

Properly encouraged, then, a shaman links his own fate with that of his patient. But the association is one of dependency, not equality. The shaman is the spirit familiar, the patient is the child. The shaman carries the patient's surrogate—the betel offering—as a parent carries a child. The association is further heightened by calling the cloth that is placed over the shaman's head a "toru." The toru, a broad-brimmed hat, is a quintessential symbol of the nurturing and protective parent, shielding a baby from the elements as it rides in its parent's arms or on the parent's back. In the ritual whereby a newborn is first carried from the house to the ground, a protective toru, treated with magic and medicines to insure the child's safety and well-being on journeys short or long, figures centrally (Figs. 6, 7). Should a toru be carried off by the wind or lost, the child it has protected is endangered, for with it may go the child's dream agent (*tanuana*).

In like fashion, the patient's life depends on the shaman's conduct on his journey. Should the shaman trip and fall, the patient could be harmed (Fig. 26). The shaman who is inattentive to his charge may indeed cause catastrophic results—as in the case of the daughter of a couple I knew, who was said to have possessed a fate to die at marriage. To ward off that fate, an all-night mabolong was held in conjunction with her wedding. After daybreak, the two presiding shamans got drunk and fought. A meal had been served, but when the violence broke out the plates were collected again and the food was returned to the pots. Throughout the chaos, the young woman's betel offering was bound to the back of one of the shamans. Not long after, the young woman died. Her parents saw a connection between the disruptive behavior of the shamans and their daughter's death.

In his negotiations with Pue, a shaman once again establishes both his own identification with the patient and the patient's dependence on him. The shaman and his spirit familiars "assume the debt"—that is to say, take responsibility for fulfilling a vow to Pue in return for the patient's life. So committed are a shaman's spirit familiars to a patient that if the patient should die before the vow is fulfilled, the familiars may abandon the shaman to follow the ghost of the dead. The shaman must then summon them back so that they will prove efficacious again. I have seen this done with a small resin torch and a toru. The torch for this rite is auspiciously constructed with seven securing ties. The shaman makes three circles with the burning torch beneath the toru and four above to summon back the spirit familiars, much as one summons back an infant's soul to the protection of the toru. The shaman may similarly perform a rite over the coffin of a patient at the gravesite to prevent his familiars from joining the dead person.

SUMMARY

Following Loisy, Valeri (1985, 67) deems sacrifice an "efficacious representation" that asserts the hierarchy of humans and their divinities. This hierarchy, he suggests, is expressed by the disproportion among the gifts exchanged. The superiority of the gods is expressed through their largess; the inferiority of mortals, by the paltriness of their offerings to the gods. Relative differences within the categories of divine and mortal gifts further elaborate the scheme. In the case of the Wana pantoo, the Owner's gift of life dwarfs the oblation of betel made on the patient's behalf, as does the shaman's willingness to risk his own life for the patient. Thus, by the magnitude of his own sacrifice in undertaking the ritual, the shaman, like Pue, asserts superiority over the patient. The comestibles that comprise the second stage of the ritual can also index the relative status of ritual participants. A large feast can testify both to the strength and prosperity of the community—of which the patients are members and on which they depend—and to the reputation of the shaman whose ritual actions have occasioned a large celebration. A shaman must follow up his transaction with Pue by negotiating with patients' families about when and how to stage a feast of thanksgiving.

It is instructive to compare this Wana "gift to god" with ceremonial gift exchange of the sort Mauss described, which involves humans on both sides of the exchange—wife-givers and wife-takers, kula partners, potlatch rivals. The pantoo, in contrast, involves humans on one side and an exogenous being on the other. Fulfilling a vow of the sort described here entails pooling resources—food, drink, betel fixings, tobacco—for a communal celebration. We can see "exchange" with a small *e* at work in the collective feast: I support your celebration and you support mine. Thematically, though, the principle operating here is not potlatch, but potluck. Fulfilling a vow means sharing food and good cheer, thereby modeling the way a community ought to be. The principle of exchange would be cited only if breached.[5]

Like gifts to gods, gifts between humans in the Maussian scheme have implications for hierarchy. In direct exchange, gifts are reciprocal; they even out over time. I am in your debt for a while, but when I reciprocate our positions are reversed. Indirect exchange among human parties can sustain hierarchy (witness Eastern Indonesia), but each party is both indebted to a giver and superior to a receiver. In a pantoo, where reciprocity between humans and a deity is negotiated by a shaman, the shaman is in principle beholden to no one but Pue, and for his efforts, his community should be beholden to him.

10

Rituals Through Time

Critics of cultural analysis frequently note that interpretive approaches too often impart a timeless quality to symbolic behavior. If culture is always so "meaningful," how and why does change occur? By examining the link between Wana ritual and politics I hope to illuminate a major source of change at work in the Wana region. In this chapter, a historical examination of the shaman's journey to Pue will suggest some changes that have occurred in Wana ritual and cosmology over the course of this century. In contrast to the summoning of spirit familiars, the treatment of patients, and requests for familiars' foods—the other three ritual sequences analyzed in the book—the shaman's pantoo appears (from what documentation there is) to represent a new development in the mabolong. In Part Five I shall link that development to changes in ritual practice and political conditions that may have heightened the profile of Wana shamanship in the twentieth century.

What is the evidence that change in the ritual has occurred? First, nowhere in Kruyt's lengthy 1930 report on the Wana do we find a supreme god who matches the conception of Pue I found current in the 1970s. Second, that article makes no mention of the pantoo in the context of shamanic ritual. Finally, whereas the shaman's journey to the Owner in the mabolong appears to be an abbreviated version of the molawo ritual described above, Kruyt does not cite the latter, except as the name of an episode in another, larger ritual.

What might explain the differences between Kruyt's account and my own? The inconsistencies could, of course, reflect the fact that Kruyt was in the Wana area for two months, whereas I was in residence for two years, and that most of his information came from interviews rather than participant observation. Yet the high quality of Kruyt's article, his interest as a missionary in religious and ritual matters, and his decades of familiarity with the language and culture of the Poso people—close relations of the Wana—make his article a valuable and trustworthy document.

Another possibility is that the differences in our accounts reflect regional variations in Wana culture. To be sure, Kruyt's informants included several Wana from the southwestern villages of Toronggo and Ula, an area with which I am unfamiliar and my informants lacked ties. The community where I spent most of my time was composed heavily of To Barangas from the Manyo'e area far to the north. Kruyt omits the To Linte, another Wana branch, from his account, whereas they figured among my sources. Still, there is significant overlap in our accounts, for we both drew on informants from Watu Kanjoa and Ue Kauru; some of my associates even recognized names and faces in Kruyt's article.

It is not possible for me to distinguish fully regional from historical differences in our studies. For example, Kruyt transcribes a /tj/ sound which was totally absent in my companions' speech. Time could be responsible for some of these differences, but geography may be a factor as well. Whereas Kruyt's sources were strongly oriented to the former raja of Bungku, mine were preoccupied with Wana ties to the former raja of Tojo. This difference could reflect the fact that I worked far to the north of Kruyt's informants (although most of my neighbors had been born to the south and west of the settlements where they resided at the time of my research, and hence their parents and grandparents owed tribute to Raja Bungku). Alternatively, it could reflect the later historical significance of Raja Tojo, who was executed by the Japanese during World War II.

Admitting both the problem of relying on a single prior source (however rich) and the likelihood of regional variation, I wish to pursue the possibility that some of the differences between Kruyt's account and my own are attributable, first, to shamanic innovation that has applied conventional concepts and practice to new ritual ends, and second, to changing political and interethnic conditions in the region. Considering how to reconcile Kruyt's account and my own may well further our understanding of the place of Wana shamanship in Wana life.

DEITIES: THE ONE AND THE MANY

In his monumental comparative study of world shamanism, Eliade argued that shamanism is defined by an ecstatic ascent to the sky or descent to the underworld. In Eliade's view, ritual follows myth, not the reverse. Consequently, shamans' out-of-body journeys must be based on a belief in Supreme Beings. In fact, Eliade is able to document time and again an association between shamanic journeys and deities of the sky or the underworld. Whereas many theorists and historians of religion posit this historical emergence of a Supreme God from a prior pantheistic state, Eliade, like Father W. Schmidt, favors a reverse evolution. In the case of North and Central Asian shamanism, for example, he argues for a "prior religious ideology" focused on "faith in a celestial Supreme Being." True shamanism, in his eyes, is the archaic religion associated with that belief. Although the cult of the Supreme God subsequently died out with the onslaught of a host of new spirits, goddesses, ancestors, and demiurges, its "symbolism of ascent" persisted in shamanic practice. In Eliade's reconstruction, the core shamanic experience is thus "a survival" that continues long after its theological moorings have been dismantled (Eliade [1951] 1964, 505).

Critics have challenged Eliade's attempt to define shamanism in terms of ecstatic ascents and descents, as well as the theological premises of his model of religious development (see Reinhard 1976). Still, Eliade's theory does have the virtue of pondering just what those *dei otiosi* in so many religious traditions may signify.

My own attempt at religious reconstruction will be more modest than Eliade's. It will not be broadly cross-cultural, although it will have an interethnic dimension. Nor will it delve deep into an archaic past to uncover the origins of Wana shamanism; rather, its time depth will be the twentieth century. Even though it will not lend support to Eliade's theory about a prior cult of a Supreme Being, nevertheless it will offer a demonstration of how shamans may "transform a cosmo-theological concept into a *concrete mystical experience*" (Eliade [1951] 1964, 265).

Over this century at least, Wana notions regarding a Supreme Being appear to have moved in a direction opposite to the one Eliade proposed. In the interval between Kruyt's study and my own, Wana have constructed an omniscient creator god in line with the models presented to them by Islam and Christianity. This figure, Pue, has assumed a cultural centrality quite different from the place of the several deities depicted in Kruyt's account.

Like Kruyt, I was told of two beings, Lai and Ndara, who were siblings when the earth and sky were still connected by a vine. Also like

Kruyt, I heard accounts of Lai and Ndara that included a third sibling, Koni (the name means "eat"), whom his siblings murdered for devouring people. Koni, I was told, was the first liver-eating demon (*measa*). When the vine holding heaven and earth together was severed (one of Kruyt's accounts holds a mouse as responsible for gnawing through the vine), Lai managed to grasp the vine and climb upward. Lai became the *pue ri wawo yangi*, the Owner above the Sky, while Ndara went down to become the *pue ara ntana*, the Owner beneath the Earth. (Kruyt notes that among the Poso people to the west of the Wana, Lai is male and Ndara is female. Neither he nor I found such an association among the Wana, however. Kruyt determined them to be brothers.)

Kruyt tells another tale about Ampue, an old man who had taken root in the ground. (Interestingly, the Wana word for an elder and the word for a tree stump are identical: *tu'a*, which also means "old.") One of Ampue's sons repeatedly bumped his father's roots with firewood. Angered by his son's thoughtlessness, the elder went up to the sky to become one of the constellations by which the Wana regulate their farming cycle. Kruyt's account (abbreviated here) matches the general lines of stories that I was told. Although he reports that Ampue had seven children, I heard one version in which there were seven, while another—the best version I have—claims that the "rooted elder" (Pue Makale) had only two children.

Kruyt also recounts a story of human creation involving a deity called Pue Lamoa. In this story, a character named Pololoiso—whom Kruyt describes as either "man or god" (1930, 417)—descended from heaven along the vine and set the earth down in the sea. He then planted what Kruyt called the *parambae* tree (*parambaa* to my associates). The tall tree, however, threatened to capsize the earth, so Pololoiso went up to the sky to ask Pue Lamoa if he could chop the tree down. Permission was not granted. The tree continued to sway, and the earth again nearly capsized. Pololoiso once again requested permission to fell it. This time Pue Lamoa granted permission but ordered Pololoiso to be certain that the tree fell on land and not sea, otherwise he would become poor. Although Pololoiso did his best to fell the tree on land, it landed in the sea. Pue Lamoa pronounced: "Now the people shall be poor. They shall beat bark cloth into clothing and enjoy no well-being." From the base of the tree Pololoiso carved a man and a woman. He then went up to the sky to request breath for the pair. In his absence, a "jini" (Wana today would say *jimi*) came along and gave the figures breath.[1] Regrettably, the breath given humankind was not the everlasting breath that Pololoiso sought: thus, because of the jini's breath, humans must die. (For other stories about Pololoiso, see Kruyt 1930, 418; and Atkinson 1983.)

Once again, the stories I was told about human creation fit the general outlines of this tale. One major variation is in the god's name: my companions used the unmarked form of *pue* and *never* qualified Pue in these tales with the term *lamoa*. According to Kruyt, in the language of the Pamona-speakers of Poso (formerly known as Bare'e-speaking Toraja), the term *lamoa* refers to sky gods; Wana, in contrast, associate the term specifically with spirits of thunder and lightning (Kruyt 1930, 420). Thus Pue Lamoa, "the lord of heaven" in Kruyt's account, fells trees with lightning. Kruyt also notes that human illnesses are attributed to "fishhooks" thrown down from the sky that lodge in people's flesh (p. 422). When he asked who hurled the hooks, he received different answers. Some people said Pue; others said Indo i Dolinde or Dalinde, the ghost of an unmarried woman. But Kruyt surmised from shamanic practice that actually spirits called Sangia, associated with the rainbow, were generally agreed to be the source of the hooks. Notions about Sangia, he observes, were probably imported from the south—perhaps from the Mori or populations of Southeast Sulawesi.

To my companions, Pue was the benign *deus otiosus*, the creator and giver of breath, the ultimate justice in the universe. Pue Lamoa (or simply Lamoa), by contrast, was a wrathful and vengeful being who cast hooks, axes, and other weapons into human beings in response to reversals of intention, mixing of meats from land and water, and mockery of animals. One could approach Pue in the mabolong and molawo rituals, but a separate set of ritual procedures was reserved for victims of Lamoa. The most elaborate of these procedures was called *molawo maneo*, the "crooked" molawo, in which the performer chanted the journey of spirit familiars to the place of Lamoa. A journey to Pue, by contrast, was called a *molawo manoto*, or "straight" molawo.

In the molawo maneo, Pue Lamoa is portrayed as a great, fierce being who emits hissing sparks as he approaches the spirit familiars. The latter exhaust the deity in a contest, then search his body—his ears, armpits, stomach folds—for the missing soul parts of the patient.

They extinguish the fires at his resin tree, his grasslands, his anvil, and quell the smoky turmoil of his lake. After defeating Lamoa and quenching the sources of their patient's feverish distress, the spirit familiars engage Pue Lamoa in a reconciling meal composed of all the foods whose mixing he prohibits. (See Atkinson 1979 for more details of the rituals dealing with Lamoa.)

The point to be made here is that my associates, in contrast to Kruyt's, maintained a separation in ritual and discourse between Pue and Pue Lamoa. The former is approached with respect by mabolong performers and their walia; the latter is deeply feared (indeed, some of my associates did not want to utter the word *lamoa*) yet bullied by the spirit familiars in the molawo maneo. Whereas a mabolong attracts an audience from far and wide, rituals performed for Lamoa are shunned by all but the performer, the patient, and those wishing to learn the procedures. When I wanted to transcribe the tape of a healing ritual associated with Lamoa, I had to leave the house where I lived because one of my housemates was pregnant and thus vulnerable to the dangers of hearing the ritual. Another time after I had played a recording of a molawo maneo, a baby in the house woke up in gasping seizures that were attributed to hearing the tape. Once again I had to move my transcription site.

I did encounter the name Dolinde (identified by Kruyt's sources as a hurler of hooks) as an epithet in a ritual for Lamoa-based conditions. The performer, a knowledgeable old woman, told me that Doe Dolinde was a name for one of the Owners. As for the Sangia spirits, they (as I have noted elsewhere) were associated with a particular kind of attack by headhunting spirits. They were managed ritually in procedures quite distinct from those accorded illnesses caused by Lamoa—although a patient might be diagnosed as a victim of both Sangia, who caused excruciating pain in the head and torso, and Lamoa, whose searing weapons caused fever and chills.

In reviewing this "cast of characters" in Kruyt's account and my own, it is clear that nominally the list is the same. What differs is how these characters figure in ritual and everyday discourse.

DEITIES IN RITUAL CONTEXTS

In this section I shall explore the ways in which the gods above and beneath the earth, the benign *deus otiosus*, and the wrathful Lamoa all merge and part across ritual domains in Kruyt's account and my own. I start with a ritual procedure common to our two studies.

"Talking a Betel Offering"

Changing one's mind is for Wana an act that invites divine wrath. In this my companions explicitly identified Pue Lamoa as the agent of retribution. Yet to divorce the person from the dreaded consequences of this proscribed act, a betel offering is made not to Pue Lamoa, but to the Owners beneath the Earth and above the Sky. Kruyt documents this rite as well. The procedure is carried out by someone versed in the formal invocation—usually, but not necessarily, a shaman. The performer of the ritual "calls out" to each of the two Owners in turn. To the Owner beneath the Earth the performer says: "If you are lying on your stomach, roll over on your back and listen to me." To the Owner above the Sky the speaker says: "If you are lying on your back, roll over on your stomach and listen to me." (Kruyt's partner, N. Adriani [1932, 190–215], transcribed an identical charge from the Poso area.) By shifting their positions, these *dei otiosi* come a little closer to human life.

The performer then suggests that the patient on behalf of whom the offering is made may be vulnerable to spiritual retribution on account of some past words or attitude. To take a common example, just before a young boy has his penis incised, an offering is made in case the child has experienced doubts or fears about the procedure. To quote part of an invocation at such an occasion:

> I am chewing betel because perhaps there are some words of. . . Linus, perhaps just a word when he was still very little. He said "I don't want to be incised for I feel it will hurt." That's why I am chewing betel again so that the Owner will no longer notice those words, eh, Lamoa will no longer notice those words, so Doge [another epithet for Lamoa] will no longer notice all those words, buzzing, falling about. Lift back those many words there.

After both Owners have been addressed, the officiant sets out a betel quid—one in a low place, one in a high place—for each one. In this procedure, an assault by Lamoa is offset by offerings to the Owners above the Sky and beneath the Earth, neither of whom is addressed directly as Lamoa. The invocation is directed to the Owners Below and Above, but it mentions Pue, Lamoa, and Doge with the hope that they will ignore the words and refrain from casting their weapons. The last two terms are synonymous; as for the first, Pue, it is unclear whether the term is being used synonymously or whether it refers to another deity.

For a patient already smitten by Lamoa's vengeful blows, a pantende ritual may be held. The pantende, varieties of which both Kruyt and I found, is devoted to detailing Pue Lamoa's arsenal and removing its effects from the patient. My texts of the ritual identify the two Owners as agents of wrath (one representative passage itemizes "eh, the hook of the Owner up above, eh, the hook of the Owner down below"). Thus, just as the pair of Owners are cited as a preventive to Lamoa's vengeance, so Lamoa's vengeance entails the weapons of the Owners Above and Below. Both the pantende and the betel offering described above are directed at releasing the patient from something— words in one case, sources of pain in the other. One might argue that appeals to a divided pair of deities, each relegated to opposite extremes of the cosmos, underscores the ritual theme of separation and distancing. A further observation (one I shall pursue later) is that neither of the procedures detailed here is a shamanic act: although shamans *may* perform them, these procedures are merely "talk," involving no direct and personal contact with a spirit realm.

Deities and Vows

To see how shamanic practice may be implicated in transforming a ritual, let us look specifically at how vows are made. Just as the cosmic Owner depicted in the shamanic journey to the sky is not the focus of the rituals described so far in this chapter, neither is that deity present in the formulation of vows outside shamanic ritual.

Kruyt makes no mention of the shamanic vow, but he does speak of a practice called *mantoo*. That word puzzled him. He speculated that it might be related to the word *manto'o*, meaning in the Poso language "something spoken." But he reported that he did not hear its root, *to'o*, among the Wana; instead he heard the word *tuntu*. By the time of my fieldwork, *to'o* was part of common parlance. I, like Kruyt, suspect a relation between *to'o* and the term *pantoo*, although no linguistic principle in the Wana language accounts for the transformation of the word by the omission of the glottal stop. Similarly, Kruyt does not identify *nia* as a synonym for *pantoo*; *nia*, from the Indonesian *niat*, may well be a more recent borrowing.

As Kruyt describes it, a mantoo is performed if a patient fails to respond to treatment. A ritual practitioner places betel and tobacco on a copper tray and covers it with a length of fine cloth. The speaker then places the tray on the ground, faces the east, and summons the Owners beneath the Earth and above the Sky. The orator asks pity for the patient and promises a great feast if the patient recovers, specifying a number of chickens to be slaughtered. A dueling contest may also be promised, which is done in broad daylight and involves ritual preventives to sangia attacks. If the patient recovers, he or she then uses the sarong; if the patient dies, the sarong is used to wrap the corpse. Here again we see the invocation of the Owners Above and Below, with no mention made of Lamoa or Pue. The feast is familiar from the mabolong episode, although Kruyt specifies only two elements: the chickens and the dueling.

My neighbors performed a variant on the vow described by Kruyt. They call it a *pantoo mako'o*, a "hard vow" (*nia mako'o*, I was told, being synonymous), and it too is performed outside the context of a mabolong. Like the invocation cited earlier, it involves summoning three times each the Owners Above and Below, then promising that if the patient recovers certain things will be done. Typically one promises to slaughter chickens and pour rice beer, placing a betel offering in a metal betel case or a tin can as a token of the vow. Vows of this sort can take different forms. For example, one couple I knew promised to set afloat an offering consisting of a blouse, a sarong, and a plate with a betel offering in it if their daughter recovered from an illness. This resembles a practice Kruyt describes that did not seem to carry the label *mantoo* but was intended to rid a community of an illness by floating an offering downstream to the spirit owners of the condition. Of the transcripts presented in Chapter 8, one involved a vow to slaughter three chickens over the feet of a mother and stepdaughter who had survived difficult childbirths and to share a plate of food with close friends. We note once again the invocation at the fulfillment of a hard vow to the Owners below the Earth and above the Sky.

In the same invocation, the performer, Apa Mene, narrated the history and power of his speech. His oratory can be compared to a shaman's invocation of his spirit familiars. In both, a performer is identifying the sources of his powerful knowledge for his audience;

but instead of invoking personal familiars, Apa Mene couched his recitation in the conventions of Wana mythology.

e pantuntuku maya rato'o palalaeesong etu
My speech, it can be said, is Palalaeesong's.

pangantuntu maya rato'o nabi etu pantuntu etu
The speech, it can be said, of the *nabi*, that speech.

panto'o etu wali etu
That talk there is effective.

pansombo pansombo etu
A legacy, a legacy,

maya rato'o pololoisong etu
it could be said, of Pololoisong,

se wetu se maya pantima tuwu
and that's why it can obtain life.

e sambengi e pai seo etu
Eh, by night, eh, and by day,

pansaningku etu to etu
that knowledge of mine there.

se panto'o nu nabi to etu
It's the speech of the *nabi* there.

se maya rato'o sombo i ngkasi etu
It can be called the legacy of Ngkasi,

ia e nayua joe ntana etu
he who went to the end of the earth.

to etu se e rasombo etu
That's what [he] stored,

nse naka to etu kuika aku
and that's why I do what I do.

apa kiyako ngkasi etu
Because Ngkasi's departure,

e maya rato'o joe ntana etu
eh, it could be said, to the end of the earth,

mangkeni maya rato'o sugi etu
carrying what could be called wealth,

e omo patanya walia etu
and only those spirit familiars,

e sombonya jamo to etu
only that did he store behind—

to'o wali raika untuk to etu
talk that works when it is performed,

e tiroo wali raika untuk
and still works when it is performed,

maya rato'o tuwu nu manusia
it can be said, for the life of humankind,

maya rato'o katuwu ngkaju liano
it can be said, the life of the tree crop,

e katudu e mpue etu to etu
that which the Owner put down.

The allusions in this text are familiar in Wana mythology, for they refer to the creation of humankind and to the departure of "knowledge, power, and wealth" from the Wana land. Pololoiso (called variously Palalaeesong and Pololoisong here for rhetorical effect), it will be recalled, is the culture hero who went up to the Owner in search of breath for the human figures he had carved from the parambaa tree. Thus Wana call themselves the Owner's *kaju liano*, which, as best I understand it, means the crop or descent of the tree. The story of Pololoiso concerns the severing of an *axis mundi*; like the story of the rat who gnawed through the vine holding sky and earth together, its theme is the partition of a prior unity into divided realms.

In his invocation, Apa Mene shifts from the creator hero Pololoiso who journeyed to the sky to the trickster Ngkasi who departed for the end of the earth with "knowledge, power, and wealth." This departure spelled an end to the age of magical power, the time of *adi adi* or *wali mpanto'o*, when words had the power to conjure themselves into being. Like the stories of the kaju parambaa and the severed vine, the story of the departure—what Wana call the "separation" or "parting" (*poga'a*)—is a story about "lost plenitude" (Traube 1989). Apa Mene's speech, however, focuses not on what was lost, but on what was retained in the Wana land. Like coastal regencies that have their sacred regalia (*posaka*)—magical swords, flags, umbrellas, and the like—from which their owners derive great power (see Errington 1989), so too was a treasure left to the Wana: this is the power of "spirit familiars," "talk that works when it is performed," "performed for . . . the life of humankind." In using this talk to invoke the Owners beneath the Earth and above the Sky, Apa Mene accepts the conditions of a divided world.

If the hard vow acknowledges the separation of earth and sky and the consignment of Ndara and Lai to either extreme of a now-severed *axis mundi*, the "vow" as it is made and fullfilled in the mabolong does not. Instead of making priestly offerings to two deities separated from each other and distanced from earthly affairs, a mabolong performer rejects those divisions and re-establishes direct connections with Pue, the creator, using the spirit familiars who stayed in the Wana land after the parting. He does not restrict himself to the effectiveness of words, however. Like Pololoiso, the shaman goes in search of life-giving breath; if it cannot be the eternal breath that Pololoiso sought, at least it can extend life for a while.

I am proposing, then, that a vow made in a shamanic context involves a single deity because a shamanic journey challenges the divisions of the world on which an appeal to an Owner Below and an Owner Above is premised. In support of that claim I would note that the formulaic dualism of Lai and Ndara washes out not only in the move from a pantoo mako'o to a vow made in a mabolong, but also in the move from the pantende ritual to the molawo maneo. The pantende, which does not involve a spirit journey, is laced with references and appeals to the Owners Above and Below, whereas the molawo maneo, which features a journey to Lamoa's place by the spirit familiars, focuses on a single ferocious giant. In both the molawo maneo and the mabolong vow, the shamanic contingent mediates directly between the human level and a single ultimate arbiter.

My argument here converges with one made by Eliade. He too identified a contrast between shamanic and nonshamanic communications across the divide of the severed *axis mundi*, and Wana stories about the prior connection of sky and earth and the subsequent felling of that axis are duplicated many times in his work. He also recognized that offerings are the conventional form of communication between humans and deities across the divide of heaven and earth. Elaide contended that whereas ordinary people make offerings and sacrifices across that divide, shamans bridge it through ecstatic experience:

> In the archaic cultures communication between sky and earth is ordinarily used to send offerings to the celestial gods and not for a concrete and personal ascent; the latter remains the prerogative of shamans. . . . What for the rest of the community remains a cosmological ideogram, for the shaman . . . becomes a mystical itinerary.
>
> (Eliade 1964, 265)

Setting aside the question of whether ecstatic experience defines shamanism, Eliade and I differ in our investment in a historically prior significance of a celestial Supreme Being in shamanic practice. Instead of reflecting a prior "cult" of either a celestial Supreme Being or a pair of celestial and uranian Supreme Beings, stories of Lai, Ndara, and Ampue were part of a cosmogonic discourse distinct from shamanic practice. The "priority" these figures hold in creation stories cannot be extended to a priority in shamanic practice. Kruyt gives no evidence that Wana shamans in the early part of this century were making spiritual voyages to "Supreme Beings," although they very definitely had a tradition of traveling to spirit realms. Eliade might argue, of course, that a historical proliferation of spirits had eclipsed an earlier cultural centrality of these deities, but there is no evidence to either support or counter such a hypothesis.

The evidence that does exist might help us to address the curious absence of shamanic journeys to Pue and Pue Lamoa in Kruyt's account and their visibility in my own. I shall attempt to reconstruct, in a preliminary and speculative fashion, some changes that may have come about.

Kruyt (1930, 438–39) describes a hierarchy of Wana shamanic practice. The lowest level is *walia mangepe*, in which practitioners, without the intervention of spirits, can locate intrusive objects (Kruyt calls them "poisons") in the body and suck them out. (In mabolong performances a shaman typically uses his special shaman's cloth to attract and draw out intrusive objects from a patient's body, instead of sucking them out with his mouth.)

Next in Kruyt's shamanic order is *walia mantende*. The meaning of *mantende* in Kruyt's research and my own is very close: the word refers to procedures to remove the hooks and other weapons associated with Pue Lamoa. Then follows *walia moganda*, corresponding to the mabolong ritual I have described here. (*Ganda* was a popular substitute for the term *bolong*, or "drum," in the shamanic texts I collected.)

At the top of Kruyt's hierarchy are *to walia mamparada woto ntongku*, "the priests who climb the mountain slopes (where the *walia*-spirits live) along a ladder. These priests thus do not await the arrival of the helping spirits, but seek them out in their habitat (pp. 438–39). Kruyt does not mention traveling to the Owner. He goes on to explain that the spirit familiars let down a ladder for the shamans to use to reach them. This mediation take place in the *mosalia*, a great ritual performed at most once a year to promote the health and well-being of a community.

Neither Kruyt nor I ever witnessed a salia. Kruyt (p. 450) described it as a great feast that was held "in olden times" when people still lived among their clanmates. Similarly, I knew the salia as a ritual that had all but died out in the Wana region.[2] That Kruyt and I each—a half century apart—should have known of the salia as a ritual on the wane raises two questions. First, why was it in decline in Kruyt's time? Second, why did it persist in one area of the Wana region into the last quarter of this century? The first question must be answered, I think, against the political background of the nineteenth and early twentieth centuries, a matter I shall consider in Part Five. As for the second question, although I shall touch on it too later, only further fieldwork could confirm my hunches.

A salia was staged not for an individual patient but for an entire community.[3] It was held not at times of illness or misfortune, but instead after the harvest when rice supplies were abundant. In accord with its aim of promoting the health and well-being of all the participants, several ritual specialists would systematically drive out all hidden threats to people's health and call back the souls of everyone present. The ritual lasted three nights (although I was told that seven nights was possible) and was held in a building called a *bombaru* (a popular term for "house" in shamans' speech during my fieldwork) that seems to have been built for the event to accommodate the large gathering.

A heap of cordyline branches was placed on the floor adjacent to two lango, which Kruyt (1930, 450) describes as copper trays with feet, filled with betel fixings. The ritual specialists used one lango, the feastgoers the other. (By contrast, at a mabolong shamans and audience members alike take betel and tobacco from the same lango, and then it is a woven winnowing tray, not a copper tray.) On the evening of the first day, the feastgoers seated themselves in rows inside the house. The officiants walked up and down the rows, striking each person on the head six times with a cordyline leaf and calling the walia spirits on the sand and on the mountain (using the phrase *oo wurake*, which refers to spirits of the air in the Poso language and which Wana of my day used in their Lamoa-related chants). The performers then proceeded to chant the entire night as the feastgoers slept.

On the following day, mothers of young children who (as I can reconstruct the ritual) had not yet heard the salia took those children and one chicken for each child to the bombaru. The chickens were killed and their blood dripped over the pile of cordyline leaves. (The chickens were then used for the day's feast.) Next an officiant cut the comb of a living bird and rubbed the blood on the foreheads of everyone present; it was then released, not to be killed. The use here of the blood of slaughtered and living chickens resembles what I witnessed in both Wana farming ritual and the study of magic. Wana use "living blood" (*raa tuwu*) to promote continuing life and efficacy. The use of blood from live chickens in the salia in connection with young children is consistent with this association.

The officiants then decorated a *pomaku*, a tall carrier used for transporting foodstuffs, and placed the cordyline leaves in it along with a plate of betel fixings. So arranged, the pomaku was now called the *rare* (a word that in Poso, according to Kruyt, may refer to magical plants wrapped in cordyline leaves) and represented the "strength of the place" (*roso nu lipu*).

The women brought plates of rice to the carrier along with tiny packets of rice called "food of the dream agent" (*baku ntanuana*), one for each child, whereupon the officiants repeated the act of striking all the participants with cordyline branches. Then a woman known as the "pincher" (*to mongkisu*) sat by the carrier, placing the rice packets around the carrier and emptying the plates of rice onto a leaf-covered winnowing tray. Next the feastgoers handled the mass of rice in an act called "pinching the rice," and the rice—called the *baku mwalia bae*, "the rice of the great walia"—was redistributed on the plates. A cry went up for the "side dish" to be "pinched" as well. The meat of the chickens slaughtered earlier was brought out, the to mongkisu placed chicken meat on each family's plate along with the family's packets of rice, each woman then reclaimed her plate, and her family ate of it. Whereas the baku mwalia bae before had been handled by the entire community, now only members of the household that owned the plate might eat of it, lest the tiniest children of the household die.[4]

Once again the officiants chanted all night.

The next day each feastgoer was again struck on the head with the cordyline and on the back with an officiant's hand, had a cordyline leaf blown onto his or her head, and finally was sprinkled with water from a cordyline leaf. The significance of this "massage," as it was called, was to drive off the sources of illness (and, I would suspect, to restore vital elements to the person: note that the head and the back—the sites of the two major kinds of soul parts—are involved here). Following this all-day procedure, the rite of "pinching" the rice was repeated at the evening meal.

The third day involved a grand feast to which people from other areas came bearing food as well, with the "pinching" of the rice repeated in the morning. In the late afternoon, each family brought an item of apparel and hung it on a line attached to the carrier. The officiants then dressed in these clothes and, taking the cordyline leaves and chanting the single word *tanuana* ("dream agent"), proceeded to the door of the house, descended onto banana leaves placed there, faced the east (the auspicious direction of the rising sun), and cried out *lelelele* three times. The drum and gongs were then set up and the officiants returned, carrying the cordyline leaves, to do a dance described as "mock fighting with the cordyline leaves" (*mampomoseka taba*). This dance was done six times (again, not seven, which would represent a completed life). Mothers then brought their babies to the officiants, who blew along the leaves onto the babies' crowns. (As in the mabolong when a performer blows along his cloth onto the crown of a patient, this gesture was no doubt to give life and strength.)

Finally, a broad-brimmed toru was placed over the carrier, and the officiants passed the cordyline branches over it three times and sang. (Kruyt indicates that the walia were sent off to their homes in this way.) Another meal was held, after which people danced all evening. Packets of steamed rice were divided among all the participants and each officiant was given carriers full of rice packets and live chickens provided by the families whose babies were treated. With drums beating, the officiants departed, carrying these bundles on their backs. The mothers and babies would follow them a ways, then go back to the feast house, entering by a different door, and be greeted as strangers from afar. (Such a greeting meets newborns after their first descent to the ground; its aim is to deceive the spirits who might do them harm.)

The officiants (whom my informants called "people of the cold hearth," *tau loto rapu*; see Graham 1987, 137, for an Iban variant) kept the chickens and treated them as surrogates for the children. As for the cordyline branches, they were planted again on the third day after the feast.

From this account, it is clear that the salia was a celebration of community. The emphasis is on strengthening the lives of all celebrants, particularly the newest among them. Nowhere does Kruyt clarify the point about performers ascending by ladders to the homes of the spirit familiars. He does note, however, that the all-night chant performed by the salia officiants is called *melawo*,[5] observing that among the Poso people the word *melawo* refers to the recital of a chant by a shaman who sits under a tent constructed of barkcloth. Although Kruyt provides no details of the molawo chant in the context of the Wana salia, his associate Adriani (1932, 203–10) supplies excerpts from the chant of the Toraja "priestesses," whose task it was to make journeys to the "Upperworld." In some of these chants, Adriani notes, the visit to the Uppergod is unelaborated; in others it is described in vivid detail. For example, when the priestess's party rouses the Uppergod, he stands, accepts the offering they have brought to him, and conducts an inquiry to discover which spirit may have stolen the patient's "soul stuff" (p. 207).

Unfortunately, Kruyt does not tell us whether the melawo performed at the salia resembles the Poso spirit journeys of the same name and, if so, whether and how Pue may have figured in them. Given Adriani's account of the Poso melawo and the modern Wana use of the same term to refer to a detailed litany of a shamanic journey to the sky, it is tempting to assume that the salia performers' chants depicted such a journey. Whether it culminated in a visit to the Owner, we do not know.

Curiously, Kruyt makes no mention of the molawo apart from the all-night chant during the salia. By contrast, I found the molawo to be a ritual in its own right. Just as Kruyt found the salia to be the most sophisticated form of Wana shamanic practice, my companions regarded the molawo as highly "esoteric" (*masusi*) and indeed spoke of it as "the mother" (*indo*) of shamanic rituals (*momago*). As for "going to Pue" in the manyomba (supplication) segment of the mabolong, they regarded this as simply a "fast" way to make the journey that takes molawo performers all night.

What are we to make of this, then? It could well be that the Wana molawo was in times past performed on a small scale for a patient, as in the case of the Poso molawo, as well as in the context of the salia. Another possibility is that the molawo has been detached from the salia and is now performed as a ritual in its own right. Why this might have happened is easy to deduce. A salia requires a community willing to host a three-night feast for more than one hundred people;[6] a molawo performance requires only an after-dinner gathering of a roomful of people and a performer willing to sit up all night to chant. In either case, elements of the two performances I saw (as well as accounts I heard) carry the collective emphasis of the salia. For example, each family was represented by areca nuts, and in one of the two performances the shaman's spirit familiars returned soul parts not only to the patients, but to everyone in the room.

I cannot resolve the issue of whether Pue figured in the salia. The negative evidence is Kruyt's and his sources' silence on the subject: if "going to Pue" had been the focus of the molawo, I suspect it would have been mentioned. The positive evidence comes from the Poso molawo, in which a shamanic journey sometimes entailed engaging the Uppergod. What may have changed since Kruyt's time, however, is the institution of a spirit journey in the context of the mabolong, a journey whose single purpose is to petition a high god. This petition in turn appears to be a shamanic enactment of the "hard vow" (*pantoo mako'o*), which transcends the partitions of a formerly united cosmos and simultaneously seems to reject the notion of a divided pair of deities in favor of a single ultimate arbiter.

My reconstruction draws principally on elements internal to Wana ritual. If in fact a single *deus otiosus* has gained prominence in Wana ritual in recent decades, it has done so in a time of pressure from adherents of world religions and the Indonesian government. Wana relations with Muslims go back to precolonial times; Christianity arrived more recently—after World War II, within the memory of my acquaintances. Since Indonesian Independence after World War II, the nationalist government, in an effort to unite the diverse populations of Indonesia, has promoted what to members of five world religions looks like religious choice, but to ethnic minorities whose traditional cosmologies and rituals fall outside the government's model of a world religion looks like religious coercion. As defined in the Pancasila, the "Five Principles" of the state, Indonesians are expected to *bertuhan*, to worship a single God. Of the recognized religions, only two—Islam and Christianity—in fact conform to a Middle Eastern monotheism (although non-Christian Indonesians occasionally call into question a pantheism inherent in the concept of the Christian Trinity), whereas adherents of the other acceptable religions such as Buddhism and Confucianism must endeavor to conform to a monotheistic discourse. As I have documented elsewhere, pagan Wana are under considerable pressure to convert to a world religion as a gesture of their acquiescence to and membership in the nationalist enterprise.

Pagan Wana asserted the identity of Pue with the "Pue" of Islam and Christianity. Christians and Muslims in the region, however, were not always willing to do so. I suspect that criticism from advocates of world religions may help to explain why my neighbors claimed that a shaman who negotiates with Pue at the Opo Bira Lima does not in fact "see" Pue but instead deals with Pue's intermediary (*liang mpue*). One has only to contrast the obeisance of the shamanic party at the Opo Bira Lima to the "uppity" behavior of the crew that confronts Pue Lamoa to see that the former has acquired the lofty dignity of an all-knowing and powerful creator, whereas Pue Lamoa is just a big bully whom the spirit familiars are free to whip into shape.

In this chapter I have proposed that shamanic mediation with a high god in the context of the mabolong may have developed in the twentieth century. Indisputably, the waning of the regional salia ritual has allowed the mabolong to emerge as the dominant ritual for sustaining human health and well-being, a shift in ritual emphasis that is related to a simultaneous shift in political authority (see Part Five). Before I explore this connection between ritual and political authority, though, it is necessary to examine more closely the nature of shamanic authority in the mabolong itself.

PART FOUR

11

Foods for the Spirit Familiars

> For the time being we should simply bear in mind that this
> openness of practice to the future, an openness which lends or
> reascribes a meaning to it, is undoubtedly a characteristic of
> ritual activity in general; the carrying out of a ritual act entails
> a risk, for the one who orders that it be done and for the one
> who executes it, in so far as its efficacy must itself be practical
> if it is to exist as symbolic.
>
> Augé, *The Anthropological Circle:*
> *Symbol, Function, History*

At the start of this book I noted that a mabolong involves several
performing shamans. It is easy to lose sight of that fact as one reads the
transcripts of shamans' songs presented thus far. These texts convey a
vivid sense of a lone performer concentrating powerful spirits around
him as he undertakes heroic deeds. *As texts*, the songs analyzed in the
first three sections of this book are indistinguishable from solo performances of healing rituals that go by other names. The potudu—a
ritual that is essentially a mabolong without the drum, dance, and
drama—involves a single performer who sits by an offering tray as he
treats a patient; his song matches the transcripts presented in Part One
and Two. Likewise, the text of a mabolong performer's journey to the
Owner is, as explained in Part Three, simply an abbreviated version
of the molawo, a ritual performed by a single shaman seated at an
offering tray.

For the purposes of healing, a potudu or molawo performance
could be substituted for a mabolong. The potudu is said to be insufficient in some instances because a potudu performer cannot travel far
to investigate directly the "sources" (*pu'u*) of a patient's condition. By
simply switching the style of singing, however, a knowledgeable
potudu performer could transform the occasion into a molawo, the
"mother" of Wana shamanic ritual. In short, the mabolong is not
required simply on therapeutic grounds.

Be they part of a potudu, a molawo, or a mabolong, these shamanic songs *presume* the validity of the performer's claims to shamanic power. With power unquestioned, the texts are ostensibly directed at concentrating that power and applying it to the treatment of patients. Yet as the mabolong is actually practiced, matters are commonly reversed.[1] Validation of shamanic claims overshadows healing as a dominant issue; after all, other ritual means exist for the management of illness. A mabolong not only offers reassurance to patients and their immediate kin that powerful shamans are working on their behalf, but it also provides an arena for performers to create, augment, and sustain reputations as "people with spirit familiars."

Why must mabolong performers press their shamanic claims? Might this not simply be a political "add-on" to the "real" purpose of the mabolong? Let us pause for a moment and reflect on what the label *shaman* means in social terms. Roger Rouse (1978), in a useful critique of the literature on Amazonian shamans, pointed out that anthropological extension of the word *shaman* seems to suggest a professional specialization corresponding to the term in all societies with shamanic practices. In other words, by applying social scientific notions of roles and statuses to societies like the Wana, we make the matter of "being a shaman" more cut and dried than it in fact is. Although Wana do speak of experienced performers of mabolong, potudu, molawo, and salia rituals as "people with spirit familiars" (*tau kawalia, to walia*),[2] nevertheless there is no formal office of shaman, no limits on the number of tau kawalia there may be in a community, no explicit procedures for determining who is a shaman and who is not, no definitive rite of passage, and no insignia or badges of membership in a shamanic fraternity. Just how a person comes to be recognized as an effective "person with spirit familiars" is a subtle and long-term process, much of which is conducted in the mabolong arena. More people dance at mabolong than sing; of those who sing, more summon spirit familiars and treat patients than make journeys to Pue. Whether those who dance go on to sing, and whether those who sing eventually undertake dramatic travels to the sky, depends in part on the individual and in part on the reception the performer meets with over time from his or her fellows (a matter to be explored further in Part Five). Although the etiquette of the mabolong demands that audiences respect all performers, in practice certain ones claim audience concern and attention, and others do not. Thus, what is presumed in shamanic singing is precisely what a performer must convincingly achieve through performance.

Wana notions of ritual efficacy deny the relevance of audience engagement and participation to the success of shamanic endeavors. Likewise, the songs of shamans—as they summon spirit familiars, examine patients, and make trips to the Owner—are ostensibly directed toward a spirit audience, not a human one. Mabolong performers operate in a realm from which their human audience is cut off. A shaman's actions—as he summons his familiars, investigates hidden dimensions of human conditions, and makes forays into hidden realms—derive their efficacy from hidden sources: neither the attention nor the participation of a human audience (including patients) is required. As mabolong performers go about their tasks, others in the room divert themselves by chewing betel, smoking tobacco, and visiting with neighbors. Their disengagement, however, poses a challenge to mabolong performers, whose shamanic reputations ultimately depend on audiences acknowledging their claims. Whereas Roy Rappaport (1979, 177) asserts that "dramas have audiences, [but] rituals have congregations," I have deliberately used the word *audience* to apply to the assembly of people at a mabolong to underscore the point that Wana shamans are performers who must attract—and can never presume—the interest, attention, and commitment of others in what they are doing.

The episode that follows offers performers one way to exact from an audience a demonstration of commitment to their shamanship.[3] If performing a ritual is to accept its premises, as Rappaport (p. 193) contends, to respond to a performer's requests is, for Wana audiences, to acknowledge his shamanic endeavor.

FOODS FOR THE SPIRIT FAMILIARS

The reader may recall that Apa Mene, on his journey to the Owner examined in Chapter 7, spoke directly to his human audience at several points in his song. Each time he did so it was to make a request. First he asked for the hair decorations on a war shield. Then he asked for moss. When neither was forthcoming, he issued some directives to the drummer. Finally, as he stood speaking at the Owner's place, he indicated a desire for some beer.

When shamans address their audiences directly, it is usually to request baku mwalia—"rice" or "food" for his walia, or spirit familiars. The term applies generally to the contents of the lango that is prepared to host mabolong performers and their hidden associates, which, along with betel fixings, tobacco, and rice beer, include a variety of plant materials that the performing shamans' familiars are known to prize (Fig. 11). As a shaman performs he may sniff sprigs of basil (*wunga*, a standard ingredient of every lango) and rub it on himself. He may likewise taste, smell, mix with water and drink, or in other ways partake of the other plant materials to indulge his familiars. The implication is that the shaman has been transformed by the presence of his hidden allies: his being merges with theirs. Hence his expressions of desire and delight as he partakes of these substances are theirs as well.

But the appetites of spirit familiars are not limited to what has been placed on the offering tray. As the evening progresses, various familiars may "arrive" (*sonda*) with distinctive requests. For this reason, it is incumbent on at least some portion of the audience to attend to a shaman's singing and to remain alert to his spirits' desires.

When his familiars desire something, a shaman addresses his song to his human companions. His singing style remains constant, thereby signaling that his involvement with spirits is ongoing. Consistent with this style, his requests are couched in the verbal disguises of shamanic speech. So, for example, instead of asking for *ue raya mwua*, the liquid contained in a young areca nut, a shaman may ask for *salu kansoe ri rawa*, "water swinging in the air." (Both *salu* and *rawa* are words unique to shamans' songs.) Instead of asking for a banana, a shaman may request *lemba ntompuso maloe*, "the corpse of a suspended *tompuso*." (A *tompuso* is a being whose body has turned into a feature of the landscape; thus topographical features across the Wana land, including certain rocks and petroleum pools, are said to be the visible remains of mythical figures of an earlier age. According to legend, plant foods such as coconut palm, bananas, and tobacco are also tompuso. Once, it is said, a child cried for a food that did not then exist; when its parents failed to grant the wish, the child transformed itself into that food, thereby introducing it into the world. Hence the shaman who requested "the corpse of a suspended tompuso" was in fact asking for a banana. In a related metaphor, the shaman who asked for *salu pojene ntompuso*—"bath water of a *tompuso*"— wanted the sweat that forms on the lid of a rice pot.)

Sometimes a shaman's request is familiar to members of his audience because he or another shaman has made it before. Other times it is unfamiliar. If the audience does not understand the request, a guessing game ensues between the performer and his audience, like the following one involving Apa Linus:

solu to ri rapa bente	The One at the Fortified Crest arrives,
to tu'a mupewe wegaku	the Old One in a Loincloth, my spirit,
biasa momense wega	accustomed to dancing, spirit.
kono naendo nsuola	The familiar happens to remember,
wegangku mo raju ntuo naponowe wega	my spirit strongly desires to sniff, spirit,
wondu ntayu nja'u ma'i wega	the scent of the person over there who comes, spirit.
raju ntuo naponowe wega	Strongly desires to sniff, spirit,
wondu ntayu njo'u mai	the scent of the person who comes and goes
yako ri tidangi	over at the border.
rianya nayande	It's not to eat.
ojo raju naponowe wega	The spirit only wants to sniff
wondu ntayu njo'u ma'i	the scent of the person who comes and goes
ungka ri tidangi	as far as the border.
wondu ntayu nja'u ma'i wega	The scent of the person over there who comes, spirit,
ungka ri tidangi wega	as far as the border, spirit.
wega nsuola mananya	Spirit of the experienced familiar,
to la'u pobete	the One Down at the Sunset,
to pongkami reme	the One Who Guards the Light.
o raju ntuo naponowe wegangku	Oh, my spirit greatly desires to sniff
wondu ntayu nja'u ma'i	the scent of the person over there who comes
ungka ri tidangi wega	as far as the border, spirit.
nanu monayamo kutotae wegangku	Something I'm used to requesting, my spirit.
panewa kuporaju muni	At last I desire it again.
kono naendo nsuola wegangku	The familiar, my spirit, happened to remember it.
to la'u pobete	The One Down at the Sunset.
to ri naga nreme	The One at the Serpent of Day
raju ntuo naponganowe	greatly desires to sniff
wondu ntayu nja'u ma'i	the scent of the person over there who comes

ungka ri tidangi	as far as the border.
ane panta joa solu	If all the followers come,
ane panta joa sonda	if all the followers arrive,
to ri pondoboi	the ones at Pondoboi
mampolemba wonti wega	disguised as monkeys, spirit.
suola monanyamo	Experienced familiars,
suola monaumo	accustomed familiars.
ojo suola raponunde	Only a familiar who was taught,
pai naka suola	and in that way became a familiar.
pai namalanya nanganti	But this one can recover soul parts
nau ri luo saluo suola	even if they are off in another place, familiar.

Performers often boast about familiars they have won through personal quests. Apa Linus is indicating here that the spirit making this request is one he obtained by studying with another shaman. His use of the epithet "One at the Serpent of Day" makes me suspect he is alluding to spirit familiars from Apa Mene, who possessed special knowledge of a mythical serpent, *naga* (who derives ultimately from the Indian *nāga*). Associating his knowledge with a shaman of Apa Mene's stature may reflect well on this junior shaman.

nanu kutotae segi wega	What I mention here, spirit,
panta nggita mansosulu wega	each one we see, spirit,
e pantamo kudange wega	each one I hear, spirit.
kusosulu seja wega	I can see them also, spirit,
njo'u lino	over there in the world.
raju ntuo naponowe wega	The spirit greatly desires to sniff
wondu ntayu nja'u ma'i	the scent of the person coming and going
ungka ri tidangi	as far as the border.

At last a member of the audience ventures a guess.[4] Is the desired item a photograph? I think the questioner suspected the shaman wanted to see a photograph of my husband, who was back in the United States. The guess implies that a photograph, like a scent, is a trace of a person; it also captures the sense that my husband was a traveler who came to and went from the Wana land.

rianya to ele wegangku	It's not that, my spirit.
to ele taariemo natae wegangku	That was not what my spirit said,
yande nsuola mononyamo wega	the food of the experienced familiar, spirit.
wei panewa kutae muni . . .	But before I say it again . . .

Someone then proposes that he is asking to sniff a bar of soap.

rianya to ele wegangku	It's not that, my spirit,
wei simbau simbajumo	but something similar,
kutotae segi wega	I say now, spirit.

"Hair oil?" someone volunteers. It seems from the guesses that people are taking the reference to "coming and going" to mean that the desired substance is not indigenous to the Wana land but has its origins on the coast.

rianya to ele wegangku	It's not that, my spirit,
wei simbau simbajumo	but something similar.
wei kutotae segi wegangku	But I say now, my spirit,
ia la'u seja nowenya	It's down there also, its odor.
ia mongkami liano	This one guards the crop.

There is another guess, inaudible on my tape.

e rianya seja to ele wegaku	No, it's not that either, my spirit.
dange ja kutotaeka nggomi wegangku	Listen to what I tell you, my spirit.
ane ia mangkami liano wega	If this one guards the crop, spirit,
taa maoe petuwunya	the life of the latter will not be good.

Here the performer has offered a broad hint and someone guesses he is asking for a *nango*, a small green insect that destroys rice and in the process leaves a distinctive and unpleasant smell.

bara i ele mo ratae wegangku	Perhaps that is what was said, my spirit.
suolangku suola sala suola	My familiar, familiar, not the familiar.
sonda to ri pondoboi wegangku	The ones at Pondoboi arrive, my spirit,
mokarai wonti	dressed as monkeys,
raju ntuo naponowe seja	greatly desiring also to smell
wondu ntayu longko	the scent of a far-off person.

As this example indicates, a "food" for a shaman's familiars is not limited to the edible, even though Apa Linus's clarification that "it's not to eat" (*rianya nayande*) highlights the convention of speaking of the request as a food. Shamans may in fact request substances to eat, to look at, to feel, to listen to, to smell, or to use in other ways. A familiar's "food" may be any substance found in the everyday world for which the familiar, through a shaman, expresses a craving.

If the request is understood and granted, the shaman will accept the proffered treat, savor it momentarily, then resume his other activities. Both in song and in manner a performer may—as he partakes of the substance—express the pleasure and glee of the spirit familiar as though it were his own. At such a moment, the shaman's persona and his spirit familiar's are fused.

THE THREAT OF "SMALL FEELINGS"

What is at stake if the request is not granted? In principle, a great deal; but in practice, matters vary. If the shaman's request is not immediately understood, a riddle session will ensue as in the text above. If the request is deciphered but proves impossible to grant, or if the request is neither deciphered nor heeded, trouble may lie ahead. Although sometimes a shaman will simply drop the request and proceed with his performance, he and his spirit familiars may interpret the failure to grant their request as a lack of support for their efforts. They are said then to express "small feelings," or *kodi nraya*, an emotional state that, if it cannot be appeased, will have dire consequences. Acutely pained by the audience's callous inhospitality, the shaman's soul will depart for distant realms in the company of his spirit familiars, whereupon the shaman falls unconscious (*poso*). At this outward sign of the spirits' flight the shaman becomes a patient (Fig. 28). Other shamans should now attempt to "lock" (*kunsi*) his body so that his remaining vital elements do not escape, and then undertake spirit journeys to recover the shaman's soul parts and restore them to their owner. If they are not successful by daybreak, the shaman—in theory—will die. In short, the failure of an audience effectively to demonstrate their support for a shaman and his spirit familiars may put an end not only to the ritual occasion, but indeed to the shaman's life.

In light of these risks, audiences at a mabolong must take special care not to offend a shaman. When a performer requests "food" for his familiars, the request should be heeded. If it can be granted, well and good. If it cannot—either because it cannot be deciphered or because the substance is not available—the shaman's feelings must be assuaged. Indo Lina, the daughter of one shaman, wife of another, and an expert at deciphering shaman's requests, articulated the art of soothing a shaman. One should, she said, instruct the shaman to inform his familiars not to take it badly, that the audience is not intentionally depriving them of what they want; suggest to the shaman that he encourage his familiars—who are, after all, "sharp of eye" and "fast of foot"—to go off and find the desired substance themselves.

From the preceding transcript of Apa Linus's request and my sketch of cultural expectations pertaining to the episode, it should be apparent that this segment of the ritual is not directly associated with the treatment of patients. It appears, rather, to be a diversion—slightly comic, potentially tragic—from the main action of the evening. What are we to make of this episode?

I wish to advance three claims. First, like a "ritual of rebellion," this episode is a key to understanding the structural logic of the mabolong: it highlights the very ritual order it threatens to disrupt. Second, a shaman's appeal is potentially the most compelling part of the ritual for mabolong audiences. At this point a performer is no longer autonomous from his audience, but dependent on it. By couching his experience in familiar idioms of emotional experience, he appeals to others to identify with his plight and respond to it. By placing his well-being in the hands of others, he makes himself vulnerable. In contrast to other portions of the ritual, this interlude is highly improvisational and unpredictable, qualities that enhance its dramatic potential.[5] Finally, the epsiode has political dimensions: it provides a moment for the articulation of both a performer's relation to the audience and his relations to his fellow shamans.

The rest of this chapter will be devoted to a reading of the structural logic of this episode. In the next chapter I shall explore three transcripts in depth to show how the episode's dramatic and political possibilities unfold in mabolong performances.

THE LOGIC OF THE RITUAL ORDER
AND CHALLENGES TO IT

Schieffelin (1985) has recently argued that symbolic meaning is emergent in performance. True enough. But performative effect is itself highly dependent on ritual structure. The baku mwalia episode possesses an intricate relation to the structural logic of the mabolong, a logic that can be sketched in the following way:

People enlist the services of a shaman to serve as their advocate in
spirit realms. They host him in the hopes that he in turn will
host his spirit allies and that together they will work on the patient's behalf.

The performer summons powerful agents from afar to congregate
around him in order to address the patient's problem.

The patient's condition is precisely the reverse of the shaman's.
Whereas the shaman represents the concentration of hidden exogenous agents from distant realms, the patient represents the
dispersal of hidden endogamous elements to distant places.

Empowered by his hidden allies, the shaman recapitulates the flight
of his patient's hidden soul parts.

By the same agency he is able to counteract the centrifugality of
those soul parts.

Through the concentration of his own exogenous spirit powers, he
is able to reassemble his patient's endogenous vital elements of
being.

When a shaman requests a "food" for his spirit familiars, he turns
the tables on his audience.

Whereas earlier the audience through the shaman had been requesting favors from the spirit familiars, now the spirit familiars request a favor from the audience.

Whereas earlier he had been acting as an advocate of human interests, he is now acting as an advocate of spirit interests.

Whereas earlier he had addressed his spirits, now he is addressing
his human audience with his song.

The appeal is an emotional one. The shaman expresses "small feelings" to the audience. To avert catastrophe, the audience is expected to demonstrate "big feelings" (*bae raya* or, as shamans
may put it, *bangke ndanda*) for the performer and his familiars.

If the audience fails to satisfy the shaman and his spirit familiars, the
shaman's vital elements will flee to distant realms with his spirit
familiars. In other words, the shaman's condition will resemble
that of a patient whose soul parts have fled.

Because the shaman's identity is fused with that of his spirit familiars to work on a community's behalf, the threat that he may die

can work on several levels: first, it posits the loss of a human life; second, it threatens a withdrawal of spirit assistance; and third, it imperils the community's existence.

THE EMOTIONAL IDIOM
OF THE EPISODE

In contrast to the other parts of the shaman's performance, emotions are front and center in the baku mwalia episode. Ordinary Wana discourse about emotions centers not on the hidden elements of being described in Chapter 5, but on one's "inside," or *raya*; this word, which I often translate as "feeling," may be further modified by terms for happy, sad, angry, worried, and so forth. The emotional state called *kodi nraya*, or "small feelings," then (which receives a good deal of cultural elaboration in other contexts as well), is precisely the state a shaman threatens in this episode.

Earlier chapters have stressed how a mabolong is an occasion for people to demonstrate kasintuwu, the value of living together in harmony and mutual support. Although kasintuwu is highlighted through participation in life-crisis rituals, its texture comes from people's willingness to share necessities and treats in "the practice of everyday life." Daily traffic in edibles, wearables, chewables, and smokables is not tallied as instances of exchange but rather is read as expressions of solidarity. People who care for (*poraya*) one another share with one another—at least in principle. In a subsistence-based economy in which luxuries are few and supplies often tight, people who have a little more are frequently pressed to give; at another time these same people may find themselves in need and dependent on the generosity of others. Arriving in the field during a time of famine, I had ample opportunity to study the delicate ways in which requests for food were both formulated and deflected.

The baku mwalia episode plays on the value of community solidarity and the consequent social and emotional complexities of sharing. The shaman and his spirits ask for food. If the audience does not provide the desired item, the shaman and his spirits interpret that failure as deliberate withholding and thus experience "small feelings."

In ordinary life "small feelings" are played out according to a cultural "script." People whose "feelings are small" on account of insult, rejection, or neglect are likely to withdraw or retreat from those who have caused them emotional pain. Such social withdrawal is called *kawu*, which I gloss as "going off hurt." It is a standard explanation given when people separate from others. Young lovers whose marriage plans have been overturned by recalcitrant elders, for instance, may absent themselves for days, weeks, or months on a "journey of small feelings" (*linja ngkodi nraya*). Likewise, the decision of households to break off from a community and move elsewhere is often blamed by those left behind on kodi nraya, as is a threatened or actual death, especially of a tiny child.

The similar use of kodi nraya to explain the vulnerability of infants and shamans derives from the fact that both are people whose emotional sensitivity is augmented by hidden agents. The feelings of a small child are said to be monitored by a personal spirit called a nabi. Thus a baby who is slow to be born or who is sickly may be *kodi nabinya*: its "spirit is small" on account of rejection, neglect, or abuse. Likewise, a performing shaman will experience "small feelings" and respond by "going off hurt" because his spirit familiars influence his sensitivity. In this way, a performer's emotional displays can be read as indicators of his hidden alliances.

I shall have more to say later about the emotional dimensions of a shaman's appeal. For the moment, however, I want to point out that in a ritual whose ostensible aim is to restore the metaphysical order of patients, "small feelings" on the part of the performer and his familiars pose the threat of chaos on several levels.

Because the emotional retreat of an offended shaman is metaphysical rather than social, it invokes an image of death, the disintegration of a person's vital elements of being. What some in the room fear for themselves or their loved ones, and what is fundamentally anguishing about the human condition, is vividly confronted in the person of the shaman.

The possibility of the shaman's death in turn raises the specter of social rupture. For one thing, "small feelings" are culturally identified as reasons for the actual breakup of social relations. For another, by causing offense the audience bears some responsibility for the death. Audience members—often older women—explicitly raise the possibility that a shaman's relatives will avenge his death on those in the room. (I have heard such fears of retaliation expressed even when the performer was closely related to his audience. Indeed, some Wana I know claim to be so upset at the sight of an unconscious shaman that they flee the house the instant a shaman collapses.) The implication is that the death of a performer could be the death of a community, an association that essentially extends the ritual logic by which a shaman is the sustainer of order. If a shaman dies, people and communities fall apart.

Finally, a shaman's withdrawal suggests the withdrawal of spirit aid. Such a desertion of the community parallels the stories detailed earlier of the mythical departures of "power, knowledge, and wealth" from the Wana land. It also parallels accounts that attribute a loss of spirit assistance to "small feelings," such as the story in Chapter 2 about the Bolag who took offense at the stinginess of their Wana hosts. The parallel to the mabolong episode should be evident: just as inhospitality toward the Bolag resulted in their aid being withdrawn, so can failure to host a shaman and his familiars adequately provoke their desertion.

Here I have sought to describe how the conventions of a baku mwalia episode are fine-tuned to the structural logic and cultural premises underlying the mabolong ritual. As the next chapter will show, however, the impact of an actual episode is more than a matter of being symbolically apt.

12

Emotional Performance

> A whole social milieu may be affected by the mere fact that
> a magical act is being performed in one part of it. A circle
> of impassioned spectators collects around the action being
> performed. They are brought to a halt, absorbed, hypnotized
> by the spectacle. They become as much actors as spectators in
> the magical performance—rather like the chorus in Greek
> drama.
>
> Mauss, *A General Theory of Magic*

Shamans' requests for "foods," like other episodes in the mabolong, are based on certain premises and carry certain cultural implications. The logic of these episodes, however, does not unfold automatically. Much depends on whether and how a particular performer approximates his audience's notions of the "shaman as hero" (Lévi-Strauss 1963a). Despite these commonalities, more is at stake in the baku mwalia episode of the mabolong than in the other three, because a performer who requests a "food" for his spirits engages his audience directly, thus giving up a significant measure of control over the ritual action. By sharing the stage with human partners who can guide the outcome of the episode, the performer encounters new risks as well as expanded possibilities for dramatic improvisation.

A request for a "food" for one's spirit familiars entails a sounding of a performer's relation both to his audience and to other performers, for what this ostensible negotiation of the shaman's "feelings" (as transmuted by his spirit familiars) ultimately involves are his very claims to shamanship. To show how these observations figure in ritual practice, I shall examine in close detail two episodes in which a mabolong performer took offense and required the intervention of other shamans to bring him around. Then I shall treat another segment of text that reveals how performers may engage each other in expressions of solidarity and dependency. The three transcriptions are drawn from two mabolong performances that took place within the same week, with two of the three performers appearing in all three segments.[1] Taken together, the texts give an extended view of the dynamics of shamanic partnership. Although these segments are lengthy, Western readers should find their focus on riddles, feelings, and relationships more immediately accessible than the focus on spirit epithets, pursuit of soul parts, and dramatic journeys to the sky in the transcripts examined in earlier parts of this book.

Because of the complexity of the relationship between speaker and text in the following transcripts, advance clarification of my identification of speakers in this chapter is called for. When I refer to a performer by name—or more accurately, by teknonym—I am referring to the shamanic persona of the performer, unless I explicitly invoke a nonritual context. By "shamanic persona" I mean the performer as a human whose identity is currently augmented by hidden agents.

PLACATING A FELLOW SHAMAN

In the first episode, a young performer, Apa Miin, expresses unhappiness when his request for "food" for his familiar is not granted. His first cousin Apa Mene, a prominent shaman in the community, intervenes, even though he was in "real life" exhausted and in no mood to devote his evening to restoring his cousin should Apa Miin fall unconscious. Indeed, he indicates as much below. Apa Miin's older brother, Apa Linus, joins Apa Mene in "instructing" the younger man on how to accept the fact that his request has been denied.

We begin with Apa Miin's request. Just as it appears bluntly before you on the page, so too a shaman's request may suddenly come to the attention of audience members. In fact, the performer may have been singing his request for some time under the din and distractions in the room. Since it is not imperative for the audience to heed a shaman when he is summoning familiars and treating patients, it may take a while for members of the audience (including the ethnographer with her tape recorder) to grow alert to the fact that the shaman is in fact addressing them.

salu pojene langgiwo e wega   Bath water of the ghosts, eh,
                                     familiar.

Someone guesses that he desires water to be poured over a flint (*ue watu pandingku*).

rianya to ele wega	No, it's not that, spirit.
sabengi to sabengi segi wega	One night after another now, spirit,
pane nja'u sonda muni	until at last the one from over there appears again
pai rajunya mongande	and wants to eat.
o wega kono naendo nrayaku	Oh, spirit, I happen to remember,
maria mwegimo ia wega	it's been many nights that this spirit
layo layo ngkalidonya	has been alone, alone, by himself.

The last line conveys a sense of estrangement. The term *layo* has positive connotations when used to refer to a young unmarried person or to a young couple as yet unencumbered by children, but in general, to be alone and unconnected to others is a negative and potentially dangerous condition. "To go off alone" (*yau ngkalio* or, as the shaman renders it, *ngkalido*) is a phrase for seeking spirit alliances through personal quest, although the phrase can also serve as a euphemism for dying.

Apa Mene, sensing from his words and manner that Apa Miin is decidedly unhappy, intervenes with these words:

dange kutaeka nggomi	Listen to what I say to you,
suola taawa monau	spirit familiar not yet accustomed,
suola taawa mananya	spirit familiar not yet experienced,
yakowa momata	still fresh.

Note how Apa Mene establishes himself as the senior shaman by speaking of his fellow performer as inexperienced. The reference to the latter's "freshness" (*mata*, a word that expresses the efficacy of magical knowledge) may offset the apparent "put-down" of this remark.

lo'a ja layo layoda	Look at Layo Layoda.
lo'a ja lele naugi	Look at Lele Naugi,
taamo napeasi wuri	who no longer waits for dark,
wegaku	my spirit familiar.

Apa Mene offers himself as a model for Apa Miin: Layo Layoda and Lele Naugi are his own spirit familiars and thus part of his own shamanic persona. (Apa Mene's allusion to his spirit Layo Layoda may have been triggered by Apa Miin's expression of estrangement, *layo layo ngkalidonya*.)

ojo kutaeka nggomi wegaku	I simply say to you, my spirit familiar,

siko to kusarumaka	you to whom I delegate,
ne'e bojombojo	don't take offense.
suola sansala to tuatuama	The companion spirit familiar, the older one [here Apa Mene is referring to himself],
koro liu katungkonya	indeed has passed the point of pain,
koro liu kaledonya	indeed has passed the point of exhaustion.
saeo sandodi taa mangande	For a day, he has virtually not eaten.
ojo paka dole dole	He has simply acted cheerful.
ojo paka doendongi o wega	He has simply acted pleasant, oh spirit.
ane puramo ratae wega	If the request has been fully stated, spirit,
pei taarie nabanda ntayu to randa bombaru	but the people in the house haven't given anything,
ne'e kojo mesonaru	don't you dare leave it to others,
ne'e kojo bojo bojo	don't you dare take offense.

Apa Mene is being quite blunt. He portrays himself as weary and in no mood to revive a faltering companion.

Apa Miin continues:

sabengi to sabengi si'i	One evening after another now,
rajunya monsibu	the spirit has wanted to sip.
rianya to ele wegangku	It's not that, my spirit,
pai simbau simbajunya	but something like it.
rianya to ele [. . .]	That's not it [unintelligible].

Someone in the audience has apparently guessed wrong as to his (or the familiar's) desires.

solu ana saru biasa manangu	Here is Ana Saru, accustomed to swimming,
owo bengi to sabengi segi	Only an evening, this one evening,
pane nja'u rango muni	till this one arrives back from afar.

Apa Miin is in a holding pattern after Apa Mene's counsel. He returns to the fact that what he has requested is not forthcoming, fields a guess from the audience, then shifts his focus from the request to the spirit familiar.

At this point his older brother takes up where his cousin left off. Apa Linus sings:

taa siwee nundanda	Not much is felt.
ane ratae wega	If it is spoken, spirit,

ane taarie naanti ntayu wega

if people don't get any, spirit,

bangke randa mangabanda

great is the desire to give,

wei taarie randa bumbaru

but there isn't any in the house.

rianya taarie rabanda tayu wega

It's not that people give nothing,
spirit,

wei taarie raanti

but there is none to be had.

wetumo nggita suola wegangku

It's just that way for us shamanic
familiars, my spirit familiar.

In translating this passage, I have tried to convey Apa Linus's reliance
on passive verb forms and the avoidance of second-person pronouns.
After using no pronominal forms whatsoever in the first seven lines,
he then introduces the inclusive first-person plural *nggita (kita* in
ordinary speech) to link Apa Miin's experience to his own, which he
then proceeds to detail.

nggami kuporaju seja mangande
wega

We, I also wanted to eat, spirit.

wei natotae ntayu wega

But people said, spirit,

taarie naanti

there isn't any to be had.

wei taa siwee nunraya

But feelings were not hurt.

e ojo rapaka gondo nggindanda
wega

Eh, feelings are just made good,
spirit.

soba nasulu nsondilo wega

Try to look and see, spirit.

to nja'u ri bolag wega

The one over there in the *bolag* land,
spirit.

ia rajunya mangande wega

That one wanted to eat, spirit.

wei natotae ntayu wega

But people said, spirit,

ne'e nuporaju yande wegangku

don't wish for a food, my spirit.

nggita narumpa nsukara wega

We here are experiencing difficulty,
spirit.

naka taa nasigena yande segi

That's why we're out of food here.

koro bangke randa ntayu

Great indeed is people's

mangabanda wega

desire to give, spirit.

wei mbenumo raanti segimo

But where can [the food] be
obtained now,

burimo njo'u

off there in the dark?

Apa Linus has shifted his focus from Apa Miin's immediate situation
to an earlier one of his own by referring to one of his familiars, a Bolag
spirit, whose desire was not met. He then characterizes an audience
expressing regrets to a spirit familiar in terms applicable to a farming
community that lacks the resources to share with a visitor. This image
moves the focus of discussion further from Apa Miin's grievance.

   Apa Miin seems to accept this comfort:

| naj'u lengke mwuri | Over at the shadow of darkness |
| dua marimbanga mai | come two people approaching. |

(As transcribed, Apa Miin continues to sing, but the content suggests that the next few lines belong to Apa Linus, who had asked earlier that evening for *jole pisi mwana*.)

e ojo nutotaeka tayu wegangku	Eh, just tell the people, my spirits,
ane re'e nasosulu	if they see any there,
nabandaka nggita wega	give it to us, spirit.
ane taarie nasulu wega	If none is seen, spirit,
bangke randa mangabanda	great is the desire to give,
wei mbenumo raika manganganti	but when it is done, obtaining,
e mo lo'a nggami nantotaeka	eh, watch us tell [them],
i yadu wega	I, spirit,
rabanda jole pisi mwana wega	*jole pisi mwana* be given, spirit.
wei natotae ntayu	But people said
bangke ndanda mami	great is our desire to give, spirit,
mangabanda wega	
wei mbenumo raika manganganti	but from where can it be gotten?

Apa Miin either continues or takes over:

e pai kutotaeka nggomi	Eh, but I tell you,
salu pojene langgiwo	bathwater of the ghosts,
pei simbau simbajumo	but something like it.
pai kutoleka nggomi salu pojene	But I tell you, bathwater.
embaku biasa mangangu	My friend, accustomed to swimming
ndeku lengku nsalu	up at the stretch of water,
pai mojaya laya mbatu'e	who travels on starlight
pai naj'u rango ma'i	and from over there comes forth.
manopa ntuo kusulu wega	Clearly indeed I see [it], spirit,
naj'u ri luo saluo	over in another place,
pai taarie kuronggeni wega	but there's none I bring, spirit.

By the end of this exchange, Apa Miin seems somewhat placated, but not fully resigned to the fact that no one is giving him what he and his spirit (the swimming starwalker) desire.

EMOTIONS AND INTENTIONALITY

A baku mwalia request signals a shift in the relation between performer, audience, and text. This shift raises a much debated issue in the literature on shamanism. When a mabolong performer makes demands on his audience on behalf of his familiars, is he engaging in a form of spirit possession? Mircea Eliade ([1951] 1964), whose definition of shamanism centered on ecstatic journeys to the Upper and Lower Worlds, adamantly argued that spirit possession, whereby a spirit occupies the body and consciousness of a ritual specialist, is not a feature of true shamanism. Where it occurs in Central and North Asia—the shamanistic heartland—he views it as a later historical overlay. For Eliade, a shaman is a mediator between the human and spirit worlds, but not a medium for spirits to communicate with humans.

So when a Wana kawalia requests "food" for his spirits, does he shift from being a shaman to being a spirit medium? After all, his emotions and behavior in such instances seem to be subject to the fancies of his spirit familiars. Has he indeed lost his own agency, his own willful control, the quality that Reinhard (1976) argues distinguishes a shaman from a medium?

The issue I raise here is one not of definition, but of drama. This episode calls intentionality into question, not only for the analyst, but for Wana audiences as well. Who is speaking here, and what is the speaker's relation to both words and audience? A premise of the ritual is that performers are at once ordinary mortals *and* spiritually empowered beings. Through most of a performance, audience members are passive witnesses to the alliance of shamans and spirits. When a performer (literally, "someone with spirits") demands something of an audience, the audience is called upon to respond directly to someone who in appearance resembles a person they know but whose consciousness has been transformed through powerful association with spirit familiars. It faces, in essence, a double image: a human companion and an assortment of alien spirits. The paradox is expressed well in the conventional expression shamans use to refer to themselves as they perform—*suola sala suola*, "the familiar not the familiar."

Culturally it would be an error to reduce exchanges like that involving Apa Miin, Apa Linus, and Apa Mene simply to the performers' personalities and to the relations these individuals have to one another and to their audiences in ordinary life. These episodes— the most improvisational of the mabolong—have a dynamic of their own. The feelings the performers express are not thought to have a one-to-one correspondence to their feelings in everyday life; in fact, it is often precisely the lack of correspondence that provides the humor and wonder of the incident. People note how under the influence of spirit familiars the performer, a grown man, is reduced to tears because he is denied a flower or some other seemingly trivial item. Such peculiar behavior can be excused by attributing it to his spirit familiars. Thus, when a performer's threat to die was imputed to his wife's falling asleep during his performance, people noted that he did not ordinarily resent a lack of attention from his wife. And the shocking custom of a shaman who, I was told, would request in his song to copulate with his wife, then leave the house to do so—a stunning violation of Wana notions of sexual propriety—was written off to his lustful spirit familiars.

Yet a performer's identity is neither entirely nor consistently divorced from the episode.[2] Revealing in this regard was a discussion I had with Apa Mene as we listened to a tape recording of a shaman in another community as he engaged an audience at great length to decipher a request for a "food." It was evident that the performer was asking for a liquid, but his companions were hard put to deduce more than that. Finally one of the more prominent men in the community was heard to remark, "Perhaps it's cow piss" (*bara yoe nsapi*). Apa Mene declared that he would feel humiliated, "put down as stupid" (*deom*), if someone said that to him as he performed.

A performer requesting a "food" has not abandoned shamanism for spirit possession; he remains in theory a mediator, not a medium, between spirits and humans. But he reveals a different and more vulnerable dimension of his go-between role by calling on his audience to confirm their commitment to his mediation.

Because an episode like the one above is focused on a shaman's sense of how others regard him, such exchanges may reveal much about both a performer's relations to his audience and his relations to other shamans. The passage above gives us little sense of Apa Miin's relation to his audience (apart from conventionalized estrangement); it does, however, reveal some fascinating dynamics among the three shamans who partake in the exchange. Apa Mene is clearly the senior shaman present: he actively calls on his seniority and authority to contain his younger cousin. By contrast, Apa Linus expresses camaraderie by identifying with his brother's experience. He speaks at first in general terms. His use of passive verb forms and his omission of pronouns allows him to avoid saying, "They've gotten nothing for you, they've given nothing to you." Like Apa Mene before him he offers himself as an example to follow, but he does so less directly than the senior shaman. Instead of ordering Apa Miin not to take offense and thereby create problems for the other shamans, he phrases his advice in the passive—*ojo rapaka gondo nggindanda*, "just [let] feelings be made good." At the same time, he underscores the desire ("great feelings") of people in the room to provide what is asked for and suggests that Apa Miin encourage his familiars to look for the desired substance themselves.

Sometimes the dynamics of such an episode are less subtle. I have seen Apa Mene delay the task of tending to a junior shaman who lay unconscious on the floor. Deflecting anxious requests from the audience that he hasten to the fallen shaman's side, he indicated that the danger of immediate death for a young and as yet inexperienced shaman was not great and that he would be along in a while ("As long as I don't die this evening, neither will he"). By contrast, when Apa Mene or one of his peers fell unconscious, shamanic aid was immediately forthcoming.

Although prominent shamans may seem cavalier when less experienced performers collapse, Wana audiences are constrained to respond with concern. After all, even the most humble performer may in fact have powerful spirit friends and could well die if left untended. I heard, for instance, stories about a poor young person who stood to dance at a mabolong performance. (In some versions the protagonist is male; in others, female.) Thinking the dancer had no spirit connections, the musicians scornfully broke off their playing, whereupon the dancer fell to the floor. People assumed that the collapse was faked and so left the dancer untreated; but when sunrise came it became evident that the soul of the scorned dancer had departed with its spirit allies. The moral of this and similar tales is that performers must always be treated as though their spirit claims are valid—for they very well could be.

In practice, however, this advice is variously heeded. Not long before I arrived in the field, a young novice collapsed with his head in the lap of an eligible woman he clearly admired. Instead of treating him, people in the room joked that his penis was erect and threatened to hammer it. The performer came instantly to consciousness unaided—a sure sign that his collapse had been faked. In another instance which I witnessed, a retarded youth from a distant settlement fell unconscious in a roomful of strangers. Although his collapse was greeted by many of those present with derision, one old woman—the mother of several performers and aunt of another—insisted that he be treated, arguing that the youth's father was a renowned shaman who would sorcerize the community if the young man proved in fact to have spirits and should happen to die untreated. Because of her insistence help was rendered, but the senior shamans present left the task to their juniors.

"HURT FEELINGS"
IN DEFENSE OF SHAMANSHIP

A performer's unhappiness is not always as neatly contained as was Apa Miin's. In the transcription that follows, Apa Linus and his spirit familiars express displeasure at being ignored by audience members, and transcriptions of other mabolong over a several-month period reveal that his complaint was ongoing. The previous year had been difficult for Apa Linus, beyond the ritual context. He had repeatedly coughed up large quantities of blood and had been unable to work effectively, which caused him to curtail his shamanic activities for some time. Now that he was feeling stronger, he was performing more often. But (as I read it) he sensed that some adolescent boys in the community were deriding his efforts. When these teenagers would beat the drum with no regard for shamans who were trying to make their requests heard, he and his spirits became angry.

ane momense sangkio	Having danced a little,
mayontomo muni	stop now.
sonda to ri pondoboi	The Ones from Pondoboi arrive.
nggita wega mampolemba wonti	We spirits disguised as monkeys.
kono naendo nraya	[We] happen to recall
kaju layo nja'u tida	the lone tree off at the border.
suola sala suola	The familiar not the familiar
kono naendo nrayanya	happens to remember
kaju layo nja'u tida wegaku	a lone tree off at the border, my spirit.
o pantamo suola mantae wegangku	Oh each spirit has spoken, my spirit.
nau ojo naoamo	Even if only deceiving,
rianya suola mamporaju wega	It's not a familiar who desires, spirit.
lemba baju mamporaju wega	The exterior body desires, spirit.

This passage makes a number of odd shifts. First it identifies with the inclusive first-person form a union of "spirits disguised as monkeys" who chance to remember a "lone tree off at the border." Next that memory is attributed to "the familiar not a familiar," a term often used to distinguish the performer from his spirit allies. Then the possibility of deception is raised, with the wish attributed not to spirits but to the outward body of the performer. (As discussed in Chapter 6, the external body [*lemba*] is culturally disparaged.) Apa Linus has now introduced the sort of doubt that skeptics might hold—namely, that it is not his spirit familiars who want something, but only he himself.

Apa Mene, realizing that his comrade is distressed, attempts to engage him:

kita ane kasuola	For us, if we have spirit familiars,
taarie taa rabanda	it's not that nothing is given,
pei taarie randa bombaru	but that there is none in the house.
longko luo naka layo	It's a far place to go alone.

It is evident that Apa Linus has been requesting something for some time but has been neither heard nor heeded. Apa Mene explains that the only reason a shaman is not given what he asks for is that none is available.

Apa Linus answers:

ane yadu mantolulu	If I go off to follow,
sonda to ri pondoboi	I'll arrive among those at Pondoboi
nja'u ri luo saluo wega	off in another place, spirit.
kami to tae seja ngena	We who also mentioned earlier
liano nto tu'a mupewe	the crop of the Old One in the Loincloth
sipaondong nu lino	which causes one to forget the world.

He alludes here to something he asked for earlier—I suspect a wild tuber (*ondo*) that makes one dizzy or faint if one eats it raw.

taa nabandaka ntayu	People didn't give it.
taa maria wei	We didn't take offense.

In his defense, Apa Linus notes that he has responded with equanimity to a previous failure by his audience to grant his wishes. At the same time, however, his words can be read as a threat to die. Earlier he alluded to a "lone tree by the border"; now he speaks of following his spirit familiars to their land and recalls his desire to consume a substance "that causes one to forget this world."

matungko nggita suola segi	Pained are we, the familiars here.
mangantae yande wega	We request a food, spirit.
taarie tayu mampodangeka	No one listens.
wei bia boakamo wegangku	But never mind, let it be, my spirit.
wenumo nggami suolaku	That's what we're like, my familiar.
ojo ratae yande wega	A food is simply mentioned, spirit,
pai raromba muni kuntinya	and their drum is beaten anew.

Apa Mene takes over:

bela dange kutaeka nggomi wega	Friend, listen to what I tell you, spirit.
ponundeka nggomi	I'll instruct you.
panta to tae _	Each request is spoken,
pai taarie rabanda	but none is granted.
longko ntuo lo luonya	It's far indeed down to its place.
gondo ragondoka sondilo	It's good to be good to look.
tu'a masowo omo rakenika toko	The Old Goitered One is brought only a staff.
taa siwee nundanda	Offense isn't taken.
wetumo kita suola wegaku	We familiars are like that, my spirit.

Apa Mene begs to differ: all that the audience gives his spirit, the Old Goitered One, is a walking stick—but he does not take offense.

Apa Linus continues his lament and in so doing asserts his shamanship:

koro matungko masusi wega	Oh, it is painful and difficult, spirit.
kita mangantae yande	We speak a request.
paka suola mangantae wega	It's a familiar who speaks, spirit.
mbenumo napangantae	When it has been spoken,
ia momense seja	he dances too.
wei rataeka wega	But it's spoken, spirit,
to ronta bombaru wega	to those in the house, spirit.
taarie nadange	No one listens.
ojo kuntinya naromba wegaku	They only beat their drum, my spirit.
ane nu dange nggomi wega	If you are listening, spirit,
ne'ewa raromba kunti wega	hold off beating the drum, spirit.

Instead of complaining in general terms about the "people in the house," Apa Linus is directing his unhappiness specifically at the young people gathered around the drum and gongs. Note how in his song he repeatedly attaches the third-person possessive suffix *-nya* to the word *kunti*, "drum." Yet in fact, drums are treated as community property. To speak of this instrument as *belonging* to a social "other" is a peculiar and startling usage in the context of a mabolong and thus underscores a sense of alienation.

lo'a mata to mali	Look at Mata To Mali
jaya pindurai	who travels on the rainbow.

Apa Mene alludes here to a spirit or mythical character who is known for his drumming—an apt allusion, given the current debate.
  Apa Linus resumes:

nggami suola	We are familiars,
tayu masangangi seja	happy people also.

  Apa Mene sings at the same time:

to pongkoli janji	who moves fates.

  Apa Linus asserts that he displays equanimity when he is not being drowned out by the drum:

nggami ane ratae yande wega	We, if a request for food is spoken, spirit,
pai taa raromba kuntinya wega	but their drum isn't beaten, spirit,
taa siwee nunraya	we don't take offense.

  Apa Mene offers counsel:

ewa ele kutaeka nggomi	It's like that, I tell you,
kuponundeka nggomi wega	I teach you, spirit.
nggomi to taawa monau	You who are not yet experienced,
komi yakowa momata	you who are still fresh.

As he did for Apa Miin, Apa Mene asserts his own superiority but takes the edge off the assertion by alluding to the "freshness" of his companion's shamanic skills.
  Apa Linus continues:

o wei matungko masuli	But it's painful and difficult
naka pei koro kutae wegangku	so that indeed I say, my spirit,
nggita mangantae yande	we request a food,
ojo kuntinya raromba	only their drum is beaten.

baramo suola segi poraya	Maybe the familiar here desires,
bara ojo rani momense wegangku	maybe only wishes to dance, my
	spirit.
matungko koro liu ngkaroronya	Exceedingly pained is his body.
ojo paka suola ja	It's only another familiar
mangandange wega	who listens, spirit.

Apa Linus notes that no one but another shaman heeds his complaints; others, he charges, seem to think he wants only to dance, and so they beat their drum.

Apa Mene holds himself up again as an example:

to tu'a masowo	The Old Goitered One,
liu ntuo kaledonya	excessive indeed his weariness,
ledo sala ngkaledo	weariness not weariness,
kutae nande	I request a food,
taarie rabanda wegaku	None is given, my spirit.
banda sangkio tinumbo	Give a little beer.
taawa niyonto	He's not yet finished.

Apa Linus goes on the offensive, asserting that four of his spirit familiars have been ignored:

dange ja ruyu wegangku	Listen here first, my spirit.
pantamo nggami opo sala	Each of the four of us
mangantae yande wega	has requested a food, spirit.
taarie kojo rapondangeka wega	No one at all listened, spirit.
ojo kuntinya raromba wega	Only their drum was beaten, spirit.
to ruyunya suola manayamo	The remainder of the experienced
	familiars
mangantae seja	also made requests.
ane tayu to ronta bombaru	As for the people in the house
taarie nadange ojo kuntinya	nothing was heard, only their drum
naromba	was beaten.

Now Apa Mene tries to divert the discussion by calling attention to the fact that another shaman—his brother-in-law, Apa Weri—who had been sleeping on the floor, is getting up:

lalu ane suola sansala	It's better if the fellow familiar
ia bangu katibangu muni	has gotten up again,
wega kupobelo	spirit I befriend.
koro liu kaledonya	Indeed surpassing, his conduct,
liu naendo ntuo	surpassing indeed in memory.
dua isa dua nsala	Two one two on a path

taawa miyonto momense
i we'a ntiara
ia leta la'u lante
bangu katibangu muni

not yet weary of dancing.
Oh, Woman of the Pearl,
lying down on the floor,
is getting up again.

He refers to his companion and dancing partner by the epithet of one of the latter's familiars, We'a nTiara.

Not to be diverted by Apa Mene's effusive expression of praise and admiration for another shaman, Apa Linus asserts his own shaman-ship before resuming his complaint:

yadu segi wegaku
ane rapodangeka ja sangkio
suolaku tayu gondo seja wega

si'a ojo naoamo
wei nggita mangantae yande
ojo kuntinya naromba
koro matungko suola wega
nau nempo naliumo wegangku
taamo mayonto natotole wega

koro liu ngkakodinya

Here am I, my spirit,
if it may be heard a little.
My familiar is a good person too,
    spirit.
This isn't just deception.
But we asked for food.
Only their drum was beaten.
The familiar is pained indeed, spirit.
Not even if passed by, my spirit,
he will no longer leave off saying,
    spirit,
exceeding, indeed, his small
    feelings.

Apa Linus's objections are at last registering. One of the teenage boys who had been at the drum claims that it was little children who were playing the instruments and drowning out Apa Linus's re-quests.[3] Apa Linus answers him:

rianya pomuli wega
nanu kusulu nsandilo wegangku

taarie kudange nempo pomuli wega

nau kusulu seja wega
wei taa rapodangeka
nggita mangantae yandeta
ane rianya suola mananyamo

rapangamposoba soba wegangku
posoba soba wegangku
wei reija suola mananyamo
    wegangku

It was not the children, spirit,
whom I saw and observed, my
    spirit.
There were none I heard, even
    children, spirit.
If I saw also, spirit.
But it was not heeded
when we asked for our food.
If there were no experienced
    familiars,
it could be tested, tested, my spirit.
Test, test, my spirit.
But here is an experienced familiar,
    my spirit.

The word *soba* alludes to "testing" people's knowledge and hidden powers by sorcerizing them. To so "test" a person who actually has spirit connections, however, is to risk being sorcerized in return. Apa Linus's words here, as I read them, are thus a challenge to those who would doubt his shamanic claims.

Referring to himself with his familiar's epithet, Apa Mene resumes his instruction:

ane sarumaka	If you depend on the
to tu'a matoko	Old One with the Staff,
dange kutaeka nggomi	listen to what I tell you.
nabi masigoli mananya mangkoli	Nabi Masigoli, experienced at moving fates,
ne'ewa nakodi	don't yet have small feelings.

I do not understand the reference to Nabi Masigoli here. It may be extraneous, it may be an invocation of one of Apa Mene's familiars, or it may allude to an ally of Apa Linus. The advice, however, is clearly directed to Apa Linus, who expresses his reliance on Apa Mene:

nggami segi	We here,
ane rianya nggomi	if there weren't you,
suola monanyamo	the experienced familiar

Here the dialogue breaks off.

In this text the reader can detect a passion not evident in the soliloquies examined in Parts One, Two, and Three. Apa Linus's sense of injury is palpable. By obsessing at length about his audience's offense, he commands and manages to sustain the care and attention of the leading shaman in the room, and eventually he captures the attention of his purported offenders. He indulges in a variety of postures: abandoned, pathetic, even suicidal at one moment; assertive, confident, menacing at another. He is not simply displaying his shamanship; instead, he is calling it fundamentally into question.

I speak of "his" feelings and actions here. Who is "he" in this case? This is of course the issue. In principle, a shaman is "a person of spirits" when he performs, meaning that his feelings, as well as his perceptions, are augmented by spirit familiars in the mabolong context. This very augmentation by spirits makes it incumbent on an audience to cater to a shaman's wishes and needs. By not heeding the desires a shaman expresses, an audience can be charged with implying that the performer is not a "person with spirit familiars." It is just this implication that the performer has drawn and publicly articulated in this case. His lengthy and indulgent display of pathos, anger, and injury on his own behalf and that of his spirit familiars is to be read as a repudiation of that charge.

LATE-NIGHT DIALOGUES

As the evening advances, sleep is likely to overtake mabolong audience members and performers alike. Several keyed-up performers, obligated hosts, and other night owls may continue the proceedings amid the sleeping bodies of the less resilient. Occasionally shamans become annoyed at the sleepers, but usually not so long as a small cadre of attentive individuals remain awake, alert, and involved in what the shamans are doing. What they *are* doing in the predawn hours ranges from treating patients (some of whom must be aroused from sleep if a shaman is inspired to attend to them) to discoursing on cosmic matters. Some shamans, skilled at the art of conjuring images of people in cups of water, may apply their skill to solving mysteries regarding thefts and sorceries. The late-night hours are also times for performers to surrender to an emotionally wrought state.

The final transcript I shall present—one that does not fit neatly into my fourfold categorization of mabolong episodes—contains a late-night exchange between Apa Linus and Apa Mene. Were categorization a goal in itself, this text might fall into a fifth pigeonhole, labeled perhaps shamanic dialogue or shamanic instruction. Yet such a category would not be discrete. Clearly the last two transcriptions involving baku mwalia involved exchange and instruction among shamans. Such dialogues result from the fact that a mabolong is a circus with more than one ring; because of the danger that a lone performer could take offense, lose consciousness, and become a patient himself, mabolong performances require more than one shaman.

How these multiple concentrations of power—the shamans and their respective spirit familiars—interrelate is a delicate matter. When unfamiliar shamans perform together, they make a point of introducing their spirit familiars to one another. (They are also likely to use a good deal of defensive magic to prevent being sorcerized.) When close acquaintances who are peers perform together, they may express affection and solidarity—as Apa Mene did in the text above in reference to his brother-in-law Apa Weri. When the relationship between performers is familiar but unequal, we may find assertions of authority and dependency interwoven with expressions of devotion.

In the following text, Apa Mene and Apa Linus have just returned from a jointly undertaken journey to Pue. Apa Mene claims to be teaching Apa Linus the secrets needed for such an adventurous shamanic act. He alludes here to his role as Apa Linus's mentor:

ojo pata ewa ele	Only just that much
kutaeka nggomi wega	I tell you, spirit.
komi kuponunde	You I instruct.

Apa Linus indicates his willingness to be taught:

imba nggomi mamponunde nggami	Whatever you [will] teach us.
bara letamo ri lante	Even if [I'm] lying on the floor.
ojo ele kutotae	Only that I say.
taawa leta	[I] won't lie down yet,
taawa yore	[I] won't sleep yet.

Apa Mene resumes:

sei to tu'a matoko	Here is the Old One with the Staff.
is rasombo mangkami luya	He's been placed to guard the betel offering.

At the end of a performance, a shaman may post his spirit familiars to protect his handiwork. The following phrases are sung together:
Apa Linus:

ane ewa ele nu tae	If it is spoken like that.

Apa Mene:

rasombo mangkami luya	Posted to guard the betel offering.

Apa Linus then continues:

ane wenumo wegangku	If it's like that, my spirit.
nggami nempo taa mangande	even though we haven't eaten,
gondo ntuo gindandangku	happy indeed are my feelings.
ane taawa leta nggomi	If you do not yet sleep,
nggomi kusosarumaka	I'll turn matters over to you.

Even though he and his spirits have not been granted their earlier requests, Apa Linus indicates he is going to stop performing and get some sleep.

Apa Mene replies:

ewa ele kutaeka nggomi wega	It is like that I tell you, spirit.
pai kuponunde yami nggomi	But I instruct you in advance
ane layo tu'a masowo luo saluo	in case the Old Goitered One goes
	off to another place
pai ronta salu injongi nggomi	and your tears fall.

Here the elder shaman announces that he is teaching his younger companion the secrets of shamanship in the event that he himself should die.

Apa Linus responds with a declaration of devotion:

ane nggomi pai layo	If you should go off alone,
taansa gana togo mwengi	three nights would not pass
kutolulu njo'u seja	before I too followed [you] there.
yaumo nggami	We would be gone.
pai kutolulu yau nggomi	But I would follow you.
nggami bara taamo momense	We would likely no longer dance.

(Note how Apa Linus shifts between singular and plural pronouns. I take this to mean that he is at once a person and a person with multiple spirit familiars.)

As Apa Linus sings these words, Apa Mene joins in:

i ele pai kuponunde yami nggomi	That, but I instruct you in advance,
tompo seiwa to tu'a matoko	while the Old One with the Staff is
	still here.
sei to tu'a masowo	Here is the Old Goitered One.
naka taawa layo to tu'a matoko	For the Old One with the Staff has
	not yet gone off alone.
taawa layo to tu'a masowo	The Old Goitered One has not yet
	gone off alone.
kuponunde yami nggomi	I instruct you in advance.
kuponunde panta panta	I instruct each and every one.
paka belo belo	Take care.
ne'e sala yongko	Don't make an error in bouncing.
ne'e sala lodu	Don't make an error in bending.

("Bouncing" and "bending" refer to the manner in which spirit familiars propel their vehicle on a journey to the Owner and to the style of the shamans' dance [*motaro*].)

Apa Linus now:

koro matungko masuli	It's painful and difficult indeed.
maranjoeni kuendo	Far I recall.

kudonge nu totae	I hear what is said.
ane nggomi ewa ele	If you were like that,
ane rianya nggomi	if there were not you,
nggami bara taamo namense	we probably would dance no more.

Apa Mene responds to his companion, who is now in tears:

yakowa momense	Still dancing,
sei to tu'a mosowo	here is the Old Goitered One.
sei to tu'a matoko	Here is the Old One with the Staff.
e wega donge kutaeka nggomi	Hey, spirit, listen as I speak to you.
ojo paka belo belo	Just take care, care.

Apa Mene's song has stressed the relationship of teacher and student. Apa Linus's song has stressed the devotion of a younger shaman to his older companion, whom he would follow to the death. Apa Mene now switches ground by breaking into ordinary speech:

sei naka potundeka yami siko oli	That's why I instruct you in advance, Oli,
tompo da si'iwa aku	while I am still here.
ane to pondomo aku	When I have died,
taamore tau da potundeka siko	there will no longer be anyone to teach you.
omo da nu liwu ngkalio	[You'll] just search on your own.
paka taaroowa aku	While I'm still here,
o siko si'i kawaliamo	oh, you here are one with spirit familiars.
pei salaakinya mandakedake	But the techniques of climbing upward [i.e., going to Pue]
taawa ansani	you don't yet understand.
sei naka patundeka yami siko	That's why I instruct you in advance.

Apa Mene's bluntness here underscores his authority. He has switched from shamanic speech to ordinary speech, from subtle indirection to frank assertion. He addresses his companion neither in the language of shamanic song as a "fellow spirit familiar" (*suola sansala*) nor with the respectful teknonym "father of Linus" (Apa Linus) but with his name. To use a person's name as a term of address can be an intimate or a patronizing gesture. Here it is both. Assured in his sense of superiority, Apa Mene proceeds with a critical assessment of his companion's shamanic claims. Yes, you are a shaman, he says, but you have a lot to learn and you are dependent on me for that knowledge.

Apa Linus pauses, then sings acceptance of his partner's judgment of his own dependency. Yet his very declaration to follow Apa Mene in death is itself an assertion of shamanic power, for it implies that his feelings are augmented by powerful spirit agents who would lead his soul in pursuit of Apa Mene's.

wega maronta salu ijongiku	Spirit, my tears fall
mangadange suola manau	as I listen to the experienced familiar
mangantataeka yadu mo	speaking to me.
e ane ia pai rugi wega	Eh, if he is ruined, spirit,
nggami bara kutolulu seja	we, probably I, will follow too.
ane ewa elemo nggami wega	If it's like that, spirit,
taamo seja meka	we too no longer will fear.
nau nempo ewa ele nu totae	Even if it is as has been said,
pai yadu taamo seja meka	I too am no longer afraid.
ane ia pai mowale	If he departs,
yadu kutolulu seja	I shall follow also.

A text of this works in multiple ways. My comments have high-lighted its political dimensions. At the same time, Apa Mene's asser-tion of shamanic authority and Apa Linus's concession of shamanic dependency are couched in the language of mourning and loss. One shaman reduces another shaman to tears by foretelling his own death, while simultaneously both shamans invite their audience to imagine what it would be like if the two of them were to die. Apa Mene phrases the loss in terms of knowledge: without him as teacher, Apa Linus will be forced to rely on his own resources. That loss extends beyond Apa Linus to the community, which without Apa Mene would be bereft of the aid of his powerful spirits. By proposing to die himself, Apa Linus (whose powers to date are admittedly fewer than his companion's) threatens to compound the loss for the community. In addition to embodying concentrations of spirit power, Apa Mene and Apa Linus are kinsmen and companions of virtually everyone in the room. Apart from the specifics of who and what the performers represent, this exchange may also be read in the abstract as an enact-ment of grief and longing. Performers, patients, and audience mem-bers alike could well project into the episode fears of death and the pain of mourning (Atkinson 1987). A dialogue of this sort has the potential not only to evoke different facets of loss and bereavement but to constitute shamanic reputations as well.

CONCLUSION

Each shaman both initiates and ends his own performance. When he wishes to stop, he urges his familiars to continue to work on his patients' behalf. Tying his shaman's cloth into a knot—with the hope that the restoration of his patients' beings will be likewise firm—he may issue instructions to the kin of the patients regarding special prohibitions to insure recovery. When all the performers have stopped for the evening, the drum is given a final tattoo as the instruments are taken down. Dawn does, however, occasionally find shamans and companions still drinking and reveling. Women then hasten to prepare an early-morning meal lest there be a shaman who wants to continue his performance past dawn—a dangerous extension because, some say, a performer who falls unconscious after sunrise may never be revived.

The festive atmosphere, theatrics, and suspense provided by episodes like the ones presented here make the mabolong the most popular of contemporary Wana rituals. If need for treatment is urgent, supplies of rice beer short, or interest in revelry low, a potudu may be substituted. As for the esoteric molawo, shamans are typically reluctant to perform it.[4] The molawo chant of the shamanic journey to the sky and back must be sung through from beginning to end to insure the well-being of performer and patients, whether anyone is paying attention or not. Shamans of my acquaintance complained of having to sit still with their hands on the betel offering and sing all night while everyone else dozed off. I was told of one molawo performer who would prop himself up against a pillow tied to a housepost; another had himself bound to the housepost so that he would not topple over from sleepiness as he sang. In contrast to the mabolong, the molawo requires minimal engagement of the audience; audience members are not required to play the drum and gongs, to support shamans physically as they dance, to humor importunate or despondent shamans and their hungry familiars, or to attend to the drama of the event. As one person put it, "When one performs a molawo, others are free to sleep." Although any experienced shaman who can make the journey to Pue in the mabolong controls the basics of the molawo, most do not want to be bothered. Even renowned molawo performers commonly insist on performing a mabolong instead, for all but a few patients to whom they are deeply devoted.

Students of kinship have contrasted "ego-focused" and "socio-focused" kin networks. Transferring the distinction to ritual, a "liturgy-focused" (or -centered) ritual would be one whose ritual action is dominated by an order that is collectively recognized and observed by its participants. A "performer-focused" ritual would be one like the mabolong, in which different performers work according to their own agendas. In doing so, they strive to capture the attention and commitment of audience members for their efforts to create and sustain ritual authority.

PART FIVE

13

Shamanship and Leadership

> The question of the functional or dynamic relationship
> between ceremonial and ordinary, non-ritualized social action
> and the question of the nature of the structure of ceremonial or
> ritual itself must, then, be seen as aspects of the same question,
> not distinct and mutually independent questions as they have
> almost invariably been treated by anthropologists.
>
> T. Turner, "Transformation,
> Hierarchy, and Transcendence"

At the start of this book I stated that my aim was to show how the mabolong articulates a cosmic order and at the same time constitutes a political one. Parts One through Four have explored the cultural premises, structural logic, and ritual practice of the mabolong. In this final section I shall develop my claim about the political dimensions of the mabolong by showing how this ritual not only symbolizes but is also integral to the very workings of Wana society. The argument developed here for a peripheral Southeast Asian population will address the relation between cultural forms and social action, an issue germane to both the recent literature on more complex Southeast Asian political systems and the discipline of anthropology at large.

First, it will be useful for what follows to recap my analysis of the mabolong itself and the issues it raises. Part One considered the ritual as an occasion for publicly invoking and displaying power, as defined in cultural terms. Wana notions of power are not partitioned into religious versus secular categories;[1] rather, culturally, power involves access to exogenous resources, including special knowledge and hidden agents. At first blush that view seems quite alien to social scientific concepts of power. Yet if power in the social scientific sense is defined as the ability to control other people's actions, then an overlap, if not full identity, does obtain between the two. In the Wana context one comes to control people and events in the world by tapping exogenous resources. For this reason it is neither reductionistic nor cynical to analyze the mabolong as both a religious event and a political one.

255

Giddens (1979, 93) observes that "power relations. . . are always *two-way*, even if the power of one actor or party in a social relation is minimal compared to another." Among the Wana, the "power" that people can wield over one another derives principally from claims of personal control over exogenous resources, including magic, spirits, and knowledge of customary law. For this reason, the relational dimensions of power are particularly evident: a person has "power" in social terms only insofar as others acknowledge it. By taking (or being given) charge in collective ritual (both shamanic and nonshamanic), certain individuals can gain recognition as persons with authority.

Part Two examined the nature of shamanic experience and cultural notions of personhood, health, and illness as they operate in Wana ritual. Two points are particularly striking about the model of the person as a concatenation of vital elements prone to disperse at the slightest provocation. First, it underscores a person's reliance on shamanic mediation by restricting direct access and control over these vital elements to individuals with shamanic powers. And second, it reveals a homologous relation between person and polity. Like a healthy person, the Wana homeland is depicted as having thrived at a time when knowledge, power, and wealth resided at their point of origin; with these elements dispersed, the land languishes like a person experiencing soul loss. Hence millennial visions posit a revitalization of the Wana region only when knowledge, power, and wealth return to their source. The oscillation between concentration and dispersal fundamental to models of person and polity is, as we shall see, also evident in social practice and in the Wana experience of community life as temporary aggregations of households that are easily dissolved. The homology permits the mabolong ritual to invoke simultaneously issues for the individual, the community, and the cosmos.

Consideration of shamanic experience revealed the liminal nature of the shaman as mediator between human and nonhuman realms. To overcome the centrifugality of his patient's vital elements, the shaman must transcend the otherwise discrete domains of Wana and spirit communities (see T. Turner 1977). Wana terms for shaman (*tau walia, tau kawalia*) reveal that fusion of separate domains, human and spirit. So too does shamanic conduct.

In the journeys to the Owner, discussed in Part Three, shamanic mediation assumes an explicitly hierarchical form. The geography of power that figures in other aspects of the mabolong is largely horizontal: most of the spirits that cause illness, as well as the spirit familiars who help combat it, are of this earth, lying beyond the bounds of human communities, sometimes in elevated places like mountains. Whereas the geography of power is primarily outward in other phases of the mabolong, when a shaman makes a pantoo it is upward. Verticality here involves rank as well as altitude. Whereas spirit friends and foes on the human plane require no deference, to approach Pue a shaman and his spirits must take careful ritual measures to avoid the condition of buto, brought on by violations of rank.[2]

By intervening with a higher power on a patient's behalf, a shaman necessitates a future demonstration of social solidarity (*kasintuwu*) by the community. Shamans who can claim responsibility for continuing and extending the lives of others thus instigate and perpetuate community events that celebrate their own management of human lives. Just as they assemble spirit familiars at a mabolong, so too do they initiate collective events that bring together people to support their mediation with higher powers.

And yet the shamanic centrality and influence implied in these three segments of the ritual are not achieved by every mabolong performer. Claims to shamanship are not a given but rather a goal of performance. The mabolong serves as a public arena in which reputations may be asserted and tested. Summoning spirits at a mabolong is to conjure hidden powers before an audience of one's peers. Being asked by others to investigate the sources of their own and their children's conditions is to have one's powers acknowledged by others. To undertake a journey to Pue is to display the confidence and authority to approach the godhead. To ask one's human companions for "foods" is to call for affirmation of and commitment to one's shamanic endeavors. Such requests underscore the fact that shamanship is not a unilateral matter: to be a shaman, a performer requires the acceptance, support, and encouragement of others. For this reason, I have argued, the baku mwalia episode holds special fascination for an audience because it can occasion an improvisational articulation of a performer's relations both to other shamans and to the community at large.

RITUAL AND POLITICS
IN ISLAND SOUTHEAST ASIA

Having considered the internal dynamics of the mabolong, we are now in a position to ask how the models of power, community, authority, autonomy, and dependence created in the ritual context may translate into the rest of Wana life. As Errington (1989, 49) has observed, a traditional "division of labor" in scholarly investigations of Island Southeast Asia has accorded the study of courtly elites to historians and the study of commoners, peasants, and hill populations to anthropologists. The result has been a vision of the region as a scattering of Hindu-Buddhist kingdoms floating atop an autochthonous "soup" of local cultures. In her monograph, then, Errington has sought "to correct the vision of the Indic State as a different sort of entity from a hill tribe in Island Southeast Asia."

In a related effort, the historian O. W. Wolters (1982) has drawn on ethnographic analogy to propose a political evolution from a Southeast Asian equivalent of Melanesian "big men" to dynastic kings who legitimated their rule through Hindu symbolism. I shall focus here on Wolters's model of politics in early horticultural communities that match some conditions of contemporary Wana social organization— namely, small clusters of households isolated from one another by great forests, subsistence practices based on "forest efficiency," and cognatic kinship systems with no corporate kin groups.

By no means does studying shamanic ritual in twentieth-century Sulawesi offer an unobstructed window on ancient Southeast Asian politics. As Anna Tsing (1987) has demonstrated for a similar population in Kalimantan, local culture and politics in the hinterlands are profoundly shaped through interaction with the nation-state. In the final chapter of this book I shall argue that the political significance of ritual in the Wana area has been shaped as well by contact—both direct and indirect—with local manifestations of the *negara*, the royal political center that once dominated the Indonesian Archipelago. Here I shall apply Wolters's model to more recent political dynamics.

Wolters hypothesizes that political integration within and between early horticultural communities of Southeast Asia was provided by what he terms "men of prowess." In the absence of corporate kin groups, influential leaders mobilized people through cognatic and neighborhood networks to carry out joint endeavors. These men of prowess owed their leadership, Wolters (1982, 6) suggests, to the fact that others attributed to them an abnormal amount of personal and innate "'soul stuff,' which explained and distinguished their performance from that of others in their generation and especially among their own kinsmen."

Political integration within and beyond settlements occurred as people allied as dependents of influential men of prowess, whose success was gauged not only by their own achievements but also by those of their followers, presumably in such activities as warfare, feasting, and ceremonies. Focused as they were on the leadership of individuals, such networks typically did not survive the deaths of their central figures. Wolters proposes that cults built around dead leaders were one way that would-be successors could attempt to draw on political capital from a former generation, and the importation of Hindu political concepts was a further means of enhancing the possibility of dynastic succession.

Wolters leaves the details of this evolution vague. His achievement is in recognizing the continuities in political leadership across levels of sociopolitical integration in Southeast Asia and in clarifying some of the commonalities of the shaman of the periphery and the raja of a center. What he does not do is specify the conditions that might promote political integration on local and regional levels or account for regional variation and change. In Chapter 15 I shall attempt to specify those conditions for the Wana and to account for change in that corner of Sulawesi.

With a bit of tailoring, Wolters's model applies admirably to Wana political processes. On the basis of his familiarity with the Southeast Asian literature, Wolters posited "soul stuff" as the sine qua non for "prowess" as regionally defined. For the Wana, prowess is epitomized by magical knowledge, the prerequisite for success at any enterprise. Thus Wolters's suggestion is by no means wide of the mark: as we have seen, power, knowledge, and soul stuff are as integrally related for the Wana as for other peoples in the area—only the configurations differ. Among the Bugis of South Sulawesi, for example, spiritual potency or soul stuff is inherited: the more noble of birth one is, the greater is one's potency (Errington 1983). By contrast, Wana "souls" are equal; what differs is people's achievement in the quest for magical knowledge—a quest that, among other things, confers control over other people's souls.

Like Wolters's soul stuff, magical knowledge is a key social value through which Wana relations of power and dependence are culturally articulated. As an intangible quality derived from sources exogenous to mundane social existence, its possession must be publicly iterated and validated. Whereas Wana presume that everyone possesses *some* magic, shamans have in addition personal ties to spirits, the sources of magical knowledge. The mabolong, then, is the paramount occasion for shamans to display evidence of those spirit ties. Like other politically charged theatrical spectacles in Island Southeast Asia, the mabolong provides an arena for performers to strive to match their culture's ideals of power. Given this aim, such endeavors are highly self-reflexive, by which I mean that they highlight the relation of a performer to attributes of power. Herein lies a contrast between Southeast Asian "men of prowess" and the Melanesian "big men" to whom Wolters compares them.[3] Big men's reputations for magic, oratory, and bravery support their entrepreneurial efforts to accumulate and distribute vast amounts of wealth in intergroup exchanges. In much of Melanesia, moreover, "agonistic" exchanges among social actors are mutually transformative for the participants involved; political reputations are built through public exchanges with competing rivals. By contrast, in many Southeast Asian theatrical displays the focus is on the connection between a political actor and a spiritual quality, such as soul stuff, spirit familiars, or deities. Relational dimensions of rituals, and hence their dialectical potential, are suppressed. One might say that politics of this sort posits audiences instead of adversaries; it is theatrical rather than transactional.

What are the consequences of theatrical performances beyond the ritual context? In the case of the exchanges of Melanesian big men, ritual displays and economic production are linked. Noting a correspondence between big man politics and the generalized exchange of women (whereby wealth, in the form of pigs and the like, may be exchanged for wives), Godelier (1982, 1986) has argued that Melanesian big men control the reproduction of human life and kinship through the grip they exert on economic production.[4] Wana shamanship, in contrast, confers no control over production or marriage. In this regard, Wana politics resembles the "great man" pattern outlined by Godelier rather than the familiar Melanesian "big man" pattern. Godelier coined the term *great men* to characterize influential political actors among the Baruya of Highland New Guinea. Although individual Baruya may achieve recognition as outstanding warriors, shamans, or hunters, these successes do not translate into control of production and distribution of wealth in Baruya society. For both the Baruya and the Wana, political reputation and influence are a function of personal control over prestigious resources exogenous to the social system (such as spirits, enemies, and game), not of material production and exchange.

SETTLEMENTS, SHAMANSHIP, AND THE
CREATION OF COMMUNITY

Wana shamanship does not offer control over economic production, but it does play a part in constituting Wana communities. To understand how this is so, it is necessary to consider the nature of a Wana community and the processes of its formation and dissolution.

Wana build their houses in their swidden fields: in a single large clearing of contiguous swidden sites there may be anywhere from from two to ten, twelve, or more houses. This pattern of many households sharing a single swidden site is unusual for swidden farmers in Island Southeast Asia. More commonly, smaller areas are cleared and farmed by fewer households. In Wana judgment, however, the more households in a swidden settlement, the better.

Each house is usually occupied by a conjugal couple and their dependent relatives, both old and young. Occasionally two or more conjugal couples will share a house; a fairly common arrangement is a combined household of parents and a married child with spouse. The occupants of a house may change over the course of a year—for example, two families may share a dwelling during the early part of a farming year, then separate when the men have time from their work to build individual houses. There is also a good deal of visiting within and between settlements for friendship, courtship, healing, celebrating, and pursuit of rice and trade goods.

Just as household composition may change over the course of a year, so may settlement composition change considerably over several years. Settlements are relocated each year after the harvest and before planting time. How near or far the new swidden site will be from the old is a function of many factors, including proximity of suitable farming land, the success of the previous harvest, the health and happiness of residents over the past year, and local concerns about Indonesian governmental policies regarding minority populations. Decisions about where to move are made by community farming leaders in consultation with both neighbors and oracles.

Not all householders may choose to accompany their neighbors to the new site. Residential mobility is permitted by swidden farming practices, the absence of private ownership, a lack of pressure on available farmland, and options for households to attach to new settlements where their members have kin or friends. Morever, a Wana-wide practice of exchanging a fixed amount of unhusked rice and a midday meal for a day's farm labor makes it possible (and, if supplies are low, desirable) for people to relocate, often over long distances, *during* a farming cycle as well as after it. Thus, although the future of settlement composition is most in question after harvest time, splintering can and does occur at other times.

Residential mobility has also been enhanced historically by a succession of coastal regimes in this century, which have sought (with varying degrees of success) to impose resettlement, corvée labor, taxation, religious conversion, and other unpopular policies on the Wana (see Atkinson 1979, 1984a, b). Kruyt put the matter simply: "The Wana are known to be a much plagued people." Their traditional enemies, known to them as the To Lage and to anthropologists as the Bare'e-speaking Toraja, marveled at their seemingly magical ways of disappearing—by making themselves so small they could hide under tree leaves and by transforming their fires into red tree ants when their enemies approached. The Wana "always had to be prepared for flight, and for this reason provided their pigs with nose rings . . . something that sounded ridiculous to Toraja ears; with these nose rings people could pull these domesticated animals along with them with every rumor of an enemy approach" (Kruyt 1930, 403–4). (I saw precious few domesticated pigs during my time in the Wana region, the difficulty of transporting them with every move being a possible reason for their absence.)[5]

Wana openly acknowledge their cowardice as a people. Apa Iki, the father of the shaman Apa Mene and head of the settlement in which I worked, told of his paternal grandfather, Liwa, himself the head of a settlement, who would lead others off into hiding at a moment's notice. It was Liwa's habit to eat a full meal early in the morning, so that if there were something to fear he wouldn't have to flee hungry. Apa Iki's sister-in-law recalled how once Liwa led them all in flight in the middle of the night on account of a dream. And one of Liwa's close friends and drinking companions, known as "Tall Fellow" (Ngkai Malangang), composed the following verse (*kiyori*) for him:

> baru yangu yangu la'u
> anumo pei inu yau
> ane ma'imo nsa tau
> siko Liwa lampu yau
>
> There's the beer sloshing back and forth.
> Come on and drink it down.

> If a stranger should arrive,
> you, Liwa, will go feral.

Liwa's timidity had its roots in the endemic regional warfare of the nineteenth century. In the regional game of headhunting, the Wana were often the heads, the victims of neighboring peoples (see Kruyt 1930, 505). There is also evidence that the coastal raja of Tojo and Bungku instigated war against the Wana to force their submission (Kruyt 1930, 403, 467). Subsequent history brought new trials for Liwa and his contemporaries. As Kruyt documents, pressures on Wana settlements did not cease with pacification. Although the imposition of direct Dutch rule in the region at the beginning of this century put an end to raiding, it inaugurated a new form of local terrorism. Kruyt (p. 404) recounts:

> In the beginning of the occupation, the Administration supposed that these shy people should come to know order and law most easily if they were forced to live near the coast. But they did not wish this, and the result was that—from the north by the government official of Poso as well as from the south by the administrator of Bungku and Mori— patrols of soldiers were sent repeatedly into this land to draw the people down [to the coast]. The result of all this was that a small portion of the people settled themselves in the vicinity of Bone Bae; another portion made villages close by the coast of the Moluccan Sea, but most chose an uneasy existence in the forest. Whenever the pressure of the patrols became strong in the north, people yielded from there to the south. When danger threatened from the south, then people moved to the north. The distress of these people must have been great. Of those who had let themselves be forced to live by the coast, many died.

Some of my older acquaintances were children when this Dutch effort took place, probably in the 1910s. By the late 1920s, when Kruyt conducted his survey, the policy had changed. People who wished to return to the interior were granted permission to do so, but only if they registered as members of villages or kampung. Some chose to settle near Bone Bae in the north; the coastal settlements in the south were generally abandoned. At the time of Kruyt's visit in 1928, "hundreds of Wana [were] still unregistered in the mountains and woods" (p. 404). Dutch patrols continually endeavored to "uncover" settlements of unregistered Wana. Offenders would be taken to the government capital at Kolonodale to become familiar with "society," whereupon they would be allowed to return home on the condition that they "build a village at a mutually agreed upon place." After such treatment, though, Kruyt (p. 405) noted, "most disappear again into their inaccessible hiding places."

Opportunities for trade, not government coercion, have brought Wana into willing contact with the coast. In the years leading up to World War II and once again in the 1950s and 1960s, a regional market in resin engaged Wana, who energetically tapped wild damar trees and traded resin for cloth, knives, pots, salt, and other coastal luxuries. Holdouts who refused to register in villages traded in turn with the more courageous village registrants, who had direct access to markets. At various points coastal traders would come into the interior as well to obtain forest products in return for coastal trade items.

After World War II, traders brought horses to the Wana region to enable people to bring out resin in quantities too great for a person to carry. Villages apparently thrived with this trade. Many Wana were willing to put up with taxation, corvée labor, and other impositions of the government when they saw benefit as well as hardship. With political turmoil in the wider society, however, they would easily return to their reclusive ways. World War II and the presence of seven Japanese soldiers in the area sent village people into hiding. So too did the Indonesian political turmoils of the 1950s and 1960s.[6] Both resulted in millenarian movements in which whole communities would vanish into remote areas of the woods. Three large settlements in the vicinity where I worked, for example, including the one in which I lived, were composed largely of refugees from one such movement in the late 1960s.

In the 1970s the Indonesian authorities engaged in an endeavor reminiscent of the abortive Dutch efforts to relocate the Wana population as the Social Ministry created new settlements along the northern coast in which to settle upland residents. Opposition to these plans was widespread among Wana, who felt that the coastal plains were unsuitable for farming, feared exploitation by local officials, and were anxious about forced conversions to Islam and Christianity. Plans to resettle interior peoples replaced any government interest in sustaining interior villages; they also provoked withdrawal by many Wana who would have been willing to cooperate with the government so long as they be allowed to remain in their homelands. Thus both external policies and historically conditioned skittishness have fostered residential instability in the area.

Like Wana models of personhood and homeland, Wana settlements exhibit centrifugal tendencies. A verse attributed to an influential Wana leader portrays his constituency as a flock of birds lighting on a tree, but likely to fly off at any moment.

COMMUNITY, RITUAL,
AND LEADERSHIP

In light of this picture, one might well ask if there is anything to counterbalance the centrifugal tendencies of Wana settlements. Two factors seem critical: one is a sense of community, built on histories of familiarity, cooperation, and affection; the other is a reliance on leadership and the protection of key individuals. At work in everyday life, both factors are manifested and joined in collective ritual.

The factor I am calling community is epitomized by the term *kasintuwu*, which refers to the moral quality of living together. People to whom the adjectival form *masintuwu* can be applied are mutually supportive: they share with one another and come to each other's assistance. Kasintuwu, which is part of the moral texture of quotidian existence, is highlighted as a primary social value on collective occasions when people are expected to come together.

Settlementwide gatherings take place on two kinds of occasions: the first predictable and associated with the farming cycle, the second unpredictable and associated with the life cycle. In the first category are a series of four annual farming celebrations held at the beginning and end of the planting season and the harvest season. Depending on the success of the harvest, the final harvest feast may attract celebrants from many settlements. These four celebrations are scheduled and directed by a community leader known as a *woro tana* (literally, the one who "bores the ground"), a mature man usually, who is a successful farmer and possesses knowledge of rice ritual and magic.

The second category of collective occasion includes funerals, marriage feasts, and mabolong performances. Like harvest feasts, these can be occasions when people gather from many settlements; but they may be smaller affairs, drawing principally on the residents of a single settlement. Whereas woro tana assume a centrality in farming festivals, experts on customary law (*ada*) occupy center stage in marriage negotiations, and shamans dominate mabolong, which may be held in conjunction with other kinds of festivals as well.

Attending a collective celebration is a demonstration of kasintuwu. Contributing food or rice beer is a further demonstration of neighborly commitment. Although it is expected that residents within a settlement will participate in collective events, between settlements attendance is a more fluid and overtly "political" matter. Funeral feasts and harvest festivals in particular are occasions when representatives of settlements within a radius of several miles make a point of appearing in order to demonstrate kasintuwu.

The spirit of collective gatherings, whether they involve members of a single settlement or of several, is cooperative, not competitive. In situations where opposition might be expected—for example marriage, in which at least some of the guests are associated with the bride's side or the groom's—formal procedures are designed to establish a sense of harmony and consensus among all who have gathered. Even ada discussions to settle disputes over adultery, divorce, and other disagreements work on this principle. This is not to say that political competition and rivalry are absent from Wana gatherings; but the articulated goal of a collective event is not to defeat or to shame a rival, but instead to celebrate community. As I noted earlier, political performance in this region is self-reflexive. So, for example, one local leader planned to stage a large harvest festival, a woman explained to me, because he wanted his community to have "great news" or "great fame" (*bae kareba*). Individuals and communities compete with others not by defeating them in explicit contests, but by outshining them.

Collective celebrations reflect on both a settlement and its inhabitants. The larger the settlement, the wider the personal networks of its members; and the greater its prosperity, the more brilliantly it will shine on festive occasions. A settlement with poor harvests will likely keep its collective celebrations to itself. It is also not going to attract people willing to trade farm labor, cloth, and other desired goods in return for rice, nor will its farming leader, shamans, and ada experts be able to increase their regional profile by being at the center of collective celebrations. Should fortunes change—should harvests improve, should people be attracted from elsewhere not simply to work or trade but to settle—the new situation can boost the reputations of prominent individuals who in various ways can take credit for community prosperity.

Farming Authority

Abundant harvests reflect well on the people who coordinate community farming decisions and ritual. Although bad harvests can be blamed on a variety of factors, ranging from pestilence to sorcery from other settlements, a woro tana can take credit for successful harvests. To become woro tana, one must be an effective and successful farmer, as well as a cooperative and persuasive neighbor whom others can trust. In addition—and this is critical—one must possess knowledge of ritual and magic handed down from one generation to another that people consider vital to the success of their own fields. Put another way, many Wana are effective farmers and cooperative neighbors, but not all claim to know the magical knowledge and ritual procedures to make their own and their neighbors' crops thrive. Vital as that expertise is to Wana life and livelihood, proximity to an admired woro tana is cited as an important consideration in Wana residence decisions.

Legal Authority

Just as association with a prominent woro tana lends a measure of security in matters of subsistence, so association with an effective legal orator provides assurance of another kind. The Wana possess a system of ada, or customary law.[7] They regard this system as a historical importation, maintaining that sometime after Wana submitted to the raja of Bungku in the last century three Wana went to Bungku and there were given ada. Without ada, they claim, "people would kill people"; with ada, disputes can be settled peacefully within a shared legal framework. The code specifies in metaphorical language payments to be made to settle matters of marriage, marital infractions, and a host of social breaches including slander, theft, and murder. That the code originated under the hierarchical conditions imposed by coastal sultanates is evident in the fact that the size of payments varies according to the social rank of the parties involved. In the Wana region in the nineteenth century, the various rankings consisted of the chiefs (*basal* or *makole*) and their kin, ordinary commoners, and debt slaves; in the 1970s, then, descendants of these former leaders could still be expected to pay more than others.

A variety of sanctions surround the use of the ada code. These sanctions place limits on the power of ada specialists. One must never claim to "know" ada; instead one should only allude to having heard others discuss a point of ada in a particular way. This stipulation mitigates against exclusive claims of authority and correctness on the part of ada experts. Furthermore, one must never accept rice in exchange for ada objects. This stipulation asserts a separation between ada exchange and subsistence production. To violate these principles results in the debilitating condition of buto.

What promotes adherence to the ada code? Principally the negative sanction that without it, vengeance taking would be rampant: if people did not submit to ada, it is said, they would kill each other. Regarding adultery, a more specific and fearsome sanction is at work. An act of adultery gives rise to "constricting" afflictions as a "monkey" (*kuse*) grips the guilty parties or their innocent relatives. The withholding of neonates or placentas in childbed is a classic form of kuse. In times of serious illness or difficulties in childbed, people may be quizzed about any affairs they might have had that could account for the problem. Confession and payment of a fine should release the grip of the "monkey" and restore the patient to health.

As I saw ada in operation, legal discussions were held principally over matters of marriage—the establishment, violation, and dissolution thereof. Ada provided a forum for willing parties to come together to resolve a matter of mutual concern. When parties were unwilling to talk, threats to report matters to coastal authorities a four-day hike away were sometimes made (but, in the interior, rarely acted upon). One of my neighbors, who had grown up in a community with powerful ada orators, observed that although I had achieved a thorough understanding of Wana shamanic practice, I had lacked the opportunity to make a comparable study of ada. I would agree. Ada practice is, I believe, livelier in settlements located at the "Old Mountain" (Tongku Tu'a), the Wana homeland, than in the region where I worked. The settlements I knew best were composed in the main of people who had moved away from the Old Mountain into wider expanses of land across the Bongka River to the northeast. There they settled near the To Linte, the northern branch of the Wana who in the past were subject to the raja of Tojo and a somewhat different code of ada. A lack of long-standing relations with others in the area and a low concentration of authorities versed in the same form of ada may therefore have dampened the enthusiasm of local experts for seeking out reasons to "talk ada."

Ada specialists are people with the confidence to engage in public deliberations, an activity that requires familiarity with highly embellished legal oratory, a quick wit, and people to depend on one's advocacy. It also requires access to objects suitable for payment, which one obtains by being party to prior ada discussions and through a double exchange pattern. For although one finds barriers to direct conversion of ada objects into rice, there are no barriers to exchange of ada objects for cloth; people who can acquire substantial stores of cloth through trade either of forest products like rattan and resin or of rice, then, can thereby obtain copper trays and china dishes to use in ada exchanges. They can also use cloth for some payments as well. (The possibility of translating cloth into ada payments gives men an advantage over women in this arena because men participate more actively than women in long-distance coastal trade.)

The importation of ada from the kingdom of Bungku was related directly to the institution of debt slavery in the Wana region (see Chapter 15), since in the nineteenth century people who could not pay their legal fines became the slaves of those who paid the fines for them. Although debt slavery ended in the colonial era, indebtedness to ada experts persists. People who marry, divorce, or become embroiled in complicated extramarital entanglements involving people in other communities may find themselves in need of an effective orator and assistance in paying large fines. If someone else pays a large fine on one's behalf, people say, the person who was rescued should make a point of residing near the benefactor and offering assistance occasionally. Although an ada expert has no recourse if a dependent chooses to move away, a follower may be persuaded to stay by the thought of future assistance from a past benefactor. Thus, paying fines for others is one way of invoking their allegiance. Slavery this is not; but dependency it most decidedly is.[8]

Shamanic Authority

Just as knowledge of rice ritual and ada attracts and sustains a following, so too does effective shamanship. Besides endeavoring to restore integrity to persons through ritual means, successful shamans can combat the centrifugal tendencies of Wana communities by encouraging the dependence of others on their skills.

The "shaman as hero" (Lévi-Strauss 1963a) is a dominant theme in both ritual and nonritual contexts. The action of the mabolong features a shaman as a powerful protagonist leading a spirit cohort in a struggle to save patients' lives. The private side of shamanship involves pressing beyond the limits of ordinary experience to engage alien and dangerous powers. Stories of heroic shamans abound—such as Towambo, a shaman so powerful that he was said to "defeat the Owner" by bringing people back to life even after forest had regrown on their gravesites. Although no living shaman can equal Towambo, people look for—and, I will argue, create—powerful ones to depend on.

In times of illness, Wana rely not simply on shamanic mediation but on mediation by particular shamans. Dependence on one special shaman comes about if people feel they owe their lives or the lives of their dear ones to this person who fought against all odds to save them, once or on numerous occasions. Shamans may impress on others this dependence. "If it weren't for me, this person would not be alive today" is a boast that shamans often make in the hearing of their patients. Patients and their families may likewise voice their reliance on a particular shaman. Children grow up being told that they owe their lives to the efforts of one shaman or another. In this way shamans and patients make reciprocal claims on each other, the shamans asserting their patients' dependence, and the patients insuring future assistance from the shamans.

SHAMANSHIP AND LOCALITY

Contrary to the biblical dictum that a man cannot become a prophet in his own land, it is precisely in one's own neighborhood that a shamanic reputation must be cultivated. In characterizing Javanese notions of power, Anderson (1972, 22) observed: "Perhaps the most exact image of the ordered Javanese polity is that of a cone of light cast downwards by a reflector lamp," its intensity being strongest at a central point and diminishing gradually as one moves outward toward the periphery. (This image has historical roots; see Moertono 1968.) Not only in Java, but elsewhere in the archipelago as well, political efficacy diminishes with distance. As Kiefer (1972) argued some time ago, this pattern is a function of the ego-focused networks through which political coalitions are created in this area. Wana followings of shamans, rice magicians, and ada specialists alike comprise first and foremost the people (generally close cognatic kin) who reside in the same swidden settlement. Beyond that cluster may be people in other settlements who periodically express commitment to those influential people but do not interact with them day to day. And still further beyond are acquaintances and strangers whose attitudes toward these persons of influence may be neutral, competitive, hostile, or denigrating.

The immediate neighbors of a prominent shaman stand to benefit most from his skills. Their advantage is not only logistic but also political. Established shamans use their reputations to attract people to their settlement, for only those who live nearby have primary claims on a shaman's services. The way in which access to a powerful shaman can serve as an enticement and a justification for residence choice is illustrated in the following case. (Given the potential sensitivity of the case, I have changed the names of the parties involved.)

Dodi and her husband Ngalo were a young married couple who had resided for several years with his parents, not hers. Dodi's parents were Christian converts who lived in a government village near the coast. Relations between Dodi and her parents were somewhat strained, and Dodi claimed that she preferred to live with her in-laws, despite Wana sentiment that married daughters should live near their parents. After considerable pressure from her parents, Dodi and Ngalo decided that once their harvest was completed, they would go to farm by her parents.

During the harvest season Dodi and Ngalo's infant daughter fell sick. Ngalo's brother, Apa Leru, a prominent shaman, along with Apa Jampu, the brother of Ngalo's sister's husband and the leading shaman of a neighboring community, took charge of the case. After a succession of mabolong and potudu performances and other healing measures, the baby showed some improvement. Apa Jampu instructed the baby's father to summon him to perform again in fourteen days. When the time came, though, the child was much better, and the father neglected to fetch Apa Jampu for a follow-up mabolong. Soon after, the child fell sick again; the relapse was attributed to the failure to perform the required mabolong. Once again Apa Leru and Apa Jampu made a heroic effort to save the child, and the parties concerned vowed that if the child lived to make the trip to her maternal grandparents, Dodi and Ngalo, with the help of Apa Leru, would set an offering afloat in the river. The child survived, and as the family set off on their journey the vow was fulfilled.

Not long after, Ngalo returned to his parents' settlement for a funeral feast. During his stay, a messenger arrived with an urgent request from Dodi that Ngalo and his shaman brother Apa Leru should come immediately: the baby had fallen sick again, and Dodi was terrified. Although Dodi's father was a shaman, there was fear that the baby's condition would not respond to his treatment but awaited that of her uncles. Ngalo left immediately, but Apa Leru declined to make the long journey; instead he sent his spirit familiars to investigate the child's condition and take proper measures. The child's paternal grandmother made a vow for the child's recovery, amid much negative talk insinuating that Dodi's parents were putting the child at risk by demanding that she be taken away from the shamans on whom her life depended. The point was apparently not lost on Dodi's mother and father. Within a week the young family returned, with the blessings of Dodi's parents, for it had been shown that the child could not live apart from the shamans who had sustained her life.

Dodi and Ngalo's choice of residence involved issues of religion, farming considerations, and family sentiments. Its resolution was not framed in terms of those issues, however, but rather in terms about which all parties could agree—namely, the welfare of the child and her dependence on the powers of particular shamans.

REMUNERATION AND SHAMANSHIP

To attract others to him, a shaman must present himself as being indispensable to their life and health. He also must appear to be doing more for them than they are for him. This stance cannot, however, be maintained indiscriminately. Instead it is cultivated for a core following and allowed to diminish with social distance.

A consideration of direct remuneration for shamanic treatment shows how this process works. Within a community, a shaman receives no special payment for shamanic performances or treatments with spells, although he is hosted with betel, tobacco, and rice beer, and occasionally a meal as well. For certain procedures a gift may be required to protect the shaman and his family or to encourage his spirit familiars. These prestations are phrased as spiritual requirements and sharply distinguished from wages.

Shamans from other settlements may require a more direct incentive to perform. An *oko mwiti* ("to take the feet") is a gift given to entice a shaman to travel to help a patient. Similarly, if there is social or spatial distance between a shaman and those in need of his services, a gift of clothing is in order. Once again, a distinction is made between this gift, which demonstrates "whiteness of heart" (*buya nraya*) to encourage a shaman's spirits, and payment or "wages" (*gaji*).

Shamans who demand payment for healing are viewed as "crooked" (*maneo*), in contrast to "good" or "decent" (*magao*) shamans who do not. Yet the matter of remuneration, be it phrased as buya nraya or gaji, is more a matter of social relationship than of personal character. A shaman may be judged as "decent" by those to whom he is committed, with whom he is engaged in the ongoing "give and take" of community life, and as "crooked" by those whom he feels no obligation to assist and from whom he has no expectation of future remuneration.

Although generous shamans will ostensibly work selflessly on their neighbors' behalf, people who depend on a certain shaman's services often do find ways of reciprocating. One woman, for instance, periodically brought supplies of piper leaf and areca nut to the shaman whose aid was continually requested by her household of six. Portions of meat, fish, fruit, and the like may also be directed to the households of prominent shamans. In one settlement, I was told, residents on one occasion went so far as to join together to help an old shaman with his farm work to compensate him for his tireless efforts on their behalf.

In general, such remuneration is subtle and evident only in the breach. For example, I overheard a prominent shaman and his wife discuss the fact that a neighbor had allegedly found some honey and neglected to share it with the shaman's household. Sometime, they noted, the neighbor would ask the shaman to perform, and he would decline.

The same couple was involved in another incident I witnessed. One day the shaman's sister-in-law brought her infant by for a visit. In a style of baby talk used among women in the company of infants, she declared that her husband was irritated because his brother (the shaman) was picking his piper leaf. The shaman's wife answered, also in baby talk, "Don't criticize, so he'll be willing to treat us [*kita*] with spells." The use of baby talk kept the exchange on a joking level; moreover, the use of the inclusive first-person pronoun (*kita*) delicately avoided an opposition between the two women.

Should a shaman's household become too tactless about its expectations of remuneration, people may seek shamans elsewhere. I did note that people, used to patronizing one shaman, would visit another when the first had been less than gracious about helping. Uncooperativeness was also cited as a reason why some had chosen not to live near one powerful shaman who in his old age had refused, I was told, to perform without payment.[9]

To sum up, shamans themselves underscore the dependence of others on them and demonstrate a particular willingness to help those who choose to live nearby. Others, for their part, are attracted to the neighborhood of a prominent shaman and often see it as in their best interest to be generous with such a person if he will reciprocate when they need shamanic attention.

So far I have focused on the fact that an alliance with a powerful shaman assures assistance in times of illness. Significantly, however, illness may according to Wana etiology have human as well as spirit sources; thus, to protect their followings shamans must defend not only against illness-bearing spirits but also against human sorcerers. The cliché that the best defense is a good offense applies aptly here: sorcery is an important part of an expert shaman's medical—and political—kit, and one that often comes into play beyond the ritual context.

SORCERY AND SHAMANSHIP

Like other cognatic peoples in the region, Wana distinguish a sense of "usness" based on social and spatial proximity through contrast to an undistinguished "them," referred to sometimes simply as *tau*, "people," or more definitively as *tau yusa*, "other people" (see Errington 1989). This contrast is morally charged. The rules of conduct that should hold among people who view each other as "us" break down as interaction with strangers comes into play. Within a community of "us," sorcery should not be used. In fact, the rare accusations of intrasettlement sorcery that I heard of always coincided with and were used to fuel the breakup of a residential cluster. Sorcery, in short, comes from "other people," those beyond the margins of one's moral community.

Sorcery is not, however, the weapon of the socially marginal. Instead, as a form of special knowledge, it is at its most powerful among powerful people. Anyone thought to possess magical spells should be presumed to know sorcery; mature and influential men especially warrant both respect and caution on this account. People with sorcery need not be people with spirit familiars, but there can be no doubt that people with spirit familiars are people with sorcery. After all, included in the category of spirit familiars are precisely those creatures who make a practice of "eating out people's insides." Whereas anyone can study sorcery spells for self-defense or malicious intent, shamans necessarily cultivate ties with the spirit agents of sorcery, whether their intentions are to heal or to harm.

Except in playful boasting and serious challenging, people with spells commonly deny that they know or use sorcery (a category of magic labeled *doti*, a term borrowed from the Buginese). Rather, they say that they possess "walls of the body" (*rindi ngkoro*)—spells used to defend against sorcery. Even people with reputations for powerful sorcery, when asked, are likely to say that they strive "to support the lives of [their] companions" (*potuwu yunu*), not to harm people. When incidents of alleged sorcery are raised, people may solemnly observe, "The Owner is not blind," suggesting that divine justice condemns sorcery. But such ethical judgments are applied relativistically, not universalistically. Wanton use of sorcery is condemned, defensive use is not—a judgment that in any given instance depends on the evaluator's place in the social field. Thus a man whom neighbors consider to be a champion and protector may be regarded as a deadly sorcerer by people in other communities.

Sorcery, like other forms of special knowledge, can be used to benefit a following. Because a shaman defends his community from dangers emanating from human as well as nonhuman sources, sorcery, used in retaliation for suspected sorcery by others, is one means shamans have of protecting those close to them. Thus sorcery is integral to the shamanic endeavor.

Politically, the value of sorcery derives not from its actual use but from its *potential* for use. A reputation for sorcery is an advantage when persuading others to do what one wishes them to do. Consider the place of a shaman's reputation for sorcery in the following dispute.

Apa Bale had an orphaned niece, Neli (both pseudonyms), who lived far away in another settlement. He and his wife were elderly and wanted the girl to come live and work with them. He visited the girl's guardians and intimated that his son, a powerful shaman, would be "angry" if the girl were not allowed to reside with him, an anger that might translate into sorcery if the request were not granted. Not long after, one of the girl's guardians developed a terrible stomach pain, the source of which was determined to be a "crab" (*bungku*) sent into his body by Apa Bale's son, who was renowned for this particular sorcery technique. The girl was sent to live with her uncle and later married into his community. (Apa Bale told me this story; I do not know how Neli's guardians would have explained their decision to give up the girl. The value of Apa Bale's account is the light it casts on the plausibility of using sorcery as leverage in achieving compliance from others. Note that it was Apa Bale himself, not his shaman son, who used the younger man's reputation for sorcery in these negotiations.)

In an incident that I witnessed, a shaman's stepmother instructed a relative returning to a distant settlement to tell people there that the shaman would "be angry" if they did not hand over a gong to which the shaman's community felt entitled. Like the previous example, this incident shows the perceived advantage of a reputation for sorcery, not simply for the person who holds it but for those allied with that person as well.

As it turned out, the woman's threat did not bring about the immediate return of the gong. People may worry about intimations of sorcery, but they do not automatically capitulate when so threatened. More likely, they take stock of their own defenses, for possessing sorcery themselves or being allied with someone who does effectively diminishes such worry. For example, when a marriage proposal came for a young woman whom I will call Lina, both Lina and her parents were distressed. All were opposed to the match, but the suitor's mother and stepfather were widely regarded as powerful sorcerers. Although Lina's father was a shaman, he feared retribution from this powerful pair if the suit were rejected. As Lina's relations discussed the matter, however, they reassured themselves with the knowledge that Lina's brother-in-law and *his* brother-in-law were powerful shamans who could rebuff any vengeance the suitor's parents might wreak on Lina and her community. The proposal was rejected.

Like rice ritual, ada, and shamanic prowess, sorcery is an important form of knowledge on which others in a community may come to depend. Because of the intrinsic relation between sorcery and the shamanic pursuits, sorcery is a means whereby the authority achieved through mabolong performance can be carried over from ritual to nonritual contexts.

LIMITS TO THE SYSTEM

In characterizing early "men of prowess" politics in Southeast Asia, Wolters hypothesized that political constituencies, focused as they were on powerful individuals, were likely to collapse at the death of their leaders. Indeed, the Wana lack effective measures for perpetuating authority intergenerationally. In contrast to societies such as the Sa'dan Toraja of South Sulawesi, with their famous funeral rituals directed at transferring status and property rights from the dead to the living (see Volkman 1985), the Wana seek to defend the integrity of the living against the contagious dangers of the dead; instead of occasioning orderly succession, death calls for collective measures to ward off physical and psychic threats to the survivors. The powers that a shaman concentrates about himself in life dissipate at his death, like the dead man's own soul parts. Only by keeping vigil at his grave (and so risking death themselves) can would-be successors hope to intercept a few of his spirit allies.[10]

CONCLUSION

This chapter has considered the ways in which knowledge of rice ritual, ada expertise, and shamanship figure in the creation of communities. People who develop reputations in these three specialties can attract followers who depend on them to sustain the life and health of their crops and themselves, and to serve as advocates in social and spiritual matters alike. In highlighting how each specialty comes into play, I have spoken as though these were three separate categories of social actors. Yet although the forms of knowledge and practice are culturally discrete, their social control is not: there is nothing about expertise in one domain that prohibits expertise in another. In fact, there are good reasons for the same person to possess expertise in more than one domain. First, all three forms of expertise are highly prized; hence it is desirable and enviable to control them. Second, because each form requires the memorization and articulation of lengthy formulae, people who can master one domain have the mind and verbal skills to master another. Finally, all three forms confer a measure of political authority. If people well versed in one area develop expertise in one or both of the others, they may free themselves and their associates from dependence on the expertise of others.

Developing authority in any of these domains seems to be a social, not an individual, matter. Not every person seeks full independence of everyone else; consociates generally prefer to look to each other rather than outside for advocacy in human and spirit realms. It is in this spirit that a senior shaman urges "the little children" (*ngana miyunu*)—his own children and those of his siblings and cousins—to seek shamanic knowledge so they won't have to "pay" others for help in time of illness. It is in this spirit as well that people seek special knowledge from aging relatives, lest a community be left bereft not only of its "great old people" (*tau bose tu'a*) but also of their expertise.

14

Shamanship, Gender,
and the Life Cycle

Habitus, as the social inscribed in the body of the biological
individual, makes it possible to produce the infinite acts that
are inscribed in the game, in the form of possibilities and
objective requirements. The constraints and requirements of
the game, although they are not locked within a code of rules,
are *imperative* for those, and only those, who, because they
have a sense of the game's immanent necessity, are equipped
to perceive them and carry them out.

> Bourdieu, quoted in Lamaison,
> "From Rules to Strategies"

The ideal of shamanship promotes the image of a powerful agent
surrounded by passive but appreciative dependents. The last three
chapters should have dispelled the notion that all performers are
equally powerful and appreciated. Only some can match the self-
characterization of one renowned shaman who declared, "As for those
who defeat me, there are none. Only those who equal me are there"
(*ane to manangi taare ane kasiwajuka re'e*).

What does it take to achieve such a profile of shamanic agency?
Culturally, success is attributed to possession of secret knowledge and
spirit alliances, an achievement that is in turn attributed to individual
qualities of bravery, industry, and good fortune. Yet in practice,
shamanic claims entail social negotiation. As Giddens (1979, 93) put
it, "Power relations are relations of autonomy and dependence, but
even the most autonomous agent is in some degree dependent, and
the most dependent actor or party in a relationship retains some
autonomy." Although shamanship may look like an individual
achievement, I will argue here otherwise: first, that a shaman is powerful only insofar as others attribute power to him; and second, that
motivation for shamanship does not rest solely with the individual
but rather derives from, and is promoted by, the interests of wider
social groups.

To develop this argument I shall consider the relations between two categories of people, one from which a disproportionately large number of shamans come and another that is poorly represented in the ranks of mabolong performers. The imbalance between the shamanic achievement of men and women suggests unequal access to key resources on which ritual and political authority depend.[1]

For Morton Fried (1967, 33), the inequality of which I speak was a nonissue: "An egalitarian society is one in which there are as many positions of prestige in any given age-sex grade as there are persons capable of filling them." That differences of age and gender should entail unequal access to positions of prestige does not imply for Fried the inappropriateness of the label *egalitarian*. Age, of course, is mutable: a person may attain eligibility for various forms of prestige and privilege at different points in the life cycle. But what of gender? Are Wana forms of prestige simply structures of male privilege, as Ortner and Whitehead (1981) might argue? Or are there separate and incomparable hierarchies of prestige and privilege for women and men in Wana society (see Leacock 1978; Weiner 1976)? Or is it perhaps the case that Wana women simply become enamored of hegemonic forms of male domination despite their own best interests (see Llewelyn-Davies 1981)?

When I initially undertook fieldwork among the Wana, I intended to examine the gendered division of religious specialization. Among the neighboring peoples of the Poso region, men's headhunting and women's shamanship appear to have been complementary endeavors (Adriani 1932):[2] men insured the vitality of their communities by their expeditions on a worldly plane, while women protected people's lives and health through trips to the Upper and Lower Worlds. The only men to engage in these shamanic journeys were those who forsook male pursuits and lived as women. By contrast, Kruyt found Wana shamanship to be the purview of men, except among the Barangas group where some women did serve as shamans.[3]

As I discovered, to examine Wana shamanship with questions of gender in mind conflicts decidedly with a Wana perspective on the matter. People objected to phrasing ritual specialization in gendered terms. When I asked who could become a shaman, people told me *anyone* could, provided that person was "industrious" (*madota*) or "brave" (*makoje*) about seeking shamanic knowledge and possessed the "fortune" (*dale*) or "palm line" (*ua mpale*) to succeed. It was obvious to me that almost without exception those anyones were men.[4] When asked to explain why most shamans were men, people resisted the suggestion that gender was a qualification for shamanship or other ritual activities.

If not articulated as a categorical rule, however, differences in social practice create a pattern whereby access to shamanic skills—a highly valued form of cultural expertise—is differentially accorded by gender. A close look at the cultural construction of Wana shamanship reveals that its emphasis on physical mobility and the external derivation of secret knowledge conform more closely to the contours of male rather than female experience in Wana society.

As we have seen, the sources of shamanic power are not contained within society but lie beyond it, an externality that translates into spatial terms. It therefore follows that a person in pursuit of shamanic knowledge should ideally frequent remote reaches of the forests and mountains. Culturally, it is deemed coincidental that these are more typically the sites of men's activities than women's. Both men and women tend swiddens and children close to home; both make regular trips through the forest between old and new swidden sites; and both venture into the forest to collect food and materials used in the manufacture of household items. Typically, however, men travel farther and faster than women. (Hunting, gathering resin for coastal trade, and making long trips to coastal markets are distinctively male activities and require long absences from settlements.) Moreover, it is appropriate for men to travel alone, but not women. Solitary trips to the forest are portrayed as dangerous by men and women alike. People continually admonish others, "Don't go out alone. A feral cat may come"—"feral cat" being a euphemism for a liver-eating demon, precisely the kind of spirit a shaman may seek as a familiar.

A shaman, then, is someone brave enough to confront murderous demons. Men, people say, tend to be braver than women. It therefore makes cultural sense that there are more men than women in the shamanic ranks. Thus construed, this imbalance appears to be the outcome of a statistical, not a mechanical, model (Lévi–Strauss 1963b)—a result dictated by probability, not fiat. Wana undercut the suggestion of male superiority on this score by freely characterizing themselves as a timid and cowardly people. (Recall that Liwa, described in Chapter 12 as a man who fled at the slightest provocation, was a respected Wana leader.) By braving hidden dangers, shamans represent exceptions; and in describing their solitary vigils in the forest or by newly dug graves to a wide-eyed audience, even shamans openly confess their fright.

Women have something additional to worry about when walking through the forest. "Feral cat" is a double entendre, applying not only to liver-eating demons, but to genitals—both male and female—as well. A women should avoid solitary journeys in the forest lest she encounter a feral cat of one sort or another. But what of a man? Does the pun work the same for him? While gender differences are suppressed in matters of procreation, they assert themselves in the initiation of sexual intercourse (Atkinson forthcoming): a woman who encounters a man alone in the forest is considered vulnerable to his sexual initiative (cf. Tsing forthcoming). Wana cautions on women traveling alone are not comparable to the Mundurucuu threat of gang rape,[5] but they do identify a limit on women's access to the very realms in which knowledge and power are to be found.

In fact, women *do* go to the forest in search of spirits. What is more, despite the stereotype of the solitary shaman keeping vigil in a remote place in the forest, in practice many male shamans obtain their knowledge closer to home. Some simply study with human teachers. Some, like Apa Mene, claim that new familiars seek them out at home in their own settlements. Apa Linus, to many people's amusement, occasionally called on spirit familiars he encountered in the sweet potato patch. And a woman called Indo nTiti, a generation older than my oldest acquaintances, could sit in a room and pluck medicines, gifts from spirits, out of thin air. As these examples show, the disproportion between men and women shamans cannot be explained simply as a functional outcome of the fact that shamanic resources lie beyond human settlements and men travel farther than women. However people obtain shamanic powers, exercising those powers proves to be more consonant with male experience than female experience.

As I explore elsewhere (Atkinson forthcoming), Wana women do not possess a unique sphere of comparably elaborated power. Men's and women's procreative and household roles are closely matched in cultural terms; nurturance is cast as a parental, not a uniquely female, act;[6] and both women and men are food producers. Women and men are conceived to be fundamentally the same—but *some* men, by pressing beyond the limits of ordinary experience, are somehow more so. Because notions of gender are constructed as a continuum rather than as a set of dichotomies, shamans can exploit a range of behavioral styles without couching their actions in transvestite imagery. For example, the nurturing stance of a shaman toward a patient is parental, not feminine, and by no means incongruent with the warrior persona the shaman may adopt in the same performance.

Although men's access to the forest gives men an edge over women in achieving shamanship, this edge is not categorically stated. By no means are all Wana men shamans. In contrast to societies in which all adult men participate in special flute cults, headhunting, or initiatory activities that exclude women, the line between shaman and nonshaman does not divide women and men in Wana society. Nor is a man who is not a shaman likened to a woman. Rather, a man who does become a shaman stands out from other men and women. Thus the gendered dimensions of the "prestige structure" are blurred.

SHAMANSHIP AND THE LIFE CYCLE

Having asserted that shamanship fits, in some way, the contours of male experience, I want to look more closely at how people become involved in shamanic activity. I will begin with the observation that in 1976 among residents of the settlement I know best, at least sixteen of the twenty-five males over the age of twelve had taken some steps toward becoming shamans. Of the sixteen, six were recognized as shamans, six more were still pursuing shamanic knowledge and experience, and four had given up their shamanic aspirations (two perhaps only temporarily). Of the twenty-four women past puberty, at least fourteen had danced the aesthetically pleasing salonde, the female version of the shaman's dance, or motaro. Of these, several did so with express hopes of gaining shamanic powers; none was yet a mabolong-performing shaman. Besides the obvious gender divide, we need to account for the waxing, waning, and sustaining of shamanic commitment and ambitions over a lifetime.

Wana children are born into a world of shamanic activity. Far from being cut off from this prestigious adult domain, they are its center, figuring prominently among the patients treated at a mabolong (Fig. 21).[7] Understandably concerned, in this area of high infant mortality, about children too young to articulate what ails them, parents rely on shamans and their spirit familiars to monitor their offspring's welfare. Whether or not a child displays symptoms of illness, parents engage shamans regularly to check for problems that may be pending. Many of the vows (*pantoo*) made by Wana shamans represent extensions of life for children. Another factor is responsible for turning children into patients: I observed that aspiring shamans who were not in great demand as healers at mabolong often devoted considerable time and attention to treating their own children, whether these youngsters were ailing or not.

Not only do children learn early to submit as patients to shamans' ministrations, but they are also playfully coached in shamanic activities. Infants of both sexes are bounced up and down in explicit imitations of shamanic dancing, at mabolong and other times as well. Toddlers are sometimes urged to motaro, to the delight of their elders. Playing shaman is a common childhood pastime. Although they are not allowed to beat the drum and gongs lest real demons come or the instruments be damaged, children make do with bamboo zithers and perhaps a pan lid or two. Little children also learn early to sing in the style of a shaman. Shamans' songs are likened to lullabies. (As one mother explained the difference, the former require magical spells and the latter do not.) Intriguingly, I observed young children on different occasions adopt the shaman's song style to express feelings of hurt, resentment, and self-pity, shifting from ordinary speech like shamans experiencing "small feelings" to voice their alienation.

Besides participating as patients and experimenting as shamans, children take part in the festive aspects of mabolong (Fig. 10). A mabolong is a social event for children no less than for their elders. Like adults, they don new clothes, apply makeup, and affect new hairstyles before a performance. From an early age, seated on laps or toddling to and fro, they are in the thick of things. One treat for a small child is to share a beater with an adult gong player, and older children commonly monopolize the instruments during lulls in the evening until adults shoo them away. Because gong playing is easier than drum playing, preadolescent girls may accompany older players at an age when boys still lack the requisite drumming skills.

Little girls also begin shyly to dance the *salonde*. By contrast, boys in my experience do not motaro in public until adolescence. This difference may reflect the fact that the salonde (meaning literally "something beautiful") serves as sheer aesthetic entertainment, whereas the motaro is not ornamental but specifically implies shamanic intent (Figs. 14, 15). The salonde allows women to dance without appearing to assert shamanic claims—although it can also mask a woman's intention when she *does* want to have her shamanic aspirations recognized.[8] Whereas older women may hold sessions to instruct their daughters, nieces, and granddaughters in the art of salonde, I never heard of comparable sessions for teaching boys to motaro.

Shamanic endeavors begin in earnest in adolescence, when young people (both boys and girls) begin to study spells, seek advice from established shamans, set off to the woods in search of spirits, and dance at mabolong. These quests for spells and spirits coincide with young people's increased mobility. Boys at this age may begin to hunt, to travel to coastal markets, and to visit other settlements in search of work and lovers. Girls, too, travel to other settlements in the company of relatives, and some go to the markets.

Adolescent dabbling in magic and shamanship generally has nothing whatever to do with healing, however; instead, it often has to do with courting. Adults joke that young people foolishly seek love magic instead of more important and useful forms of special knowledge. Indeed, a reputation for spells implies to a potential lover that one has the power of irresistible attraction as well as the power for cruel punishment through sorcery for trifling with one's affections. People occasionally joke about the inspiration of youthful mabolong performers, saying that they are possessed by "the spirit familiars of people who want to make love." A reputation as a budding kawalia can enhance a young man's prospects with both a lover and her parents, who may see shamanic potential as an asset in sons-in-law. (I have seen too few young girls overtly display shamanic aspirations to know how young men and their families view them.) Whether one's goals are courtship or shamanship, the initial steps may be the same.

Becoming a shaman means putting secret knowledge and spirit connections to work in the context of mabolong. When I would ask why more women with knowledge of magic and associations with spirits do not perform at mabolong, people typically said that women were "embarrassed" or "shy" (*mea*) about doing so. Their attitude suggests that public performance is tacitly structured in a way that excludes women from shamanic camaraderie and competiton. Unlike healing rituals involving a single performer (such as molawo, pantende, posuyu, and potudu), a mabolong is an occasion for performers to converse, carouse, cooperate, and compete. An aspiring performer must find a place among the coterie of shamans who dominate the performance. Established shamans invite male companions to the offering tray (*lango*) to drink and to talk. (Women, in contrast, congregate around the lango in the capacity of hosts and patients, not drinking companions or shamanic peers.)[9] As they perform, shamans summon novices to their side for instruction, perhaps planting special amulets in the novices' bodies to serve as "bridges for spirit familiars" (*tete mwalia*) and in other ways make them attractive to spirit benefactors. They may encourage these young people to dance along with them (Fig. 19). During my field stay, Apa Mene was sponsoring several nephews and his son in this way. Meanwhile, his orphaned niece was seeking spirits in the forest and dancing alone at mabolong without his encouragement or assistance.

Apart from tacit assumptions about gender and shamanship, notions of sexual propriety interfere with the formation of mentor-student relations between men and women. The relationship of mentor and student, like that between shamanic colleagues, involves public allusions to shared secrets and experiences and is demonstrated through loving exchanges of words and embraces. When mapped onto cross-gender relations, such behavior may convey more than a teacher-student relationship in this society where even husbands and wives avoid overt demonstrations of affection. Significantly, women appear in greater numbers among performers of rituals that imply no backstage secrets or adventures with mentors, rituals that can be learned by listening to the performances of others in a public setting.[10]

Marriage is regarded as a potential disruption in shamanic pursuits. The spells and spirit familiars one possesses before marriage may lose their potency after marriage—they are said to be "squeezed by the white thigh" (*rumpit mpa'a buya*). To restore their efficacy, one must "seek back companions for them" (*liwuka muni yununya*), that is, go out in pursuit of new spells and spirit familiars to revive the old. Simply put, one must renew one's shamanic commitment.[11]

This cultural perception of a decline in shamanic prowess after marriage may relate to several factors. For one thing, the shamanic efforts of young people are closely tied to their increasing mobility and romantic inclinations. Marriage should bring an end to courtship, and thus to shamanic pusuits. What is more, marriage introduces new responsibilities for both men and women as farmers, householders, and, eventually, parents.

To continue shamanic pursuits as a married adult is to engage in something more than youthful dalliance. If one is taken seriously as a mature shaman, one will be asked to treat others. The therapeutic side of shamanship involves sacrifice and a tedium absent from the dancing, drinking, and revelry that novices enjoy at mabolong. Despite its prestige, the possession of shamanic powers is not an unmitigatedly enviable proposition. It means being called away from work or sleep to perform, going to the aid of others "in spite of darkness, in spite of rain, in spite of heat of day, in spite of distance." People express distaste at the notion of sucking forth intrusive objects from ringworm-infested bodies. Indo Lina characterized a shaman as "a dog of many people" (*asu ntau boros*). As the daughter of one shaman and the wife of another, she is fully aware of how a shaman must work to serve and maintain a constituency.

Parenthood, however, introduces a new incentive for shamanic pursuits. Acquiring the means to heal small children is a concern for both mothers and fathers. New parents seek knowledge of minor spells and amulets and cultivate ties with established shamans. Some chafe at their dependency on others: I have heard shamans claim that as young fathers they went in search of special powers so they would not always have to seek help from others. Whether one relies on others or becomes a shaman oneself depends on a variety of factors, including gender and temperament. Another consideration, I suspect, is the relations one has to other shamans, a factor that can work two ways. On the one hand, if one has close ties to powerful shamans, one need not "pay" for shamanic services from unfamiliar people. On the other hand, having close ties to powerful shamans also means access to mentors, should one care to study.

Having established shamans nearby can be both an asset and a liability for an aspiring kawalia. In a community with such *kawalia tendamo*, "experienced people with spirit familiars," younger men are commonly regarded as novices; not yet "shamans indeed" (*kawalia kojo*), they are instead "shamans just becoming accustomed" (*kawalia owo pomananyang*). The exchanges between Apa Mene and his younger cousins examined in Part Four exemplify the difference. Apa Linus and Apa Miin gain credibility from their association with Apa Mene, but they are also patronized. As long as they must defer to local experts, they cannot establish their autonomy as prominent shamans in their own communities.

Both Apa Linus and Apa Miin have more leeway performing in

other settlements where being related to Apa Mene enhances their reputation but his presence does not cramp their style. Apa Mene's younger brother, too, almost never performed in his own settlement during my field stay, but reputedly did so elsewhere. By contrast, Apa Mene and his brother-in-law Apa Weri perform together as equals and bosom buddies. It is my hunch that a shaman who marries into another community away from senior kinsmen with shamanic reputations may exercise and develop his shamanic claims more freely than one who lives with those elder kin.

Eventually, however, older shamans must give way to younger ones. Because of age, infirmity, or weariness with continual requests to perform, they defer to younger, more active shamans. In Apa Mene's neighborhood, for example, the eldest shaman was Apa nTode, father-in-law to Apa Mene. Apa nTode complained of painful joint and back problems, performed infrequently, and deprecated his own talents in comparison to his son-in-law, himself a grandfather. Nearby, PaimBela, a young father of four, became the principal shaman for his own small settlement and for farming clusters across the Bongka River when his shaman stepfather, PaiGete, began to express a reluctance to travel about and perform.

PROVING ONESELF

As powerful factors molding shamanic careers, gender and age are relational constructs. Shamanship favors men over women, senior over junior dependents, active juniors over dependent or soon-to-be dependent seniors. Yet if Wana shamanship favors mature men, it is not simply a reflection of or a gloss for the power of age and masculinity in Wana society. There is more to achieving a shamanic reputation than meeting criteria of gender and age.

A married man who continues his shamanic activity confirms that he does so not as a carefree youth out to impress would-be lovers, but as a mature, responsible, and potentially influential adult man. His is a bid not for a lover, but for recognition within and beyond his community. The public test of shamanic confidence and proficiency comes in mabolong performances.

One might imagine that shamanic success would correlate with therapeutic achievement. As it turns out, attributions of therapeutic success are jointly negotiated by shamans and constituencies—rarely conclusively. No immediate signs of recovery are expected from a patient at time of treatment. What is more, over the course of a serious illness it is uncommon for a patient to be treated by a single person. Indeed, anyone and everyone with any claim to healing knowledge—shamans or not—may be asked to help the patient in both ritual and nonritual contexts. Alternative possibilities in diagnoses of conditions, healing measures, and justification of outcome further complicate matters.

For example, let us say that a patient experiences a relapse immediately after being treated by a shaman. Numerous causes could be asserted. Perhaps the shaman erred in his diagnosis or treatment. Alternatively, the relapse may have been a predictable reaction to the shaman's spirit familiars, with full recovery following shortly; or perhaps the patient or a close relative has violated some prohibition on diet or conduct. It might also be claimed that the shaman has corrected only one source of the patient's condition, and another still requires treatment. In short, what dictates therapeutic success is control over discourse, not disease—and that control is negotiated between shamans and their communities.

Two cases illustrate how prominent shamans can be absolved of responsibility when a patient's condition takes a negative turn. In the first, a tiny baby with a high fever was treated by two shamans. Within a day or two of treatment, the child's condition worsened. The child's family—close kin and neighbors of the shamans—attributed the downturn to a dogfight that had taken place in their house: frightened by the dogs, the child's soul parts had fled again after the shamans had restored them. In the second case, a shaman had treated his aunt for chest pains and she seemed to rally. Shortly thereafter, though, she died. As the shaman explained it, he had mended the problem in her chest, but then the woman asked a visitor from another community to treat her for pain. In examining her and administering spells, the young man bungled the repairs that the shaman had effected; hence the woman died. For those who depend on a shaman, it is preferable to attribute error or ignorance to someone else.

Judgments of success or failure are contingent and political. Furthermore, no consensus is sought in these matters. Take for example the case of Apa Weri, who experienced a lengthy bout of incapacitating pain in his head and ears. Two shamans—Apa Eri, his brother, and

Apa Mene, his brother-in-law—treated him repeatedly and eventually claimed to have healed him. On a visit to another settlement, however, I heard Apa Jango (a pseudonym) boast that actually he had healed Apa Weri when the shamans around him had been stymied. He was alluding to a brief visit he had made to Apa Weri's settlement during the latter's illness. One night when Apa Weri was experiencing considerable pain, he asked Apa Jango to treat him with a spell; the visitor did so and Apa Weri said he felt better. To members of Apa Jango's community who relied on his shamanship, his boast no doubt rang true, yet to a resident of Apa Weri's community, Apa Jango's treatment was not a decisive event. Claims of therapeutic success, then, can be seen as a form of coup-taking that is heavily governed by impression management.

Even a patient's death need not reflect badly on a shaman's skills, if he can effectively assert knowledge and control of the situation. I was told of one shaman who failed in this and continued to dance in search of a patient's wandering soul parts after the patient had expired on the floor nearby. A more fortunate or more alert shaman, aware that death is near, may decline when asked to perform, or he might declare on the authority of his familiars that nothing more can be done to save the patient. Apa Mene possessed a "no-lose" spell: if the patient was fated to die, treatment with the spell would bring on death within a week; if the patient was destined to live, survival for seven days was an equal indicator of the spell's efficacy.

Such authority in matters of life and death is not the purview of young and inexperienced shamans. The idea of having a loved one die without the care of a powerful shaman is grievous. In such a case, it is said that the surviving relatives will "not stop thinking about it." Fear of an unattended loss is one reason given for settling in the vicinity of a prominent shaman. Engaging the talents of a renowned shaman validates the outcome of an illness, be it life or death.

Creating the authority to validate fate in this way cannot be accomplished solely through performance in ritual. The mabolong does, however, provide a public arena for asserting and testing one's reputation, with the various ritual segments serving particular functions. Summoning spirits at a mabolong is to conjure hidden powers before an audience of one's peers. To be asked by others to investigate the sources of their own and their children's conditions is to have one's powers engaged and acknowledged by others. To undertake a journey to Pue is to display the confidence and authority to do so. To request "foods" from one's human companions is to call for affirmation of and commitment to one's shamanic endeavors. In this fourth àct we see that shamanship is not a unilateral matter. To be a shaman a performer requires acceptance, support, and encouragement from others. For this reason, I have argued, the baku mwalia episode holds special fascination for an audience; it has the potential to occasion a spontaneous negotiation of relations between performer and audience, and among performers as well.

If successful shamanship entails convincing others of one's claims, it also entails convincing oneself. A reputation for shamanship carries with it danger—the danger that other people with hidden powers may test one through sorcery. Pursuing shamanship requires having the confidence in one's own magical defenses to withstand the sorcery of rivals. Because such attacks are likely to come not from one's own community but from beyond it, some people perform only in the company of those they know well. But the more prominent one becomes, the more likely a target one is for others beyond one's coterie of close associates.

Even if a shaman is "tough" (*mapene*) enough to withstand attacks of sorcery himself, however, his close kin are vulnerable. Illnesses of a shaman's wife and children are frequently diagnosed as attacks by rival shamans who want to test his mettle. Thus, individuals with doubts about their ability to protect themselves and their families from sorcery are likely not to assert themselves as experienced shamans. They may perform potudu rituals for their own households, treat neighbors with spells, and perform at local mabolong when no prominent visitors from other settlements are present, but they are unlikely to perform in the company of strangers or to boast about their prowess. By contrast, those who are "shamans indeed" (*kawalia kojo*) have confidence that they can match their rivals. They are the ones who can claim, "As for those who defeat me, there are none. Only those who equal me are there."

In contrast to political leaders, the shamans of Poso protected their communities by ascents and descents to spirit worlds above and beneath the earth. Through these journeys, women could transcend the fact that their mundane activities and experience did not extend far beyond their settlements. Whether or not upward ascents to Pue are a recent addition to the mabolong (see Chapter 10), Wana shamanship seems decidedly more earthbound; also in contrast to Poso, it is not explicitly restricted to one gender. Yet as a spiritual and political form that shapes and protects local constituencies, Wana shamanship promotes leaders who are mobile, brave, and experienced in confronting strangers and negotiating with them. As it turns out, these mobile, brave, and experienced individuals are likely to be mature men.

SHAMANIC DEPENDENCY

As I have sought to establish in this analysis, the Wana version of "men of prowess" politics relies heavily on self-reflexive display that casts others in the role of audience, not agents. Wana shamans are active, their patients passive. Power is culturally perceived as a function of the relation between a shaman and exogenous agents; two-way negotiation between a shaman and his constituency is unelaborated. It would be wrong, however, to take this cultural emphasis on the agency of the shaman and the passivity of his constituency at face value.

To be a shaman is to be recognized as a shaman by one's close associates. Every successful shaman has a following of supporters who praise his talents and thereby support his reputation. In addition those shy or ambivalent about their shamanic pursuits may, sometimes to their embarrassment, be talked about by others as promising shamanic talents. Shamanic reputations depend on such talk, so much so that there is reason to ask where in fact the motivation for shamanship lies. Instead of ascribing political initiative solely to political leaders, I would argue that Wana communities seek—and thus create—their shamans every bit as much as individuals strive to become shamans on their own.

One does not become a shaman through deeds alone. Deeds must be revealed to others and remembered if they are to contribute to a performer's reputation. Shamanic actions take two forms: hidden and public. The former involve secret dealings with spirits; the latter can include both ritual performances and public behavior in nonritual contexts. Private encounters with spirits must be made public if they are to enhance a shamanic reputation; public demonstrations must be recalled if they are to sustain a shaman's standing. Shamans' deeds, as communicated to and among shamanic constituencies, must be cast in terms of culturally intelligible scenarios or scripts.

Shamans themselves may make revelations of private shamanic experience. These might take the form of storytelling or boasting at large gatherings such as mabolong or of confidences to one or two peers, who may then pass the story along to others, as in a game of "telephone," in which alterations and additions to the original message are made along the way. (Indeed, Wana millenarian expectations of the sort to be described in Chapter 15 probably originate not so much as the promises of a movement's leader, but as the escalating hopes that attach to the leader's words as they are passed from person to person.)

Accounts of private shamanic experience often do not derive from the shaman or would-be shaman, however. Instead they may be projections by others of their expectations onto a person's silence or lack of details. An unexplained absence from the settlement, a new possession whose source is unidentified, a report of an odd occurrence—all may provoke speculation about shamanic adventures. Even if the person about whom the stories are told denies them, the denial may not be accepted. Apa Linus, for example, told one day of climbing a tree to escape an anoa (a forest ox unique to Sulawesi). When someone suggested that the animal had been a spirit in disguise, Apa Linus dissented—but this did not stop speculation about his encounter. Similarly, his younger brother Mpaa, a strong and handsome young man, was teased for his trips to the forest; even though, embarrassed, he denied shamanic intent, others persisted in attributing it. Unlike Mpaa, some invite speculation about what they have been up to. One night Apa Mene was discovered by his parents in a tree outside their house. People concluded that he had been traveling through the sky, as powerful shamans are wont to do, and had caught himself in the branches.

Shamans and their constituencies play on the difference between what ordinarily happens and what *may* happen, according to cultural expectations about shamanship. Indo Lina often tells of the time she and her family went one day to fetch rice from their old swidden. Her husband, Apa Mene, vanished for a while. When he returned, she detected the smell of rice beer. She commented that he had been drinking, but he denied it, telling her to go count the bottles of beer they had stored at their granary if she doubted him. The conclusion she drew was that Apa Mene had gone off to the woods to drink with his spirit companions. The case illustrates that a shaman need not always fill in the details of his hidden adventures; by dropping a clue he may insure, advertently or not, that others will supply the details the clue implies.

Although individuals may prompt interpretations of their behavior, they cannot control what those interpretations may be and how they may be used. For example, I was told of one man who wished to create the impression that he could travel through the air. This he did by arriving at a mabolong one night and dropping broad hints about the unconventional route he had taken. Alluding to fresh scratches on the man's body, someone jokingly asked if there had been sharp grasses on his path too. In a real sense, people who would gain recognition as shamans are at the mercy of their audiences, who serve as arbiters of their claims.

And who constitutes those audiences? Everyone—men, women, and children. But the relationship of constituents to shamans may differ greatly according to age and gender. Given the centrality of men in Wana shamanship, it is noteworthy that my best authorities on the subject were often neither shamans nor men. Contrary to the passive or willful silence Edwin Ardener (1975) would have us expect from women who do not play actives roles in their societies' dominant institutions, Wana women proved insightful, enthusiastic, and engaged commentators on shamanship. By contrast, although male shamans articulate critical dimensions of the Wana social system through their performance, structural articulation does not necessarily lead to verbal articulation. Indeed, I often found shamans to be less articulate—or, perhaps better put, more guarded—in discussions of shamanic practice.

For a man to talk about another man's shamanship necessarily involves issues of relative prowess. If he is not a successful shaman, building another's reputation underscores his own lack of power. But for women, who generally have no direct stake in shamanic competition, there is freedom and pleasure, it seems, in sharing stories and opinions about performers and performances. As girls sizing up suitors, as mothers seeking protectors for their children's lives, and as noncompetitors in the mabolong arena, women hold a privileged place as critics and commentators on shamanic performers.

For their part, shamans are quite conscious of women in their audiences. Whereas a youth with courtship on his mind hides sexual motives in the guise of shamanship, an established shaman may freely engage in ribald joking and flirtation in the course of a performance. To do so is read not as a sign of his "real" motivation, but rather as the temporary influence of his spirit familiars. Sex is a matter that ordinarily is kept out of the public spotlight; the fact that powerful shamans engage in sexual joking is one way they demonstrate their prerogative to exceed the conventional bounds of community life, in the process of controlling life itself.

But flirtation as a motif may also speak to issues besides a shaman's temporary release from conventional propriety. Performers must seduce their audiences. Just as adolescents seek to attract lovers, mature performers strive to impress a public—of which women are an important sector. They and their children constituted roughly three-quarters of the patients at the thirty-four mabolong for which I have good records. A shaman's portrayal of himself as an attractive man with sex on his mind may be tacit acknowledgment of the significance of women's support. It is perhaps because of their role in shaping shamanic reputations that women were particularly open, willing, and informed in discussing shamanship. And it was perhaps for the same reason that Apa Mene kept his distance from the transcribing sessions in which my companions and I played and replayed mabolong tapes and "talked lies" about the performances.

Although they are largely absent from the ranks of mabolong performers, women are key players in creating and sustaining shamanic reputations. Upholding the centrality of shamanship in Wana social life does not cost Wana women control or ownership over what they produce, in the way that supporting the hegemony of warriorhood seems to disadvantage Maasai women (Llewelyn-Davies 1981). Nor does it support a ritual complex that explicitly denigrates their womanhood. Instead, Wana women promote an expertise that offers them protection from dangerous agents, both human and nonhuman, lying beyond their moral communities. That men may sometimes threaten or coerce them using that very same expertise is not sufficient cause for them to reject the system, but only to seek protectors against such violence.

In a valuable paper on Melanesian political systems in which differential control of knowledge is shown to be the basis for political inequality, Lamont Lindstrom (1984, 304) declines to answer "why women and more-or-less exploited social classes allow others to define their realities." In the Wana case, nonshamans—including most women and many men—allow shamans to define some of their realities because political inequality does not pervade all cultural domains and social contexts, because shamanic authority is experienced as being more beneficial than oppressive, and because followers do indeed wield a measure of control over those whose authority they support.

15

Bringing History to Bear

> And so far am I from thinking with some philosophers, that
> men are utterly incapable of society without government, that
> I assert the first rudiments of government to arise from quar-
> rels, not among men of the same society, but among those of
> different societies.
>
> Hume, *A Treatise on Human Nature*

In a 1952 article, "The Shaman's Tent of the Evenks and the Origin
of the Shamanistic Rite," the Soviet ethnographer A. F. Anisimov
developed a richly textured analysis of a Siberian shamanic ritual. At the
same time, he discerned a political dimension to Evenk shamanism.
Although Evenk shamans portrayed themselves as suffering on behalf
of their followings, Anisimov perceived that they in fact enjoyed
social privilege as a consequence of their special access to spiritual
resources. Thus the Evenk, like the Wana, represent an instance
of a small-scale noncentralized society in which special knowledge
serves as a basis for political inequality (see Godelier 1982; Lindstrom
1984; Myers 1986; and T. Turner 1979 for comparable analyses).

Having recognized a form of inequality implicit in Evenk shamanism, Anisimov invoked the "scientific" tenets of historical material-
ism to explain it. In an abrupt switch from a contextualist to a reduc-
tionist mode of argument (see White 1974), Anisimov contended that
Evenk society had evolved from an egalitarian condition of totemic
clanship to an inegalitarian one in which shamans monopolized access
to spiritual resources.

The present chapter will also examine issues of shamanship and
political change. Unlike Anisimov, however, who treated the development of Evenk inequality as an endogenous process, I shall ground
an understanding of Wana political change in a regional context
and show how political inequality has been shaped historically by
Wana interactions with neighboring peoples and polities. Instead of
looking past symbolic forms to locate political reality, I shall retain

my view of ritual as an inextricable element of Wana political relations (see Sherzer 1987).

In the final paragraph of his essay that so jarringly contrasts his sensitive rendering of Evenk ritual, Anisimov asserts that Evenk shamans showed their true colors as exploiters of their people by resisting Soviet reforms in order to protect their own political privilege. By regarding the Soviets as liberating the Evenk from their shamans, Anisimov ignores the possibility that, whatever the differences that divided Evenk shamans and their followings, all may have shared a common outlook regarding Soviet encroachment on their local autonomy. This reading—one that Anisimov (1963, 112) would surely condemn as being "of a subjective-idealistic, populist tendency"—could lend insight into one way that a noncentralized population can mobilize against external threats.

My own analysis of Wana political leadership will show how, historically, Wana have relied on "men of prowess" with special access to exogenous knowledge to promote social cohesion and to cope with the hegemonic advances of a succession of coastal regimes—a trend that has only gained in strength in recent Wana history. My aim in this chapter, then, is to develop a historical analysis of the relations between Wana leadership and ritual in the context of changing systems of political organization in the region. For a time at least in the last century, there existed in the Wana highlands a ranked political system with chiefs, commoners, an debt slaves—quite unlike the comparatively egalitarian nature of more recent Wana organization. In each of these areas, ritual has been integral to the creation and maintenance of polity and authority. The former chiefdoms, I will argue, made special use of liturgy-centered rituals conducted by priestly functionaries to consolidate constituencies above and beyond the settlement level. Hence, in the absence of chiefly sponsors, contemporary communities rely heavily on charismatic ritual leaders to lend cohesion and direction to settlement life.

The first step in my analysis is an exercise in conjectural history—namely, the reconstruction of nineteenth-century Wana political organization. The single major source on the Wana for that period is A. C. Kruyt's rich account, over two hundred pages in length, based on his visit to the Wana area in 1928 and published in 1930. Although Kruyt's portrayal of Wana political organization is vulnerable to the charge that it presents a "top-down" view of the Wana political system as seen by high-ranking informants, nonetheless Wana in the 1970s painted a very similar—and no doubt also idealized—picture of the politics of an earlier age. In practice the system was probably more fluid than either Kruyt or my Wana sources recognized. To his credit, Kruyt was sensitive to political changes in the area (although he did not connect them to the colonial presence and his own part in it), and consequently his report offers valuable clues as to what was transpiring in the region.

By the end of the nineteenth century, the Wana appear to have possessed a system of what Service (1975, 74) might call "embryonic chiefdoms" (see also Carneiro 1981). Kruyt details the political ascendance of nineteenth-century local leaders with ties to coastal Muslim polities, in which ideology of rank, political use of ritual, a corner on the system of legal payments, and an economic pipeline to the coast were critical factors. This system was deflated instantly by the Dutch, who instituted direct rule in the first decade of the 1900s and removed the external bases of economic and political leverage that had briefly upheld the authority of local chiefs.

But notions of power and dependency persist—for reasons to be explored. Unlike similar populations in regions of the Philippines that lacked relations to royal centers or *negara* (the Hanunoo and the Ilongot, for example), the Wana maintain a sense of hierarchy, of the mystique of rank, and of the prestige of the entourage. Differential claims to knowledge, unbolstered by economic clout or the authority of the negara, produce relations of autonomy and dependence. These relations are as much the creation of followers seeking security in the authority of leaders as they are the creation of leaders working to attract followings.

Extending my conjecture, I propose that the political significance of Wana shamanship in contemporary times has been fostered by a political vacuum created by the dismantling of the incipient chiefdoms in this century and by the failure of colonial and nationalist governments to extend their authority to the Wana interior. Specifically, I intend to show how both local-level politics and resistance to colonial and Indonesian hegemony have been fortified by the memory of precolonial associations with coastal polities, which are invoked to enhance the authority of Wana leaders.

In so arguing, I offer a local case study to the wider literature on the development of political inequality. Instead of starting "from the ground up" with factors standard to the literature on political change like population density, production, warfare, and exchange, this study began with cultural notions of power. Now I shall read those notions back into a changing social and historical context.

Contemporary Wana talk about power has a history, at least some of which is recoverable. My aim here is not to engage in "chicken and egg" debates about the priority of cultural or material factors in political evolution, but instead to show how a cultural pattern of Wana political authority has figured in a constellation of factors effecting political change in the Wana region for more than a century (see Hastorf forthcoming). After all, culturally intelligible ways of "making claims over other people" (Baker 1990) must be part of the negotiation of asymmetrical relations in political systems (Giddens 1979). An examination of nineteenth-century Wana politics will reveal how contemporary Wana leaders and followers may strengthen their claims on each other by drawing on shared assumptions about power deriving from an earlier political discourse, one that has retained its importance as an idiom for promoting both social unity and resistance against subsequent forms of coastal domination.

HISTORICAL ROOTS OF
WANA IDENTITY

The very fact that the Wana population possesses an ethnic identity testifies to its history of interaction with outside rivals and authorities. The word *wana* itself has an external derivation: ultimately from the Sanskrit, *wana* means "forest" in many Indonesian languages. For the Wana themselves, the word has no meaning apart from its use as the name of the land near the Old Mountain, suggesting that the Wana have adopted outsiders' identification of them as "people of the forest."[1]

The history of Wana interaction with outsiders has been a bloody one (see Chapter 13). Kruyt (1930, 505) puts it simply: "The To Wana have never had a peaceful life; as from the east as from the west they were ever being pressed." Until Dutch pacification in this century, the Wana suffered attacks from the To Lage, their neighbors to the west. Kruyt's evidence and my own conversations with Wana suggest that some of the Wana population moved east and south in response to these attacks. Occasional peace treaties were struck with To Lage and their relatives, the To Lalaeo, who had spread along both the northern and southern coasts that border the Wana region, while on the east Wana fought unceasingly with the Loinang people (Kruyt 1930, 505–6).

During—and perhaps because of—these struggles with other populations, the Wana, in historical memory, maintained a measure of internal peace. Kruyt (p. 507) asserts that intersettlement warfare was lacking in the Wana area; although feuds might lead to occasional deaths, these would be settled with fines, not chains of vengeance killings. The key to this *Pax Wana* seems to have been a system of chiefly authority, heavily dependent on ritual, that was in effect at least in the nineteenth century.

WANA CHIEFS
AND THEIR CONSTITUENCIES

A chiefly constituency was a grouping which Kruyt called a "clan." According to Kruyt (p. 459), the Wana of the upper Bongka were divided into four main "clans": To Barangas, To Kasiala, To Untu nUe, and To Pasangke.[2] These "clans" (what the Wana, using a word borrowed from the Indonesian, call *bangsa*, meaning "people" or "group") resemble the *be:rtan* that R. Rosaldo (1975) has described for the Ilongot—namely, descent constructs based on cognatic kinship and locality. Like the Ilongot be:rtan, these Wana groups played an important part in warfare.

How such bangsa might have arisen is evident in the ongoing processes of local group identification that I witnessed in the 1970s. For certain purposes, people identify themselves by their current place of residence. Hence people farming a locale known as Wata nSuyu may speak of themselves as "the people of Wata nSuyu"; if they and their children should stay in that area for a long time, then, their descendants may become generally known as To Wata nSuyu. More likely, they would identify themselves with reference to a large topographic feature of the vicinity, such as Mount Barenge, in which case they would be known as To Barenge. At the same time, these people may still remember that they or their parents had come from the locality of Barangas or Untu nUe and so for certain purposes might identify themselves as To Barangas or To Untu nUe.

I found during my fieldwork that older people from the southern half of the Wana region identified themselves as members of the "clans" named by Kruyt, but younger people often did not. These categories had little salience in contemporary life except in reference to historical relations to coastal raja. It is my guess that the ongoing processes of local group identity were frozen by the political circumstances of the nineteenth century to produce the more enduring fourfold "clan" identity described by Kruyt.

These circumstances—involving regional warfare and political patronage—very likely promoted hierarchization and centralization of authority and leadership in certain parts of the Wana area. By the late nineteenth century, three of the four southern Wana "clans" described by Kruyt had a leader called a *basal*, and in the case of Kasiala, a *makole*. Kruyt (1930, 460) guesses (correctly, I think) that the term *basal* is a borrowing of the Malay word *besar*, meaning "big" or "great"; the term *makole*, he notes, derives from Pamona speakers to the north. The use of foreign terms to identify this political personage may point to external factors that led to its creation.

A basal or makole was chosen from a particular "family" (*geslacht* is Kruyt's term), along with a subordinate, the *bonto*, whom people approached to intercede with the basal (Kruyt 1930, 461–62). *Geslacht* is perhaps best glossed as "kindred." Kruyt (p. 462) indicates that a basal would marry a woman of his own geslacht—a close cousin, I would suspect—although he could also take an additional wife from the "multitudes" (*tau maborosi*). Kruyt does not address the relative ranking of children by each wife, or the range of kin who could claim prerogatives associated with the basal. What is clear is that for a time the Wana possessed a system of rank whereby an elite distinguished itself by birth from the common folk.[3]

According to Kruyt (p. 460), a basal was selected from the "*basal* family" by members of his "clan." In making their decision, people sought a leader "in a position to defend the interests of the clan." Thus, a basal was selected on the basis of personal achievements, not of ascribed criteria of descent (beyond basal rank) or birth order. (In this respect, the case conforms to Wolters's model discussed in earlier chapters.)[4] How in fact the decision was made, who participated in the decision, whether there was jockeying, campaigning, and competition for the position, whether leaders were ever overthrown, is unknown. Nor does Kruyt clarify what it might mean "to defend the interests of the clan" or what qualifications might be important for this task. From his article, however, we can identify the arenas in which a basal operated, suggest how prospective leaders might come to lead, and determine the ways in which ritual was used to create and uphold chiefly authority.

Kruyt's account emphasizes the chief's role in military and legal affairs. (p. 523). Yet a *talenga*, the leader of a war party, would if possible be chosen from the family of the basal (p. 462). Successful warriors were publicly distinguished: anyone who had killed a person was permitted to wear red and blue (or green) feathers in his turban;[5] one who distinguished himself as especially brave could in addition wear a special headcloth and tie a hank of human hair to the hilt of his sword (p. 526). Undeserved appropriation of the trappings of a "brave person" (*tau makoje*) would, I was told, result in buto, the debilitating condition characterized by a bloated abdomen, jaundice, and chronic weakness brought on by violations in rank. Presumably commoners as well as relatives of the basal could achieve a reputation as a tau makoje. For someone to become basal, I suspect that this achievement was an imperative.

According to Kruyt (pp. 507–11), Wana raiding parties had two leaders—a *tadulako* and a *talenga*. The former acted as an "aggressor" and led the charge against the enemy, while the latter—the one who might be of the chiefly family—acted as a "protector." The talenga directed the attack from the rear (often at the camp from which the raiders set out), performing offerings and ritual procedures to insure the warriors' success. Responsibility for the warriors' safety lay in his hands.

My companions, several generations removed from actual warfare, spoke only of talenga. The fact that *talenga* is a Loinang term, whereas *tadulako* is common in many upland languages of Central Sulawesi, led me to suspect that Wana originally used these two terms (one familiar to their enemies on the east, the other familiar to their enemies on the west) for a single kind of war leader. Just as Wana spirits and legal payments may proliferate through the use of multiple metaphors, so, I suspected, did headhunting leaders as well. But further thinking about the Wana system of rank inclines me to accept Kruyt's account. If a talenga was likely to be of noble rank and to be a contender for the position of basal, it makes sense that he might have served as the brains and not the brawn of the raid. By successfully protecting his warriors through ritual and rhetorical means, a talenga could demonstrate his qualifications as defender of his people.

Kruyt does not directly state what role the basal played in initiating a raid. He does, however, assert (p. 524) that the To Pasangke, who had no basal, would not go off on a raid without the "knowledge and consent" of the basal of Untu nUe. Presumably, then, members of groups that *did* have basal would consult their leaders about intentions to raid.

Kruyt (p. 524) is clearer about what happened after a successful raid. The victorious warriors returned to the house of their basal carrying pieces of their victims' scalps on palm branches. Three days later a feast would be held, at the house of either the talenga, who had managed the raid, or the basal. Kruyt rationalized that because most settlements had only one large house and talenga were often kinsmen of the basal, "these two functionaries might well have used the same house during the feast time." Whether the host was a basal or an eligible candidate for that office, hosting a headhunting festival was certainly a way to call attention to his own achievements and those of his followers.

Besides basking in the glory of their followers' military successes, basal had a role to play in negotiating peace and enforcing ada. If there were a quarrel within his constituency, the basal had authority to mediate the matter. When people could not settle a dispute among themselves, they would refer it to the bonto, who would then bring it to the basal. Basal apparently conferred about disputes involving members of different bangsa as well. Large-scale feuds that could not be settled in such as manner could be referred to a coastal raja (Kruyt 1930, 526–27).

Speculating on what we know about the relation of basal to warfare, peacemaking, and negotiation, it seems likely that a young male relative of a basal could enhance his chances of becoming basal himself by distinguishing himself as a warrior and eventually being selected as the talenga responsible for raids. His success as protector of numerous war parties (publicly celebrated at headhunting festivals) could testify to his ability to "defend the interests of the clan." Once he became basal, his role would switch from war leader to negotiator and peacemaker.

A parallel could be drawn to "men of prowess" among the Ilongot, a Philippine population lacking the notions of rank held by the nineteenth-century Wana. M. Rosaldo (1980) examines how, in cultural terms, the youthful display of passion in headhunting is the condition for a mature man's exercise of knowledgeable authority in directing matters of war and peace. Among the Ilongot, this pattern operates on the local level with no superordinate authority beyond it. In parallel fashion, among nineteenth-century Wana local *tau tu'a*, or "older people," distinguished by their maturity and experience, probably held authority over their juniors, just as they do in Wana settlements today. The basal rank, however, added a level of authority beyond the local community.

LEADERSHIP AND RITUAL

The basal were set apart from others in several ways. Disrespect shown them would be punished by the debilitating condition of buto; offenders could then atone for their actions by paying four copper trays, called *dula*. Basal and their families, in turn, owed higher ada payments for marriage and for wrongdoings. Their funeral rites would be grander and different from those for ordinary people in a number of respects, including the precipitation of headhunting expeditions, which themselves generated lavish celebrations.

Some of these differences are differences of degree, not kind, from the privileges mature Wana parents are owed by their children and children-in-law. The risk of buto is strong for offenses against parents-in-law; funerals of respected local elders, too, attract wider attendance that funerals of younger, less prominent people. Yet by virtue of local and regional networks, the basal could clearly marshal far more assistance and stage far grander celebrations than ordinary Wana householders or local elders. Whereas older people can expect some assistance with housebuilding and farming from their resident children and children-in-law, chiefs were to receive such assistance from their entire constituencies.[6] This additional labor should have increased the size of a chief's house, granary, and stores of rice beer, and thus enhanced his ability to host large feasts and rituals.

Basal received more, but they gave more too. Like chiefdoms elsewhere, this system was a redistributive one. Although Wana worked for their basal—building their houses, tending their farms, and, as we shall see, assembling tribute for presentation to coastal raja—they gained in return, sharing in the achievements of their leaders, who provided them with identity, peace, and prosperity. Sponsoring large feasts and rituals was one way a basal could promote his stature. Hocart (1970, 104), for one, argued that "the clan is partly artificial:

it is a family cut and trimmed and adjusted to one particular purpose, the feast." And indeed, what Kruyt called Wana "clans" seemed to assume their shape in the context of celebrations staged by their basal.

I have already mentioned the association of headhunting festivals with the basal, the cultural rationale of which was to promote the vitality of crops: "If we don't go raiding, the rice does not succeed," said Kruyt's (1930, 507) sources. In this area where rainfall is highly unpredictable, seasonality is determined by the order in which wild fruits appear. Shedding blood through warfare insured that wild trees would bear fruit. In this formulation, the achievements of headhunters were culturally linked to the regulation of the rains, a critical matter for Wana farmers. By negotiating matters of war and peace, and by hosting victory celebrations, the basal asserted their influence over regional prosperity.

The salia, the three-night regionwide ritual discussed in Part Three, was performed "to procure good health for the clan, or so people put it: so there shall be no pale faces and weakness among us" (Kruyt 1930, 450). Although Kruyt does not link the salia directly to the basal, the ritual was performed expressly for the benefit of this leader's constituency.[7] And tellingly, Kruyt's unusually detailed description of the ritual came from the basal Apa nTjabo, "'the father of Sabo,' [who] gave me in his calm manner an orderly account of the feast" (p. 450).[8] We can infer that a basal could provide the coordination of labor required to construct the giant building for the ritual and, with his large stores of rice and rice beer assured by the labor of commoners and debt slaves, could underwrite the elaborate festival. The fact that the salia waned in tandem with the power of the basal is further evidence of the tie between this ritual and the political authority of the basal.[9]

Finally, the death of a basal occasioned an enormous funeral and complicated set of observances that engaged not only his own following but others as well. It precipitated in addition a headhunting raid, an endeavor directed at insuring future prosperity and no doubt orchestrated by his would-be successors. Such a raid might also be staged at the death of a family member of the basal; in this way a basal could translate his kindred's grief into warfare and victorious celebration—both achievements that would reflect on the glory of his followers and himself.

CHIEFLY AUTHORITY
IN A REGIONAL PERSPECTIVE

Over time certain Wana leaders gained access to exogenous sources of power and wealth that certainly altered their relations with their followers. The Wana had a long-standing exchange relation with the polity of Banggai to the east (Kruyt 1930, 466): each year one or more of the basal would lead a contingent of Wana to Banggai to present a mat, seven bunches of onions, and a barbed spear. Kruyt could not determine just how Banggai reciprocated. The relationship was not one of lord and subject, but of elder and junior in which the two groups pledged mutual support (of a military nature, I would guess).

A more significant political alliance took shape in the middle of the nineteenth century. The southern Wana submitted to the authority of the raja of Bungku, whom they acknowledged as "owner" or "lord" (*pue*). This relationship was decidedly unequal, with both economic and political consequences. Raja Bungku recognized one basal—the makole of Kasiala, the first Wana leader to yield to Bungku—as paramount (a matter that did not sit well at all with Kruyt's Barangas informant; p. 465). Each year Raja Bungku sent cotton cloth worth eight silver coins to this *makole tongko*, as he was called. The makole in turn divided the cloth among his fellow Kasiala. In return for cloth worth half a silver coin, the recipients had to give the makole four pieces of beeswax, each the length of a hand. The makole then presented the beeswax as tribute to the raja.

As Kruyt (p. 467–68) tells it, the Kasiala leader, backed by the military force of Bungku, pressed Barangas to assist with the tribute. Later the other two groups followed suit. The tribute came to include, in addition to beeswax, a small gift of rice and a white chicken from each household. The makole of Kasiala led a delegation to present this tribute to the raja of Bungku at the coastal village of Tokala in the south.

From Kruyt's account, (pp. 467–69), it is hard to gauge the magnitude and economic significance of the tribute, but it does suggest that basal could derive power by negotiating exchanges with coastal royalty. In addition, it demonstrates that they could draw on the power of a coastal raja to intimidate their neighbors.

From this account, one may legitimately ask why Wana submitted to Bungku. Even if some leaders recognized the political desirability of exchange relations with exogenous polities, how and why did their followings support them in forming these relationships? The conventional Wana answer to this story, Kruyt (p. 468) tells us, is the same one "that we find all over Central Celebes":

> When the Bungku people were back in their capital. . . , they sent a buffalo horn to the Wana with a challenge to hack it with a single blow. The Wana cooked the horn, and when it was soft, they hacked it with a single blow. In turn the Wana now sent to Bungku a *noti buya*, a piece of white wood that as long as it is fresh is easy to work, but when it becomes dry, can no longer be chopped because of the toughness of its fiber. In this [exchange] the Bungku were no match for the forest people. Then the Bungku sent the Wana two pieces of leafstalk from a sago palm, bound together in the shape of a cross, with the charge to chop the pieces with a single blow. The Wana were so crafty that they didn't chop it but sliced it into pieces. Then the raja of Bungku acknowledged the superiority of the Wana and he came with a great boat to Tokala as a sign of his homage. He let a great cannon be fired that was named *ndindi wita*, "that which makes the earth shake." The Wana heard this and they said to one another, "People who can cause such a condition must be gods. They should also bring us misfortune if they render honor to us; let us do so to them." And in this way raja of Bungku because the lord of the Wana.

This story pits the craftiness of the interior people against the military power of the coastal sultanate. It explains the submission of the uplanders as being a rational calculation based on an established sense of hierarchy (gods should not defer to mortals) rather than a military defeat. Indeed, it is unlikely that the forces of Bungku could have subjected the entire Wana population any more effectively than the Dutch and the Indonesians have succeeded in doing during this century. What is more, from what we know of Indonesian negara, it seems unlikely that subduing the hinterlands would have been an objective as it later was for colonial and nationalist authorities.

Why, then, did the Wana submit instead of hiding out in the hills? Those seeking to form a tie with Bungku could have persuaded others by the claim (widely held in the region) that raja bring fertility and prosperity to their domains, and they certainly cited the military threat from Bungku. (Recall that actual military pressure had allegedly been brought to bear on the Barangas by the Kasiala leader.) Association with a raja may also have offered some hope of protection against attacks by other upland populations who perhaps paid tribute to the same raja or one of his relations.

Finally, we do not know if indeed all Wana participated fully in this tributary relation to coastal authority. Was in fact the political effectiveness of the basal, like that of the raja, greatest among their close associates, and did it diminish with physical and social distance? Did basal have to exercise persuasion and threats to secure the cooperation of people beyond their immediate circle? Were there evaders of raja and their upland representatives, just as there were, and are, evaders of subsequent coastal authority? I have no answers—only questions—regarding these matters.

Besides engaging in tributary exchanges with coastal rulers, the basal were implicated in a more perfidious exchange as well (Kruyt 1930, 460–61). According to Kruyt, until the Wana yielded to Bungku there was no debt slavery in the Wana region, but after that the basal parlayed the Wana ada system into a source of people for the regional slave trade (see Reid and Brewster 1983; Bigalke 1981). If a person could not afford an ada payment, a wealthy person could pay the fine and claim the person as a debt slave (*wotua*). Wotua consituted the bottom tier of the three-step system of rank composed of nobles, commoners, and debt slaves.

Some debt slaves were kept as dependents to work for their owners. Others were sold to Bungku for twenty-five pieces of unbleached cotton. Because one length of cotton at the time could also bring one copper tray, a key object in ada exchange, payment for debt slaves could thus be fed back into the ada system, which in turn generated more debt slaves. The makole of Kasiala (the one whom the raja of Bungku had elevated above the other basal) was particularly active in the slave trade. The basal were not, of course, the only people to claim debt slaves and to play the regional slave market—other wealthy people did the same; but the ties of the basal to the coastal kingdoms no doubt enhanced their role in this traffic.

It is telling that the system of ada, which made debt slavery possible, was allegedly given to the Wana by the raja of Bungku. What is more, the raja—to whom basal had special access—was the source of objects used for ada payment such as copper trays and cloth. Kruyt's (1930, 471) sources (as mine) were well aware of the potential for abuse in the ada system, speaking of legal corruption as *alibiru* (from the Malay *harubiru*, meaning "to stir up mischief or confusion"). Today's "corrupt" use of subtlety in legal debate payments can result in high fines and indebtedness to ada experts; in the past it could make one a slave (in the Southeast Asian, not the Euroamerican, sense; see Bentley 1986; 291). I suspect that judgments of alibiru, like judgments of a shaman's goodness or "crookedness," were and are conditioned by one's place in the social field. Like a shaman or a modern ada expert, then, a basal would be regarded as honorable by his supporters and as less so by those at a distance from him.

Basal were chiefs, not dictators. They cast their actions in an idiom not of despotism but of beneficence. In Kruyt's account (p. 460)— much of which seems to come from an individual who was himself a basal—basal assumed the role of protectors for debt slaves: "If someone did something for which people would kill him, then he'd take refuge with the basal. People must then threaten his life no more; the matter would be settled with a fine which was paid mostly by the head, after which the culprit would remain with him as a slave." Thus, enslavement was couched as a form of assistance. People who required such "help" were likely to be without large and influential kindreds to assist them with legal fines. When, for instance, a human sacrifice was required for peacemaking ceremonies, the victim would likely be an orphaned slave, not a profligate debtor whose kinsmen were important members of a leader's constituency.[10]

Kruyt (p. 461) does hint at rebellious acts by debt slaves, but these were rebellions directed at individual masters, not at the system of debt slavery itself. And once again basal figure as protectors in his account:

> If a slave were beaten a great deal, or was given too little to eat, or was mistreated in some other way, he could flee to the *basal* of his own or another clan and destroy some things in this person's house. In such a case, those among whom the slave had climbed would claim such a high compensation for the destruction that the old master found it preferable to permit the refugee to live in the new house. Sometimes, however, he would pay the required fine to get the slave back, then sell him to Bungku in revenge.

CENTRALIZATION AND CHRONOLOGY

Just how long the incipient chiefdoms I have described were in place in the Wana region is not clear. Apa nTjabo, "the last basal of Barangas," told Kruyt (pp. 465–66) that his grandfather had taken the first tribute to the raja of Bungku. Kruyt placed his Apa nTjabo's age between fifty and sixty years in 1928. Assuming that the man's grandfather was a mature Wana leader when he traveled to Bungku, this tribute could have been offered in the mid-1800s or later. Whatever the chronology, if it was the tie to Bungku that gave Wana basal economic and political leverage over their subjects, this sytem was in effect for no more than two generations. Prior to that time we can imagine that there were Wana "men of prowess," resembling very much the "great men" whom Godelier describes among the Baruya—prominent men whose influence, based on dealings with exogenous agents (such as enemy warriors and spirits), did not translate into direct control over people and production.

What elevated some of these "great men" into basal? One important factor may have been a chronic condition of regional warfare to which Wana responded by developing intersettlement defense networks. The basal—modeled perhaps on the leaders of the enemy To Lage—were critical nodes in these networks. The further transformation of basal into nobles probably came about as these leaders allied with coastal polities that backed them with regal ideology, prestigious exchange, and military power.[11]

Local Wana reactions to the ascendancy of their basal are hard to gauge. A hint of ambivalence regarding these leaders is contained in Wana trickster tales, in which Ngkasi the trickster is forever turning the tables on the makole (the other term for basal) who represents the dominant coastal culture. My familiarity with these tales, of course, is modern. One wonders when the genre began and if it carried the same weight at an earlier time. Whatever sense of oppression may have been brewing at the turn of the century, however, was soon to turn to nostalgia.

THE ENCROACHMENT OF THE STATE

Like a cake that falls when the oven door is opened, these incipient chiefdoms collapsed abruptly with the arrival of the Dutch. In the 1890s the missionaries A. C. Kruyt and N. Adriani established a base in the Poso region to the west of the Wana; by 1908 the Dutch formally controlled this area of Central Sulawesi (Kutoyo et al. 1984, 107). In Chapter 12 I described the initial efforts of the Dutch to resettle the Wana in areas where they could be governed effectively. Kruyt's account offered one view of Wana resistance, but it did not clarify Wana views on the new situation, nor did it give a sense of Wana strategies for coping with crisis. The history of Wana relations with outsiders makes clear the reasons for initial fear of the Dutch. Once Dutch intentions became clearer to the Wana, further objections can be understood: the Dutch were replacing chiefdoms with a state.[12]

The changeover was experienced locally in the Dutch attempt to organize Wana into villages. Village membership involved paying taxes, performing labor, maintaining a house, and meeting other government demands. The eventual development of coastal markets for forest products offered some compensation for the burdens imposed by village membership. But the benefits of involvement in coastal trade were offset by taxes, regulations, and indignitites at the hands of coastal authorities. Later, Indonesian authorities would impose further demands, including conversion to Islam or Christianity and participation in a feared election system, as demonstrations of commitment to the nation-state.

Dutch rule spelled an end to the regional integration of Wana settlements through affiliation with basal; it also removed some of the conditions that had promoted such integration, notably regional warfare. As a result of Dutch policies and the subsequent turmoil they produced, political authority in many areas reverted to the settlement level.

Structural reversion, however, does not mean historical reversion. The return of political leadership to locally influential tau tu'a ("elders") did not restore the Wana to a pre-basal condition. For one thing, the newfound "autonomy" of local communities was now under the shadow of the state, whose designs on the Wana were more comprehensive and far-reaching than those of the coastal chiefdoms that preceded it. What is more, the historical consciousness of the Wana population had been transformed.

CONTEMPORARY SHAMANSHIP
AND ITS TIES TO THE PAST

We can now reconsider contemporary Wana shamanship in light of the foregoing reconstruction of the nineteenth-century Wana political order and its twentieth-century aftermath. Kruyt provides little sense of the political dimensions of shamanship in the 1800s. Did shamans wield political influence locally or regionally? Were basal ever shamans? There is no definitive answer. I shall argue that with the dismantling and disappearance of some other forms of traditional leadership, along with twentieth-century unrest, shamanship has assumed increasing political significance. (This is not to say that formerly Wana shamanship lacked political significance, only that in recent times its political dimensions are no longer combined with, rivaled by, or superseded by chiefly structures.)

Both the Dutch and the Indonesian nationalists who followed imposed a new system of political authority that obtains in settlements near the coast. Under the new regimes Wana give, but they do not receive. The government does not appear to be their protector and defender, nor is it a fount of life and vitality for people and crops. The new system, moreover, is distinctly at odds with Wana-style leadership. In the former, orders are given top down, and subordinates are simply expected to follow. In the latter, a leader must attract followers and maintain their conviction that they benefit by their dependence on him. He must appear to be doing more for them than they are for him; if he cannot sustain that conviction, they can simply choose to follow someone else. Of course, a government-appointed village head who is *also* a respected shaman, ada expert, or farming leader can compensate to a degree for the governmental demands he must make by serving his constituency in other ways. Hence, it would be desirable from the government's point of view to appoint mature and respected leaders as headmen—and indeed, this tactic has been used. But such individuals do not always match modern nationalist notions of what a progressive village administrator should be. Nor are they always willing to serve.

One persuasive technique used by leaders in both traditions is to emphasize external threats to the followers' well-being. A shaman may stress potentially fatal attacks by spirits and human sorcerers that only he can ward off. A millenarian leader (see below) may claim that only those who follow him will be preserved from the impending destruction. And a village headman may assert that people who flee from villages will be rounded up, even massacred, by government troops. But unlike a shaman or a millenarian leader, a village headman is at a disadvantage in convincing his following that he offers the protection and benefits they desire—and invoking the state as a threat to exact compliance does not instill nationalist sentiment in Wana villagers.

Whatever the realities of life in an earlier age, Wana glorify a prior era to emphasize the misery and powerlessness of the present. *Katuntu*, or stories of a mythical past, celebrate a former era of magical power, *baraka*, associated with the former royal centers. In these stories, voicing one's wishes makes them happen. Poor Wana men wind up marrying the daughters of makole. The present is negatively contrasted to that former age: the earth now is "worn out" (*mariwam*), the rice does not grow as it used to. There have been "many layers" (*malagi ntapim*), many generations; people are smaller and weaker. Pestilence—for crops and people both—has multiplied. The "great old people" (*tau bose tu'a*) are dead. The old stories are no longer known. Efficacious knowledge has been lost.

On the surface, this new consciousness suggests a linear notion of time. But time in this conception is really a journey that begins with a departure and ends with a return. The prior age of glory coincides with the presence of "knowledge, power, and wealth" in the Wana homeland; the era of impoverishment coincides with their absence. Their return to their homeland at the Old Mountain will be the resolution. This model of history can be compared both to a shamanic journey and to the plot of a Javanese *wayang* play. As Becker (1979, 225) shows, the wayang constitutes "movement out and back, a trip": its plot must begin and end in a royal court; its middle part transpires "in the forest on a mountain, but sometimes, too, in or beside the sea." By posing the Old Mountain, not a regal abode, as the center, Wana history presents itself as the inverse of the negara—"power to the periphery." Shamans in their performances establish their own centers, call on powers from both forested mountains and royal courts, and journey out and back on behalf of their followings. As mediators between the near and the distant, the visible and the hidden, they possess privileged insight into what others cannot know.

POWERFUL RESOURCES

Whereas basal leadership became the locus of growing political authority in the nineteenth century, shamanship has, I suggest, been a locus for political leadership among upland Wana in the twentieth century. A contrast can be made to a similar population, the Ilongot of the Philippines. Ilongot shamans are said to have died off during World War II, whereas Ilongot political authority continued to reside until the 1970s in effective warmaking and peacemaking. In contrast to the Wana, Ilongot were able to hold outsiders at bay through headhunting; hence, directing raids was a vital element of effective political leadership. Because the Wana learned early in their dealings with outsiders that they could not resist militarily, shamanship rather than military leadership became a major avenue for creating and maintaining polities.

A closer look at privileged forms of knowledge suggests why shamanship in particular has assumed political significance in the twentieth century. Although "knowledge, power, and wealth" are absent from the homeland, lesser forms of exogenous resources are still available to Wana. One form is magic and ritual from the past. Another (like that controlled by the basal) consists of prestigious ties to coastal polities. And yet another is found in the knowledge and allies of the forest.

The past is the source of valuable knowledge for sustaining the lives of crops and people. The authority of *woro tana*, farming leaders, is based on knowledge of magic and rituals going back to creation, knowledge that is passed from one generation to another.[13] Much healing magic and ritual is similarly derived. For example, the ritual experts who officiated at the salia gained their knowledge by listening to their elders, and in the same way people learn how to make offerings to the Owners Above and Below and to perform chants to heal the victims of Lamoa and the malevolent tambar spirits. Possessing these forms of special knowledge from the past is a matter of conservation, not innovation and augmentation. Knowledge of ada derives from the coast, from the far-off kingdom of Bungku. The same is true of a historical succession of authority that backed both basal and modern village officials. The ultimate authority, however, lies far beyond the coast at the "end of the earth": this is the "knowledge, power, and wealth" that had their origin in the Wana land, then departed, leaving the land and its people wretched.[14] Only their return will eclipse present-day coastal authority and revitalize the homeland.

Although the most powerful "knowledge" has departed the land, some knowledge can still be had either through study with older people or through personal quest. There are reasons why an emphasis on winning knowledge and spirit alliances "on one's own" has been particularly strong in the area where I worked. First, I did not reside at the "navel of the world" in the vicinity of the original Wana homeland. The fact that locally there was no grave of Pololoiso or sacred rocks, the transformed bodies of the "powerful people" who had gone off to the end of the world, may have engendered greater reliance on newly discovered knowledge than on mythical ties to the past. Second, many of the people with whom I worked had participated in a millenarian gathering a decade earlier that itself had been above all an exercise in encountering spirits. The powerful shaman who led the gathering encouraged his followers—both women and men—to seek knowledge in the forest. (People joked that what people in fact obtained in so doing were babies, as spirit quests often turned into romantic trysts.) Although the movement failed, many of its members came away with shamanic skills and experience in gaining knowledge "on their own." Thus local history may have accentuated the importance of knowledge obtained in the forest over other kinds of knowledge for the communities I know best. Nevertheless, more general dynamics in Wana shamanship promote this emphasis as well.

The principal one is the necessity for a shaman to, in Weber's (1963, 32) words, "keep up his charisma," and in Wana terms, maintain the "freshness" of his shamanic powers. To do so he must provide his following with evidence that he is actively engaging spirit familiars. Long absences from the settlement, stories told by himself or others about adventures in the forest, as well as the introduction of new spirit epithets and requests for foods during shamanic performances are ways of demonstrating an ongoing commitment to shamanic pursuits.

Pressures on shamans to uphold their reputations simultaneously promote innovation and sustain continuity in Wana shamanship. Shamans are expected to pursue new knowledge and skills, and the premium placed on shamanic entrepreneurship virtually guarantees the incorporation of both the exotic and the novel. Formulae from Muslim and Christian prayers, words from foreign languages, all manner of spirits and sorcery enter shamanic practice in this way. At the same time, however, Wana performers must be convincing to their audiences. Therefore, whatever they introduce in their public practice cannot remain either idiosyncratic or alien, but must be rendered in a way that impresses others as a sign of genuine shamanic potency. By encouraging both enterprise and intelligibility, Wana audiences insure the ongoing regeneration of Wana shamanship.

Among the ways shamanic authority sustains its interpretability is through links with past forms of authority. The Wana "shaman as hero" (Lévi-Strauss 1963a) participates in the heroics of two forms of leadership now gone from the scene: warriorhood and chiefly authority. Because of gaps in our knowledge about past ties among shamanship, warriorhood, and chiefly authority, it is difficult to say whether the overlaps we find are continuations or appropriations of the past.

Regarding the past relationship between warriorhood and shamanship, Kruyt (1930, 512, 525) tells us that shamans performed at the departure of headhunting parties and that the drum was played as part of headhunting festivities. And indeed, warlike bravado survives today in Wana shamanship. Contemporary shamans dance to the drum songs of headhunters. Some are possessed by the ghosts of headhunting victims, the very same spirits that would possess a warrior and make him kill. Vows made by shamans on behalf of patients may be fulfilled by grand performances of ritual dueling at which only the powerful magic of the presiding shamans can prevent murderous attacks by the headhunting sangia spirits. Through acts of courage— epitomized by lonely spirit quests—shamans gain the powers to serve as protectors and defenders of their communities. No longer threatened by headhunting raids, contemporary Wana fear sorcery from strangers and enemies; thus shamans must acquire special proficiency in *sangka langkai*, "men's accoutrements," to do battle with hidden forces.

The relationship between shamanic authority and chiefly authority is more complicated to trace. Kruyt does not indicate whether the same individuals ever possessed both. He does, however, present a hierarchy of shamanic skills in which the spirit familiars associated with the mabolong ranked below the spirit familiars associated with the salia.[15] The mabolong was and is held locally on behalf of sick individuals, whereas the salia was a regional celebration held for the chief's constituency. In the mabolong, performers engage familiars won through personal quest or study; in the salia, performers sang of traditional spirit familiars associated with the ritual chant. The mabolong highlights shamanic initiative, while the salia featured priestly function. The ritual authority of salia performers apparently derived from their knowledge of a highly prized liturgical form and from the chiefly authority of the basal under whose auspices the ritual most certainly took place. By contrast, the mabolong performer must create the conditions of his own authority.

Given the challenges of constructing ritual authority, it is revealing that the contemporary mabolong appropriates salia elements. As seen in Part Three, the mabolong performer's journey upward on behalf of individual patients may have been lifted directly from the salia. Although the Wana no longer offer tribute to coastal lords, in this segment the shaman and his familiars, in the manner of a basal and his following, carry tribute to a rajalike deity at a place called an *opo*, a term associated with a ruler's locality. In so doing they must observe the etiquette for approaching royalty to ward off the debilitating condition of buto brought on by violations of rank. Even the word *pue*, or "lord," applies to both a raja and a high god.

In the ritual more generally, the shaman is the leader of a spirit entourage and negotiates on equal terms with the spirit leaders of other followings composed of "many handsome dependents"—a phrase recalling *katuntu*, epic stories of the mythical past, and the molawo ritual, itself apparently an offshoot of the salia. Among the spirit familiars touted by contemporary shamans, moreover, are those that figure in the salia. Even though there are no more basal to initiate regionwide rituals, by making vows (*pantoo*) for their patients, mabolong performers initiate future mabolong that may attract audiences from afar to celebrate their own mediation with higher powers.

Contemporary Wana shamanship is a vital link between a glorified past and an uncertain future. To create and sustain their authority, shamans must continually innovate. At the same time, their activities must be rendered comprehensible and compelling in cultural terms. By acting as leaders of spirits in the manner of war leaders and chiefs, shamans can couch their present-day initiatives in the terms of leadership carried over from an earlier age of glory.

MILLENNIAL DREAMS IN ACTION

To what end? This question was posed in a conversation I had with several of the least fortunate members of a Wana settlement, one a crippled widow, another a semi-invalid. All were deeply dependent on others for assistance with food and health. "What is the goal to be sought?" one asked rhetorically. "The life of food? Each day one eats and the result is excrement." The point of the search, the three agreed, should be a "life of another sort." Their remarks implicitly criticized the leading shaman of their community, a prosperous farmer whose commitment at the time was to the status quo. His spiritual quests were limited to sustaining the health and well-being of his local settlement. Yet his critics wanted more—at the very least, a release from their present travails. They personally were seeking a fundamental transformation of the conditions of their existence. Should they do so collectively and pin their hopes on the spiritual endeavors of someone less conservative than their current leader, the result could be a millenarian movement—what Wana call a *ngua*—a tradition dating back at least to the arrival of the Dutch.

The Wana saw very quickly the futility of resisting the Dutch with violence. (Wana claim to have fought Dutch troops at a site called Pindu Loe in Bungku Utara.)[16] Soon convinced that blowguns and spears were no match for rifles, they adopted a different strategy. From Kruyt's perspective, the strategy was simply to flee—but in fact, the organization of Wana disappearances was internally more complex than the act of fading into the woods would suggest.

These disappearances were organized around leaders who people hoped could provide an escape from their present plight. The leaders of such gatherings—what today are called *ngua*—were thought to have special access to information about the fate of the Wana land, information that would be predicated on the scenario outlined in Chapter 2. In a prior age, the Wana homeland thrived. Then, however, "knowledge, power, and wealth" were carried off to the "end of the earth." At some point they will return to their source, a return that will be accompanied by war and cataclysm. Those who heed the portents and take proper precautions will survive to participate either in the revitalization of the Wana land or in a paradise removed from the destruction.

Ngua leaders were and are those whom others view as possessing special knowledge about what is to come and what is to be done about it. This knowledge and its accompanying action are typically reworkings of Wana stories and rituals. For example, one prized form of esoteric knowledge at Wana ngua has consisted of the names of the "powerful people" who left the Wana land along with "knowledge, power, and wealth." In the past ngua participants have recited these names over an offering table to summon back these beings and revitalize the Wana land. They have also performed rites at the alleged grave-site of the culture hero Pololosio, in anticipation of the millennium. In this way ritual "foreshadows" (*mampolengke*) old stories in the hope of changing the present order. These old stories, associated with an ear-lier age, were expressly intended to counteract the present one.

In the 1930s a Wana named Nau, the appointed district head of Bungku Utara, hiked in the company of a village secretary and a basal into the interior to break up a ngua. The three men met their deaths at the hands of ngua participants who hoped that, with this sac-rifice, the new order should arrive. (This incident was told to me early in my fieldwork by an old man who had hosted the trio on their fateful journey. I did not grasp its significance at the time and hence did not pursue the matter of murdering a former basal.) Violence is rare at ngua, but its possibility heightens tensions between Wana who remain in the villages and those who go off to join a particular gathering.

In 1941 a great ngua was held in the Barangas region. It was so large that it attracted not only the Dutch troops but also the raja of Tojo, to whom the northern branch of the Wana paid tribute, who made the long hike in from his coastal residence. One might suppose that the raja went to prevent violence and put an end to the gathering, but I was told repeatedly that he actually went to side with his people if this was indeed the moment for the fighting to begin, the Dutch to be vanquished, and a new order to be installed. One story alleges that the raja crafted a metaphor (*ligi*) to request that the women and children be removed from the scene so the battle could take place; according to my source, however, his meaning was missed, and the gathering was peaceably dispersed. But the Dutch troops guided the hands of village heads who had joined in the ngua and forced them to sign their names to documents they did not understand.

Within a year the Japanese had overtaken Sulawesi and executed the raja of Tojo. During my fieldwork it was widely believed that this action had been taken because Wana village leaders had signed a deposition implicating him in the insurrection against the Dutch. (That the Japanese would punish the raja for opposing Dutch rule is an inconsistency of which my companions were unaware.) People anticipated the return of the raja to call in the "debts" of those who had betrayed him, and a ngua held while I was in the field had the return of the raja as its theme.

Although ngua often anticipate a new order on earth ("after the dogs have swum in blood on the Old Mountain"), some feature hopes of escape to another realm—either heaven (*saruga*) or the realm of the Bolag spirits. Here the wish is literally to vanish, to leave this earth. People tell a story of a ngua held in a house suspended on the edge of a cliff. When the desired deliverance by spirits did not come, someone cut the bindings, and the building with its sleeping occupants tumbled into the ravine. In this way they achieved collective salvation, albeit not in the manner they had planned. One person stated the matter flatly to me: Death, he said, was the best way to escape the government.

The ngua is the one form of collective action, apart from the staging of more conventional rituals, that can cause Wana to gather together in a concerted endeavor. Potentially they can do so on a larger scale than in ordinary ritual. When a government official asked a Wana acquaintance of mine how the Wana could be got to cooperate with a government plan, my friend proposed that the plan be turned into a ngua. One millenarian movement, in the plot of which Indonesian officials may or may not have been involved, was built around a coastal resettlement project in the 1970s. A Wana man prophesied that the end was coming, that the Wana land would soon be consumed in flames, and that only those who joined the project would be saved. What sound like religious texts, with pictures of people burning in hell, were offered as demonstrations of what was to come, and the movement leader promised goods—supplies furnished by the Social Ministry—to lure prospective members. Here we see a ngua leader drawing on the external resources of the state to attract a following.

Millenarian leadership resembles closely the forms of political leadership outlined in Chapter 13. People pin their hopes on a leader who appears to possess special knowledge from exogenous sources. The leader must continually demonstrate to his following that their trust is warranted. This is often achieved through innovations based on conventional ritual forms. The offering table mentioned earlier is an example. At one ngua in the 1960s, participants held periodic celebrations on *eo jamaa* ("*jamaa* day," a twist on the Indonesian term *Hari Juma'at*, or Friday, the Muslim sabbath) as well as a salia. Mabolong, too, are a standard element of ngua. Another ngua developed a new and more democratic form of shamanizing, in which all the participants could experience shamanic vision; the movement died, but the style of performance, called *walia makore,* "the standing spirit familiars," persists in some areas.

Ngua leaders sometimes receive material support from their followings, somewhat in the manner of the basal of old. When people so assemble, it is generally in the hope that the present world order is at an end. They abandon their farms, kill their chickens and pigs (if they have any), and pour their rice beer liberally at the ngua festivities. Some people stay for a day, a week, or a month. Only when the anticipated end is not in sight do they grow cynical and leave, although others may be persuaded to stay longer and after a time make new farms in the vicinity. Sometimes these communities last several years. One ngua leader I knew stopped farming altogether and was supported by his followers, until a scandal involving his sexual relations with a number of young girls at the ngua caused others to become disillusioned.

Although not every ngua organizer is a shaman, both are charismatic leaders who through negotiation with hidden agents generate a sense of community and common purpose for their followers. Both shamanic and millenarian enterprises are framed culturally as struggles against the centrifugal tendencies inherent in the order of things. What shamans attempt for individuals and farming settlements—namely, reintegration and revitalization—ngua leaders attempt in times of crisis for the Wana homeland. Thus the same form of charismatic leadership, one based on negotiation with hidden agents, can serve more or less simply to sustain a farming community; or, when constituencies require leaders to manage eschatological traumas rather than merely quotidian concerns, it can inspire escalation into a wider social movement.

MILLENARIAN PROSPECTS

I have argued that in the twentieth century shamanship has served as a means of creative and effective local leadership. It has operated in the wake of a system that had privileged noble birth, tributary relationships, and achievement in warfare and has offered an alternative to an alien system that privileges education, wealth, and knowledge of— not to mention connections in—the nationalist culture.

Center-periphery relations in the 1980s reveal a new twist. The New Tribes Mission, an evangelical organization devoted to conveying the Christian gospel to Fourth World peoples, established three bases in the Wana area. The people of Ue Bone, once the seat of the paramount Wana chief, were the first to receive New Tribes personnel. The mission magazine, evocatively entitled *Brown Gold*, published the following account of the missionaries' welcome in Ue Bone, which begins with a Wana story:

> "Many years ago, long before our time, two men came flying into Uebone [*sic*] on an umbrella. These two men came to make the Wana people prosperous. The Wana people, of course, welcomed these two men and were very happy to have them live here. One thing these men did not seem to like was a lot of noise. The people were warned to be careful around these men and not to disturb them. On a particular day, a lady warned her husband that when he brought the firewood into the house he should be quiet and be sure not to drop it. The husband did not pay much attention to his wife's words and came into the house noisily and dropped the firewood on the floor. The two men then got on their umbrella and flew away, to the regret of the Wana people."
>
> We here have been overwhelmed at the reception these people have given us. Many times we have wondered why they are so happy to have us here. One day we asked a Wana fellow down at the coast the reason for all of their kindness and the above is the story we got. These people evidently believe Vic [another New Tribes missionary] and I are the two umbrella men and have returned to live among them. Our airplane undoubtedly is our umbrella in which we have come. This story answers our question of why at times they have apologized for making noise and why they always lay the firewood down quietly. I guess we have come to make them prosperous, too. Some day, Lord willing, in the near future, these folks will have the Gospel, "as having nothing, and yet possessing all things." We just praise the Lord for the way He has prepared their hearts for us.
>
> (Ed Casteel and
Jeanne Casteel 1980, 8)

This account gives a fine sense of the intersection between two millenarian traditions. The tale of the umbrella people, as recounted by the missionary couple, fits the genre of Wana tales of the departure of "knowledge, wealth, and power" from their land. Like other *tau baraka*, or "people of power," the two "umbrella men" take offense and depart by magical conveyence, presumably to the end of the world. Like some characters in epic stories, theirs seems to be what Wana call "the path of the *toru*," referring to the Wana *toru*, or broad-brimmed hat.

The story also recalls the tale of Ampue, the elder whose thought-less son repeatedly jostled his father by dragging firewood over his rooted limbs and thereby provoked his father's departure from the Wana land (see Chapter 10). Strangely, however, the two umbrella people in the Casteels' account do not have their origins in the Wana homeland, and in this respect they are quite unlike Ampue and the other tau baraka of the epic age and more like the succession of high-status foreigners with whom Wana have had dealings in his-toric times. The benefits these umbrella people bring, moreover, are of foreign, not autochthonous, origin.

By this report, the people of Ue Bone regard themselves as having a second chance to benefit from the presence and prosperity of these foreign visitors. In 1974, their fear of two Americans resulted in the pair going elsewhere—a consequence that many residents of Ue Bone subsequently regretted. The next time they had a chance to host people from afar they acted differently, and in so doing precipitated the possibility of vast changes in their world.

In the last century, a Kasiala leader took an initiative that sig-nificantly altered political relations in the region. The joint initiative of the New Tribes Mission and the Kasiala people may once again trans-form relations between centers and peripheries in the region. High-status representatives of a world religion—one strongly opposed to the magical and shamanic nature of traditional forms of powerful Wana knowledge—are now locally based. Advanced technology in the form of airplanes, radios, and computers challenges the physical isolation of the Wana people, and a missionary presence offers media-tion between the Indonesian government and the upland population. The possibility for education in the national language at last seems genuine. It remains to be seen whether and how these new conditions may further shape the ritual and politics whose historical development this book has traced.

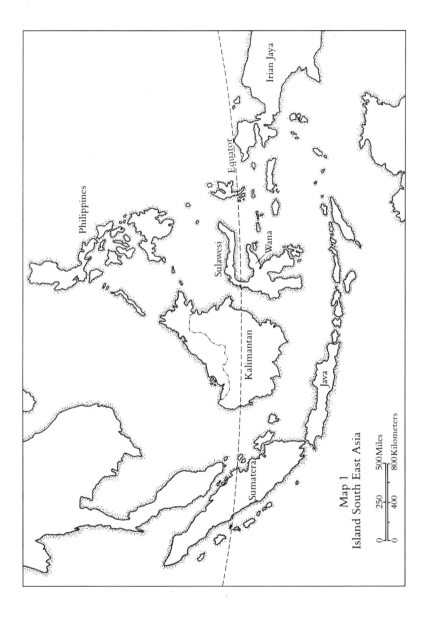

Map 1
Island South East Asia

Philippines

Sulawesi

Wana

Kalimantan

Sumatera

Java

Equator

Irian Jaya

0   250   500 Miles

0   400   800 Kilometers

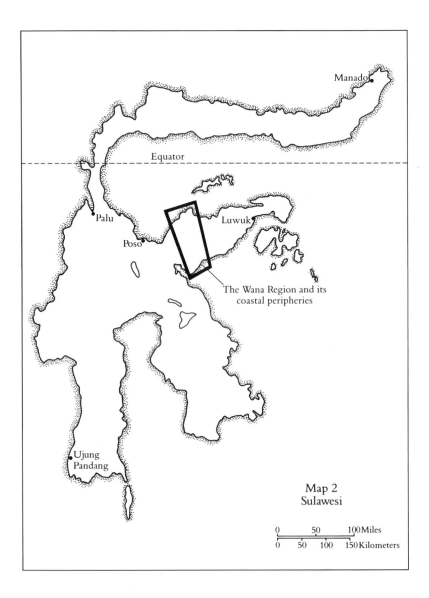

Manado

Equator

Palu

Poso

Luwuk

The Wana Region and its
coastal peripheries

Ujung
Pandang

Map 2
Sulawesi

0   50   100 Miles

0   50   100   150 Kilometers

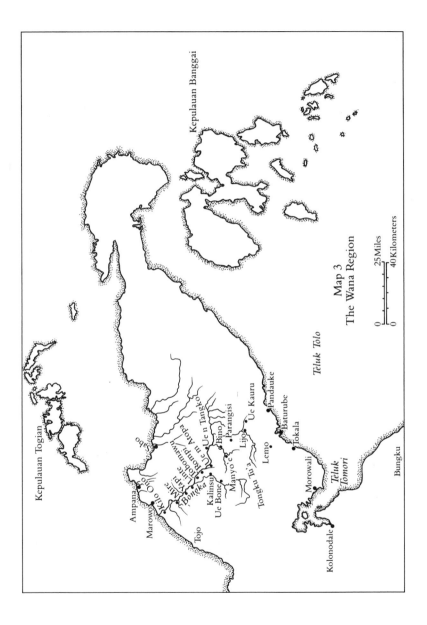

Kepulauan Banggai

Kepulauan Togian

Ampana

Tojo

Marowo

Kilo

Tojo

Sabo

Kasiguncu

Kapi

Mire

Lipu

Lobonawu

Kolonawu

Bongka

Kalinsu

Ue Bone

Ue m Alopa

Kompi

Ue n Tangko

Manyo'e

Bino

Parangisi

Lijo

Ue Kauru

Tongku lu'a

Lemo

Pandauke

Baturube

Tokala

Morowali

Teluk Tomori

Kolonodale

Bungku

Teluk Tolo

Map 3
The Wana Region

25 Miles

40 Kilometers

0

0

Notes

INTRODUCTION

1. Uplanders expressed bewilderment at the way the label *suku terasing* divided people who shared physical distance from the coast and identical modes of livelihood into two distinct groups based on whether or not they were affiliated with a world religion. The Dutch had not required religious conversion as a condition of kampung membership; to the consternation of people who had long been affiliated with kampung, then, Indonesian authorities specified that adherence to either Islam or Christianity was a sign of commitment to nationalist principles. In the 1970s, pagan kampung members were therefore in an anomalous position. For a discussion of Indonesian religious policy and and its effects on the Wana, see Atkinson 1983, 1984a.

Estimates of numbers of pagan, Muslim, and Christian Wana are exceedingly difficult to make, in part because, for topographical and political reasons, there is no accurate census of the Wana region and in part because many people move in and out of religious affiliation depending on their proximity and orientation to coastal life, factors that are quite labile (see Part Five).

2. Adult Wana are conventionally known by their teknonyms, as the mother or father of someone. Thus Indo Lina is "the mother of Lina," and Apa Nedi "the father of Nedi." Childless people may be identified as aunts and uncles. A teknonym is a term of respect. As older people's children themselves come of age and assume their own teknonyms, the elders may come to be known by epithets—such as "the old white-headed one"—that avoid mention of their adult children's names. (Thus for example, Apa Iki, whose son Iki—Apa Mene—is cited frequently in this book, was often referred to in oblique ways that avoided mention of his prominent son's name.)

3. The Mori are a largely Christian ethnic group located to the southwest of the Wana.

4. After several major northern kampung were relocated to near the coast at the end of 1974, the trails through Ulu Bongka became overgrown. We therefore switched to the southern route through Bungku Utara, which had the advantage of clear paths and inhabited settlements. From long and taxing hikes in and out of the field, I grew acquainted with a wide swath of the Wana region.

5. Sensitivity to the intersubjective nature of ethnography might prompt one to ask whether the presence of a fieldworker with interests in ritual may

have provided an additional incentive for mabolong performances. Except for our first evening in Ue Bone, I was never aware of a mabolong being staged specifically for my benefit. But over time my presence did attract visitors— some of them prominent shamans—from elsewhere and thus heightened local interest in festivities.

6. The royal centers with which the Wana had dealings were by regional standards quite minor. The image of a raja of Tojo (described in Adriani and Kruyt 1950, 1:71) holding gambling parties at his house at which he would tax fighting cocks and charge fees for lamps, betel, and other treats offers an undignified contrast to descriptions of courtly grandeur in larger principalities. Nevertheless, these centers, which supported themselves by extracting forest products from upland people like the Wana and selling them to coastal traders, were buttressed by regal ideology and symbolic trappings derived from more powerful realms in the archipelago.

7. Geertz's 1980 book *Negara: The Theatre State in Nineteenth-Century Bali* is an exception to this statement. The first three-quarters of *Negara* focus on the political workings of precolonial Bali. Only the final chapter addresses the symbology of royal ritual and ceremony. Geertz's contention is that the cultural model of the exemplary royal center, promoted by courtly ritual and ceremony, was continually undermined by the practice of Balinese social life. To make this point, however, Geertz stresses political symbolism at the level of the royal courts and political practice in the local and regional levels of Balinese life, a polarization strongly criticized by Tambiah (1985d).

8. Edward Schieffelin (1985) and I (Atkinson 1987) have both made sport of the fact that the words of the Kuna shaman's chant to which Lévi-Strauss (1963a) attributed symbolic efficacy were likely to be unintelligible to Kuna patients. And yet, as Sherzer (1983, 134) emphasizes, "while ordinary Kuna may not understand an *ikar* [healing chant] in absolute detail, they are quite aware of its purpose and general structure." In the Wana case, people bring to a mabolong knowledge and assumptions about what will transpire. Hence they do not need to heed every word a shaman sings but are free to tune in and out, much as do Javanese audiences at *wayang* performances (Keeler 1987) and Achehnese audiences at recitations of epics (Siegel 1978). When they do tune in, however, they can follow the details of performers' songs.

9. Although Wana I talked with insisted that gender is not a criterion for shamanship, nearly all Wana mabolong performers are men. I use the masculine pronoun here to acknowledge that fact, one that will receive detailed consideration in Chapter 14.

10. Victor Turner (1981, 154) granted that ritual can offer what Moore and Myerhoff termed "a declaration of form *against* indeterminacy," although he maintained that such a declaration, minus *sparagmos*, is "ceremony," not "ritual."

11. I recorded performers only with their knowledge and compliance. Generally performers cooperated. On one occasion a visiting shaman seemed suspicious, but finally he consented to my use of the tape recorder. When I tried to replay his performance, the tape was blank; mysteriously gloating, the shaman intimated that he had defeated my machine.

CHAPTER 1

1. In Polynesia the word *malae* refers to a "village green or sacred enclosure" (Hocart 1970, 255), that is, a center for the community—or its high-status representatives—to congregate. Wana use the word to describe participation in festive gatherings that manifest community.

2. This *patoe* by Apa Mene was taped during a *potudu* performance, an abbreviated version of the mabolong to be discussed in Chapter 4

CHAPTER 2

1. A shaman's spirits are invisible to nonshamans in the audience, but shamans claim to see each other's spirit familiars during a performance.

2. Despite the doubts that have been voiced about Carlos Castaneda's writings, they *do* reveal keen insight into the private side of shamanic experience. They do not clarify, however, how a shaman puts private experience to work in the service of a human community.

3. The Bolag spirits may very well be borrowed from the Poso peoples, former enemies of the Wana. Adriani and Kruyt (1912, 1:235–36) mention *bolagi* spirits in their account of that population.

4. Schieffelin (1976) also employs a concept of "scenario," but he uses it in reference to structures of social action rather than structures of narrative in Ortner's sense. In this chapter I focus on narrative structure. Later I intend to delineate the intersection of narrative structures and conventional social practices.

5. The fact that a protocol exists for the recitation of stories suggests that storytelling may once have been more important than it is today. There is reason to think that recitation of powerful stories may once have been a part of offerings made at sacred places in the Wana landscape.

6. As Errington (1987) has recently analyzed, Indonesian myths of primordial incest take different forms across the archipelago. In the Wana version, a brother and sister were separated as children, only to meet again in adulthood, first as strangers, then as lovers. Their forbidden act led to cataclysm and chaos in the natural order: only their separation could restore calm. Today the pair is kept at opposite ends of the sky, where one is the morning star and the other the evening star. (The astronomically inclined might note a covert unity in that "separation"!) Whereas among the Mambai the division of the primordial Lone House leads to the formation of separate houses linked through marital exchange (Traube 1986), for the Wana the separation of the original sibling pair leads to no well-defined prescriptive system of exchange but only to the perpetual threat of cosmic collapse should the siblings meet again.

7. The *adi adi* formulation implies that the speaker's knowledge is superior to his or her parents' knowledge. To assert superiority over one's parents in Wana society is to invite sanctions of illness. I sense that the suggestion of insubordination heightens the rhetorical potency of the phrase.

8. Several Wana characterized a pabriik to me as a small object that spewed

forth material wealth. As one who had hitherto unreflectingly regarded the concept of organized human labor in a mechanized workplace as self-evident, I was stopped short by their vision. From their vantage, commodification had indeed obscured the social nature of production.

9. Most of my fieldwork was conducted in interior settlements whose members were pagan. Some of these people had converted to either Islam or Christianity at various points in their lives in compliance with government demands. To be a pagan in the 1970s was not to be unacquainted with world religions, but rather to adhere consciously to an "earlier religion." For a discussion of the politics of conversion, see Atkinson 1983, 1984a.

CHAPTER 3

1. In a work on Southeast Asian history, Wolters (1982, 52) develops a concept he calls "localization" to characterize the way in which "Indian [cultural] materials tended to be fractured and restated and therefore drained of their original significance . . . before they could fit into various local complexes of religious, social, and political systems and belong to new cultural 'wholes.'" The reader will note many instances of "foreign materials retreating into local statements" (Wolters 1982, 63) in the Wana context. These materials are drawn from the Sanskrit tradition (e.g., *guru*), Islam (e.g., *nabi*), and from wider Indonesian culture (e.g., *pontiana*).

2. Fredrik Barth launched a particularly cogent attack on the interpretability of symbolism. Striking at both Victor Turner's interest in native exegesis and the British enthusiasm for a variant of French structuralism, Barth (1975, 228) argued that "the translation of non-verbal messages into a verbal code introduces a schematism and productivity into the communication which all too easily carries away both informant and anthropologist." Barth himself was studying a ritual system that relied in the main on secret and nondiscursive symbolism whose power, he argued, lay primarily in use, not meaning. Barth's insights, even if true for the Baktaman, cannot be generalized to all non-Western peoples. I think it no accident that a highly word-oriented approach to cultural analysis has been advanced by ethnographers of Island Southeast Asia (among them Clifford Geertz, Michelle Rosaldo, and James Siegel), where ritual discourse and oratory abound and people engage one another in speculative exegesis, with or without the prodding of anthropologists.

3. This point converges with Mauss's ([1902–3] 1972, 124) observation that "all over the world where magic flourishes, magical judgments existed prior to magical experience."

At the risk of committing what Evans-Pritchard (1965, 24) termed the "if I were a horse fallacy," I shall mention here how Wana scenarios of spirit quests shaped my own experience on one occasion. About a year and a half into my fieldwork, I fell sick with a respiratory virus combined with what may have been malaria. As I lay on the floor of a field hut late at night, a black-spotted yellow feline some three feet high appeared beside me and recited some words in the Wana language. Part of me recognized this as a hallucination, but I did not resist it. After the apparition vanished and I fell asleep, the episode played itself over and over in my dreams. The feline's words assumed the form of a Wana spell. Later when I told others about it, they explained that this was one of the spirit owners of the magic Apa Mene had been teaching me. My illness was said to have been brought on by my violation of a food taboo associated with my shamanic knowledge.

Several frameworks structured this experience for me. At the time of this episode I was well acquainted with scenarios of encounters with spirit familars, including the maxim that confusing messages from spirits will be clarified in a subsequent dream. I had recorded many Wana spells and hence knew what form a spell from a spirit should take. Finally, Wana commonly refer to liver-eating demons (*measa*) as "feral cats" (*tute lampu*). That the tute lampu who visited me resembled more a cheetah or a leopard than Wana cats or civets reveals how my own cultural background impinged on my experience.

CHAPTER 5

1. In a pair of articles on the Mentawei, Loeb drew a distinction between shamans and seers, although in doing so he acknowledged that "naturally a choice of words is only a way of making a distinction." Loeb's distinction, but not his choice of words, prevailed. He defined the "seer" much as Eliade and subsequent writers have defined the "shaman": "The essentials of the seer are the obtaining of a vision and, with the vision, a guardian spirit or spirits. The seer is then able to communicate with these spirits, who aid him in curing" (Loeb 1929, 62). In Loeb's formulation, spirits speak "through" shamans and "to" seers. What Loeb calls a shaman, we would call a spirit medium. Shamans (in Eliade's usage) or seers (in Loeb's) are specialists who exercise their own will in dealing with spirits, in contrast to spirit mediums, whom spirits use to their own ends.

2. In a tantalizing commentary on Radcliffe-Brown's speculative thoughts on rhythm and ritual, Tambiah (1985c, 123–24) makes the following observations: "Fixed rhythm and fixed pitch are conducive to the performance of joint social activity. Indeed, those who resist yielding to this constraining influence are likely to suffer from a marked unpleasant restlessness. In comparison, the experience of constraint of a peculiar kind acting upon the collaborator induces in him, when he yields to it, the pleasure of self-surrender. The peculiarity of the force in question is that it acts upon the individual both from without (as a collective performance) and from within (since the impulse to yield comes from his own organism)."

The incessant pulse of the drum and gongs at a mabolong performance is powerful and compelling. But people engage it in different ways. Some bounce babies; some take turns playing the drum and gongs; and some—girls and women of all ages—dance attractively, not shamanically. Others—mostly adolescent boys and men—dance in a deliberate effort to bring on spirits: should they fail to accomplish that end, over time they will resist the urge to dance. Some nondancers cite embarrassment. And a few (Indo Lina is one) insist that the music never moves them to dance. It is tempting to suggest that for those who stifle the urge to respond physically to the drum and gongs, a shaman's vigorous surrender to the driving beat may enact an inclination and thereby provide vicarious engagement and pleasure.

3. The old woman who told me about the murder of the kameasa mother and daughter also told me that as a child she had been given a piece of human scalp as medicine. She did not raise the possibility that she might have become a kameasa as a result. As I understood it, she chewed it as part of a betel quid, in which case it would not have been swallowed.

CHAPTER 6

1. See Graham (1987, 54–58) for an examination of Iban ritual practices involving the *ayu*, a spirit double tended by either human or spirit shamans much in the manner of the Wana *balo nosa* described in Part Three. Both the Iban and Wana concepts of ayu phrase human well-being as dependent on the treatment of one's soul at a distance from one's self.

CHAPTER 7

1. The shift from a religious to a medical emphasis in the study of shamanism in the last two decades has been underwritten and promoted by foundations and granting agencies in the social sciences with interests in channeling funds into research projects with a medical focus.

2. For a fuller discussion of how the therapeutic efficacy of the mabolong is contingent on other dimensions of the ritual, see Atkinson 1987.

CHAPTER 8

1. The term *pue* means "to own" or "possess" something. In glossing the term as it applies to Wana deities and coastal raja, I am torn between the English terms *Lord* and *Owner*. Although *Lord* correctly connotes the "feudal" quality of the relationship between the Wana and these "overlords," it also connotes for English speakers the Jewish and Christian deity. My preference for glossing the term as "owner" is not a romantic effort to make the familiar strange; instead, the word *pue* has an everyday meaning in contemporary Wana life, in contrast to *Lord*, which in English carries archaic overtones.

2. *Opo* also means "four." The possible association of "four" and "five" in the phrase *opo bira lima* recalls Tambiah's (1985a, 253) discussion of simplified mandala schemes among "tribal lineage-based segmentary" swidden societies in Southeast Asia. In some societies of this sort, a "quinary formula called *mantjapat* ('five-four')" applied, among other things, to "the arrangement of four village tracts around a fifth central one." Wana society is not segmentary and lacks lineages. However, the same coastal ties that gave rise to

the *makole* of the nineteenth century (see below, Chapter 15) could very well have produced a term for a ritual-political unit that resembles those of segmentary societies of Eastern Indonesia. (Suggestive in this regard is the Wana claim that the first raja to hold dominion over them was the ruler of Ternate.)

3. Like the central peak (*tambalang*) of a Wana rainhat (Figs. 6, 7), the sky also has a peak (*tambalang yangi*), where Pue resides.

4. In addition to the two molawo performances mentioned here, I also transcribed a *molawo maneo*, a "crooked" molawo, in which the spirit familiars visit the dreaded Owner of thunder and lightning, Pue Lamoa.

5. It is because of such divergence of opinion that I cannot neatly distinguish the performers of molawo and mabolong as "bards" and "shamans," as has been done in Bornean ethnography (see Graham 1987).

6. *Winayo* was on one occasion described to me as what sounded like decorative copper sheeting. The word *pinayo* elsewhere in Sulawesi Tengah refers to headhunters. The connection is suggested by the fact that the warriors of Poso, the dreaded enemies of the Wana, wore caps with copper-clad horns (Kruyt 1930, 509).

7. The Wana did not build *lobo*, or "temples," but their neighbors to the west did.

CHAPTER 9

1. Mauss ([1925] 1967, 14) briefly considered a contrasting form of exchange between human and spirit that "does not require this human support." His one example comes from the westerly neighbors of the Wana where, Kruyt reported, people "purchase" use rights over trees and land from spirit owners. The case intrigued Mauss because it suggested that the "purchase" of spiritual boons could precede a developed sense of economic purchase. But he did not speculate further on such contracts, probably because they did not conform to his sense of a fully social exchange.

2. My translation of this invocation does not include all the stutter words (*e*) which are a characteristic feature of Wana oratory, of which spoken invocations to spirits are a form. The Wana text reveals where those words occur.

3. Wana references to Raja Ternate may refer back as far as the seventeenth century when the Portuguese had lost their grip over the Spice Islands and the ruler of Ternate was recognized as "lord of seventy-two islands," including the northern and eastern regions of Sulawesi (Schrieke 1975, 236). To what degree the tributary relations between Ternate and coastal polities of Sulawesi actually affected the Wana, I cannot say.

4. Valeri (1985, 65–66), a structuralist, dismisses van der Leeuw's phenomenological explanation of sacrifice. Without attributing explanatory power, I note here the similarity between Wana phenomenology and van der Leeuw's own.

5. The shaman's wife who requested assistance with the harvest in return for a mabolong performance was citing the principle of exchange in its breach.

From her perspective, the woman's household expected the shaman to serve its members but would not live in the shaman's settlement and engage in quotidian give and take.

CHAPTER 10

1. Jimi exemplify the process Wolters (1982) calls "localization." The Wana term *jimi* derives ultimately from the Arabic *jinnīy*.

2. Salia were still occasionally performed in the 1970s by Kasiala people in the region of Ue Bone. I suspect this was one reason I had been urged to base my research there.

3. The salia resembles community rituals such as the Toraja *ma'bua'* (Volkman 1985) and the Iban *gawai* (Graham 1987). Wana sometimes used the term *gawe* to refer to the salia. My summary of the ritual is drawn from Kruyt (1930, 450–59).

4. The common meal shared by families at the salia is reminiscent of the common meal shared by warriors at a victory celebration (see above, Chapter 5).

5. The difference in prefix between *molawo* and *melawo* should not be semantically or syntactically significant.

6. Just how many people were hosted at a salia is not clear. Kruyt indicates that the throng numbered over one hundred, but he was going on informants' impressions, not precise tallies. The salia was a "clan"-sponsored event, but we do not know how many members these local descent groups contained or how many members of a group would attend a salia. There were four of these groups in what is now Bungku Utara and a fifth in Ulu Bongka. Estimates of the Wana population in the 1970s were in the range of five thousand people. If in fact the "clan" membership approached an average of one thousand, these groups far exceeded the size of Ilongot *be:rtan*, a comparable social unit in northern Luzon (R. Rosaldo 1980). Part Five will suggest some reasons why these Wana *bangsa* might have been large.

CHAPTER 11

1. Whereas the mabolong highlights shamanic pyrotechnics, the potudu generally concentrates more on the patient's condition, as do the varieties of rituals (*pantende, molawo maneo*) performed for victims of Lamoa, the thunder spirit. The molawo highlights the aesthetics, not the politics of shamanship. The salia, of course, was not performed in the event of illness; its emphasis was celebrating the health and vitality of the ritual community. In Chapter 15 I shall consider the political dimensions of this emphasis.

2. The word *walia* refers to "spirit familiars" or "helping spirits" whose assistance is publicly elicited by performers of the mabolong, potudu, molawo, and salia rituals. To perform as a "person of spirits" is to *momago*. A distinction is made between *momago mabolong*, "performing at a mabolong," and *momago maroti*, "performing quietly" as in a potudu or molawo performance. Whereas there was consensus that experienced mabolong performers were "persons of spirits," I found different opinions about people who per-

formed only molawo or salia rituals—probably because the last two consist of chants that one can learn by listening to others. Whereas some performers of these rituals seem to maintain special relations to walia, others do not. It is the personal tie to hidden beings that seems to distinguish "persons of spirits" from liturgical experts.

3. An abbreviated version of this argument is presented in Atkinson (1987).

4. In contrast to the shamans' requests, audience guesses are spoken, not sung. Usually someone in the audience simply calls out a word or says, "Perhaps it is such-and-such."

5. One might counter this point with the claim that whether or not a patient recovers is at least as unpredictable. Although ultimately it is, dramatically it is not. Mabolong performers go through their paces of restoring vital elements as though the patient is going to recover.

CHAPTER 12

1. The three transcripts are presented here in chronological sequence. The first two derive from a single evening's performance. Note that Apa Linus, who had been consoling his younger brother earlier in the evening, becomes disconsolate himself later on. The third transcript derives from a performance six nights later.

2. Tambiah (1985c, 156) uses the Peircean terms *indexical symbol* and *indexical icon* to clarify how ritual elements may convey cosmological meaning and simultaneously implicate the contextual situation of the ritual participants.

3. Here, because I did not catch the speaker's exact words, others explained to me what he had said as we transcribed the tape.

4. It was only in my last few months in the field that I was able to hear and record molawo performances. Apa Disa, a wonderful old man from the region of the Old Mountain, came to visit the settlement where I lived, and his relatives there urged him to perform a molawo for my benefit and their enjoyment. Not long after, Apa Eri, a local shaman, performed one himself. Unfortunately I did not know about it and hence did not attend. Then I visited Apa nSempa, an old blind shaman, whose relatives convinced him to perform a molawo during my stay. Finally I prevailed upon Indo Lale to let me record a molawo maneo, a journey to the feared spirit Lamoa. This was the only ritual of any sort—other than that first mabolong at Ue Bone—that was performed solely for my sake. I was planning to leave the field shortly and wanted very much to hear it. As the molawo maneo is considered to be exceedingly dangerous for anyone other than a victim of Lamoa to hear, our only audience was Indo Lale's deaf husband. Because they drive people away, the Lamoa-based rituals do not serve as "proving grounds" for aspiring shamans. Indo Lale is an expert in these rituals; yet although she dances (*salonde*) superbly at mabolong and is known to encounter spirits on her own, she does not choose to serve as a shaman in mabolong contexts. Why she and other women may shun that arena is a question to be addressed in Chapter 14.

CHAPTER 13

1. As Anderson (1972) has observed for Europe, such partitioning occurred with the demise of the divine right of kings. Only then in Western tradition did the exercise of mundane power become a question. As heirs to that tradition, social scientists find an analytical distinction between sacral and political power useful. Indeed, contrary perhaps to the opinion of their critics, cultural analysts resort to this distinction regularly. It is quite evident, for example, in Geertz's 1980 analysis of the Balinese *negara*, which explores the challenge of sustaining the symbolics of power in political practice. The argument of cultural analysts is not that a sociological or political concept of power cannot be used to analyze a culture which lacks that concept; instead, they hold that it is wrong for the analyst to confound cultural and analytical concepts of power and assume that cultural actors are "rationally" orienting their action to the latter.

2. The spirit contingent that approaches Pue Lamoa in the molawo maneo must take identical measures to avoid buto.

3. I am indebted to Marilyn Strathern for drawing my attention to the contrast between Melanesian exchange and Indonesian theatrical display.

4. Godelier (1982) speculates that the difference between "great men" and "big men" politics may derive from the different ways in which Melanesian men exchange women. Jane Collier (1988) has developed a complex set of models to account for the relations between marriage and political inequality. In future work I plan to investigate the connections between marriage practices and political inequality over the last century in eastern Central Sulawesi.

5. Another reason for the scarcity of pigs in many Wana settlements may have to do with decades of millenarian gatherings in which pigs were slaughtered as part of collective feasts.

6. From the 1950s until the mid-1960s, Sulawesi was wracked by struggles between guerrilla insurgents and government forces. For a vivid account of the impact of the rebel movements and nationalist counterinsurgency around Lake Lindu, an upland area of western Central Sulawesi, see Acciaioli 1987. Although the Wana did not suffer directly from the warfare, they were aware of the turmoil. At one point, Wana men in the district of Ulu Bongka were summoned to appear with their blowguns to hold off rebels in a battle that did not materialize.

7. *Ada* is the Wana rendering of *adat*, a term used throughout Indonesia for similar systems of law and ritual custom.

8. Tambiah (1985a, 278) has made the point that an understanding of debt slavery in Southeast Asia is better framed in the terms of factionalism and patron–client relations than in the terms of Euroamerican slavery.

9. When I knew him, this once-influential man was living in a settlement consisting of two households and including only four adults besides himself.

10. Weiner (1980, 1985, 1989) has developed important insights regarding processes of societal regeneration across different political formations in the Pacific.

CHAPTER 14

1. See Atkinson (forthcoming) for a detailed treatment of Wana constructions of gender.

2. Adriani's use of the term *shaman* matches that of Loeb (1928, 1929),
who equated the term with spirit possession. Adriani (1932, 192) writes: "The
priestesses among the Bare'e-speakers are never shamans. They do not allow
themselves to be possessed by a spirit entering them, but they do separate
their innermost essence from their body in order to go off to the sky. They go
as humble supplicants with a prayer and an offering for the gods, and they
behave thus not to bring themselves into a cataleptic state, which in shamanism slips easily into all sorts of depravity.

3. Kruyt (1930) does not make it clear whether the Barangas women
shamans were mabolong performers or experts in other rituals, such as the
salia and the molawo. I knew several older Barangas women—Apa Mene's
stepmother, Indo Ngonga, among them (Fig. 7)—who performed a variety
of healing rituals and danced the salonde at mabolong but would never
summon spirit familiars in the mabolong.

4. Of the scores of Wana shamans I met who performed regularly at
mabolong, only two or three were women. Note that I specify mabolong
performance here. Occasionally people applied the term *tau kawalia*, "person
of spirit familiars," to individuals who did not serve as shamans at mabolong
but were skilled at the *molawo maneo*, a chant in which spirit familiars go up to
the place to Pue Lamoa and which can be done with or without shamanic
vision. Some women perform this ritual but refrain from performing at
mabolong (see note 3).

5. See Atkinson (forthcoming) for a case in which a young woman seeking
spirit familiars in the forest was threatened with rape.

6. Elsewhere I describe how Wana identify men's and women's roles in
procreation. Meeker, Barlow, and Lipset (1986) have argued that in Oceania
male political leadership is framed in the idiom of female nuturance and propose different ways in which extracommunity ventures can offer men bases for
authority apart from women's functions. By their argument, Wana men could
be seeking to compensate for women's centrality as bearers and nurturers of
life through adventures in distant and dangerous places. Although these
authors have captured some distinctive aspects of gender symbolism in the
Pacific, I think that their argument relies too heavily on a presocial definition
of women and men. Nurturance, for example, they take to be intrinsically
female, something that men can only emulate and appropriate—a claim that
strikes me as "unreal" as the Wana assertion that men menstruate. Furthermore, Meeker, Barlow, and Lipset seem to presume that the male-female
hostility found in the Melanesian area constitutes a natural divide that under-
lies cultures everywhere. Instead of generalizing that hostility as the bedrock
of human gender relations, I would argue that it is socially and culturally
generated in the Melanesian context and not universally generalizable.

7. Taking thirty-four mabolong performances for which I have good

records on treatments, I have tallied the numbers of women, men, and preadolescent children who were treated as patients (with shamans who were treated for "small feelings" excluded from these figures): the results are sixty-seven women, forty-seven men, and seventy-nine-plus children.

8. One young unmarried girl took to dancing frequently at mabolong performances. One night she began to cry as she danced and had to be helped to her knees by an aunt (Figs. 16, 17, 18). Later some women in the community said that the girl's dead mother—herself a shaman—had appeared to the girl as she had danced. The senior shamans in the community took little note of her efforts. One uncle dismissed her adventures in the forest as an attempt to create a millenarian movement, although another uncle, a junior shaman who perhaps desired a protégé, seemed more sympathetic to her shamanic aspirations.

9. Many Wana women express a distaste for rice beer, although they enjoy eating the fermented mash from which it comes. Women who drink at all typically do so in the company of other women. I have seen no women do so frequently enough to deplete seriously the stocks of rice beer they endeavor to have on hand to serve at shamanic performances and other festive occasions. Robert Netting (1964, 379) has noted that through fermentation, the nutritional value of the grain from which beer is made is enhanced. This process, called "biological ennoblement," yields B vitamins, ascorbic acid, and proteins. By eating fermented mash, then, women and children may obtain these nutrients without indulging in the brew itself.

10. Although women are rare in the ranks of mabolong performers, they are common among the practitioners of other forms of healing rituals. More than half the performers of both Lamoa-based rituals and the salia whom I met or heard of by reputation were women. These forms—as well as the posuyu and molawo, which women also perform—are learned by attending to the performances of others. All are liturgically focused rituals that do not call for shamanic self-aggrandizement. Also, with the exception of the salia, these rituals are not notably political. As for the salia (as we shall see in Chapter 15), its performance likely served to highlight the reputations of its organizers, not of its ritual specialists. It seems, then, that women avoid performing in the mabolong not because women should not have spirit familiars, but because the mabolong is a competitive arena in which political reputations and alignments as well as human welfare are at stake.

11. Apa Mene's own daughter, Indo Non, is a woman whose shamanic aspirations may have been blocked by marriage. According to her stepmother, Indo Lina, Indo Non would have become a shaman if it were not for the fact that her husband, a Muslim with some schooling, discourages her attendance at mabolong.

CHAPTER 15

1. Kruyt (1930) restricted his account of the Wana to the residents of the upper Bongka River drainage, an area that is now the district (*kecamatan*) of

Bungku Utara. He does mention a northerly branch of the Wana known as the To Linte, who reside today in the district of Ulu Bongka. What perhaps distinguished the To Linte from the groups Kruyt chose to treat in his study was the fact that the southern Wana groups were claimed as subjects by the raja of Bungku, whereas the more northerly To Linte were claimed by the raja of Tojo. Because Kruyt's account focuses on Wana who were subjects of Raja Bungku, Wana relations with Raja Tojo figure little in my account.

The *Sejarah Daerah Sulawesi Tengah* (Kutoyo et al. 1984, 107) distinguishes between Suku Wana and Suku Kayumarangka. If I am correct, the latter group is the same as the Kajumarangka in the western interior of the Wana region. The elasticity of the term *Wana* is, I think, due to the fact that labels for people in this area begin as labels for places. The To Wana, or Wana people, are those who live in or come from a place called Wana. For coastal peoples, *Wana* appears to mean the rugged forested uplands. Interior peoples make finer distinctions: for them, *Wana* refers specifically to the vicinity of the Old Mountain. Because many upland dwellers trace their origin to this place and because the term sets them apart from coastal culture, *Wana* offers an identity for most of the interior residents of three administrative districts— Bungku Utara, Ulu Bongka, and some of Barone.

It should be pointed out to those familiar with other Austronesian languages of this area that there is a distinction between the Wana term *tau*, "people," and *to*, which corresponds to the Indonesian term *yang*, meaning "who" or "which." It is equally correct to speak of the *tau wana*, "the people of Wana," and the *to wana*, "those of Wana." Whereas Kruyt speaks of the To Wana, I refer simply to the Wana. It should be understood, however, that Wana is, strictly speaking, a place name.

2. The word *clan* is inappropriate for the Wana case for various reasons. For one thing, Wana kinship is cognatic, not unilineal: whereas "clan" constructs generally trace descent from a mythical ancestor, these Wana groupings do not. Also, no rule of exogamy is associated with the Wana groupings, as there often is with clans.

3. Ties to former basal may be invoked today in ada discussions. People with claims to basal rank are subject to higher marriage payments and legal fines than those descended from commoners.

4. Wolters (1982, 28–30) discusses how the Vietnamese deviated from this pattern when they adopted Chinese dynastic principles.

5. Wana use a single term, *maliwuyu*, for colors in the range of blue and green.

6. It is my hunch that labor for basal was extracted not as onerous tribute but as part of work parties (*gawe*) in which participants would be hosted with food and drink. Significantly, my older acquaintances were familiar with such a practice, but as far as I can tell nothing of the sort occurs today.

7. Whereas the mabolong confers prestige on successful performers, the salia apparently confers prestige on the basal, whom I suspect of organizing it and whose constituency it celebrates. What of the salia performers themselves? It may be significant that the ritual leaders of the salia seem to have

performed as liturgical experts, not as personal possessors of spirit familiars. Many appear to have been women. These facts suggest to me that the salia performers ("people of the cold hearth," *tau loto rapu*), although they were highly respected, did not engage in the "men of prowess" politics we find in the mabolong.

8. In the 1970s, /tj/ was not an element of Wana phonology: where Kruyt transcribes /tj/, Wana in my experience pronounced /s/. Whether what is at work here is some regional variation of which I am unaware, a historical shift in phonology, or interference from Kruyt's own fluency in the closely related language of the Poso people, I cannot say.

9. Two decades after the Dutch asserted control, Kruyt (1980) described the salia as extinct. In the 1970s I learned that salia were still held occasionally in the region of Kasiala. It may be significant that this ritual should persist only at the former seat of the paramount Wana makole. One would need to know more about the dynamics of local leadership in that neighborhood to understand whether and how people may be appropriating the past for contemporary claims.

10. In the last peace settlement between the Wana and the To Lage, the Wana killed a young girl as their part of the bargain. It was explained to me that she was an orphan about whom nobody cared. Kruyt (1930, 527) discusses the practice of killing humans as part of peace settlements.

11. My explanation for the emergence of Wana chiefdoms resembles Carneiro's (1981) model, which identifies warfare (or its threat) as the factor responsible for the development of chiefdoms.

Perhaps there were more bangsa and basal in the Wana region before relations were established with Bungku. One could speculate that smaller groups and weaker leaders may have consolidated with stronger groups and more powerful leaders as external ties were constructed.

In theory, the process I have described thus far could have happened more than once in Wana history. But before proposing an ongoing oscillation between centralized and decentralized political authority in the region (cf. Leach 1954), I would want an opportunity to investigate further the history of political systems in Central Sulawesi, including the effects of indirect as well as direct colonial rule.

12. Hocart (1970, 223) offers a perceptive account of a parallel instance for Fiji: "I was the witness of such a rapid adaptation in Fiji. The inhabitants of the Windward Islands had asked Government to establish a school, and had agreed to support it. The government, obsessed with the idea that the Fijians are lazy, insisted that the people should support their school in the good old way by supplying food and free labor. Unfortunately it could see only one side of the good old way, the contributions and the labor; it forgot the compensations, the feasts and the gifts. Had it commandeered the labor and the yams by a special envoy bearing whale's teeth, had it awaited the freights of yams with feasts, with bales of cloth and mats, and with dances, had it fed the staute-labourers [*sic*] in chiefly wise, liberally, and with ceremony, had it done all this, all might have been well, and the change over might have been slow.

As it was, it merely gave orders on foolscap, and expected to receive without giving. It did not realize that, so far from upholding the good old custom, it had carried out a revolution; it had substituted a one-sided take for a balance of give and take."

13. Older people expressed the sense that Wana rice rituals had declined in elaboration and efficacy from earlier times. I would not be surprised if this decline were related to an earlier involvement of basal with farming rituals. We do know that headhunting, over which basal had authority, was culturally related to farming success. Some people also attributed success in rice culture with giving tribute to the rajas. Given the involvement of basal with other kinds of ritual, I would be surprised if basal did not organize and sponsor rice rituals.

As for the Wana sense that rice production has declined since the era of raja and basal, it could be that chieftainship, with its system of tribute and incentives of the greater glory of a chief's constituency, may have spurred farm production beyond subsistence levels. As Hocart (1970, 206) asserted for another case, "The chieftainship braced the Fijians to greater efforts than they would endure for the sake of private gain."

14. Although these prized entities are thought to have a Wana "source" (*pu'u*), the terms for two of them are foreign: *baraka*, the magical power Wana associate with royalty, derives from the Arabic; *kasugi*, meaning "wealth," derives from the Buginese. Only *pangansani*, or "knowledge," is autochtonous conceptually and linguistically.

15. Graham (1987, 121) has rightly criticized the tendency of early scholars to force diverse shamanic styles into hierarchical frameworks. Kruyt's ordering in this case seems to reflect differences not in the relative skill of mabolong and salia performers, but in the scale of the ritual itself.

16. Kruyt (1930, 467) was told that the forces of Bungku laid siege to the Barangas people at a site called Pinaloe. It would make sense that encounters with both the Bungku and the Dutch would have happened at Pindu Loe, a defensible spot along a southern trail leading into the Wana region.

Glossary

ada	The Wana code of customary law.
adi adi	A magical formula associated with an earlier age that insured instant fulfillment of a wish.
agama	A governmentally sanctioned religion.
ate	Liver.
baku	Cooked rice, a meal. *Baku ragi*—a special meal consumed by successful headhunters; *baku mwalia*—food of the spirits, the refreshments offered to and/or requested by a shaman's spirits.
balo	Bamboo. *Balo nosa*—tubes of breath, both within a person's chest and at the Owner's residence, which shamans manage on behalf of their patients.
bangsa	A kind of people; an ethnic group or nation.
baraka	Magical power associated with an earlier age that departed from the Wana land in the company of knowledge and wealth.
basal	A chief. Also called *makole*.
baya nia	To repay a vow.
bayar	To pay.
bayo	A shamanic term for "shadow."
bolag	A population of benign spirits who inhabit the Wana region.
bolong	A double-skinned drum.
bombaru	A shamanic term for "house."
bonto	A title for a chief's subordinate, who served as an intermediary between the chief and his following.
bui	Center of the midriff, corresponding to the xiphoid process, which is subject to attack by malevolent beings.
bunga bunga	Ornamentations, decorations, embellishments.
buto	A condition of illness brought on through violations of hierarchy, including unwarranted claims to rank and acts of disrespect. Typical symptoms include bloating of the abdomen, yellowness, and physical weakness.
buya nraya	Literally, "whiteness of heart." Gratitude; a gift given to demonstrate gratitude.
do'a	A spell.

doti	Sorcery.
epe	To feel; to experience as a sensation.
gaji	Wage, payment.
ganda	Another word for *bolong*, drum. *Ganda mokio*—"the summoning drum," the name of a place on a shaman's journey.
guru	Teacher.
inda	Debt.
jampu	The power to become invisible.
janji	A fate to die.
jaya	Path, route. Also a means of conveyance.
jimi	A mischievous, lascivious spirit who befriends humans in search of special knowledge.
joe ntana	The end of the earth.
juru tulis	A governmentally appointed village scribe.
kabuya nraya	See *buya nraya*.
kakayuka	To enact something so that it will come about. In particular, the funeral rites for a person's soul or dream agent carried out by ghosts.
kameasa	A person possessed by a demon (*measa*) who eats the livers of other humans.
kampung	A governmentally sanctioned village.
kaju parambaa	A tree important in Wana mythology.
kantar	A war shield.
kapongo	A betel quid (consisting of a slice of areca nut, a piper leaf, and lime); an offering of betel to a human or spirit. *Kapongo gana*—a kind of betel offering known as a "complete" kapongo that is made to the Owner on behalf of a patient.
karamat	Spiritual power associated with the former sultanates.
kasintuwu	The value of living together in harmony and cooperation.
kasugi	Wealth.
katuntu	Epic stories about the mythical past.
kawalia	See *tau kawalia*.
kawu	To feel hurt and rejected; to withdraw; to go off hurt.
keni kapongo	The ritual act of carrying a betel offering to the Owner.
kepala kampung	A governmentally appointed village head.
kodi nraya	A state of feeling hurt, or "small inside," in response to insult, injury, or neglect.
kunsi	To lock.
kunti	A shamanic term for "drum."
koro	A living body (as opposed to a corpse); a soul that resides in a person's back and survives the body after death. *Koro tongo, koro nonong, koro samba'a, koro uli* are among the varieties of souls referred to in shamanic practice.
lambuwu	Cyclone, whirlwind. A place on the shamanic route to the Owner.

Lamoa	The vengeful owner of thunder and lightning.
langgiwo	A ghost. Also called *wonggo*.
lango	An offering tray prepared for rituals like the mabolong.
leangi mpue	The Owner's intermediary who speaks with a shaman's spirit entourage.
lemba	External body; corpse; disguise.
ligi	Metaphor; verbal disguise.
luo langgiwo	"The place of the ghosts"; a site on the spirit familiars' journey to the Owner.
mabolong	A shamanic ritual performed with drum and gongs.
mangerus	To treat with a spell.
magao	Good, honest (referring to a person's character).
makole	A chief. Also called *basal*.
mandake	To go uphill. In shamanic performance, to make a journey to the Owner's place.
maneo	Crooked.
mangaku	To take upon oneself; to assume responsibility.
mangou	To commit suicide.
manyomba	To supplicate; to pay homage to the Owner or a raja.
masintuwu	To live together in a spirit of mutual support and cooperation.
mata	Eye; fresh.
measa	A liver-eating demon.
moguru	To study.
molawo	A highly prized and esoteric ritual chant, performed by a single singer, depicting the travels of spirit familiars. *Molawo maneo*—a "crooked" molawo, a molawo chant that follows the shamanic path to Lamoa; *molawo manoto*—a "straight" molawo, a molawo chant that follows the shamanic path to the Owner.
motaro	To jump up and down; the principal style of shamanic dance.
nabi	Tutelary spirit.
nia	A vow.
nosa	Breath. See also *balo*.
oko mwiti	Literally, "the taking of the feet." A gift given to a shaman to persuade him to visit another settlement.
opo bira lima	The Owner's place, located above the sky.
pangansani	Powerful knowledge.
pangepe	Removal of an intrusive object by sucking.
pantende	A ritual performed to ward off punitive attacks by Lamoa.
pantoo	A vow.
papolonsu	A cloth used by a shaman to handle patients' vital elements of being.
patoe	A summoning; a shamanic invocation.

pela mwo'o	Scalp.
pesolo	A small bamboo tube filled with rice and chicken feathers that is included in offerings to repay vows.
poga'a	Separation. In Wana myth, the term refers to the departure of knowledge, power, and wealth from the Wana land.
pokuli	A substance, usually a plant, used for medicinal or magical purposes.
polobiang	Techniques of divination.
pompobuuka	Thought.
poso	Fall unconscious.
posuyu	A healing ritual performed for victims of headhunting spirits, including the Sangia, Tau Sampu'u, and the Tambar, and named after the small resin torch (*suyu*) that is used in its performance.
potudu	Descend. The name of a healing ritual resembling the mabolong, but performed without drum and gongs and usually by a single shaman.
po'us	To fasten, lash, bind together.
pue	Owner. When capitalized in this text the term refers to the Wana deity.
pu'u	Source, origin, base, foundation.
rapiyara	Domesticated.
raa	Blood. *Raa tuwu*—"living blood," blood taken from a live chicken, symbolizing renewal and continuation of good fortune.
raja	Ruler. The raja familiar to the Wana can be described as chiefs who adopted the regal trappings and ideology of rulers of more powerful polities in the archipelago.
ransong	An intrusive object sent into a person's body by a spirit or a human with spirit assistance.
raya	In, inside, within; feelings.
rodo	Still; settled.
roso	Strength.
saki	A legal fine.
sala	Wrong; wrongdoing; responsibility. In shamanic usage, path, vehicle, conveyance.
salia	A ritual held on a grand scale to insure the continued health and well-being of all its participants. This festival has waned in the twentieth century.
salonde	Women's style of dance at mabolong.
samata	A succulent plant used in ritual to invoke freshness.
sambiaa	Belonging to one's "vine" or stock.
sanga	Name.
sangia	A variety of warrior spirits.
saruga	Heaven.

sauju	Inappropriate marriages that disrupt generational authority.
serita	Stories of the past.
soba	Pestilence.
suku terasing	Indonesian label for isolated upland pagan populations.
sule	Heart; pulse. Also a dream whose ostensible events are paired with and forecast events in the waking world.
tabang	Cordyline, a plant used in the salia, molawo maneo, and pantende rituals.
tadulako	A war leader who led the charge against the enemy.
talenga	A war leader who performed rituals and offerings to protect warriors on a raid.
tambar	Little yellow-haired spirits, related to the Sangia and Tau Sampu'u.
tanuana	Dream agent that resides in the top of the head.
taru	Beeswax.
tau	Person.
tau baraka	People possessing great spiritual power; such people once inhabited the Wana land and are expected someday to return.
tau maborosi	"The many people," an expression referring to commoners, those not of chiefly rank.
tau makoje	Literally, "a brave person." A warrior.
tau sampu'u	A variety of warrior spirits.
tau tu'a	Older person; parent-in-law; community leader.
tau kawalia	A person with spirit familiars, a shaman. Also called *tau walia, to walia,* or simply *kawalia.*
tolowu	Vital elements residing in a person's hands and feet; small stones derived from spirits and used as amulets.
toloniu	Rice spirits.
tompuso	A dead person who has been transformed into a feature of the landscape; a feature of the landscape said to be the transformation of a magical person (*tau baraka*) from the past.
tonii	The dead.
toru	A broad-brimmed hat worn for protection against rain and sun.
to walia	See *tau kawalia.*
tu'a	Old; an old person.
tuka	A fate. See also *janji.*
uta	Brains.
walia	Spirit familiars. *Walia mangepe*—spirits who assist people in the removal of intrusive objects; *walia mantende*—spirits who assist in the performance of the pantende or mabolong.
wali mpanto'o	Literally, "the becoming of the word." The realization of a

	spoken wish, a characteristic of *adi adi*, the magic of an earlier age.
wega	An appellation of spirit familiars used in shamanic song.
wonggo	Ghost. Also called *langgiwo*.
woro tana	One who coordinates farming decisions and performs rice rituals on behalf of a community.
wotua	Slave.
wunga	Basil, used in ritual to attract spirit familiars.

Bibliography

Acciaioli, Greg. Forthcoming. "Nets and Networks: Principles and Processes in Bugis Migration Strategies to Lake Lindu, Central Sulawesi." In *Ties That Bind: Bugis Modes of Authority*, edited by Kees van Dijk and G. Acciaioli.

Adriani, N. 1932. "De toradjasche vrouw als pristeres." In *Verzamelde geschriften*, 2: 190–215. Haarlem: De Erven F. Bohn.

———. 1932–33. *Bare'e-verhalen*. Vols. 1 and 2. The Hague: Martinus Nijhoff.

Adriani, N., and A. C. Kruyt. 1950. *De Bare'e-sprekende Toradjas van Midden-Celebes*. 3 vols. Rev. ed. Amsterdam: Noord-Hollandsche Uitgevers.

Anderson, Benedict, 1972. "The Idea of Power in Javanese Culture." In *Culture and Politics in Indonesia*, edited by Claire Holt, 1–69. Ithaca, N.Y.: Cornell University Press.

Anisimov, A. F. 1963. "The Shaman's Tent of the Evenks and the Origin of the Shamanistic Rite." In *Studies in Siberian Shamanism*, edited by Henry N. Michael, 84–123. Toronto: University of Toronto Press.

Ardener, E. 1975. "Belief and the Problem of Women." In *Perceiving Women*, edited by S. G. Ardener, 1–17. London: Dent/Malaby.

Atkinson, Jane Monnig. 1979. "Paths of the Spirit Familiars: A Study of Wana Shamanism." Ph.D. diss., Stanford University.

———. 1983. "Religions in Dialogue: The Construction of an Indonesian Minority Religion." *American Ethnologist* 10: 684–96.

———. 1984a. "Wana." In *Muslim Peoples of the World*, edited by Richard Weekes, 2: 849–52. Westport, Conn.: Greenwood Press.

———. 1984b. "Wrapped Words: Poetry and Politics Among the Wana of Central Sulawesi." In *Dangerous Words: Politics and Language in the Pacific*, edited by Donald Brenneis and Fred Myers, 33–68. New York: New York University Press.

———. 1987. "The Effectiveness of Shamanship in an Indonesian Ritual." *American Anthropologist* 89: 342–55.

———. Forthcoming. "How Gender Makes a Difference in Wana Society." In *Power and Difference: Studies in Gender in Island Southeast Asia*, edited by J. M. Atkinson and Shelly Errington. Stanford, Calif.: Stanford University Press.

Augé, Marc. 1982. *The Anthropological Circle: Symbol, Function, History*. Cambridge: Cambridge University Press.

Baker, Keith Michael. 1990. "Introduction." In *Inventing the French Revolution: Essays on French Political Culture in the Eighteenth Century*, 1–11. Cambridge: Cambridge University Press.

Barth, Fredrik. 1975. *Ritual and Knowledge Among the Baktaman of New Guinea*. New Haven, Conn.: Yale University Press.

Becker, Alton. 1979. "Text-Building, Epistemology, and Aesthetics in Javanese Shadow Theatre." In *The Imagination of Reality: Essays in Southeast Asian Coherence Systems*, edited by A. Becker and Aram Yengoyan, 211–43. Norwood, N.J.: Ablex.

———. 1989. *Writing on the Tongue*. Michigan Papers in South and Southeast Asia. Ann Arbor: University of Michigan Press.

Bentley, G. Carter. 1986. "Indigenous States of Southeast Asia." *Annual Review of Anthropology* 15: 275–305.

Bigalke, Terence. 1981. "A Social History of Tana Toraja, 1870–1965." Ph.D. diss., University of Wisconsin–Madison.

Bourdieu, Pierre. 1977. *Outline of a Theory of Practice*. Translated by Richard Nice. Cambridge: Cambridge University Press.

Cannon, Walter. 1942. "'Voodoo' Death." *American Anthropologist* 44: 169–81.

Carneiro, Robert L. 1981. "The Chiefdom: Precursor of the State." In *The Transition to Statehood in the New World*, edited by Grant D. Jones and Robert R. Kautz, 37–79. Cambridge: Cambridge University Press.

Castaneda, Carlos. 1971. *A Separate Reality: Further Conversations with Don Juan*. New York: Simon & Schuster.

Casteel, Ed, and Jeanne Casteel. 1980. "Indonesia: Wana Tribe." *New Tribes Mission: Brown Gold*, April, 8.

de Certeau, Michel. 1984. *The Practice of Everyday Life*. Berkeley and Los Angeles: University of California Press.

Collier, Jane. 1988. *Marriage and Inequity in Classless Societies*. Stanford, Calif.: Stanford University Press.

Eliade, Mircea. [1951] 1964. *Shamanism: Archaic Techniques of Ecstasy*. Bollingen Series, no. 76. Princeton, N.J.: Princeton University Press.

Errington, Shelly. 1983. "Embodied Sumange' in Luwu." *Journal of Asian Studies* 52: 545–70.

———. 1987. "Twins and the House Societies of Insular Southeast Asia." *Cultural Anthropology* 2: 403–44.

———. 1989. *Meaning and Power in a Southeast Asian Realm*. Princeton, N.J.: Princeton University Press.

Evans-Pritchard, E. E. 1929. "The Morphology and Function of Magic: A Comparative Study of Trobriand and Zande Ritual and Spells." *American Anthropologist* 31: 619–41.

———. 1937. *Witchcraft, Oracles, and Magic Among the Azande*. Oxford: Clarendon Press.

———. 1965. *Theories of Primitive Religion*. Oxford: Clarendon Press.

Ferguson, Charles A. 1987. "Prayer of the People: Group Construction of a Religious Genre of Formatted Discourse." Unpublished manuscript.

Fox, James. 1988. *To Speak in Pairs: Essays on the Ritual Languages of Eastern Indonesia*. Cambridge: Cambridge University Press.

Frake, C. O. 1980. "Interpretations of Illness: An Ethnographic Perspective on Events and Their Causes." In *Language and Cultural Description*, 61–82. Stanford, Calif.: Stanford University Press.

Fried, Morton H. 1967. *The Evolution of Political Society*. New York: Random House.

Geertz, Clifford. 1973. *The Interpretation of Cultures*. New York: Basic Books.

———. 1980. *Negara: The Theatre State in Nineteenth-Century Bali*. Princeton, N.J.: Princeton University Press.

———. 1983. *Local Knowledge: Further Essays in Interpretive Anthropology*. New York: Basic Books.

Gesick, Lorraine, ed. 1983. *Centers, Symbols, and Hierarchies: Essays on the Classical States of Southeast Asia*. Southeast Asia Monograph Series, no. 26. New Haven, Conn.: Yale University Press.

Giddens, Anthony. 1979. *Central Problems in Social Theory*. Berkeley and Los Angeles: University of California Press.

Godelier, Maurice. 1982. "Social Hierarchies Among the Baruya of New Guinea." In *Inequality in New Guinea Highlands Society*, edited by Andrew Strathern, 3–34. Cambridge: Cambridge University Press.

———. 1986. *The Making of Great Men: Male Domination and Power Among the New Guinea Baruya*. Cambridge: Cambridge University Press.

Graham, Penelope. 1987. *Iban Shamanism: An Analysis of the Ethnographic Literature*. Canberra: Department of Anthropology, Research School of Pacific Studies, Australian National University.

Gregory, C. A. 1980. "Gifts to Man and Gifts to God: Gift Exchange and Capital Accumulation in Contemporary Papua." *Man* 15: 626–52.

Hallowell, A. Irving. 1967. *Culture and Experience*. New York: Schocken Books.

Hastorf, Christine. Forthcoming. "Negotiating Political Inequality in the Sausa of Peru: One Path to the Heights." In *The Evolution of Political Systems*, edited by Steadman Upham.

Helman, Cecil. 1978. "'Feed a Cold, Starve a Fever'—Folk Models of Infection in an English Suburban Community and Their Relation to Medical Treatment." *Culture, Medicine, and Psychology* 2: 107–37.

Hocart, A. M. 1970. *Kings and Councillors: An Essay in the Comparative Anatomy of Human Society*. Edited by Rodney Needham. Chicago: University of Chicago Press.

Hubert, Henri, and Marcel Mauss. [1898] 1964. *Sacrifice: Its Nature and Function*. Translated by W. D. Halls. Chicago: University of Chicago Press.

Hume, David. [1739–40] 1888. *A Treatise on Human Nature*. Oxford: Clarendon Press.

Kapferer, Bruce. 1979. "Entertaining Demons: Comedy, Interaction, and Meaning in Sinhalese Healing Ritual." *Social Analysis* 1: 108–52.

———. 1983. *A Celebration of Demons: Exorcism and the Aesthetics of Healing in Sri Lanka*. Bloomington: Indiana University Press.

Keeler, Ward. 1987. *Javanese Shadow Plays, Javanese Selves*. Princeton, N.J.: Princeton University Press.

Kessler, Clive S. 1977. "Conflict and Sovereignty in Kelantanese Malay Spirit Seances." In *Case Studies in Spirit Possession*, edited by Vincent Crapanzano and Vivian Garrison, 295–331. New York: Wiley.

Kiefer, Thomas M. 1972. *The Tausug: Violence and Law in a Philippine Moslem Society*. New York: Holt, Rinehart & Winston.

Kruyt, A. C. 1930. "De To Wana op Oost-Celebes." *Tijdschrift voor indische taal-, land-, en volkenkunde* 70: 398–625.

Kutoyo, Sutrisno, et al. 1984. *Sejarah Daerah Sulawesi Tengah*. Jakarta: Department of Education and Culture.

Lamaison, Pierre. 1986. "From Rules to Strategies: An Interview with Pierre Bourdieu." *Cultural Anthropology* 1: 110–20.

Leach, Edmund. 1954. *Political Systems of Highland Burma: A Study of Kachin Social Structure*. Boston: Beacon Press.

Leacock, Eleanor. 1978. "Women's Status in Egalitarian Society: Implications for Social Evolution." *Current Anthropology* 19: 247–75.

Leeuw, Gerardus van der. 1963. *Religion and Manifestation*. Translated by J. E. Turner. New York: Harper & Row.

Lévi-Strauss, Claude. 1963a. "The Effectiveness of Symbols." In *Structural Anthropology*, 181–201. Translated by Claire Jacobson and Brook Grundfest Schoepf. New York: Anchor Books.

———. 1963b. "Social Structure." In *Structural Anthropology*, 269–319. *See* Lévi-Strauss 1963a.

———. [1950] 1987. *Introduction to the Work of Marcel Mauss*. London: Routledge & Kegan Paul.

Lewis, G. 1980. *Day of Shining Red: An Essay on Understanding Ritual*. Cambridge: Cambridge University Press.

Lindstrom, Lamont. 1984. "Doctor, Lawyer, Wise Man, Priest: Big Men and Knowledge in Melanesia." *Man* 19: 291–309.

Llewelyn-Davies, Melissa. 1981. "Women, Warriors, and Patriarchs." In *Sexual Meanings: The Cultural Construction of Gender and Sexuality*, edited by Sherry B. Ortner and Harriet Whitehead, 330–58. Cambridge: Cambridge University Press.

Loeb, E. M. 1928. "Mentawei Social Organization." *American Anthropologist* 30: 408–33.

———. 1929. "Shaman and Seer." *American Anthropologist* 31: 60–84.

McKinley, Robert. 1979. "Zaman dan Masa, Eras and Periods: Religious Evolution and the Permanence of Epistemological Ages in Malay Culture." In *The Imagination of Reality*, edited by Alton Becker and Aram Yengoyan, 303–24. Norwood, N.J.: Ablex.

Mauss, Marcel. [1925] 1967. *The Gift*. Translated by Ian Cunnison. New York: Norton.

———. [1902–3] 1972. *A General Theory of Magic*. Translated by Robert Brain. New York: Norton.

Meeker, Michael E., Kathleen Barlow, and David M. Lipset. 1986. "Culture,

Exchange, and Gender: Lessons from the Murik." *Cultural Anthropology* 1: 6–73.

Moertono, S. 1968. *State and Statecraft in Old Java: A Study of the Later Mataram Period, Sixteenth to Nineteenth Century.* Ithaca, N.Y.: Cornell University Press.

Moore, Sally F. 1975. "Epilogue: Uncertainties in Situations, Indeterminacies in Culture." In *Symbol and Politics in Communal Ideology*, edited by S. F. Moore and Barbara Myerhoff, 210–39. Ithaca, N.Y.: Cornell University Press.

Moore, Sally F., and Barbara Myerhoff. 1977. "Secular Ritual: Forms and Meaning." In *Secular Ritual*, edited by S. F. Moore and B. Myerhoff, 3–24. Assen, Neth.: Van Gorcum.

Myers, Fred R. 1983. "What Is the Business of the 'Balgo Business'? A Contemporary Aboriginal Religious Movement." Unpublished manuscript.

———. 1986. *Pintupi Country, Pintupi Self.* Washington, D.C.: Smithsonian Institution.

Netting, Robert. 1964. "Beer as a Locus of Value Among the West African Kofyar." *American Anthropologist* 66: 375–84.

Ortner, Sherry B. 1973. "On Key Symbols." *American Anthropologist* 75: 1338–46.

Ortner, Sherry B., and Harriet Whitehead. 1981. "Introduction: Accounting for Sexual Meanings." In *Sexual Meanings: The Cultural Construction of Gender and Sexuality*, edited by S. B. Ortner and H. Whitehead, 1–27. Cambridge: Cambridge University Press.

Otto, Rudolph. 1950. *The Idea of the Holy.* Translated by John W. Harvey. 2d ed. Oxford: Oxford University Press.

Prince, Raymond. 1982. "The Endorphins: A Review for Psychological Anthropologists." *Ethos* 10: 303–16.

Rappaport, Roy. 1979. *Ecology, Meaning, and Religion.* 2d ed. Berkeley: North Atlantic Press.

Reid, Anthony, and Jennifer Brewster. 1983. *Slavery, Bondage, and Dependency in Southeast Asia.* New York: St. Martin's Press.

Reinhard, Johan. 1976. "Shamanism and Spirit Possession." In *Spirit Possession in the Nepali Hamalayas*, edited by John Hitchcock and Rex Jones, 12–20. Westminster, Eng.: Aris & Phillips.

Renard-Clamagirand, Brigitte. 1982. *Marobo: Une société Ema de Timor.* Langues et Civilisations de l'Asie du Sud-Est et du Monde Insulindien, no. 12. Paris: SELAF.

Ricoeur, Paul. 1971. "The Model of the Text: Meaningful Action Considered as a Text." *Social Research* 38: 529–62.

Rosaldo, Michelle. 1973. "Magic and Medicine: A Problem in Cultural Analysis." Unpublished manuscript.

———. 1980. *Knowledge and Passion: Ilongot Notions of Self and Social Life.* Cambridge: Cambridge University Press.

Rosaldo, Renato. 1975. "Where Precision Lies: The Hill People Once Lived on a Hill." In *The Interpretation of Symbolism*, edited by Roy Willis, 1–22.

London: Malaby Press.

———. 1984. "Grief and the Headhunter's Rage: On the Cultural Force of Emotion." In *Text, Play, and Story: The Construction and Reconstruction of Self and Society*, edited by Edward Bruner, 178–95. Washington, D.C.: American Ethnological Society.

Rouse, Roger. 1978. "Talking About Shamans." *Journal of the Anthropological Society of Oxford* 9: 113–28.

Scheff, Thomas J. 1977. "The Distancing of Emotions in Ritual." *Current Anthropology* 18: 483–505.

———. 1979. *Catharsis in Healing, Ritual, and Drama*. Berkeley and Los Angeles: University of California Press.

Schieffelin, Edward. 1976. *The Sorrow of the Lonely and the Burning of the Dancers*. New York: St. Martin's Press.

———. 1985. "Performance and the Cultural Construction of Reality." *American Ethnologist* 12: 707–24.

Schrieke, B. 1957. *Indonesian Sociological Studies*. Vol. 2: *Ruler and Realm in Early Java*. The Hague: Van Hoeve.

Service, Elman. 1975. *Origins of the State and Civilization: The Process of Cultural Evolution*. New York: Norton.

Sherzer, Joel. 1983. *Kuna Ways of Speaking*. Austin: University of Texas Press.

———. 1987. "A Discourse-centered Approach to Language and Culture." *American Anthropologist* 89: 295–309.

Siegel, James. 1978. "Curing Rites, Dreams, and Domestic Politics in a Sumatran Society." *Glyph* 3: 18–31.

———. 1979. *Shadow and Sound: The Historical Thought of a Sumatran People*. Chicago: University of Chicago Press.

Simmel, Georg. 1950. *The Sociology of Georg Simmel*. Translated and edited by Kurt H. Wolff. Glencoe, Ill.: Free Press.

Tambiah, Stanley J. 1985a. "The Galactic Polity in Southeast Asia." In *Culture, Thought, and Social Action*, 252–86. Cambridge, Mass.: Harvard University Press.

———. 1985b. "Introduction: From the General to the Particular and the Construction of Totalities." In *Culture, Thought, and Social Action*, 1–13. *See* Tambiah 1985a.

———. 1985c. "A Performative Approach to Ritual." In *Culture, Thought, and Social Action*, 123–66. *See* Tambiah 1985a.

———. 1985d. "A Reformulation of Geertz's Conception of the Theatre State." In *Culture, Thought, and Social Action*, 316–38. *See* Tambiah 1985a.

Traube, Elizabeth G. 1986. *Cosmology and Social Life: Ritual Exchange Among the Mambai of East Timor*. Chicago: University of Chicago Press.

———. 1989. "Obligations to the Source: Complementarity and Hierarchy in an Eastern Indonesian Society." In *The Attraction of Opposites: Thought and Society in a Dualistic Mode*, edited by David Maybury-Lewis and Uri Almagor, 321–44. Ann Arbor: University of Michigan Press.

Tsing, Anna. 1987. "A Rhetoric of Centers in a Religion of the Periphery." In

Indonesian Religions in Transition, edited by Rita Kipp and Susan Rodgers, 187–210. Tucson: University of Arizona Press.

―――. Forthcoming. "Gender and Performance in Meratus Dispute Settlement." In *Power and Difference: Studies of Gender in Island Southeast Asia,* edited by Jane Monnig Atkinson and Shelly Errington. Stanford, Calif.: Stanford University Press.

Turner, Terence. 1977. "Transformation, Hierarchy, and Transcendence: A Reformulation of Van Gennep's Model of the Structure of Rites of Passage." In *Secular Ritual,* edited by Sally F. Moore and Barbara Myerhoff, 53–70. Assen, Neth.: Van Gorcum.

―――. 1979. "Anthropology and the Politics of Indigenous Peoples' Struggles." *Cambridge Anthropologist* 5: 1–42.

Turner, Victor. 1968. *The Drums of Affliction.* Ithaca, N.Y.: Cornell University Press.

―――. 1977. "Variations on a Theme of Liminality." In *Secular Ritual,* edited by Sally F. Moore and Barbara Myerhoff, 36–52. Assen, Neth.: Van Gorcum.

―――. 1981. "Social Dramas and Stories About Them." In *On Narrative,* edited by W. J. T. Mitchell, 137–64. Chicago: University of Chicago Press.

Valeri, Valerio. 1985. *Kingship and Sacrifice: Ritual and Society in Ancient Hawaii.* Chicago: University of Chicago Press.

Volkman, Toby Alice. 1985. *Feasts of Honor: Ritual and Change in the Toraja Highlands.* Urbana: University of Illinois Press.

Weber, Max. 1963. *The Sociology of Religion.* Translated by Ephraim Fischoff. Boston: Beacon Press.

Weiner, Annette. 1976. *Women of Value, Men of Renown: New Perspectives on Trobriand Exchange.* Austin: University of Texas Press.

―――. 1980. "Reproduction: A Replacement for Reciprocity." *American Ethnologist* 7: 71–85.

―――. 1985. "Inalienable Wealth." *American Ethnologist* 12: 210–227.

―――. 1989. "Why Cloth? Gender and Power in Oceania." In *Cloth and Human Experience,* edited by A. Weiner and Jane Schneider. Washington, D.C.: Smithsonian Institution.

White, Hayden. 1974. *Metahistory: The Historical Imagination in Nineteenth-Century Europe.* Baltimore: Johns Hopkins University Press.

Wolters, O. W. 1982. *History, Culture, and Region in Southeast Asian Perspectives.* Singapore: Institute of Southeast Asian Studies.

Index

Acciaioli, G., 338n6
Adriani, N.: on ritual in Poso, 21, 162, 201; on shamans in Poso, 210, 280, 339n2
Adriani, N., and A. C. Kruyt: on ethnography of Poso, 21, 331n3; as missionaries, 311; on Tojo, 330n6
Anderson, B.: on European concepts of power, 338n1; on Javanese concepts of power, 8–9, 76, 270
Apa Iki: as community leader, 4–5; as father of Apa Mene, 329n2
Apa Linus: identity of, 21, 80; shamanic relations of, 31, 83, 237–38, 246; spirit encounter of, 293; transcripts of songs by, 80–85, 221–23, 233–35, 239–45, 247–50; treatment of daughter by, 105, 107
Apa Mene: identity of, 6, 21, 329n2, 339n3; magic of, 57, 290; references to transcripts by, 109, 113, 115, 116, 219, 236, 237–38; shamanic relations of, 34, 83, 222, 286, 287, 288; shamanic sponsorship by, 286, 340n11; spirit familiars of, 30, 31, 32, 99, 100–101, 176, 293, 332–33n3; transcripts of dialogues involving, 232–33, 240–45, 247–50; transcripts of invocations of the Owners by, 184–86, 203–5; transcripts of shamanic songs by, 29–30, 31, 85–87, 87–90, 167–75
Apa Miin: shamanic relations of, 231, 237–38; transcript of performance by, 231–35
Apa nSempa: molawo performance by, 162–67, 337n4 (Chapter 12)
Apa Weri: relation with Apa Mene, 29, 34, 185, 243–44; shamanic language of, 30–31, 33, 34; transcript of invocation by, 28–29
Ardener, E., 294
Asinimov, A. F.: on Evenk shamans, 297–98
Auge, M., xii, 217
Austin, J. L., 12

Bahasa Taa (Wana language): pronouns in, 32; transcription of, xvii–xviii, 196, 342n8
Barth, F., 332n2
Basil: shamans' use of, 25, 28, 94, 220
Becker, A. L., xviii, 314
Beer, 187, 340n9, 340n10
Bentley, G. C., 8, 310
Betel: in applying magic, 70–71; in invocations to the Owners, 201–2, 203; in molawo song, 162, 163; ritual uses of, 27, 70, 79, 93, 183; as symbol of sociability, 71, 182–83
Betel offering: patient's relationship to, 161, 178, 182, 188–89, 192; preparation of, 160; ritual significance of, 182–84; shaman's relationship to, 161, 178, 187, 190, 192, 193. See also Vow
Bigalke, T., 309
Bourdieu, P., 12, 179, 182, 187, 279
Breath: "bamboo tubes of," 109, 187; as gift of life, 109, 177, 183, 186, 189; myths about, 105, 198–99; transcripts of shaman's retrieval of, 84, 175, 178
Bungku: as source of Wana legal code, 267, 269, 309; Wana relations to, 188, 196, 307–9, 310, 340–41n1; 343n16
Buto, illness of: in shamanic practice, 190, 338n2; in social relations, 303, 305, 331n7; varieties of, 177

Cannon, W., 61
Carneiro, R., 299, 342n11
Casteel, E. and J., 323–24
Castenada, C., 37, 331n2 (Chapter 2)
Chickens: in salia ritual, 208, 209, 210; as surrogates for humans, 184, 185, 186, 210; in vows to the Owner, 177, 178
Chiefdoms, 298, 299, 302, 307–11, 312, 342n11
Chiefs: access to labor by, 305, 341n6, 343n13; and constituencies, 305, 309, 310, 311, 341n3; external ties of, 307–10, 315; in Kasialia, 307, 309, 323, 324; and the legal system, 304, 305, 309–10,

Compositor: Asco Trade Typesetting Ltd.
Text: Bembo
Display: Bembo
Printer: Maple-Vail Book Mfg. Group
Binder: Maple-Vail Book Mfg. Group